Following *The Fugitive*

Following
The Fugitive

*An Episode Guide and Handbook
to the 1960s Television Series*

by BILL DEANE

McFarland & Company, Inc., Publishers
Jefferson, North Carolina, and London

The present work is a reprint of the library bound edition of *Following the Fugitive: An Episode Guide and Handbook to the 1960s Television Series,* first published in 1996 by McFarland.

LIBRARY OF CONGRESS CATALOGUING-IN-PUBLICATION DATA

Deane, Bill.
　　Following the Fugitive : an episode guide and handbook to the 1960s television series / by Bill Deane.
　　　　p.　　cm.
　　Includes index.

　　ISBN 0-7864-2631-4 (softcover : 50# alk. paper) ∞

　　1. Fugitive (Television program)　I. Title.
PN1992.77.F79D4　2006
791.45'72 — dc20　　　　　　　　　　　　　　　　　　96-31167

British Library cataloguing data are available

©1996 Bill Deane. All rights reserved

No part of this book may be reproduced or transmitted in any form or by any means, electronic or mechanical, including photocopying or recording, or by any information storage and retrieval system, without permission in writing from the publisher.

On the cover: David Janssen as Dr. Richard Kimble, the Fugitive *(ABC/Photofest)*

Manufactured in the United States of America

McFarland & Company, Inc., Publishers
　Box 611, Jefferson, North Carolina 28640
　　www.mcfarlandpub.com

Contents

Preface		1
Introduction		3
Act I	The 1963-64 Season	7
Act II	The 1964-65 Season	56
Act III	The 1965-66 Season	105
Act IV	The 1966-67 Season	156
Epilog	The Series Finale	204

Appendices: The Show

1	Writers	209
2	Directors	210
3	Guest Stars and Support Players	211

Appendices: The Character

4	Places Visited or Lived In	218
5	Aliases Used	220
6	Occupations Held	221
7	Romances Engaged In	223
8	Injuries Sustained	225
9	Interesting Facts	226

Index	229

Preface

After two years of watching *The Fugitive* reruns, five days a week, it dawned on me: "If I'm going to spend this much time in front of the television, why not write a book about the show?"

I was introduced to this wonderful program by my mother, Edith Deane. After its four-year run in a time-slot "way past my bedtime," *The Fugitive* was shown weekday afternoons on ABC in 1967-68. I watched it every day with Mom and became hooked. Unfortunately, after this I didn't get to see the show again for 22 years. In the 1970s and 1980s networks just weren't interested in airing reruns of black-&-white television shows, no matter how good they were.

Finally, in 1990 the Arts & Entertainment cable network brought *The Fugitive* back to life, airing the show daily to a new generation of viewers. Since then fan clubs for the show have formed on two continents, the program was selected "Best Drama of the 1960s" by *TV Guide*, and it has become the subject of a megahit motion picture, with a sequel on tap.

I began working on my book in January 1992. I sat down in front of the television with a notepad, writing down the plot-lines and all the important details of each of the 120 hour-long episodes: Dr. Richard Kimble's alias, his occupation, the location of his latest adventure (which often required detective work: squinting at a state name on a license plate or an area code on a pay phone, for example). I relied heavily on the patience of my wife, Pam, and daughter, Sarah.

After I typed a rough draft of each synopsis, I took every opportunity to watch each episode again, whenever it was on, often catching details I had missed the first time. I also corresponded with two other people who were as fanatical about the show as I: Kay McAfee, and Rusty Pollard (editor of the "On the Run Newsletter," P.O. Box 461402, Garland, TX 75046-1402). By comparing all of our observations, I was able to compile the most accurate information possible without access to actual scripts of the show. Finally, I transferred all the data into a word-processor. In all, I spent some 700 hours putting together this book, a labor of love.

In addition to those people mentioned above, I am indebted to friend and fellow *Fugitive* fan Joe Dittmar; to Ed Robertson, author of *The Fugitive Recaptured*; and to Michael Katz and John M. Yodice of the A&E network.

Introduction

The Fugitive was the brainchild of writer Roy Huggins, who produced such television hits as *Cheyenne*, *Maverick*, and *77 Sunset Strip*. He wrote his series format for *The Fugitive* on September 19, 1960. Convinced that he had a hit, Huggins shared his idea with friends and television people. In his book *Tears from a Glass Eye*, Huggins recalls that "without exception, *The Fugitive* met with embarrassed silence, apathy, distress, distaste, pity, scorn, or multiple combinations thereof," until Huggins himself almost believed he had had a bad idea. "If enough people tell you you're blind," he later said, "you'd better get yourself a dog."

Finally, Huggins found an enthusiastic backer: ABC executive Leonard Goldenson. But because of academic commitments, Huggins would not be available to produce his own show. Huggins suggested that Quinn Martin (*The Untouchables*) serve as executive producer; thus, *The Fugitive* became a "QM Production," with Huggins listed as the creator. One of *The Fugitive*'s Quinn Martin touches is the breaking down of each episode into "Act I," "Act II," "Act III," "Act IV," and "Epilog." He also employed the distinctive music of Peter Rugolo. Alan A. Armer would serve as the show's producer during its first three seasons, while Wilton Schiller would take over in that role in 1966–67, the only season aired in color.

The Fugitive is the story of Dr. Richard Kimble, falsely accused of murdering his wife, Helen. After an argument with Helen, Dr. Kimble had stormed out of the house and gone for a drive. Upon returning, Kimble saw a one-armed man fleeing from the vicinity of his house. The doctor had then gone inside and discovered that Helen had been murdered. Unable to find the one-armed man who apparently had committed the crime, Dr. Kimble was convicted of the murder and sentenced to death. After all appeals failed, Kimble — accompanied by police Lt. Philip Gerard — was "en route to the deathhouse" when their train derailed. Kimble managed to escape during the resultant melee, and has been a fugitive from justice ever since. While the police (especially Gerard) trail Kimble, Kimble searches for the elusive one-armed man, who represents the only chance to prove his innocence.

Quinn Martin's biggest contribution was his choice of the show's star:

David Janssen, of *Richard Diamond, Private Detective* (CBS/NBC, 1957–60) fame. The role of Richard Kimble would be a demanding one, requiring someone who would appear in almost every minute of every episode and who could exude the brains of a doctor along with the physical prowess of an escape artist. The actor would have to be experienced, hard-working, intelligent, and athletic. Janssen was all of those things and good-looking to boot. His powerful screen presence made the show work.

Janssen was born David Harold Meyer in Naponee, Nebraska, on March 27, 1931. He appeared in dozens of feature films, mostly in bit parts, before finding his niche in television. After *The Fugitive*, Janssen starred in *O'Hara, U.S. Treasury* (CBS, 1971–72) and *Harry-O* (ABC, 1974–76), along with numerous TV movies and miniseries. Janssen died of a massive heart attack at Malibu Beach on February 13, 1980. He was 48.

The second important character in *The Fugitive* would be Gerard, "the police lieutenant obsessed with his capture." Although he would appear in less than one-third of the show's episodes, Lt. Gerard would have to be such a commanding presence that he would be there even when he *wasn't* there, so to speak. The role went to British-born actor, director, and writer Barry Morse. Morse, born in London on June 10, 1918, had played hundreds of roles around the world — in the theater and movies, on radio and television. A master of dialects, Morse would skillfully hide his accent in what he believes "was the only instance up to that time where a British actor played an American character in a TV series." Morse would later star in the syndicated *Space: 1999* (1975–76) and the CBS miniseries *Master of the Game* (1984), among other projects, but he is still best-remembered as Lt. Gerard. "People still call me 'Lieutenant' on the street," he says, "and pretend they have only one arm." Barry Morse lives in London.

Another important character was the notorious "one-armed man." Bill Raisch (who lost his right arm in World War II) portrayed the villain, although — other than in the show's weekly opening scene — he was seen in only ten of the show's 120 episodes. Raisch died of lung cancer on July 31, 1984. He was 79.

The final important figure in the show was the omniscient, unseen narrator, whose powerful, ominous voice would begin and end each episode. The job went to William Conrad, the voice of Matt Dillon in the radio version of *Gunsmoke* (1952–61), and the narrator of *The Bullwinkle Show* (NBC, 1961–62). Conrad, born William Cann in Louisville, Kentucky, on September 27, 1920, would later narrate the syndicated *Wild, Wild World of Animals* (1973–78), and NBC's *Tales of the Unexpected* (1978) and *Buck Rogers in the 25th Century* (1979–80). But he would become best-known for his acting roles as *Cannon* (CBS, 1971–76), *Nero Wolfe* (NBC, 1981), and Jason L. McCabe on *Jake and the Fatman* (CBS, 1987–92). Conrad died on February 11, 1994.

The Fugitive made its debut on ABC on September 17, 1963. It aired on

Introduction 5

Tuesday nights from 10 to 11 P.M. over the next four years. After a moderately successful first season, *The Fugitive* vaulted all the way to fifth place in the Nielsen ratings for the 1964–65 season (in the previous season, ABC had had no series rank higher than 16th). The commercial success would be joined by critical acclaim as *The Fugitive* received the Emmy Award for "Outstanding Dramatic Series" in 1966.

One of the keys to the success of *The Fugitive* was the outstanding acting talent that graced the credits week after week. No fewer than eleven past or future Academy Award winners appeared on the show: Martin Balsam, Ed Begley, Sandy Dennis, Melvyn Douglas, James Dunn, Robert Duvall, Gloria Grahame, Lee Grant, Eileen Heckart, Celeste Holm, and Dean Jagger. Many other familiar names graced the credits: Edward Asner, Beau Bridges, Dabney Coleman, Bruce Dern, Angie Dickinson, Ronny Howard, Brian Keith, Ted Knight, Jack Lord, Lee Meriwether, Vera Miles, Tony Musante, Leslie Nielsen, Carroll O'Connor, Suzanne Pleshette, Wayne Rogers, Mickey Rooney, Kurt Russell, Telly Savalas, William Shatner, Tom Skerritt, Jack Warden, and Tuesday Weld, to name a few.

In a unique (but since often-imitated) move, *The Fugitive* actually resolved the basic plot of its existence. In a two-part episode aired in August 1967, Richard Kimble, Lt. Gerard, and the one-armed man were united for the climactic conclusion of the series. The final episode aired August 29 and set a new record for viewers of a single episode of a regular series. Its 72 percent viewer-share (meaning that 72 percent of Americans watching TV were watching *The Fugitive*) remained a regular series record until the notorious "Who Shot J.R.?" *Dallas* episode 13 years later.

This work is designed as a handbook and episode guide to the TV show, which is enjoying a renaissance of interest. The book covers all 120 episodes of *The Fugitive*, including the title, original air-date, writer, director, cast, and 500- to 1,000-word plot summaries for each. It is divided into five sections: Act I (the tone-setting 1963-64 season), Act II (the highly rated 1964-65 season), Act III (the Emmy Award-winning 1965-66 season), Act IV (the 1966-67 season, the only one produced in color), and Epilog (the historic two-part conclusion).

Also included are three appendices relevant to the show itself, listing the writers, directors, and guest stars and supporting players for each episode; and five appendices relating to the Kimble character: the aliases used, jobs taken, romances engaged in, injuries sustained by, and locations visited by Richard Kimble; a ninth appendix is about both the character and the show and is a collection of interesting facts that didn't seem to fit elsewhere.

My hope is that this work will serve as an indispensable handbook for the thousands of fans following the show daily on cable.

Bill Deane, *Summer 1996*

Act I
The 1963-64 Season

The Fugitive made its television debut on Tuesday, September 17, 1963, at 10 P.M. Broadcast in black and white, it replaced *The Untouchables* (drama) and *Bell & Howell Closeup* (documentary) on ABC's fall lineup. *The Fugitive*'s competition came from *The Garry Moore Show* (CBS) and *The Bell Telephone Hour* (NBC), a variety show and music program, respectively.

The Fugitive was a drama created by Roy Huggins. It bore resemblance to Victor Hugo's literary classic *Les Misérables* and to the real-life Sam Sheppard murder case. The series' executive producer was Quinn Martin, and its original producer was Alan A. Armer. The music was composed by Peter Rugolo, and the series was narrated by noted actor William Conrad (1920–94).

David Janssen (1931–80) appeared as Dr. Richard David Kimble, the fugitive, in each of the 30 episodes (aired through April 21, 1964) of the show's first season. Barry Morse portrayed Lt. Philip Gerard in twelve episodes: numbers 1, 3-5, 7, 10-11, 14-15, 19, 26, and 30.

TV Guide awarded the Silver Bowl to *The Fugitive* as Best New Series of the 1963-64 Season, and its readers also named Janssen as Best Dramatic Actor. Likewise, *TV Radio Mirror* named Janssen as Best Male Star of the year.

Episode #1
FEAR IN A DESERT CITY
Original Airdate: September 17, 1963

Written by: Stanford Whitmore   **Directed by:** Walter Grauman

Cast: Vera Miles as Monica Welles, Brian Keith as Edward Welles, Harry Townes as Detective Sgt. Burden. (Uncredited: Dabbs Greer as Detective Fairfield, Donald Losby as Mark Welles, Barney Phillips as Cleve Brown, Paul Birch as Capt. Carpenter, Abigail Shelton as Evelyn.)

Dr. Richard Kimble has been a fugitive for six months, since escaping from a train wreck en route to his scheduled execution. He had been wrongfully convicted of murdering his wife and believes the actual murderer was a one-armed man he saw running from the direction of his house the night of the crime. Kimble travels about under assumed identities, attempting to elude the authorities (particularly Indiana police Lieutenant Philip Gerard), and at the same time searching for the mysterious one-armed man.

Kimble arrives now in Tucson, Arizona, with the alias James "Jim" Lincoln. He finds employment at the Branding Iron in the Hotel Santa Rita, tending bar for $75 per week. He begins work on a Friday night and meets his coworkers, including the pianist, Monica. Jim soon encounters an abusive customer, Ed, who seems to have eyes for Monica. Ed finally departs, leaving her visibly upset by his visit.

Jim finishes work and finds Ed physically abusing Monica in the parking lot. Jim intervenes, knocking Ed down with one punch. Ed runs off and Jim escorts Monica home. Apologizing for involving him, Monica tells Jim that Ed is her husband. She had married at 18 and soon became pregnant with their son, Mark. Ed is an influential man, owning some 250,000 acres of land, belonging to the proper social organizations, donating to the proper charities; he has even been mentioned as a potential political candidate. At home, however, he had evolved into an insanely suspicious, violent man. Not being able to take any more, Monica and Mark had fled their Phoenix home a month earlier. Until tonight she had remained free of Ed, but now he is back on his mission to possess and abuse Monica, and to teach Mark how evil she is.

Jim makes a date to spend the next day at a carnival with Monica and Mark. Jim goes home, where he is promptly visited by Ed. In a thinly veiled threat, Ed shows off his custom-made revolver. Jim suggests that Ed seek psychiatric care, infuriating Ed. He leaves after warning Jim to "Get out of my sight!"

While Ed spies on them, Jim and Monica — having quickly become fond of each other — share a nice day at Wonderland. Jim tells Monica about Ed's visit, and she suggests he call the police. Jim says he can't do that and can't explain why. Ed later contacts two local detectives, saying that Jim is breaking up his marriage and ought to be run out of town. The cops are happy to oblige such an upstanding citizen.

After another night of work and another confrontation with Ed, Jim and Monica prepare to go home. Jim is accosted by the detectives and driven away. They ask a variety of nerve-wracking questions before bringing him to his hotel room. Finally, they deliver the punch line: "Leave Tucson tonight."

Jim checks out and heads for the bus station in a taxi. He has it stop at Monica's place and knocks on her door. With the meter running, Jim tells Monica who he really is, about the night of his wife's murder, about the one-armed man with the "face I can never forget," about his 18 months in prison and his escape, and about the relentless Lt. Gerard. Jim and Monica kiss, and she begins packing to join him.

Ed visits the police station to thank the detectives, who assure Ed that Jim checked out of his room a half hour ago and is probably now at the bus station. With that problem solved, Ed goes to Monica's place, presumably to punish her. Finding it abandoned, he angrily heads for the bus station.

Jim, Monica, and Mark are boarding the San Diego bus when Ed catches up with them. Ed tries to explain to Mark what a tramp his mother is, but Mark isn't buying. Blaming him for turning his son against him, Ed turns his wrath on Jim. Ed pulls out his revolver and is about to fire when a station policeman guns him down. With more cops soon to arrive at the scene, Jim realizes he will have to separate from Monica and Mark to avoid identification. Jim bids farewell to the two and slips away.

The Tucson detectives ultimately realize who Jim Lincoln really was and contact Gerard. Gerard arrives at Ed's funeral in Phoenix and pulls Monica aside, asking her where Jim went. She says she doesn't know and realizes this must be the notorious Gerard. The lieutenant is delighted to hear that Kimble told her about him: "Excellent! He thinks of me as much as I think of him."

Episode #2
THE WITCH
Original Airdate: September 24, 1963

Written by: William D. Gordon   **Directed by:** Andrew McCullough

Cast: Patricia Crowley as Emily Norton, Gina Gillespie as Jenny Ammory, Arch Johnson as Ty Tyson, Madeleine Sherwood as Mrs. Ammory, Crahan Denton as H. R. Ammory, George Mitchell as William Sturgis, Claudia Bryar as Mrs. Sturgis, Ray Teal as McNary, Elisha Cook as "Sailor."

Now a fugitive for ten months, Kimble — alias Jim Fowler — has taken a $1.10 per hour job driving a truck for Tyson's Fuel, Feed & Supply in Hainesville, Missouri. There is veiled friction between Jim and his boss, Ty Tyson, who calls Jim "Brains." Jim has been on the job for a week, and is on his way to the Ammory farm to pick up a cord of firewood for Tyson.

Jenny Ammory, a conniving little girl with an unusual interest in witchcraft, is once again late for school and has once again failed to do her homework. Today she is trying to con a way to avoid school and the daily confrontation with Miss Norton, her teacher (and also the town's librarian).

Jenny dallies toward school, taking a forbidden, roundabout route through the woods and stopping to pick flowers. The sound of Jim's approaching truck sends her ducking into the bushes, ripping her dress. Jim, noticing a lunchbox and book on the road, stops the vehicle and searches for their owner. Jenny is beside the mill pond, having a conversation with her secret doll, Naiad. Jenny offers a Latin incantation, asking the doll to help her out of another jam. When Jim finds Jenny she denies owning the lunchbox and book, saying the true owner is not supposed to go through the woods. Jim understands and suggests Jenny go to school and bring the items to their rightful owner. Afterward, Jenny thanks her doll for "sending" Jim to figure in a perfect excuse for her various problems. Jenny offers Miss Norton her reason for lateness: a man chased her into the woods and tore her dress, also causing her to lose her homework. The teacher is concerned but hardly convinced, recalling previous excuses involving wild Indians and a monster.

Jim gets to the farm, meeting Jenny's parents: a gossipy, self-righteous woman and her long-suffering husband. Mrs. Ammory asks if Jim passed Jenny on the way; covering for the girl, Jim says he didn't. Mrs. Ammory also remarks on the amount of time (two visits) that Jim has spent at the library since his arrival in town, and she seems concerned that he might have romantic interest in the sultry Miss Norton.

Jim returns to work for his next assignment, delivering a load of coal to the school. Ty helps Jim load the truck and brings up the subject of Miss Norton, on whom Ty thinks he has some sort of claim. Ty and Jim engage in a repartee on the subject, grinning at each other through clenched teeth. Ty at last suggests that Jim "stay away from her entirely."

Jim unloads the coal in the school barn, and Jenny points him out as the man who chased her. Miss Norton goes to ask Jim about it. Two children cavort through the barn while the adults talk. Miss Norton catches Jenny eavesdropping and scolds her. Jenny runs home in tears, telling her mother she had to leave school because she saw Jim and Miss Norton doing unspeakable things in the barn. Mrs. Ammory promptly phones Mrs. Sturgis, wife of the Chairman of Elders. "It's happened, just like I always knowed it would," she begins, and word soon spreads around town. A special discussion about Miss Norton will be added to tonight's regular Thursday board meeting at the church, and she will be given 30 days' notice to leave.

Jenny finds Jim and asks him a favor: to return her overdue book to the library so Miss Norton won't think she stole it. He obliges, arriving at the library just as Mrs. Ammory and Mrs. Sturgis leave; they have just delivered the message about the meeting to Miss Norton. The two ladies cast disapproving looks at the sinful couple. Emily is very upset, telling Jim this is the fourth time she has been driven out of a town like this. Jim advises her to stop feeling sorry for herself and to fight for her job.

When Jim returns to the shop, Ty — having heard the rumor — is ready for him. Ty launches an unmerciful beating, and Jim is no match for the burly bully. McNary, the local police officer, intervenes and takes Jim to headquarters. The cop, finding that Jim's references don't check, advises Jim to leave town. McNary mentions the meeting that is in progress and the nature of the "charges" against Miss Norton. Jim promises to leave but asks for a chance to clear Miss Norton first. McNary accompanies Jim to the church.

Jim addresses the crowd. He asks about the other witnesses, referring to the two children. Learning that one of them was the chairman's son, Jim points out that whatever happened in the barn was so unimportant to the boy that he didn't even mention it to his parents. There is silence as the group realizes Jenny is lying. Desperate, Jenny tries out her other lie. Feigning fear of Jim, she shrieks that he chased her and tore her dress. A murmur goes up, just as the menacing Ty and his pals arrive. Mrs. Ammory recalls that Jenny's dress *was* torn and that Jim had denied even seeing Jenny that morning. Tyson and company move in on Jim, and he dives through a window to escape into the woods. Jim takes refuge in the mill pond.

Miss Norton talks with Jenny, trying to make her realize the danger she has put Jim in. When the Ammorys catch her in another lie, Jenny flees to the pond to discuss her troubles with Naiad. She encounters Jim, who pleads with her to get him off the hook. Ty and his gang soon surround the pond, brandishing rifles. Jenny at last admits that she was lying, and the lynch mob dissipates.

The next morning Jim tells Jenny she was a good friend to him and asks her to try to be a friend to Miss Norton as well. Thus, student and teacher start off with a clean slate. McNary gives Jim a lift to the bus station, offering to provide a reference the next time he needs one.

Episode #3
THE OTHER SIDE OF THE MOUNTAIN
Original Airdate: October 1, 1963

Story by: Alan Caillou   **Teleplay by:** Alan Caillou & Harry Kronman
Directed by: James Sheldon

Cast: Sandy Dennis as Cassie Bolin, R. G. Armstrong as Sheriff Sam Bradley, Ruth White as "Grams" Bolin, Frank Sutton as Del Jackson, Bruce Dern as Deputy Marlin, Paul Birch as Capt. Carpenter, John D. Chandler as Quimby, Hugh Sanders as Leo, Johnny Day as Masters.

Kimble is dropped off at a West Virginia hamlet, which has become something of a ghost town since the coal mines stopped producing. He stops for a beer and soon finds himself surrounded by locals who have no use for strangers in their town. They harass and rough up Kimble, touching off a playful barroom brawl. Deputy Marlin enters, seeking to restore order and vowing to lock up whoever started the melee; the locals indicate that Kimble started it. Kimble tries to escape, winding up in a fistfight with the deputy. Kimble gets the better of the lawman and is about to leave when he is clubbed from behind by Sheriff Bradley. The unconscious stranger's effects are checked, turning up no identification. While the sheriff contemplates this over a beer, Kimble regains consciousness and slips away. Bradley confiscates Kimble's suitcase for a fingerprint check whose results will be teletyped to Lt. Gerard. Gerard soon boards a TWA flight to West Virginia.

The manhunt is on, with the sheriff and his men hot on Kimble's trail up a mountain. Kimble encounters a person who seems to be following him and tackles the offender. It turns out to be a country girl, Cassie, who lives in a remote mountain cabin with her grandmother. She deduces Kimble is the man the sheriff (a relative of hers) is looking for, but it doesn't trouble her; she is happy just to have caught herself a man. Cassie convinces Kimble (whom she refers to only as "Mister") that he will have a better chance of escape if he sticks with her, as she knows "every foot of this mountain." She leads him to her grandmother's house.

Gerard arrives in town and rents a helicopter to bring him to the manhunt. He meets the sheriff, who remarks that Gerard "must want him real bad."

Grams tries to tell Cassie that she can't keep "Mister" as a pet. "I found him," Cassie points out, adding that "ain't nobody gonna take him away." This man may be her ticket to the big city on the other side of the mountain. Kimble soon realizes he is being toyed with and wants out, but Cassie reminds him that her help is indispensable to his escape.

Jackson, a deputized local, visits the Bolin house, but Cassie pulls a rifle and makes it clear that he isn't needed or welcome there. Jackson deduces that she is hiding Kimble, and retreats to tell Bradley and Gerard. The two lawmen and Marlin journey up the mountain on foot, but by the time they reach the Bolin house, Kimble and Cassie have left. She has brought the fugitive to an abandoned mine with a labyrinth of passages (which she knows well), one of which leads to the other side of the mountain. Cassie shows Kimble her "Dreamin' Room," where she often goes just to be alone with her daydreams. She asks Kimble to take her along and help her overcome her fear of the big city. Kimble says he can't but that she doesn't need him as long as she has the desire to make it on her own. Kimble makes Cassie promise she will try, and she points him on his way to the exit passage.

The mine is soon filled with the voices of Gerard and the local cops, in pursuit despite their unfamiliarity with the caves. Cassie joins the group, leading them in the wrong direction. They enter the "Dreamin' Room" and Cassie knocks down an entrance support, causing a cave-in. It will be several hours before they will be able to dig themselves out, giving Kimble plenty of lead-time.

Kimble makes it out of the mine and hitches a ride with a farm truck. Gerard flies home empty-handed. And Cassie packs, bids her grandmother farewell, and sets out for the big city.

Act I: The 1963-64 Season 13

Episodes #4–5
NEVER WAVE GOODBYE (Parts I & II)
Original Airdates: October 8 & 15, 1963
Written by: Hank Searls **Directed by:** William Graham

Cast: Susan Oliver as Karen Christian, Robert Duvall as Eric, Lee Phillips as Dr. Ray Brooks, Will Kuluva as Lars Christian, Rachel Ames as Ann Gerard, Harry Bartell as Clement Parker, Paul Birch as Capt. Carpenter, Bert Remsen as skipper, William Zuckert as navigator, Henry Beckman as passenger, Ed Holmes as Fugitive Detail Lieutenant, Lawrence Parke as Gulden, Diana Bourbon as yachting wife, Tina Menard as Mrs. Rodriguez.

Kimble, alias Jeff Cooper, has worked more than a month as a sail-maker for Lars Christian Sails of Quality in Santa Barbara, California. He decides it is time to move on, upsetting Lars's niece Karen, who has fallen in love with Jeff. Sickly old Lars tries to talk Jeff out of leaving, saying Karen should not have to "wave goodbye" to someone she loves again; she had lost her mother at age ten, and been separated from her father shortly after. Karen asks Jeff to stay a few more weeks, and Jeff agrees. This disappoints Ray, Karen's former beau, and angers Jeff's coworker Eric, who is enchanted with Karen and thinks she deserves better than a drifter.

Lt. Gerard cancels a camping trip with his son, "Flip," when he gets a report from the Los Angeles County Jail. Clem Parker, a one-armed man, has been incarcerated there for assaulting a woman. Capt. Carpenter, Gerard's boss, says, "I wish you'd close this case," but he allows Gerard to fly to L.A.

Jeff and Karen plan to accompany Ray on his yacht, *Tranquilizer*, but Ray (a doctor) is called out on an emergency. He lets Jeff and Karen take the boat out by themselves. Eric is infuriated when he hears about this and tells Lars so. Eric says he doesn't trust Jeff and thinks he is hiding from somebody, maybe the police. Who knows what unspeakable things might happen between Jeff and Karen, alone on the boat? Angry at Eric's implications Lars strikes Eric but collapses from the exertion. Jeff (who used to spend summers sailing in Maine) and Karen, meanwhile, are having a nice time together and making plans to enter the dinghy race on Sunday. Karen tells Jeff she loves him, but Jeff says he can't afford to fall in love. The trip is interrupted by a call from the marine operator, who informs them Lars has had a heart attack.

At the hospital Eric blames Jeff for helping to set off the attack and tells Jeff to leave town. Jeff reads a newspaper and discovers an interesting article: "One-Armed Vet Convicted." Lars asks to see Jeff, and Jeff goes to the deathbed. Lars asks Jeff not to leave Karen, and Jeff promises to try to stay. He first has to make a trip to L.A., and if he finds the right man, he will be back for good. Satisfied, Lars dies.

On Saturday Karen drives Jeff to the bus station, but he is being mysterious about the trip to the L.A. jail. Jeff takes the bus to Los Angeles while curious Karen decides to drive to the jail. Gerard, meanwhile, has already arrived by TWA plane.

Jeff enters the Hall of Justice, blending in with the plethora of weekend visitors. While he goes to see Clem Parker on the 13th floor, Gerard is meeting with the L.A. police three floors below. Jeff, introducing himself as an old army buddy of Palmer's, soon realizes this is the wrong one-armed man. Jeff gives the man a light from a Lars Christian Sails matchbook and learns he was in a neuropsychiatric ward in 1960 when Helen Kimble was murdered. Disappointed, Jeff boards the elevator to leave. As it makes a stop on the tenth floor, Jeff finds himself face-to-face with Gerard, waiting for an elevator going up. Jeff continues his descent, while Gerard must find another way down to pursue him.

Jeff exits the building and finds Karen outside waiting for him. He tells her to stay away from him, but she follows him onto a bus. Gerard finds a manned police car and persuades the driver to follow the bus. With Karen still tagging along, Jeff gets off at the first stop and climbs up a flight of stairs to another highway. From there, they see the bus pulled over by the police, and Karen realizes Jeff is in serious trouble. They get on another bus, losing Gerard, and finally make their way back to Karen's car. The two of them drive back to Santa Barbara, with Jeff at last telling her the truth about himself. She is sympathetic and still wants to be with him. Jeff, tired of running, says that maybe he will just stay put this time, and they won't have to wave goodbye.

Gerard interrogates Palmer, and discovers the match Kimble had used; it has the word "SAILS" printed on it. With this thin lead, Gerard decides to scour the California coast, checking sail-making enterprises.

Jeff registers for the 4 P.M. dinghy race. Meanwhile, the shark-ravaged body of Pedro Rodriguez is brought ashore. This illustrates just one of the hazards of water-travel in this area, others being high winds, thick fog, and jagged rocks guarding the shores.

Gerard stops at an awning establishment in Ventura, asking and warning about Kimble. The proprietor then phones Karen, telling her of the visit and warning her to be careful whom she hires. Karen tells Jeff that Gerard is only an hour away.

Jeff has an idea: to enter the race, fall behind, and keep going past the turning point. They will become hidden in the late afternoon fog and fake an accident, leaving behind blood-soaked life jackets as evidence of a shark attack. They will escape in the old life raft, *The Big Apple*, that Lars had given Karen many years earlier. Jeff patches the raft, saying "we'll see if Gerard will chase a ghost."

Gerard arrives at Lars Christian Sails, meeting Eric. Eric is glad to show Gerard to Jeff's room, but Jeff has slipped away. Gerard and Eric go to the harbor, but the race is already well under way. Gerard waits at the finish line for several hours before he realizes his fugitive is not returning. Night has fallen on the harbor, and Gerard will have to wait until morning before a search boat captain will consent to go out.

Jeff and Karen's boat is tossed around by the wind and encircled by sharks. The two slit their forearms to draw blood, applying it to the life jackets and tossing them to the sharks. They then capsize the boat and climb aboard the raft. Jeff declares Richard Kimble dead, and them alive — so far.

The rescue boat searches for the missing dinghy. The two life jackets are found, sufficient evidence of a fatal shark attack, according to the skipper. He plans to head back, but Gerard asks about the possibility of the two having had a life raft. The captain replies that small boat sailors don't carry rafts. Eric recalls noticing that Karen's raft wasn't in its usual place, which is sufficient evidence for Gerard to continue the search. Gerard informs the skipper about Eric's story, but Eric, realizing that Karen might be in trouble for abetting a fugitive, refuses to verify it. The captain, not wanting to unnecessarily risk his ship in these treacherous waters, turns for home. Gerard takes matters into his own hands, releasing the ship's life raft and getting aboard. He figures his raft will wind up in the same place as Kimble's.

Jeff and Karen crash into the shore of Point Doom. Jeff buries the raft and the two take refuge in a cave for a while. They then climb up toward the highway, intending to hitch a ride. From above, they see the bizarre sight of Gerard approaching the shore in his raft. Gerard crashes into the reef, is knocked unconscious, and appears doomed to drown.

Kimble's Hippocratic Oath gets the better of him. Despite Karen's pleas not to, he returns below to save Gerard's life. Kimble makes sure Gerard is out of danger but knows he will now have to move on alone. Kimble makes a deal with the prostrate Gerard: he will phone for help before escaping, leaving Karen to stay with him, if Gerard will promise not to prosecute Karen as an accessory. Gerard agrees.

Kimble and Karen kiss, and he heads up to the highway. He turns for one last look, and Karen waves goodbye.

Episode #6
DECISION IN THE RING
Original Airdate: October 22, 1963

Written by: Arthur Weiss   **Directed by:** Robert Ellis Miller

Cast: James Edwards as Joseph "Joe" Smith, Ruby Dee as Laura Smith, James Dunn as Lou Bragan, Robert F. Simon as Murphy, Edward Kemmer as Henry "Hank" Stone, Harry Swoger as Wally Wilson, Hari Rhodes as Dan Digby.

Middleweight boxing contender Joe Smith is the son of a doctor. Joe had pursued the same career, but dropped out of medical school after his second year, feeling he had a better future as a boxer than as a Negro doctor in some ghetto.

Smith suffers a cut over his eye during a victorious fight at the Los Angeles Memorial Sports Arena. Cut-man Ed Robins, having dropped the bottle of adrenaline, is unable to stop the bleeding. Robins, who had been hired upon the recommendation of Smith's sparring partner, Dan Digby, is dismissed by trainer Lou Bragan. Kimble, alias Ray Miller, comes to the rescue and manages to get the cut under control. Joe (who is preparing for a big fight with leading contender Kenny Walton) and Lou are impressed with Ray, who claims to have experience with cuts, and hire him on the spot as Smith's new cut-man. Ray gets a $15 raise over the $60 a week he was making as towel and cleanup attendant at the arena. Meanwhile, Dan is upset over the firing of his friend and directs some of his hostility toward Ray.

Joe talks medicine with Ray, who claims his medical background is limited to having served as a medic corpsman in Korea. Joe suspects there is more to the story but doesn't ask Ray about it. He has come to like and respect his new cut-man. Ray, meanwhile, notices that Joe suffers from short-term memory loss and other symptoms of brain damage. He tries to talk Joe out of fighting, saying he risks permanent damage or even death. Joe tells Ray not to say anything to his trainer or his wife of four years, Laura. Laura figures out the situation, though, and pleads with Joe not to fight any more. She says she is going home and hopes Joe will, too.

Bragan's camps have a history of illegal practices and associations, and undercover cop Hank Stone is sent to infiltrate this one under the guise of being a feature writer for *Ring* magazine. Dan, still perturbed about Ray, gives Stone a "scoop" that he believes Ray is trying to distract Joe into losing (the last time someone had "buzzed" Joe about medicine, he had become so preoccupied that he nearly lost to a second-rate opponent). Stone decides to check up on Ray, confiscating a glass the cut-man had handled. Ray's fingerprints will be checked at police headquarters.

Just before the scheduled fight on Saturday, Ray makes a final appeal, urging Joe to quit fighting and resume his medical pursuits. Meanwhile, police have learned Ray's true identity and come to the arena to arrest him. While Ray hides around a corner, Joe tells police he is not there. After the cops leave, Ray affirms his innocence of the murder rap. Joe believes him and dresses Ray in bandages so that he can escape the arena, looking like just another beaten pug fighter.

Joe's corner men return to his dressing room, but Joe stops them from pursuing Ray. He tells Lou he can't fight any more due to his physical condition and goes home to a relieved Laura. Later, Ray is pleased to read a newspaper headline: "Smith Quits Ring—Brain Damage Curable."

Episode #7
SMOKE SCREEN
Original Airdate: October 29, 1963

Written by: John D. F. Black **Directed by:** Claudio Guzman

Cast: Beverly Garland as Doris Stillwell, Alejandro Rey as Paco Alvarez, Pina Pellicer as Maria Alvarez, Peter Helm as Johnny Peters, John Milford as foreman, Mort Mills as Ranger Ritter, Pepe Hern as Cardinez, Robert Contreras as Ibarra, Ed Faulkner as Jordan, Buck Young as Pat Keenan, James Seay as fire chief, Stuart Bradley as sheriff, Barry Kelley as Harry. (Uncredited: Paul Birch as Capt. Carpenter.)

Kimble, alias Joseph Walker, is a farm laborer for Sindler & Son Produce in Hidalgo Grove, California, near the Mexican border. He doesn't know why his coworkers are hostile toward him: they suspect him of being a police spy, searching for illegal aliens like Paco Alvarez and his pregnant wife, Maria.

A forest fire has broken out nearby, and a highway ranger asks Sindler & Son men to help fight it (for extra pay). Maria wants to accompany Paco but he won't allow it, so she stows away in a truck. Doris Stillwell, a pushy nurse assigned to accompany the laborers, enlists Maria to assist her.

KRGA cub reporter Johnny Peters covers the fire fighting efforts. The fire rages out of control, and laborer Cardinez collapses at the front line from smoke inhalation. Walker rescues Cardinez and is assigned to drive him to the nurse's tent, accompanied by Paco. Walker learns why the others want him out of there and assures Paco he has more reason to hide from the police than Paco.

The three arrive at the tent and find Maria in labor. She will need a Caesarian section in order to survive. Walker drives the nurse and Maria out toward a hospital, but the entire area is now surrounded by fire. The nurse is furious with Walker for not trying to make a run through the fire; she has already decided he is just a gutless, bumbling field worker.

Walker, after some soul-searching, realizes he will have to reveal his medical background in order to help save Maria and the baby. He enters the tent and says he can help, but the nurse orders him out. She does not believe his list of credits: Cornell Medical School, internship in New York, advanced study at Guys Hospital in London, residency at Memorial Hospital in Chicago, specialty in pediatrics and obstetrics. The nurse doesn't want to jeopardize her cozy career by permitting "a field worker who walks in here and tells me that he's a doctor" to assist in the operation. Walker says Maria's life depends upon his assistance, and Paco asks him to help.

Paco tells the reporter the story, and Johnny reports that a farm-worker, claiming to be a doctor, is performing a C-section. It becomes a national news story and Lt. Gerard hears about it, suspecting Kimble is involved. He had already analyzed Kimble's migration patterns and theorized Kimble was in southern California.

Fire fighters at last break through the ring of fire, just as Walker delivers a healthy boy. The nurse is now apologetic and respectful toward Walker. Walker turns down interviews and slips away while Paco and the nurse concoct a story that Cardinez, a Mexican veterinarian, delivered the baby. When Gerard sees Cardinez being interviewed as the heroic doctor, he abandons his hunch. Paco celebrates with his coworkers, proposing a toast "to absent friends."

Episode #8
SEE HOLLYWOOD AND DIE
Original Airdate: November 5, 1963

Written by: George Eckstein   Directed by: Andrew McCullough

Cast: Brenda Vaccaro as Joanne Spencer, Chris Robinson as Miles, Lou Antonio as Vinnie, J. Pat O'Malley as Ray Lumis, Jimmy Hawkins as Carl Emory, Melinda Plowman as girlfriend. (Uncredited: Jason Wingreen as Tim Cates.)

Kimble, alias Al Fleming, works at Ray's Garage in Sierra Point, New Mexico (population 562). Ray and Al are preparing to close up when two young thugs, Miles and Vinnie, arrive to hold up the place. While the hoodlums collect a meager $35, another motorist, Joanne, pulls in. An attractive young lady, she has just left her groom-to-be at the altar. Miles goes outside to get rid of her, but, just then, a policeman also arrives at the garage. Before the cop realizes what is going on, the thugs open fire, wounding the officer and killing Ray. Vinnie and Miles take Al as a hostage and force Joanne to drive them in their getaway.

Vinnie and Miles discuss the ultimate elimination of Joanne and Al, having little further use for either. Al pulls a bluff, claiming to be a con man with a $150,000 job waiting for him in Los Angeles; perhaps Vinnie and Miles could be cut in on it. Al suggests that the thugs avoid roadblocks by taking the dirt road that leads to Flagstaff. They decide to buy a different car there, after a radio bulletin identifies their current vehicle.

Al talks a salesman down from $525 to $400 on a used car, impressing Vinnie with his smooth operational skills. Miles doesn't trust Al (whom he calls "Daddy") or his L.A. job story. Alone with Joanne momentarily, Al confides that he is on her side. The fugitives drop off Joanne's car at an abandoned house, but the maneuver is witnessed by two teenagers, one of whom contacts the police. The car is identified as the holdup men's getaway vehicle, and fingerprints are taken from it.

During a stop for food, Al stages a make-out session with Joanne. All the while, they are sharing secrets: he of his escape plans, she of her private life. After the journey resumes, a news bulletin informs the foursome of the fingerprint check. Miles notices Al's worried look, and surmises aloud that the police must have Al's prints already on file. Al confirms it.

They reach the San Fernando Valley, still negotiating on Al's "big job." Al says he has a partner in a large construction company, with a watchman's schedule, key, and combination to a safe containing $150,000. While Al does the dirty work, the partner will establish an alibi. Al offers Vinnie and Miles $5,000 apiece, one to act as lookout, the other to take care of the watchman. They are interested.

They stop for a newspaper and find Richard Kimble's picture on the front page of the *Los Angeles Tribune*. Joanne, learning the identity of her "savior," is disgusted. She rams the brakes from the passenger side and flees the car. Kimble chases her while the others circle around in the car. Kimble catches Joanne, telling her he is not guilty of murder and really is on her side. She is not convinced, but the conversation ends when Vinnie and Miles catch up with them.

Kimble stops at a phone booth to call his "partner." He sees a posted ad, featuring *Tribune* columnist Tim Cates and the paper's phone number. Kimble calls it, identifying himself as Richard Kimble, and telling Cates to meet him at Steele's Motor Lodge. Vinnie waits at the lodge for Kimble's partner, while Kimble and Miles drive off to "take care of" Joanne. Vinnie is soon visited by Cates, accompanied by a couple of police officers who arrest Vinnie.

Miles is about to shoot Joanne, but Kimble knocks the gun away and punches him out. Joanne encourages Kimble to drive to safety in the car, which he does. When the police arrive to arrest Miles and question Joanne, she points them in the wrong direction, ensuring Kimble's escape.

Episode #9
TICKET TO ALASKA
Original Airdate: November 12, 1963

Written by: Oliver Crawford   **Directed by:** Jerry Hopper

Cast: Geraldine Brooks as Anna Jonov A.K.A. Adrienne Banning, Murray Matheson as Morehead, John Larkin as Capt. Carraway, Tim O'Connor as Steve Lund, June Dayton as Celia Decker, David White as George Banning, Gail Kobe as Ruth Wyatt, Gene Lyons as Paul Vale.

The SS *Alaskan Star* (a nautical version of the *Orient Express*?) embarks on an eight-day trip from Seattle, Washington, to Ketchikan, Alaska, with a crew of 14. Among the passengers are George and Adrienne Banning, enjoying the fruits of a recent $100,000 embezzlement; Celia, having an affair with first officer Steve Lund, but not fully believing the rumor about his having a wife and two kids; Morehead, a gun aficionado; Ruth, a pistol-shooting champ; and convicted murderer Richard Kimble, alias Larry Tallman, a Larkspur Lumber Company employee. Vale, another passenger, is brought aboard from a launch six hours later, supposedly because he missed his connections on the Seattle departure.

In reality, Vale is a special undercover agent there to make an identification and arrest. During the Korean conflict, the International Brigade — a top-secret, multinational fighting unit formed by the United Nations — had been annihilated during its maiden mission. The disaster was attributed to a security leak: someone selling out to the enemy. Vale is hot on the trail of that someone. He will room with Tallman, the only other bachelor aboard.

Vale is found shot to death, and the ship goes under the jurisdiction of the U.S. Government's War Crimes Commission. While federal authorities await at Ketchikan, Capt. Carraway and Lund begin the examination and interrogation of passengers in search of a murder suspect. Tallman becomes the prime suspect when his references don't check out, and he admits to being (other than the murderer) the last person to see Vale alive. "A man with no past may be hiding one," points out the captain, who will be forced to turn Tallman over to the authorities in absence of further evidence. Tallman realizes he has just 36 hours to clear himself of the Vale murder.

Tallman asks Morehead to examine Vale's body with him, to determine the caliber of bullet used. Morehead theorizes it was a .22 or .25 caliber gun at close range, eliminating his own collection of larger weapons from suspicion. Tallman, having earlier seen a handgun spill out of Celia's purse, decides to check up on her. He finds a box of cartridges in her room and brings them to the attention of the captain, wondering how such incriminating evidence could have eluded Lund's room-by-room search. Lund confesses he didn't search Celia's room, and Celia explains that she and Lund are to be married. Carraway relieves Celia of her delusion and Lund of his duties. Celia says she did not use the pistol, that it was stolen prior to the murder.

The captain is more sympathetic toward the possibility of Tallman's innocence and of the true murderer getting away scot-free while Tallman is detained in Alaska. He agrees to help Tallman in a plan to reveal the murderer. In hopes of luring the killer into a trap, Tallman will claim to have found some possibly incriminating correspondence wedged between Vale's bunk and the wall.

Tallman makes his bluff where all can hear it, flashing a bogus envelope in the dining room. Tallman says the letters are written in Greek and that he is going down to the engine room to show them to a Greek-speaking crewman.

In the engine room Tallman is ordered to hand over the envelope by gun-toting Adrienne Banning. She admits to being the killer and the person Vale was after; she was not a communist sympathizer, merely a businesswoman. Carraway, hidden in the engine room, hears the confession, as does Morehead, who had followed behind. Morehead knocks the gun away and Adrienne is apprehended to be turned over to the authorities. Tallman is off the hook.

As they disembark, Ruth remarks to Tallman that "you just don't know who you're talking to these days."

Episode #10
FATSO
Original Airdate: November 19, 1963

Written by: Robert Pirosh   Directed by: Ida Lupino

Cast: Jack Weston as David O. "Davey" Lambert, Jr., Burt Brinckerhoff as Frank Lambert, Glenda Farrell as Peggy Lambert, Vaughn Taylor as Crowley, Paul Langton as Neil, Paul Birch as Capt. Carpenter, Henry Beckman as Brown, Garry Walberg as mechanic. (Uncredited: King Calder as David O. Lambert, Sr.)

Kimble, alias William "Bill" Carter, hitches a ride with a stranger. When the driver begins nodding off at the wheel, Bill takes over the driving. In Pikesville (population 963), a car backs into Bill's path. Bill swerves to avoid it and crashes into a parked car. Bill is arrested by the local sheriff, who saw Bill attempting to slink away from the scene. Bill is fingerprinted and locked into a cell with Davey "Fatso" Lambert, a 5'8", 260-pound simpleton who had been arrested as a drunk.

Bill befriends Davey, who tells Bill parts of his life story. He plans to return to his family's huge ranch — Oak Lane Farms in Ellsmore, Kentucky — for the first time in eight years. A letter from his mother, sent in care of a Los Angeles bar, had informed Davey of his father's serious illness.

When the sheriff opens the cell to release Davey, Bill knocks out the lawman and flees. Davey tags along with his new friend, and the two steal a Model-A car. They leave it off near a railroad, where they hop a freight bound for Springfield, some 80 miles away.

Lt. Gerard is contacted after Kimble's prints are identified, and he flies out to Pikesville. The getaway car is discovered, and Gerard deduces Kimble's mode of escape. He figures Kimble is somewhere between Pikesville and Springfield and that his traveling companion should make him easier to find.

Davey (visibly apprehensive) and Bill arrive at the Lambert ranch. They meet Davey's brother, Frank, who offers a sarcastic greeting. Davey is obviously intimidated by his brother, by the prospect of facing his father, even by the horses. He tends to deal with his fears by eating and drinking to excess.

Davey's mother is happy to see him, but his bedridden father greets him with only an icy stare. He finally speaks, sardonically: "How do you like the new barn?" Eight years earlier, while his parents were at a horse auction and Frank was stationed at the Camp Weatherton army base 15 miles away, Davey was left alone to oversee the ranch. An arsonist's fire had destroyed the barn and the horses in it, and Davey was accused of the premeditated crime. Although he didn't remember setting the fire, Davey became convinced of his own guilt and left in shame. He undoubtedly has been cut out of his parents' will in the meantime.

Bill encourages Davey to face his fears, confiding that he is a doctor who has treated cases like Davey's. Bill helps him overcome his fear of the horses, but the men are interrupted when Frank shows up aboard another horse. Going beyond his usual needling, Frank begins whipping Davey. Bill intervenes, pulling Frank off the horse and beating him in a fistfight. Frank wonders why someone who talks like a teacher lives like a bum and vows to make it his business to find out. Bill knows he will have to leave and tells Davey so, promising to write. Davey can't understand why Bill is abandoning him, so Bill explains why he is on the run. Davey wishes he could help somehow.

Mrs. Lambert gives Bill a ride out of town, telling the barn-fire story. Bill can't believe that Davey could have done such a thing and decides to do some checking. He hitches a ride with a soldier on his way to Camp Weatherton. Bill learns that Frank was AWOL from the camp on the night of the fire and had been court-martialed for the infraction. Bill returns to the Lambert ranch to share his discovery. Frank tells Sheriff Crowley that Davey is back in town with another man, reminding him that there must still be a warrant out for Davey's arrest. Crowley connects this news with the report on Kimble and contacts Gerard at Springfield. Gerard arrives and interrogates Davey who, in trying to protect his friend, confesses to the murder of Helen Kimble. Gerard has no trouble tripping up Davey on his story, and the lieutenant and the sheriff accompany Davey home.

Bill tells Mr. and Mrs. Lambert what he learned at the army base, and they realize it was Frank, not Davey, who started the fire. Just then Frank comes home, brandishing a rifle and saying the police are looking for Bill. The Lamberts aren't interested in that, wanting only to know about the barn. Mr. Lambert orders Frank over to his bedside and takes away the gun.

The police car arrives, and Bill admits that they are looking for him. Mrs. Lambert lets Bill go out the side door, ordering Frank to keep his mouth shut. Bill gets away while the Lamberts claim ignorance of his whereabouts. Some time later Davey, a new man, gets a letter from Bill.

Episode #11
NIGHTMARE AT NORTHOAK
Original Airdate: November 26, 1963

Written by: Stuart Jerome   **Directed by:** Chris Nyby

Cast: Nancy Wickwire as Wilma Springer, Frank Overton as Sheriff Al Springer, Paul Carr as Ernie, Scott Lane as Larry Springer, Ian Wolfe as Dr. Babcock, Bobs Watson as Milton Plummer, Paul Birch as Capt. Carpenter, Barbara Pepper as Matty, Doreen Lang as Anna, Harry Hickox as Charley, Sue Randall as Jen, Charles Herbert as Cal.

Kimble naps in the brush of Northoak, New Hampshire. He experiences his recurring nightmare: Gerard following him down a city street and cornering him in an alley, holding him at gunpoint with the words "Finally, Kimble ... finally." Kimble is awakened by a bang, the sound of a tire blowing out. He sees a school bus careen out of control, crash, and burst into flames. Kimble rushes to the rescue, pulling the children and the unconscious bus driver to safety. As Kimble makes his final sweep of the bus, it explodes, throwing him out the rear exit. Kimble is knocked unconscious, suffering from a concussion and blurred vision.

Kimble awakens in the home of Al and Wilma Springer, who promise him free board while he recuperates. Their son, Larry, was among the rescued children. Other townspeople fill the Springer house, all wanting to do something to help or reward the mysterious hero who saved their children. Plummer, a cub reporter for the *Northoak Courier*, arrives, seeking a photo of the sleeping hero but is turned away by Mrs. Springer. Plummer offers Larry $2 to take the picture, with the added bonus of making his rescuer famous. Larry obliges, and the next morning's edition has the picture on the front page, with the headline "Unknown Hero Saves Children." The wire services also pick up the story and photo. Despite a compress which obscures the hero's eyes, Lt. Gerard is sure the mystery man is Kimble. He calls the Oak County Sheriff's Office and asks sheriff Al Springer to send him the hero's fingerprints.

Kimble, who gives his name as George Porter, sees the newspaper photo and learns that his host is the county sheriff. Although he is in no condition to travel, Kimble decides it is time to move on. He sneaks out the window and runs off but falls unconscious a half mile away. He is found by some schoolboys and "rescued," winding up back at the Springer residence. His escape is dismissed as a delirious romp.

Al feels bad about having to fingerprint the town's hero but is obliged to do so. Wilma wonders what is going on, and Al tells her that some crazy detective thinks Mr. Porter might be a wanted killer. Al goes to make a phone call, and Wilma suddenly realizes why Porter wandered off: he *is* the wanted man, and he was trying to escape. Confronted by this theory, Porter admits he is Kimble but says he is innocent. Kimble pleads for a chance to escape, saying "Is that too much to ask, a life for a life?" Wilma, daughter of a judge, adheres to her rigid sense of right and wrong ("what's right is right" is her motto) and tells Al who Porter really is. Al reluctantly takes him to the station to be locked up, and Gerard is contacted.

Kimble awakens from his nightmare to find Gerard looking at him through the cell bars. Gerard must wait some three hours before the extradition papers come back from the capital, allowing him to take Kimble. Al invites Gerard to join him for dinner at his home while deputy Ernie is left in charge.

A victorious Gerard shares Kimble-hunting stories with the Springers. Larry leaves in tears, upset that his photo led to his rescuer's arrest. Gerard advises Wilma to "convince him that he did the right thing, just as you know that you did." Wilma reflects on her lifetime of doing the right things, and self-doubts creep in. This "right thing" will send the man who saved her son's life to his own death.

Gerard returns to the station, checking on Kimble. The two have a powerful dialog, including discussion about the one-armed man. "Your nightmare," Kimble declares to an obviously unnerved Gerard, "is that when I'm dead, you'll find him."

Al returns to the station with more than a dozen townspeople who want to bid farewell to their doomed hero. Gerard objects, but Al is still in charge. In a touching scene, the people take turns shaking hands with Kimble and offering expressions of gratitude. The last in line is Wilma, who secretly passes Kimble the cell key.

Gerard makes a final check on Kimble, seeing only a blanket-covered lump in the cell cot. He opens the cell to investigate and is knocked out from behind by Kimble. Kimble takes Gerard's gun, orders Ernie into the cell, and locks both of them in it before making his escape.

The next day, Al assembles the townspeople — one of whom presumably passed Kimble the key — at the station for Gerard's benefit. Gerard accuses Al of the misdeed, promising to charge him with aiding and abetting a fugitive. Wilma speaks up, admitting that she slipped Kimble the key. After Gerard explains the consequences of her confession, the other townspeople take turns confessing to the crime. Gerard sees that it is a hopeless situation and gives up.

Episode #12
GLASS TIGHTROPE
Original Airdate: December 3, 1963

Story by: Robert C. Dennis & Barry Trivers   **Teleplay by:** Robert C. Dennis
Directed by: Ida Lupino

Cast: Leslie Nielsen as Martin C. Rowland, Diana Van Der Vlis as Ginny Denshaw Rowland, Edward Binns as Angstrom, Jud Taylor as Floyd Bolton, Jay Adler as Arthur Tibbetts, Robert Quarry as Howard Pascoe, Dort Clark as Sgt. Kronas, Tom Palmer as D.A., Warren Parker as Lewis.

Kimble, alias Harry Carson, has worked two days in the stockroom of Denshaw's Department Store in Sioux City, Iowa. The store's president is Martin Rowland, a former all-American fullback, who got his "in" by marrying Ginny Denshaw, daughter of the store's founder. Martin has worked hard to earn his status and resents insinuations to the contrary.

Floyd, another Denshaw's employee, is assigned to pick up a couple of items at the Excelsior Club on Wednesday night. He has a hot date planned instead and asks Harry to cover for him. Harry does the errand but, as he is leaving, becomes a witness to manslaughter. Howie, an "old friend" of Martin's, had begun baiting Martin at the club, dropping remarks about his "sugar mama" and about her reputation. The discussion spills out into the parking lot and ends with Martin punching Howie. Howie goes down, knocking his head against a parked car, but returns to his feet. After Martin leaves, Howie collapses with a fatal, massive cerebral hemorrhage. Harry checks Howie's condition and takes off. Tibbetts, a vagrant, stumbles upon the scene of the manslaughter. He removes the victim's wallet and watch and proceeds on his way.

Harry anonymously calls an ambulance. The police arrive at the scene, finding Tibbetts nearby. With frequent previous arrests to go with the wallet and watch, Tibbetts becomes the prime murder suspect. Martin will later testify that Howie was standing when Martin left him, making Tibbetts's outlook even bleaker.

Harry feels for Tibbetts, unjustly accused of murder as he himself had been. Harry anonymously calls Martin, saying he witnessed the incident. Ginny listens in on another extension, and both figure the call's purpose is blackmail. The manipulative Ginny is all for paying it; not only does she want her husband free of trouble, but she fears his confession — complete with details about Martin's and Howie's argument — would make her "the filthy joke of the town." Ginny contacts Angstrom, an old family friend and former cop who is now the Denshaw's store detective. She asks her to identify the blackmailer and deliver him to the Rowlands for negotiations.

Harry types up an anonymous note to Martin: "I insist you go to the authorities at once. You can only help yourself and help an innocent man, too ..." Angstrom connects the note with the typewriter used by Floyd in the store office. Having already been suspicious of Floyd's overlong errand on Wednesday, the detective interrogates him. Floyd finally admits that Harry was the driver that night, and Angstrom heads to Harry's residence.

Harry packs his bag after reserving a seat on a bus (under the name "George Paxton") to Chicago. He then makes an anonymous call to the police, telling them that Martin killed Howie accidentally. Angstrom arrives in time to overhear the conversation, and he brings Harry to the store at gunpoint. The detective will use his influence at the police department to ensure that Harry's call is disregarded.

Angstrom delivers Harry to Ginny, whose husband is momentarily away. Ginny opens negotiations with Harry, coming on to him in the process. She offers either a lifetime job with Denshaw's (including a substantial pay raise) or $10,000 cash. Harry refuses both, saying he seeks only justice. Ginny is suspicious that Harry didn't just go to the police, and asks Angstrom to check whether Harry might have a police record. Angstrom digs up Richard Kimble's "wanted" poster at police headquarters.

Martin shows up at the store, and Harry lays a guilt trip on him. Angstrom then arrives with the poster. Kimble says he is innocent of murder, unjustly convicted just as Tibbetts will be if Martin doesn't speak up. Martin is impressed that Kimble took a chance like this, while all Martin stood to lose was "something I never really owned." Over Ginny's strenuous objections, Martin phones the police and confesses to killing Howie. He also allows Kimble to escape.

Episode #13
TERROR AT HIGHPOINT
Original Airdate: December 17, 1963

Story by: Peter Germano   **Teleplay by:** Peter Germano & Harry Kronman
Directed by: Jerry Hopper

Cast: Jack Klugman as Buck Harmon, Elizabeth Allen as Ruth Harmon, James Best as Dan Murdy, Buck Taylor as Jamie, Doreen McLean as Mrs. Hendricks, Richard Wessell as Charley Hendricks, Richard Webb as Kripps, Russ Vincent as Rufe, Billy Halop as Mike.

Kimble, alias Paul Beaumont, works as a timekeeper for a construction crew at Highpoint, in the hills above Salt Lake City, Utah. The crew, armed with heavy machinery, is literally moving a mountain to make room for an irrigational river. Paul's boss, Buck, wonders why a "college man" like Paul settles for such a low-scale job and notices that Paul seems to fear the police.

Jamie, a retarded young man, comes to the construction site, looking for work. He feels responsible for supporting his younger sister and widowed mother. Paul befriends Jamie and convinces Buck to hire him as water boy. Buck is reluctant, remembering his own difficulties of growing up with a retarded brother. Buck is even afraid to have children with Ruth, his wife of seven years, thinking that retarded offspring are genetically inevitable.

Jamie becomes the target of constant ridicule and trickery from members of the crew, particularly Dan. Paul intervenes after Dan pushes Jamie into a mud puddle. "A dumb kid like him could make a lot of trouble," Dan explains, then pushes Paul into the puddle. A fistfight ensues, with Paul getting the better of it before Buck breaks it up. Buck warns that if Jamie gets involved in any more trouble, he's through.

Ruth becomes fond of Jamie and spends afternoons helping him learn to read. She lends him the book *Robinson Crusoe* to practice with. Buck comes home, and Jamie leaves. Buck and Ruth soon get into their recurring argument about not having children. Buck storms out and leaves early the next day for work. Ruth comes to the construction site to make up with Buck. Dan, who has known Ruth since her days as a cocktail waitress in Elco, remarks to his coworkers that she is "stuck up."

Dan invites Jamie to sit up in a piece of heavy equipment, "training" him how to drive it and claiming it is Buck's idea. Dan slips the rig into low gear and it rambles away. Frightened, Jamie pulls a lever in hopes of stopping the vehicle but instead sends it into high gear. It barrels down a hill for a few hundred yards before Jamie manages to stop it. The crewmen surround the rig, and Jamie runs off. Buck, at the end of his patience, fires Jamie.

Paul finds Jamie atop a mountain where they had once hiked together. He promises to help Jamie find a new job. Meanwhile, Ruth is upset with Buck for firing the lad. One word leads to another, and they are soon back to the same old argument. Buck again storms out to get drunk.

Jamie heads for Ruth's trailer to return the book. Ruth is about to enter the shower when she is grabbed from behind by a man. She struggles with him, nearly getting strangled. She screams, but she never gets a good look at the attacker. Jamie arrives just as the villain exits through the back, having left Ruth naked, bleeding, and unconscious, suffering from shock and a probable concussion. Frightened, Jamie runs out, losing his cap. Mrs. Hendricks, a neighbor alerted by the scream, goes out just in time to see Jamie fleeing the scene. She finds Ruth and summons Buck and the police.

Buck is enraged and takes out after Jamie, the presumed assailant. Paul tries to convince Buck that Jamie is incapable of such a crime (Paul is "trained to know" such things), but Buck isn't listening. Meanwhile, Dan eggs on a lynch mob of construction workers to pursue Jamie, ignoring Paul's attempts to dissuade them. With nightfall on Highpoint, the men employ a huge arclight to search for Jamie on the mountain, his likely place of refuge.

Paul finds Jamie on the mountain, convincing the lad to come down with him. Paul promises his safety, saying that the police will take care of him. As the two descend the mountain, the searchlight finds Jamie, and Dan fires a shot at him. The police arrive and Jamie tells his story, pointing out Dan as the man he saw leaving Ruth's trailer. Scratches on Dan's arm confirm the accusation, and Dan is arrested.

Paul (the "best man at the job I ever had") later tells Buck he will be moving on. He convinces Buck that retardation isn't hereditary, enabling Buck to finally overcome his fear. Paul takes Jamie home and heads on his way, while Buck reconciles with Ruth with a bright new outlook.

Episode #14
THE GIRL FROM LITTLE EGYPT
Original Airdate: December 24, 1963

Written by: Stanford Whitmore **Directed by:** Vincent McEveety

Cast: Pamela Tiffin as Ruth Norton, Ed Nelson as Paul Clements, Diane Brewster as Helen Kimble, June Dayton as Doris Clements, Bernard Kates as Lester Rand, Jerry Paris as Lt. Jim Prestwick, Bing Russell as Officer Westphal,

William Newell as Judge, Rudy Dolan as officer. (Uncredited: Bill Raisch as one-armed man.)

Ruth Norton, from Little Egypt, Illinois, is a very attractive 23-year-old stewardess based in San Francisco, California. Four months earlier she had met Paul Clements on a flight. He called her a week later, they had dinner, and a torrid romance began. Her flight schedules enabled them to get together only once a week, usually on Wednesday evenings at a little cafe. On this Wednesday, an acquaintance of Paul's happens by and asks about Paul's wife. Thus, Ruth learns that she has been having an illicit affair with a married man. Ruth leaves the cafe in tears and speeds off in her car, driving erratically. She bashes into a pedestrian standing at the roadside, and stops, horrified. The man, who will give his name as George Browning, is unconscious, suffering from a concussion, bruises, cuts, and an injured left leg. George is taken to the hospital, and the greatly remorseful Ruth follows along.

George drifts into consciousness, finding Ruth and Officer Westphal at his bedside. The officer asks him what happened, and he says he stepped out into the road. With Ruth off the hook, Westphal leaves. George drifts off again and rambles deliriously. From these ramblings Ruth learns that George is actually Dr. Richard Kimble, an innocent man sentenced to be executed.

When George reawakens, Ruth confronts him with her knowledge. Regretful about the accident and indebted to George, she wants to help him. George had not only spared her from criminal liability but snapped her out of a mission to commit suicide. She takes him home with her, and he rests in her bedroom.

From dream sequences and flashbacks, we learn much about the events preceding and following Helen Kimble's murder. Helen had given birth to a stillborn boy, almost losing her own life in the process, and efforts to save her had left her barren. Devastated, Helen had refused to consider adoption, which she considered a "lie": if she couldn't have her own children, she wouldn't have any. This became a source of frequent, bitter arguments — overheard by neighbors — between the Kimbles. Helen (who had increased her daily alcohol intake) once fell against a bureau, badly bruising her cheek; neighbors suspected the doctor had given Helen a "face job" during one of their spats. One night, after Dick had mentioned someone from the Planned Parenthood clinic, she flew into another rage. Exasperated, Dick stormed out and drove away to collect himself. He stopped by a bridge, watching a lad (who would later testify that he hadn't seen Kimble) fish from a rowboat. Kimble returned home to see a one-armed man fleeing from his house, and discovered his wife dead on the floor. During the ensuing trial, Lt. Gerard testified that his office had interrogated 83 one-armed men — none of whom could have been at the Kimble house — within ten days of the murder. Swearing his innocence, Kimble nevertheless was convicted of murder and sentenced to execution. While en route to this appointment, Kimble's train derailed and he managed to escape. He swiped a tool (from a gas station) to file off his handcuff and jumped aboard a departing truck to get out of the area.

Paul comes to apologize to Ruth, hinting he will divorce his wife, then begins unwelcome advances on Ruth. In a subtle rescue, George appears, claiming to be Ruth's brother (thus changing his surname to Norton) visiting from out of town. Paul leaves, noting George's bum leg. On the way out Paul sees Ruth's bashed-in headlight and wonders what is going on. He asks a buddy on the police force, Lt. Prestwick, to check into any recent auto accident involving Ruth. Prestwick reports back that she was involved in an accident with a transient pedestrian, George Browning. Paul puts two and two together and gets five, theorizing that George is blackmailing Ruth over the accident, and knowing for sure that he is interfering with Paul's weekly romance. Meanwhile, George continually moralizes to Ruth about her affair with Paul.

Paul calls Ruth, directing her to have George meet him at the Red Lion bar. George goes, and Paul offers him $500 cash to clear out. George turns down the money, offering a cheaper deal: if Paul will take Ruth out to dinner and the theater in public on Saturday night, George will leave Sunday morning. Paul says he can't, as he is entertaining family and friends at home on Saturday. Paul warns that "as of now, you know more about me than I do about you," implying that that could change. On that note, George leaves.

George takes Ruth out on Saturday, being coy about their destination. They arrive at a stately house which she doesn't recognize and are greeted at the door by Paul (stammering that they are friends of his) and his wife. Ruth is crushed, Paul is livid. Ruth meets Paul's loyal wife (the perfect hostess), their two charming boys, and their circle of well-to-do friends. Ruth finally takes George aside, wondering why he would do something so cruel. "Look around," he advises. "Do you think he's going to give all this up for you?" Ruth concedes that he has made his point, and they prepare to leave. On the patio, Ruth tells Paul that she will be moving to where he can't find her. Paul, drunk, lunges for George but lands on the ground. George and Ruth have a farewell drink at the cafe. George gives his final advice on romance and thanks Ruth for "running me down." He leaves on the California-Arizona bus.

Episode #15
HOME IS THE HUNTED
Original Airdate: January 7, 1964

Written by: Arthur Weiss   **Directed by:** Jerry Hopper

Cast: Jacqueline Scott as Donna Kimble Taft, Andrew Prine as Ray Kimble, Robert Keith as Dr. John Kimble, James Sikking as Leonard Taft, Billy Mumy as David Taft, Clint Howard as Billy Taft, James Nolan as Floyd, Paul Birch as Capt. Carpenter.

Pediatrician John Kimble, the fugitive's father, has retired at age 70. The travails of his two sons, Richard and Ray, have weighed heavily on him, and Dr. Kimble recently suffered a heart attack. He has put his Stafford, Indiana, home up for sale, moving into a nearby country house at "The Meadows," and donated his prized medical library to the University of Wisconsin. Richard reads about this endowment in the *Stafford Times* and realizes something is amiss. Risking his freedom, Dick takes a bus from Madison to Stafford, his home for the first 33 years of his life.

Dick phones sister Donna with his whereabouts and sneaks into his father's abandoned house. She arranges to bring Dad there, but brother Ray refuses to join them. Since Dick's escape, Ray has become an embittered young man. His fiancée had broken up with him after a ten-year relationship, and he has lost job after job as employers and their clients discovered he was the brother of an escaped murderer. He has earned a reputation for carousing, drinking, and spending to excess. His reckless driving has gotten him many a ticket, but he has channeled this fault into a new hobby: auto racing. In fact, he is scheduled to race in his *Kimble Special* (a 1961 Porsche roadster given him by Dick) tomorrow, Sunday, at a track just down the hill from his father's new residence.

The doctors Kimble, father and son, are reunited after two years' separation. Dick promises to outrun and outlast Lt. Gerard, and Dad relates his troubles with his health and with Ray. He feels guilty for having shown favoritism to Dick during the boys' childhood, perhaps an underlying reason for Ray's problems. Donna and her husband also stop to visit Dick, and Ray finally makes a reluctant, token appearance. He greets Dick coolly, and Dick wonders what his problem is. Ray chronicles his troubles, hinting that he doesn't believe in his brother's innocence. After an argument with Dick and Dad, Ray storms out. Dick resolves not to leave town until he straightens things out with his brother.

The next morning, Ray is once again arrested for speeding. He is brought to Lt. Gerard's attention at the station. Gerard, thinking that Dick might try coming to (or already be in) Stafford, tests his suspicions by probing Ray. Despite his resentment and mistrust of Dick, Ray deflects the line of questioning. Dick *is*, after all, his brother, and Ray is not about to betray him to the enemy.

Donna brings her two boys over to the Kimble house so Dick can observe his adorable nephews without their seeing him. They play in the house, and the older boy, David, makes a neat find: Dick's bottle of hair dye. Gerard pays a visit to the Kimble house, asking Donna whether she has heard from Dick. While Dick hides in another room, Donna takes umbrage at Gerard's questions and sends him on his way. There is a near-miss as he departs: David offers Gerard a shoe-shine, but Gerard declines without seeing the hair-dye bottle.

Donna and Dad drive Dick (hiding in the back) to the Meadows residence, but Ray has already left to prepare for his race. Donna goes to the track to fetch him, asking Ray to drive off the track during a practice lap and to see Dick before he leaves. Ray doesn't want to go, but when Gerard comes snooping around, Ray leaves to warn Dick. Gerard hassles Donna some more while Ray heads for the house. Ray warns Dick to get out of there, as Gerard is nearby and may be on to him.

Dick says he can't leave with Ray thinking he is a murderer. Ray says he has tried to believe Dick and wants to, but can't. "Make me believe you!" Ray demands. "Prove it to me!" Dick walks out of the house, saying he is going down the hill to turn himself in; if even his own brother doesn't believe in his innocence, it's just not worth it to keep running. "If there was any other way to prove it," Dick says, "I would." Ray realizes Dick is telling the truth, and pleads with him not to go down the hill.

Dick says goodbye to his father for the last time, and Dad tells him that the medical books were donated under the condition that they be turned over to Dick on the day he is exonerated. Ray drives Dick away, flagging down the Madison bus. Meanwhile, Gerard — suspicious because Ray didn't return for the race — goes to the Kimble house, once again a step behind his quarry.

Episode #16
GARDEN HOUSE
Original Airdate: January 14, 1964

Written by: Sheldon Stark   **Directed by:** Ida Lupino

Cast: Pippa Scott as Carol Willard, Peggy McCay as Ann Willard Guthrie, Robert Webber as Harlan Guthrie.

When Ann and Carol Willard's father died, Ann became the sole heiress to his fortune: the house, the money, and the newspaper, the *Westborne* (Connecticut) *Clarion*. Ann was rewarded for being the loving daughter who stayed at home while Carol was roaming the world in search of good times. Harlan Guthrie married Ann for her money, becoming editor of the *Clarion*, and Carol finally came home and became the paper's photographer. Harlan and Carol have been having a steamy affair for some time and scheme for the day that they will bump off Ann, inherit her fortune, and live happily ever after.

Their first attempt is botched. Harlan "forgets" to tighten the saddle girder on a bucking bronco that Ann rides, but ranch-hand Richard Kimble (alias Sanford) comes to the rescue just as the horse is on the verge of throwing her.

Carol notices that Sanford is camera-shy. Suspicious, she goes through the *Clarion* morgue and discovers a back issue with the headline "Killer Kimble Escapes," accompanied by Sanford's picture. Carol shares her discovery with Harlan, pointing out that they have not only an exclusive blockbuster story but a perfect fall-guy for the murder of Ann Guthrie.

Harlan (claiming he doesn't have the patience to do it himself) gives Sanford a new job: to take Ann under his wing, helping her learn to ride a horse and shoot a gun like the ranch-girl she was brought up to be. Sanford and Ann seem to work well together, and Carol secretly photographs the two together. The photos will show the two, apparently very happy together, in a variety of activities. The plan is that Harlan will shoot Ann, claiming Kimble did it following the end of their affair together.

During a party on Wednesday, Carol wanders outside and finds Sanford alone. She flirts with and kisses him, dropping her purse and Sealane Motel key in the process. Harlan comes out to find Carol, and they walk away. Sanford picks up the key and goes out to return it to Carol but finds her and Harlan making out. He overhears Harlan say "until Ann is gone, we have got to be very careful."

The next day, Sanford tries to share his suspicions with Ann, but she becomes irate. She tells Harlan what Sanford said, ordering her husband to fire the hand. Harlan confronts Sanford, who says he will leave on the 10:00 bus that evening. Harlan realizes he will have to make his move tonight. Meanwhile, Ann goes to her private hideaway, a gazebo called the "garden house," to sort out her feelings.

Sanford goes to the *Clarion* office to confront Carol. He tells her that he is on to her plot, having talked to the owner of the Sealane Motel in Bayville and having learned that she and Harlan were frequent guests there. He warns Carol that, should any harm come to Ann, he will send the key with a letter to the district attorney. Carol wrestles with her options and even considers warning her sister.

Harlan meets Ann at home but, with a servant on the premises, doesn't want to execute the plan there. He tells Ann about his affair with Carol, his desire only for Ann's money, and Sanford's identity (showing her the newspaper article).

Upset, Ann flees the house. Harlan takes a pistol and goes to the garden house, awaiting her inevitable arrival there. Sanford returns to the house and finds the article on the floor and the gun drawer open and empty. He, too, heads for the garden house, hoping to avert a murder.

A woman enters the garden house and Harlan fires. Sanford, followed closely by Ann, rushes to the scene to discover that Harlan has shot Carol by mistake. Sanford engages in a fistfight with Harlan, knocking him out. With her sister by her side, Carol dies.

Sanford walks home with Ann, who promises not to mention him when she calls the police. Sanford runs off, and Ann ponders the upcoming changes in her life, including her new job as editor of the *Clarion*. One of her first editorials will be one pleading for justice for the unjustly accused.

Act I: The 1963-64 Season   33

Episode #17
COME WATCH ME DIE
Original Airdate: January 21, 1964
Story by: Perry Bleecker   **Teleplay by:** Stanford Whitmore
Directed by: Laslo Benedek

Cast: Robert Doyle as Paul Bellows, Bruce Dern as Charley Bright, Judson Pratt as Joe Bowers, John Anderson as Ed Clement, Russell Collins as Cal Shrader, Randy Boone as Benjy Bright, Virginia Christine as Cora, John McLiam as Jeff, John Harmon as Tad Crumers, David McLean as Sheriff, Diane Ladd as Stella.

Paul Bellows returns to the home of Mr. and Mrs. Bright in Black Moccasin, Tyler County, Nebraska, in hopes of procuring some money. He had robbed the Brights of $50 three years earlier, but they had declined to press charges. This time no money is forthcoming, so Bellows does the only thing a man of his mentality can think of: he murders the Brights. Bellows is seen fleeing the vicinity of the house by the Brights' sons, Charley and Benjy, as well as a couple of neighbors. An armed posse flushes Bellows out of the wheat fields, and he is brought into custody. He, along with the "witnesses," will have to be transported to the county seat for a hearing with the sheriff. The proprietor of Tad Crumers Farm Equipment is asked to supply a bus for this errand.

Crumers asks his mechanic of a few weeks, Kimble (alias Ben Rogers), to drive the bus. Rogers reluctantly complies, and is sworn in as a "temporary aide" to deputy-sheriff Joe Bowers (a notorious lush). While Rogers drives, the witnesses express their opinions about Bellows's guilt and his deserved fate. Rogers points out that Bellows is just a suspect at this point and should not be badgered like that. The group drives into a thunderstorm.

Bowers takes over the wheel, and Rogers is left to sit beside Bellows. The suspect thanks Rogers for his speech and says, "You don't know how it feels: arrested, hated, (and) you didn't even do it." This hits home with Rogers, who becomes a sympathetic ear. Bellows claims he had gone out of his way to visit and apologize to the Brights, whom he loved like parents; finding them dead, he had panicked and fled, knowing he would be blamed.

Bowers stops at a diner, picking up a jug of booze for the long ride. As the witnesses talk among themselves, passing the jug around, they realize they don't have a very solid case against Bellows. Several voices suggest that they take the law into their own hands rather than go through the wasteful charade of a trial.

Faced with a washed-out bridge ahead, the group stops at the Pike Motel for the night. Bellows is handcuffed to his bedpost, with Rogers on guard. Bellows pleads with Rogers to get him out of there before he is lynched. Bowers, trashed, comes in to relieve Rogers and promptly conks out. Rogers takes the cuff keys, detaches Bellows from the post, and cuffs him to his own wrist. They escape out the window. During their flight, Bellows hacks up his leg on a barbed-wire fence.

Rogers stops at a farmhouse belonging to Jeff and Cora, asking to use their phone. Told that the storm knocked out their phone line, Rogers cuffs Bellows to a pipe in their kitchen and walks to the nearest public phone. He calls the sheriff, 22 miles away, who is already suspicious of Rogers's role in the escape. Rogers promises that the prisoner will be there waiting for the sheriff. The lawman rounds up the posse and heads out to the farmhouse.

Meanwhile, Bellows has been calculating his escape. Jeff holds a double-barreled shotgun on Bellows while Cora attends to his wound. Noting that Bellows is no older than their own son, the sympathetic Cora sends Jeff to fetch some bandages from the barn. Jeff returns to find Bellows holding Cora hostage, her own sewing shears at her throat. Jeff obediently cuts off the handcuffs while Bellows boasts about his earlier murders. Bellows takes the gun and limps toward the state highway through two miles of woods. After Rogers returns and finds out all that happened, he sets after the killer, soon tracking him down.

The sheriff, after interrogating Jeff and Cora, takes the posse in pursuit of the two fugitives. Bellows fires two shots at Rogers but misses. He asks Rogers why he is going to so much trouble just to live up to his role as temporary deputy. "If I'm not against you, I'm for you," Rogers explains, "and if I'm for you, I'm lost." The two grapple and engage in a fistfight, which Rogers wins by knockout just as the posse arrives.

Afterward, the admiring sheriff suggests that Rogers consider a career in law enforcement, preferably at his service. Rogers politely declines and goes on his way.

Episode #18
WHERE THE ACTION IS
Original Airdate: January 28, 1964

Written by: Harry Kronman   **Directed by:** James Sheldon

Cast: Telly Savalas as Daniel Polichek, Joanna Frank as Chris Polichek, Don Keefer as Ben Haddock, Maxine Stuart as Mrs. Gaines, Connie Gilchrist as proprietor, Beverly Hills as stripper.

On Tuesday, Kimble, alias Jerry "Shelly" Shelton, is on his first day as lifeguard at the Rainbow, a resort in Reno, Nevada. Chris and several other youths are horsing around near the pool, and Shelly warns them to stop. Chris pushes a friend into the pool. The friend lands on top of a young swimmer, knocking him senseless. Shelly jumps in and rescues the boy, bringing him to safety as the youths disappear.

Shelly is called into the office by his employer, Dan Polichek. He passes the boy's parents on their way out. Mr. Gaines, the boy's father (and a lawyer on a losing streak at the casinos), has just extorted $1,000 from Polichek as a silent settlement for the mishap. Polichek wants Shelly to tell him who the "fresh young kids" that caused the accident were. The lovely Chris, who happens to be Polichek's daughter, enters the room, flirting with Shelly. Shelly says he doesn't know who the kids were but will kick them out next time. After Shelly leaves, Polichek admonishes Chris not to become involved with this lifeguard as she had with the last (costing her father $10,000 in buy-out money).

Twelve years earlier, Polichek's wife, Constance, had walked out on him with $30,000 of his money. She was granted custody of young Chris but didn't want her. Constance shacked up in San Francisco for eight months with a boyfriend, who ran out as soon as the money did, after which she took her own life at age 36. Chris had been spared the truth about her mother, whom she adored. To this day she believes her heartless father kicked out her loving mother, driving her to suicide with his jealousy, suspicion, and pride. Resentful, Chris has devoted her life to hurting and embarrassing her father.

Chris visits Shelly at poolside after hours, flirting some more, but Shelly is not interested. The tipsy Chris jumps into the pool, fully clothed, and Shelly jumps in after her. He pulls Chris out of the water, slapping her and calling her a "rude, drunken brat." Chris, upset, leaves wearing Shelly's robe.

The next morning Polichek asks Chris what happened, and she tells him. Polichek then asks Shelly, who confirms Chris's version. Polichek warns Shelly not to become involved with his daughter; Shelly calls Chris, telling her to leave him alone from now on. Ben, Polichek's "unofficial" assistant, reports to his boss that Shelly phoned Chris. Polichek orders Shelly's personnel file pulled and his references checked. Of course, they don't check out, giving Polichek ample reason to send Shelly packing when necessary.

Shelly prepares to do some errands in town, and Chris offers to drive him. He declines, so she threatens to tell her father that Shelly got out of line. Shelly reluctantly joins her, and Ben sees them drive off. Shelly learns Chris's version of what happened to her mother.

Ben approaches Shelly at a casino, handing him an envelope containing $500 "traveling money." Shelly is to take the 9:00 A.M. United flight to Los Angeles tomorrow. Ben accompanies Shelly to his room to pack, and Polichek comes to supervise. Chris storms in, telling her father that if he runs Shelly out of town, she will leave as well. After Chris leaves, Polichek threatens to dig out whatever Shelly is hiding from. "She must mean an awful lot to you," Shelly remarks. "Why don't you tell her sometime?" Shelly is brought to the Airway Motel, where he registers under the name "Wilkerson."

Chris tracks down Shelly, invites herself into his room, and proposes marriage to him. Shelly dismisses the offer, telling Chris to leave him out of her schemes to hurt her father. "You're his whole world," Shelly tells Chris, suggesting she make the first move to reconcile. She agrees, asking Shelly to accompany her for moral support. They drive back toward the Rainbow.

Polichek has discovered Chris is missing and concludes she is with Shelly. He describes Chris's car to the police, telling them that Shelly stole $500 from his cash box. Police pull the car over and take Shelly to the station, where Polichek awaits.

Shelly, desperate to get out of there, goads the Policheks into talking things out. Dan finally tells Chris the truth about her mother, and Chris realizes how much her father must love her. The family feud ended, Polichek tells the police he made a mistake about Shelly.

The Policheks see Shelly off on his flight. Dan remarks on Shelly's evident life of fear and running, calling it a good life wasted. "Not all of it wasted," answers Chris, smiling lovingly at her father.

Episode #19
SEARCH IN A WINDY CITY
Original Airdate: February 4, 1964

Written by: Stuart Jerome   Directed by: Jerry Hopper

Cast: Pat Hingle as Mike Decker, Nan Martin as Paula Decker, Addison Richards as Fred Connely, Lewis Charles as Cogen, Paul Picerni as Sgt. Al DeSantis, Arthur Batanides as Wimpy, L. Stanford Jolley as old man, Dennis Cross as bus driver, Bill Raisch as one-armed man.

Kimble has met a lady in Omaha who was beaten up by a one-armed man. If she were to go to the police, the man had warned, the same would happen to her as did to the Kimble woman. Kimble learns that the man bought a ticket to Chicago, and he does the same. Kimble spends ten days in a futile search for his quarry before seeking out newspaper columnist Mike Decker ("From the Top of the Deck"). Kimble is hopeful that Decker, who defended him in print during his trial a year earlier, can help him somehow.

Kimble calls Decker and meets him at his apartment. Decker shows Kimble his private file on the Kimble case, including an artist's sketch of the one-armed man. Decker says he is "willing to go all out to help," as long as he calls the shots. Decker, whose wife, Paula, has spent the past three months in an alcoholism treatment center, lets Kimble stay the night at his place.

Decker tries to sell the potential-Pulitzer story idea to his editor. The boss advances Decker $5,000 in expense money in exchange for Decker's guarantee of a blockbuster Kimble story—whether it be the capture of the one-armed man or of Kimble himself.

Decker's wife arrives home unexpectedly, meeting the house guest. He gives his name as George Blake, but she soon realizes his true identity. He has nothing to fear: it was she who had researched the Kimble case and encouraged her husband to write the columns. Mike comes home, excited about his editor's support. Paula recommends that Kimble get some sort of formal guarantee from Mike, but Kimble says Mike's word is good enough for him.

Decker begins passing out copies of the police sketch to various informants, including Cogen and Wimpy. Each contact is given $100 as "incentive" money, with a promise of $1,000 more for the amputee's apprehension. Wimpy, playing both sides, goes to the police with a tip that Decker is looking for the one-armed man. Lt. Gerard is contacted, and he rushes to the Windy City. He suspects that Kimble either is already in the area or will be lured there by the search for the mythical one-armed man. Area informants are to be questioned.

Cogen contacts Decker with a big scoop: he has found and met the one-armed man, who plans to leave town tomorrow. Cogen arranges a bogus deal with the amputee, who is to phone Cogen at 9 P.M. to set up a meeting. Decker and Kimble will await Cogen's call so they can be on hand at the meeting place. Moments before the one-armed man's call, however, Cogen is picked up for questioning by the police. Cogen finally phones Decker with the bad news at 2 A.M.

Decker realizes his only remaining alternative is to turn Kimble in. Paula figures out Mike's plan and blasts him for his lack of integrity. Although he prides himself on keeping his word, he has a history of screwing "friends" when he is cornered. To assuage Paula, Mike feigns repentance and offers her a drink. Unable to resist after a long, nerve-wracking evening, Paula jumps off the wagon.

Mike arrives at work that morning to find Gerard awaiting him. Gerard warns Mike that harboring an interstate fugitive would be a felony; however, if he can lead Gerard to Kimble, Mike will not only be in the clear, but have that exclusive blockbuster story. Decker brushes off Gerard but doesn't dismiss the idea. When the editor tells him he must deliver a story tonight, Decker feels he has little choice.

Cogen goes to Decker's apartment to deliver a message: the guy Mike is looking for will be at the bus station in an hour. Mike isn't home, so the inebriated Paula takes the message. After Cogen leaves, Kimble struggles to extract the message from Paula, finally succeeding. Kimble takes a taxi to the station.

Kimble checks the departing buses, seeing the one-armed man aboard one headed for Florida. After learning that the bus stops at Chicago Heights, Kimble takes a cab to beat the bus there, only to be told that the man (who had seen Kimble) had claimed illness and gotten off the bus.

Gerard interrogates Paula, tricking her into revealing that Kimble was staying there. Gerard forces Mike to cooperate, waiting at the apartment for Kimble to call or return. Kimble phones Decker about his near-miss, and Decker instructs him to come back so they can plan their next move. Gerard activates four policemen to cover the building. Paula lays a guilt-trip on the deeply-troubled Mike, asking if his column's headline will be "I Double-Crossed Richard Kimble."

Kimble arrives in a cab and buzzes at the apartment building entrance. Mike answers, telling Kimble to come on up, then correcting himself: "No! Don't! Gerard's here!" A wild stair and elevator chase ensues, but Kimble manages to escape after kayoing one cop.

Decker is arrested for abetting a fugitive and dictates a final column. Kimble, despite the frustration of it all, has new hope: he has seen the one-armed man, permitting the possibility of finding him again.

Episode #20
BLOODLINE
Original Airdate: February 11, 1964

Story by: John Hawkins & Harry Kronman **Teleplay by:** Harry Kronman
Directed by: John Erman

Cast: George Voskovec as Max Bodin, John Considine as Johnny Bodin, Nancy Malone as Cora Bodin, Parley Baer as Lee Burroughs, Dan Barton as Lt. Wally Sampson, Lew Brown as Sgt. Hackett.

Kimble, alias Dick Lindsay, has worked the past two weeks as a kennel man for Bodin Russet Kennels (established 1934) in Virginia. Max and Johnny Bodin, father and son, have spent most of the past three decades there, breeding prize-winning Irish Setters. Max is considering Lee Burroughs's offer of $130,000 for the kennels, but isn't really ready to sell. Besides, he can tack on another $10,000 to the price with a victory in the finals of tomorrow's competition. Johnny and his wife of four years, Cora, are anxious for Max to sell. Cora is simply fed up with the kennel life and wants out, while Johnny feels he can do no right in his father's eyes and that the dogs are more important to Dad than Johnny is.

Cora discovers that Colleen, a prized two-year-old setter, has hip dysplasia, indicating a possible flaw in the bloodline. She realizes that honest Max would feel obliged to apprise his prospective buyer of this flaw, plunging the price or ruining the deal altogether. Cora deliberately releases the dog, who scampers through the woods and gets herself badly hacked up on some barbed wire. Lindsay finds the dog, and Cora and Max are soon on the scene. Cora recommends that the dog be put out of her misery and Max reluctantly agrees, giving Lindsay his rifle. Max and Cora wait in the car and hear a shot, thinking the task has been performed. After dark, Lindsay returns to the scene to rescue Colleen, whom he hadn't the heart to kill. He takes the dog to his cabin, where he sutures and bandages her wounds.

Cora tells Johnny what happened, and the two go out to confirm Colleen's death. Making a dog-gone discovery, Cora goes to Lindsay's place and finds

Act I: The 1963-64 Season 39

Colleen there. Cora notes the professional workmanship, and Lindsay explains that he spent a couple of years working for a vet, Doc Anders in Carpenteria, California (contradicting Lindsay's earlier admission of no experience with dogs). Cora promises not to tell Max about Lindsay's disobedience.

Lindsay notices that there is something other than the cuts wrong with Colleen, and he diagnoses the problem with the help of one of Max's books. Lindsay also finds Colleen's choke leash, which Cora had claimed to be lost in the woods during the dog's romp. Lindsay confronts Cora and she all but confesses to the scheme, but she points out that telling Max would also implicate Johnny, thus ruining Max's life.

While Max and Johnny attend the finals, Lindsay takes the jeep into town, wanting to get Colleen to a lab for X-rays. Cora sees him leaving and chases after him, finally running him off the road. She orders Lindsay to return, or she will tell police that he stole the jeep and the dog. Noticing his reaction to the word "police," Cora follows up with some digging. She learns that there is no Doc Anders, and she calls Lt. Sampson to ask if he has a "wanted" poster on anyone with a medical background.

Lindsay is bound and determined to talk to Max, with whom he has developed a mutually-respectful relationship, but Cora tells Lindsay to start packing. Meanwhile, Lt. Sampson calls Max with the report on Cora's inquiry. Although Max assures him that his kennel man is neither a doctor nor a murderer, Sampson decides to visit the kennels with another officer.

Max goes to Lindsay's room, seeing the patched-up dog. Max realizes Lindsay must be the doctor the police are looking for, but is certain that this man—who didn't have the heart to euthanize a *dog*—could not be a murderer. Lindsay tells Max why Cora and Johnny are running him out. Johnny confirms it and explains his motivation: he hates this place and is tired of being "second dog." Max says he will sell the place, then, but Cora points out he won't get one-fourth of what it is worth. "What is it worth," Max asks rhetorically, "if it stands between (my son) and me?" Cora announces icily that she is leaving and that Johnny "can come along, or not, as you choose." She leaves, but Johnny stays. Touched that his father would give up the kennels rather than alienate his son, Johnny has new incentive. He tells his father that together they can lick the dysplasia and build the line back, even if it takes five or six years.

The police car arrives, and Max remarks that the back window has a nice view of the woods. While Max and Johnny detain the cops, Lindsay makes his escape into the darkness. The police find the cabin empty and deputize Colleen to help find the fugitive. Colleen is given an article of Lindsay's clothing, and let loose to follow the scent. She finds Lindsay, but he orders her away. Colleen goes back empty-pawed, and the police abandon the futile search.

Some time later, Max and Johnny get an anonymous package from Denver. Inside is a silver name-tag, engraved "Colleen."

Episode #21
RAT IN A CORNER
Original Airdate: February 18, 1964

Story by: William Wood   Teleplay by: Sheldon Stark & William Morwood
Directed by: Jerry Hopper

Cast: Warren Oates as Herbie Grant, Virginia Vincent as Lorna Grant, Malachi Throne as Lt. Santelli, Tommy Farrell as Det.-Sgt. Ryan, Glen Vernon as Sharp, Stewart Bradley as police sergeant, Gerald Gordon as policeman, John Mayo as technician, Barbara Perry and Ruth Packard as women.

Kimble, alias Dan Crowley, works as a clerk for Sharp's Liquor in the Youngstown/Bolton area, where there have been two fatal liquor store holdups recently. As Crowley prepares to leave for a delivery, Herbie Grant enters the store and pulls an unloaded gun. Crowley calls Herbie's bluff and tells him the cash register is empty. From the back-room, the owner hears the commotion and gets his handgun. As Herbie leaves, empty-handed, Sharp fires, wounding him in the leg. Herbie limps away, taking refuge in a car.

Crowley leaves on the delivery, then discovers he has a passenger: Herbie. Crowley checks Herbie's minor wound (while Herbie secretly pockets Crowley's Edmund Hotel key), then tells him to leave. Herbie is waiting when Crowley returns home at the end of the night.

Herbie gives a sob story, asking Crowley to help him. He knows that if he is caught, he will be blamed for the liquor store killings, which he didn't do. Crowley realizes Herbie is not a killer and sympathizes with a man liable to be wrongly accused. Herbie gives Crowley a ring, supposedly inherited from his mother (but actually stolen from his sister, Lorna), and asks him to pawn it for the price of new pants and medication. Crowley agrees, and Herbie wonders why. By consensus a "rat," Herbie can't imagine anyone doing anything decent without something in it for them.

Crowley goes to leave the hotel, but is stopped by Lt. Santelli with some questions about the would-be robber (identified by Sharp as Herbie, whose face is subsequently plastered all over the newspapers). Meanwhile, Sgt. Ryan is approaching Herbie's sister for the same reason. Lorna, a postal worker (who knows all the "wanted" posters by heart), always seems to be bailing her brother out of trouble, each time promising never to do it again.

Crowley and Lorna sit next to each other in the waiting room of the police station. Lorna recognizes first the ring (which Crowley fishes out of his pocket while searching for matches), then the bearer. When Crowley is called in, Lorna — who realizes he knows where Herbie is — warns him not to reveal Herbie, unless Crowley wants her to identify him as Richard Kimble.

Afterward, Lorna talks with Kimble, learning that he is helping Herbie. She is surprised, considering the chance he is taking. Kimble explains he is helping because he knows Herbie is innocent of the murder raps, despite being named by witnesses. "Witnesses can be wrong," Kimble says, and Lorna realizes he is talking about his own case as much as Herbie's. Kimble tells Lorna where she can find Herbie.

Herbie opens the door for Lorna, and a hotel cleaning woman recognizes the murder suspect. She phones the tip to Lt. Santelli, who notices the address matches Crowley's. Santelli, theorizing that Crowley is Herbie's accomplice, heads for the hotel. Meanwhile, Lorna tells Herbie who Crowley really is and goes to bring her car around to the front of the hotel. She plans to drive Herbie to the produce market, where he can stow away on one of the departing trucks.

Kimble has just entered the hotel when he sees the cops pull in; sensing trouble, Kimble ducks around a corner, then sneaks out when Santelli goes upstairs. Herbie is arrested and, thinking he was double-crossed, tells police about Kimble.

Lorna stops her car for Kimble (whom she has come to admire), offering him a refuge from the police. She takes him to the abandoned Kitten Club, where she used to work. She leaves him there, saying she wants to find out Herbie's connection at the produce market so Kimble can escape that way.

The police grill Herbie about Kimble's whereabouts, hinting there might be a $5,000 reward involved. Meanwhile, the real liquor store killer has been caught at Springfield and has confessed to the murders. Lorna bails Herbie out, and they head to the Kitten Club.

Lorna tells Herbie that it was the cleaning lady, not Kimble, who fingered him. The police, who have been tailing the siblings, arrive at the club. Kimble escapes up a dumb-waiter to the roof, heading for the produce market two blocks away. Herbie, in a rare moment of integrity, tells the cops he hasn't seen Kimble; by the time he has a change of heart, the cops are gone. Kimble is soon aboard a truck that will take him out of town.

Episodes #22–23
ANGELS TRAVEL ON LONELY ROADS (Parts I & II)
Original Airdates: February 25 & March 3, 1964

Written by: Al C. Ward   **Directed by:** Walter Grauman

Cast: Eileen Heckart as Sister Veronica, Albert Salmi as Chuck Mathers, Ken Lynch as Lt. Tim Craig, Sandy Kenyon as Sheriff Morris, Ruta Lee as Janet Loring, Percy Helton as hobo, Rodolfo Hoyos as Manuel, Bill Zuckert as Henry Mesta, Shary Marshall as Sherie Tallman, Jason Wingreen as Joe Friar, Burt Douglas as Sgt. Joe Lane, Lane Bradford as Sheriff Anderson, John Durren as Clete, Thomas Hasson as Lossie.

Sister Veronica, age 41, has decided to renounce her vows and leave the sisterhood. She feels she is deficient as a communicator, and is deeply troubled by the capital punishment (five days ago at Sing Sing) of one of her former students. The young Native American boy had repeatedly come to Veronica for help, and she had finally turned him away; thus, she feels a certain responsibility for his death. Veronica is trying to coax an old Model-T pickup (which had been presented to her convent as a gift) through the desert mountains of Nevada to St. Helena's in Sacramento, California. There she plans to meet with Father Carrigan and shed her habit.

Kimble has been working a couple of days as a janitor in Brady's Casino, Lincoln City, Nevada. A coworker recognizes him and contacts the police, but Kimble slips away before he can be captured. Kimble comes across a transient who has just been mugged. Taking the man's wallet (but leaving behind the cash contained in it), Kimble gains a new identity: Nicholas Walker. He jumps aboard a departing truck and gets out some time later, when the truck stops in the Nevada desert. There he comes across Sister Veronica battling with the old jalopy, which has quit on her.

Veronica regards Walker as a messenger sent from above ("what possible set of natural circumstances could have brought us together like that?"). Walker diagnoses the problem as a plugged fuel line, and Veronica offers him a ride in exchange for correcting it. The two fugitives are soon on their way westward in a vehicle that is "looking for a quiet place to die." Walker, taking over the driving responsibilities, says he is going only as far as Ravenna.

The two reach a police roadblock, which Walker realizes is for his benefit. Sister Veronica knows the policeman on duty, however, and vouches for her companion. The radiator is boiling over, and she doesn't want to be unnecessarily detained. Walker stops at the Ravenna train station and bids farewell to Veronica, but she is convinced they are destined to remain together. She will wait in the truck and "seek guidance."

Walker hops a freight train, but it turns out to be a switching freight. It goes a few hundred yards down the track, stops, reverses direction, and returns to the station. Walker gets out and meets a hobo, who tells him that police are stopping regular freights in search of a fugitive. Walker realizes he has survived another near-miss and returns dejectedly to Sister Veronica's truck. She smiles knowingly, and they proceed onward.

Veronica tells Walker she has just $1.45 with her, which, added to what Walker has on him, makes $1.45. It is obvious they will have to improve their financial situation if they hope to make it to Sacramento, so Veronica suggests that Walker find some short-term work. They stop at a pack station, but the owner advises Walker that neither she nor anyone else in this neck of the desert has work to offer. Just then, the Mountain Feed & Fuel truck pulls in with a load of hay. Walker offers to help the driver, Chuck, unload the truck for $2 per hour. Chuck agrees, and Walker unloads the bales alone while the burly, beer-guzzling driver tries to make time with the station owner. Sister Veronica bides her time sitting in the truck, reading her Bible.

Three hours later, Walker breaks up Chuck's would-be-romance to announce he is done and wants to be paid his six dollars. Chuck gives him only $3, saying the rest is in his pocket, if Walker wants to try and get it. Walker leaves disgustedly.

The Model-T gets a flat tire. Walker goes to change it but finds he hasn't got a jack. Using a tree trunk (with Veronica sitting on it) for leverage, Walker jacks up the vehicle and changes the tire. Chuck comes up behind them, his progress stopped by the tree trunk. Walker says he will be happy to move it for $3, and Chuck reluctantly pays up.

Walker and Veronica find an unlocked cabin in the mountains and hole up there for the night. The two discuss their opposing philosophies: Walker's reality vs. Veronica's fantasy. As they prepare to leave Sunday morning, a group of armed men — caretakers for the building's owner — surround the cabin and menace Walker. Veronica appears and defuses the situation, explaining their reason for staying there and their intent to leave the cabin as they found it. Assuaged, the men ask a special favor of the Sister. Car trouble has prevented them from attending church for three weeks, and they hope "one so close to God" will lead them in prayer. Veronica instead offers her and Walker's funds to pay their bus fare to church. Afterward, she finally admits to Walker her plans to renounce her vows. Walker blasts her hypocrisy and expresses hope that she will change her mind. Veronica abandons her "Providence" fantasy, and it is clear that the success of their journey is now all up to Walker.

As they drive on, two motorcycling youths harass them, finally forcing them off the road. Walker confronts the pair, but they surround him, one brandishing a club, the other a rock. Sister Veronica comes to the rescue, slapping one delinquent and shoving the other, delivering a lecture, and finally sending them on their way with their tails between their legs. Walker remarks that, for someone who can't communicate, the Sister sure got her message across to those two.

The police are still on Walker's trail. The hobo at the Ravenna station has identified him, and Lt. Craig of Lincoln City has joined forces with Sheriff Morris of Walker's current vicinity. Craig points out that, to have escaped thus far, Walker has "got more than brains riding with him — luck, maybe?"

The truck sustains a ruptured fuel pump. Walker coasts it down to a little store. There he meets up with his old buddy, Chuck, who happens to run the service station next door. Chuck is playing poker with three stooges. Walker tells him he needs a fuel pump, and Chuck offers him one for $25, double its worth. Walker offers his watch, which he says is worth at least $50, but Chuck appraises it at $10. Walker trades it for $10 worth of chips in the card game.

Walker wins more than he loses and comes head-to-head with Chuck in what turns out to be the final hand. Holding a 4, 5, 6, 8 and 10, Walker discards the high card in the remote hope of drawing an inside straight. Chuck, meanwhile, draws his third king and appears a sure winner, but Walker gets the lucky seven and wins the pot. The disgusted Chuck upsets the table and starts a fistfight, which Walker wins by TKO. Walker says he had $36 worth of chips on the table and wants his watch, the fuel pump, and $1 in change. Chuck returns Walker's watch, then pulls a pistol on him. Janet — Chuck's sister-in-law, and the store's proprietor — intervenes, apologizing to Walker. She squares up with him, then offers $10, a full tank of gas, and a night's lodging, for 12 hours of his work. "Beats playing poker with your brother-in-law," Walker says, agreeing to the terms.

While Walker works, Sister Veronica watches television. She is flabbergasted to see her companion's picture flashed with news about the escaped murderer. Meanwhile, Janet — smitten with Walker (and almost accidentally brained by him when he swings a load of firewood around) — tells him about herself. She asks him to stick around for a couple of weeks, as she could use the help and the company. Walker considers it but decides to move on the next day.

While Walker goes inside to get the Sister's baggage, Chuck swipes his wallet from the jacket in the truck. Walker and Veronica go on their way. Moments later, Chuck and Janet spot Kimble's picture on the front page of the Reno newspapers delivered to the store. Over Janet's objections, Chuck gleefully calls the sheriff and accompanies him in pursuit of Kimble's vehicle.

Sister Veronica confronts Kimble with her knowledge of his identity, and he affirms his innocence. He says he remained with the Sister because her preachings of faith were starting to get through to him: "Because of you, another side of me came up for air."

The sheriff has almost caught up with Kimble, and the chase is on. As the truck rounds a curve in Lark County, another tire blows out. The Model-T skids to a halt just a few yards short of a disabled truck, which had jack-knifed across the road. The sheriff is forced to veer around the blessed vehicle, slamming into the larger truck. Sheriff Morris is out cold, and the semiconscious Chuck babbles unintelligibly to the policeman on the scene, Sheriff Anderson. The two victims are carted away in an ambulance, while Anderson lends Kimble a jack to change his tire (yes, the old heap had *two* spares but no jack). He remarks on Kimble's luck in suffering the flat rather than crashing into the truck himself; Kimble calls it "a miracle."

Kimble and Veronica at last get to Sacramento. Veronica tells him she has changed her mind about renouncing her vows, and the two fugitives bid farewell.

Episode #24
FLIGHT FROM THE FINAL DEMON
Original Airdate: March 10, 1964
Written by: Philip Saltzman   Directed by: Jerry Hopper

Act I: The 1963-64 Season

Cast: Ed Nelson as Steven Edson, Carroll O'Connor as Sheriff Bray, Don Dubbins as Horton, Ellen Madison as Linda Morrow, Rudy Solari as Joey Morrow, John Duke as bus driver, Guy Wilkerson as desk clerk, Kathleen O'Malley as telegraph clerk.

Kimble, alias Al Dexter, has been a masseur at the Greenhurst Health Club in Michigan for the past three weeks. One of his patrons today is mean-spirited Sheriff Bray, who thinks Dexter looks familiar. The sheriff uses the club's office phone to call his deputy, Horton. Bray says the masseur resembles that doctor who murdered his wife, asking Horton to find the "wanted" poster. Steve Edson, Dexter's 35-year-old coworker, overhears and goes to warn Dexter. Bray returns, asking Dexter to accompany him to the station. Steve decks the sheriff, and he and Dexter flee the building and jump into Steve's car. Bray fires at the departing vehicle, wounding Steve in the left shoulder.

Steve parks the car in the woods near a side road, and Dexter checks his wound. Feeling indebted, he promises to stay with Steve until his injury is properly attended to. Dexter wonders why Steve stuck his neck out for him, and Steve says he empathizes with someone whose life had been left at the mercy of a jury. Just five months earlier, Steve had been acquitted of murder in Gary, Indiana, the jury ruling that he had acted in self-defense in stabbing the overprotective brother of his 28-year-old girlfriend, Linda. Steve doesn't mention that, in reality, it had been a premeditated murder. Unable to live with his conscience, Steve had fled Indiana, and he continually seeks his own punishment through self-destructive behavior.

Dexter and Steve abandon the car and board a bus which takes them to Meadville. They get a cheap hotel room, and Dexter pools their few remaining dollars and leaves to get food and medication. Steve phones Linda in Indiana, asking her to wire some money to him. Linda's surviving brother, Joey, finds out about it and resolves to do whatever is necessary to keep Steve out of her life.

Bray finds Steve's car, and deduces that the two fugitives took a bus. His job is made easier when Steve's checkbook is found on the Trans-Michigan bus, narrowing the likely search area to two towns. Determined to track down this "prize game" in this, an election year, Bray goes beyond his jurisdiction to find Kimble and Edson. The first town is checked without success.

Dexter returns to the hotel, and Steve tells him about Linda and the forthcoming money. Dexter is disturbed that Steve took the chance of contacting her. Steve is too drunk to go anywhere at the moment so Dexter, armed with Steve's ID (thus, adopting "Steven Edson" as an alias), goes to the Western Union office to pick up the $100 Linda wired. Waiting outside the office is Joey, who follows Dexter back to the hotel in expectation of being led to Steve. Meanwhile, Linda, and the police, are also on their separate ways to Meadville to find Steve.

Dexter warns Steve that he was followed by someone in a yellow sports car, and Steve hides in another room. Joey knocks on the door and Dexter answers. Dexter says Steve isn't there, first giving his own name as Paul Edson, then saying that he met Steve in a bar and stole his wallet. Steve spoils Dexter's stories by showing himself, and Joey pulls a switchblade. Steve encourages Joey to use it, but Dexter intervenes, knocking out Joey. By this time, Dexter has figured out Steve's death-wish, a manifestation of guilt for an unpunished crime. Dexter and Steve tie up Joey and put him on a bed.

Linda, having seen Joey's car outside the hotel, finds her way to Steve's room. Happily reunited with his girlfriend, Steve proposes marriage. Dexter says it is time for him to leave and suggests that Steve explain to Linda why he has been running from her. Steve breaks down and confesses to the murder of Linda's brother. The police track Kimble and Edson to the hotel. Kimble sees them coming and goes out the fire escape. He seems doomed to capture until Steve rushes out of the hotel room, bowling over Bray and Horton on the way downstairs. Steve flees the building with the police in pursuit, thinking they are chasing Kimble. Horton guns down Steve. With the cops' attention diverted, Kimble completes his escape and hops a freight out of town.

Episode #25

TAPS FOR A DEAD WAR
Original Airdate: March 17, 1964

Story by: Harry Kronman & Merwin Gerard   **Teleplay by:** Harry Kronman
Directed by: William Graham

Cast: Tim O'Connor as Joseph A. Hallop, Lee Grant as Millie Hallop, Flip Mark as Kenny Hallop, Noam Pitlik as Sgt. Bert Keefer, Nick Nicholson as bar owner, John Zaremba as druggist.

Kimble, alias Bob Davies, works this May as a rink attendant at Rollerdrome. He goes to the rescue of Kenny Hallop, who is being beaten up by four other kids. Davies is attending to Kenny's cut when Kenny's Uncle Joe comes to pick him up. Joe doesn't say anything, but he recognizes Davies as the medic whose life he saved in Chun Chan, Korea.

Kimble had been new to the 521st, Company C, when a North Korean soldier shouted "medic!" Kimble had gone out to see who needed help, finding himself facing the enemy soldier armed with a grenade. PFC Joe Hallop had leaped up from his ground position, knocking the petrified medic (who would never be able to learn who saved his life) out of the way, but suffering serious injuries in the process. To this day, Joe has an ugly scar running across his left cheek, and a gimpy right leg, and he holds the medic responsible for his disfigurement. As far as Joe is concerned, the war will not be over until he repays Kimble.

Joe returns to the Blue Diner, run by his brother's widow (and Kenny's mother), Millie. He dredges out his chest of army memorabilia, including a panoramic photograph of Company C, and a live grenade encased in clear plastic. Since his brother's death some two years ago, Joe has entertained secret hopes that he and Millie might become a couple. He even bought a house for them, although she doesn't know about it. He doesn't think Millie would want to share her life with such a freak, and is just too wrapped up in his own problems to notice that she has fallen in love with him, too.

Joe goes back to the roller rink, inviting Davies to join him for a drink. Davies unwittingly becomes involved in a barroom brawl. Although this one isn't started by Joe, he has a reputation for drinking to excess and being at the center of such incidents—"fighting a dead war."

Kenny stops at the rink the next day to thank Davies for helping him. He mentions that Uncle Joe got his scar by saving some medic's life in the 521st Army, and Davies realizes who Joe is. As Davies prepares to leave town, he meets Joe at his door. Joe insists that Davies stick around for a few weeks because "you owe me." Joe claims he is having plastic surgery on his face (not true: doctors have advised Joe that the scar is too close to his eye to operate on) in a few days, and Millie will need someone to help her at the diner. "I gave you a whole life," Joe pleads, and Davies reluctantly agrees to stay.

Kenny looks at Joe's army photo and recognizes Mr. Davies as the medic identified as "Kimble." He brings it to the attention of his mother, who realizes the significance of the discovery. Millie senses that there will be trouble—Joe might try to kill Davies and really ruin his own life.

Joe takes Davies to the house he bought, offering him rent-free lodging. There, Joe "accidentally" knocks over a bottle of muriatic acid, almost spilling it on Davies. Joe apologizes, saying he had bought the acid a year ago and forgotten about it. Suspicious, Davies later goes to Allen Drugs and learns that Joe bought the acid there just the day before. Davies also finds out that there is no operation scheduled, and realizes that Joe is out to maim or kill him. Meanwhile, Joe celebrates "the end of the war" at the bar.

Davies goes to see Millie, telling her about the acid-ent, and she wonders why he is still sticking around. Davies says he feels obliged to Joe and just wants him to know somebody cares. "Tell me about somebody who cares," Millie replies, revealing her feelings for Joe. If he kills Davies, nobody will be able to help Joe. Davies says he will leave but first wants to show Millie something. They drive out toward the house while Kenny, who has overheard everything, stays at the diner. Joe arrives there, and Kenny tells him where Davies and Millie went. Joe takes his grenade and goes off after them.

Police Sgt. Keefer, whom Millie had asked to stop by, arrives at the diner. Kenny tells him that Joe went after Davies with his grenade. Keefer and another officer rush to the scene.

Millie is overwhelmed by the house. "If he'd said ... just one word ...," she exclaims. Their tour is interrupted by shouts of "medic!" Joe has arrived, telling Davies that he plans to finish Kimble's life the same way Kimble finished his.

Kimble sneaks around and props a flashlight in a tree. Joe tosses the grenade at the light, but Kimble is safe, several-dozen yards away from the explosion. He confronts Joe, and the two engage in hand-to-hand combat, with Davies the victor. Millie comes over and, at Kimble's urging, tells Joe what she sees in him: "somebody I could love my whole life." The two secret lovers are at last united, and Joe loses his need to punish Kimble. With the cops approaching, Kimble makes his exit.

The police question Joe, who says that Millie convinced him to get rid of the dangerous grenade. Asked about Davies, Joe says he left on the Springfield bus. He was an "old army buddy of mine," Joe explains. "Saved my life."

Episode #26
SOMEBODY TO REMEMBER
Original Airdate: March 24, 1964

Written by: Robert C. Dennis   **Directed by:** Jerry Hopper

Cast: Gilbert Roland as Gus Priamos, Madlyn Rhue as Sophie, Alan Baxter as detective, Peter Mamakos as Pete, Peter Coe as Nicky, Paul Birch as Capt. Carpenter, Robert Millar as ticket agent, Maura McGiveney as travel agency clerk, Gus Trikonis as boyfriend.

Kimble, alias Johnny Sherman, has worked the past two months in the warehouse of Konstantine Brothers Distributors. His boss, Gus Priamos, calls Johnny "little brother" (causing hard feelings among his coworkers) because he reminds Gus of his younger brother in Europe. Gus knows who Johnny really is, having recently seen a magazine article ("Where is Richard Kimble?") about him and Lt. Gerard. Gus hasn't shared his knowledge with anybody.

Gus's girlfriend, Sophie, flirtingly follows Johnny into his room, but he rebuffs her. She mentions that Gus saw a doctor today, and Johnny, concerned, goes to see Gus. He finds him on the roof of his building, ready to jump. Gus has just been told that he has no more than six months to live, and he realizes that, in his entire life, "never have I done one great thing." Johnny aborts the suicide attempt, and the two go to Gus's room. There, Gus tells Johnny he knows his secret, showing him the magazine article. Gus tells Johnny he needs him and asks him to stick around awhile.

Johnny tells Sophie about Gus's condition, but she is not interested in being his nurse. Johnny suggests that she could become a "rich widow," as Gus has $8,000 in cash stashed away for a trip to Greece he will probably never take. Sophie has newfound concern for Gus's condition and begins taking care of him.

Gus devises a plan for his "one great thing": getting Gerard off Kimble's trail. Gus will give Johnny his passport, substituting Johnny's photo for his. After Johnny (henceforth using the alias "Gus Priamos") gets his visa and tickets, Gus will replace his photo on the passport and board the plane bound for Athens (via Paris and Rome; airfare, $358.60). Gerard will be notified that Kimble is on his way to Greece, and travel agency and airport personnel will confirm seeing Kimble prepare for the flight. Gerard will be forced to believe that Kimble has hightailed it to Europe and relax his search efforts at home.

Johnny goes to get the passport and money at Gus's apartment, where he runs into Sophie. He tells her Gus will not be coming back, and she becomes furious. She later happens across the magazine article, learning Johnny's true identity, and deduces that Johnny has knocked off Gus and taken his money and car (since all three are unaccounted for). She calls Gerard, who is promptly on his way there.

Gus and Johnny make the switch at the airport as planned, and Johnny heads for the parking lot while Gus waits in line to board the plane. Suddenly, Gus recognizes Gerard hovering around the ticket agent. Gus runs, hacking and wheezing, after Johnny. He finally catches him just as he is pulling out of the parking lot, and the two take off. The gate guard sees them leaving just as he gets word to be on the lookout for Kimble. Gerard has learned that Gus Priamos was the only passenger unaccounted for and is quickly piecing together Kimble's entire plan.

The stress and disappointment of the foiled plan and the gallop through the parking lot have taken a terrible toll on Gus. He is sinking fast as they race toward the river. Johnny bids farewell to his friend and gets aboard a departing ferry boat.

The police find the car, and Gerard interrogates the unresponsive Gus. Sophie then questions Gus privately and guesses Kimble's mode of escape. She is about to tell police, but Gus offers her his money in exchange for her promise to keep quiet. Gus dies having done his good deed, and Sophie — since it doesn't cost her anything — keeps her promise.

Episode #27
NEVER STOP RUNNING
Original Airdate: March 31, 1964

Written by: Sheldon Stark   **Directed by:** William Graham

Cast: Claude Akins as Ralph Simmons, Michel Petit as Jimmie Franklin, Joanna Moore as Helen "Bluebird" Simmons, Wright King as Dave Simmons, Paul Comi as Deputy Sheriff, Patrick McVey as Sheriff, Buck Young as Harold Franklin, Peggy Stewart as Mrs. Franklin, Jason Johnson as Walter Maddox, Ray Kellogg as truck driver, Maya Van Horn as woman, Jane Barclay as nurse, Carl McIntire as TV announcer.

Kimble has been working as a field hand in the beet fields of Belasco Farms, near Bellinda, New Mexico, but has decided it is time to move on. He has earned the nickname "Doc" there, due to his first-aid skills (which he claims he picked up while driving an ambulance for a while).

A man and woman having heard of Doc, ask for him at the camp. They convince him to accompany them and check on their sick boy. Doc drives off with Dave and Helen, arriving at a cabin occupied by Ralph (Dave's brother and Helen's husband) and the boy, Jimmie.

Doc soon learns that the boy has been kidnapped by the trio and is being held for $200,000 ransom. The plot was masterminded by Ralph, a former pro football player kicked out of the league because of a gambling scandal; Jimmie is the son of one of the team-owners involved in Ralph's dismissal. Helen is in on it for the money, while Dave is a reluctant partner just going along with his brother.

Doc discovers Jimmie's problem: he suffered a cut and bruise while being dragged over a wall by Ralph. This is serious only because Jimmie is a hemophiliac. Doc, whom Ralph sarcastically calls "Louis Pasteur," tells the others he will need some Vitamin K, a coagulant. Dave and Helen go out to a pharmacy.

The suspicious druggist tells the pair he has no Vitamin K, then phones the sheriff with a description of the couple and the car. Doc and Dave chat, Dave wondering if Doc is on the run, and Doc wondering why Dave doesn't pull out of this mess.

Jimmie cries out in pain, and Doc finds that the bruise on his side is worse, a possible indicator of internal bleeding. Doc says that Jimmie needs hospitalization, but Ralph won't hear of it, and he's calling all the plays. Dave is left to guard Doc and Jimmie while Ralph boozes it up outside.

Doc knocks out Dave and escapes out the window with Jimmie. He carries the boy to a farmhouse, while Ralph, Dave, and Helen chase him by car. The lady of the house speaks little English and refuses to help, so Doc hotwires her pickup and drives toward the Bellinda Hospital. He makes it through a roadblock by hiding Jimmie under a blanket on the car floor. The woman calls the police.

Doc and Jimmie arrive at the hospital to find Ralph awaiting them. Doc puts the boy down and engages in a fistfight with Ralph but is no match for the burly ex-athlete. Ralph is on the verge of strangling Doc when Dave comes up from behind and beans his brother with a bottle. With Ralph unconscious, Doc escorts Jimmie into the hospital and gives instructions to a nurse. Dave allows Doc to escape, and police pick up the others moments later.

Afterward, police ask the boy about the doctor who brought him there; his references don't check out, but perhaps Jimmie learned his name. Jimmie thinks for a moment, then recalls triumphantly: "Louis Pasteur."

Episode #28
THE HOMECOMING
Original Airdate: April 7, 1964

Written by: Peter Germano   Directed by: Jerry Hopper

Cast: Gloria Grahame as Dorina Pruitt, Shirley Knight as Janice Pruitt, Richard Carlson as Allan Lee Pruitt, Warren Vanders as Floyd Warren, James Griffith as Seth Crowley, Walter Woolf King as Judge Parker, Mary Jackson as Ellie Parker, Eddie Rosson as boy.

Kimble, alias David Benton, takes a summer job as a research technician for the Pruitt Plantation Research Laboratory in southeastern Georgia. His employer is Allan Pruitt, who occupies the stately homestead — residence of a long line of gracious women — with his wife of six months, Dorina. Allan's previous wife died less than 18 months ago, following a long illness. Their grown daughter, Janice, suffered a breakdown six months later and has been in a sanitarium ever since. She is due back home today but doesn't know about Dorina.

Janice's breakdown had followed a nightmarish experience. While picnicking with a group of children, two big, vicious dogs (running wild since their owner, a sharecropper named Potter, died) had attacked one of the lads. Janice was at the boy's bedside when he died, and the incident pushed her over the edge. The dogs were destroyed soon after the attack, but Janice maintains an irrational fear of canines.

Dorina is a manipulative woman, proud that she has elevated herself from a dirt-poor backwoods girl to the matron of a modern-day Tara. Despite outward appearances to the contrary, Dorina dreads Janice's return, remembering her grandmother's advice: "There's only room for one sow in a pen." She plots to drive Janice back to the sanitarium.

David picks up Janice at the bus station; she is disappointed that her father didn't come (Dorina had faked an injury to divert his attention). Janice is upset to learn of her father's remarriage. That evening, Allan hosts a dinner party, sort of a "homecoming" affair for Janice. Among those in attendance is Floyd, the county sheriff, who was a suitor of Janice's before her institutionalization. Dorina privately upsets Janice, and the guest of honor retires to her room for the rest of the evening.

The next morning Janice is upset by the barking of two hounds, brought over by Seth Crowley at Dorina's request. Allan wonders why Dorina would invite Seth to bring the dogs in light of Janice's fear, but Dorina claims to have invited Seth last week, before she knew Janice was returning. Seth mentions to David that Dorina actually invited him just yesterday. David confronts Dorina with his suspicion that she is trying to drive Janice away. Dorina boastfully confirms it but advises David not to interfere.

As Janice sits outside that evening, she is again terrorized by the sound of dogs (Dorina had paid Seth $100 to bring his hounds into the nearby woods for the next few nights). She screams hysterically, bringing David out of the guest cottage. David, who hadn't heard the barking over his radio, tries to calm Janice as she insists she heard Potter's dogs. David admits to Allan that he didn't hear any dogs, and they both wonder if Janice is having delusions.

Floyd visits the Pruitt home, and Dorina tells him that David has been chasing after Janice. Angered, Floyd warns David to stay away from Janice, threatening to jail him if necessary.

David packs to leave, claiming a family illness. Allan, who is going on an overnight trip to Atlanta, asks David to stay another night and keep an eye on Janice. When Dorina volunteers for that duty, David decides to stay after all.

Awakened by the dogs again that night, Janice goes outside in her nightgown. Her screams bring David, and he hears the dogs, too. Janice, convinced she is going crazy, thinks David is just patronizing her. Dorina advises David not to corroborate Janice's dog story.

Allan is disturbed to hear what happened while he was away. He asks Janice about the incident but she — hoping to preserve her appearance of sanity, but instead giving Allan more cause for concern — denies hearing the dogs. He seems resigned to the inevitability of returning Janice to the sanitarium until David speaks up. David says that he heard the dogs, too, and that perhaps somebody wanted them to be there. Dorina gasps, "I think he means *your wife*," and mentions that David was with Janice (in her *nightclothes*!) near the woods last night. Allan is totally confused.

Dorina calls Floyd, repeating the nightclothes story and also claiming that David came after *her*. Floyd comes and arrests David for "attempted assault." Floyd, David, Dorina, and Allan suddenly turn their attention to the sound of a boy crying in the woods. Janice runs out there in search of the boy, and the other four chase after her. Janice finds the boy — Seth's son — and is soon surrounded by the barking hounds. David and Floyd scare off the dogs. David finds Seth, who points out Mrs. Pruitt as the one who put him up to this. "Mrs. Pruitt," Allan says disgustedly. "Not any more!"

Floyd apologizes to David and takes Dorina away. David leaves the next morning, unpursued for a change.

Episode #29
STORM CENTER
Original Airdate: April 14, 1964

Written by: George Eckstein **Directed by:** William Graham

Cast: Bethel Leslie as Marcia (Marcie) King, Dennis Patrick as Harry Montjoy, Craig Duncan as Charlie Hannah, Robert Fortier and Clay Tanner as officers.

Harry Montjoy has embezzled $500,000 in securities and deposited the money in a bank in Rio de Janeiro, Brazil. The police are on his trail, but Harry and his companion, Marcie, have arranged for a Brazilian freighter to pick them up next week at Key Blanca, an island on which Marcie has a house. They need only to get to the house from Weber's Landing, Florida, but hurricane warnings discourage travel. They offer $100 to rent Charlie Hannah's charter boat, but Charlie refuses and leaves. Marcie spots Charlie's hired hand, Larry Phelps, and recognizes him as Dr. Richard Kimble. Surely he can be persuaded to brave the storm rather than have his identity revealed.

Five years earlier, Marcie had had an unwanted pregnancy. She had asked Kimble to perform an abortion, but he had refused on legal and moral grounds. The person who finally did the operation botched it so badly that she was left barren. Because Kimble was the last qualified M.D. to turn her down, Marcie holds him responsible for her condition.

Marcie coerces Kimble into taking Harry and her out on the boat. The storm gets worse and worse, with winds approaching 100 M.P.H., and Harry goes on deck to order Kimble to turn around. A crashing wave swamps the deck and washes Harry into the Straits of Florida, never to emerge. Marcie has lost her half-million-dollar meal ticket and gained a new reason to hate Kimble.

Kimble somehow gets the boat to Key Blanca and docks it there. Marcie pulls a gun and orders Kimble off the island, but the storm is too severe to chance another suicide run. He disarms Marcie, forces his way into her house, and makes himself at home.

The two engage in a sarcastic repartee, neither hiding their disdain for the other. Marcie attempts to call the police but Kimble disconnects the phone. Marcie's room appears in danger of collapsing, and she goes in to retrieve some valuables. Kimble pulls her out just as the room caves in, saving her and an envelope full of money she had rescued. Kimble snatches it, discovering it contains $25,000. He decides to hold on to it as "my edge," and Marcie figures she will never get it back.

Marcie connivingly suggests a truce between the two and gives a biographical (but fictional) sob story: about her growing up in a Chicago slum, her father (a mobster) having deserted the family during her infancy, and her mother's alcoholism, all forcing Marcie into prostitution. When the electricity goes out, Marcie embraces and kisses Kimble (a ruse to check whether he still has the gun and, hopefully, soften him into returning the money).

Marcie goes out to the boat, supposedly to get her suitcase. She uses the boat's radio to report Kimble to the Coast Guard. Meanwhile, Kimble slips the money into Marcie's purse, where he discovers a letter from her father: a doctor living in a fashionable section of Chicago. When Marcie returns, Kimble confronts her about her lies. Marcie discovers that he has returned her money and realizes he is truly honest — probably even about not having killed his wife. She now feels remorseful about having called the police and realizes she has developed strong feelings toward Kimble.

Kimble goes to the boat to use the radio, checking on weather conditions and leaving word for his employer. The Coast Guard radio man asks him to deliver a message to Marcie: that the sheriff got the communication O.K., and that a police helicopter will be sent out as soon as the storm clears. Marcie boards the boat and Kimble gives her the message. Apologetic and, for once, sincere, Marcie tells Kimble "I think I'm in love with you." Having no reason to trust her, Kimble replies, "You have a funny way of showing it, lady," and leaves the boat.

The wind breaks the boat loose from its mooring, setting it adrift with Marcie aboard. Kimble pulls it back but, when Marcie plunges into the water, gives up on the boat to save her again. He dives in after her, brings her inside, and nurses her as the boat drifts away.

When Marcie revives, she kisses Kimble and repledges her love. She offers an idea: for him to take Harry's passport, and the two to live happily ever after in Brazil. They will be financially set and safe from the police. He doesn't even have to stay with Marcie afterward. "I wouldn't go without you," Kimble says, "and I can't go with you." They kiss once more. The chopper arrives and Kimble hides in the house. Marcie tells the cops that Kimble skipped out on the charter boat. As they fly her back to Florida, Kimble takes a motor boat off the island and to his next stop.

Episode #30
THE END GAME
Original Airdate: April 21, 1964

Written by: Stanford Whitmore   **Directed by:** Jerry Hopper

Cast: John McGiver as Jake Devlin, John Fiedler as Sam Reed, Joseph Campanella as Lt. Spencer, Christopher Connelly as J. J. Watson, Martine Bartlett as streetwalker, Chick Hearn as newscaster, Stuart Margolin as Jimmy, Lee Krieger as vendor, Richard Chambers as photographer, Gil Frye as officer, Martin Garralaga as gardener, Ted Bensinger as man.

On Tuesday, as Kimble walks to work (second shift in the shipping department of Willoughby Carloading), he unwittingly becomes part of a shot taken by a street photographer. Through a series of coincidences, the photo winds up in the hands of a policeman who recognizes Kimble. The photographer is tracked down, helping to pin down the site of the photo. Lt. Gerard is contacted and soon arrives in town. Working with local police Lt. Spencer, Gerard sets up a stakeout and a check of local businesses.

Kimble spots the police at his workplace and he takes off on foot. The city (population 500,000) is boxed in, and Kimble's face and biography quickly make their way into the media. A woman recognizes Kimble and contacts the police. Gerard is hot on the trail, predicting Kimble's moves uncannily.

Kimble comes across a hitchhiking surfer with a portable radio. Hoping it will help him stay ahead of the manhunt, Kimble buys the radio for $40. The surfer later hears a bulletin about Kimble and realizes whom he sold the radio to, reporting this to the police. Gerard decides to use this information to his advantage: he will have bogus information broadcast over the radio waves, leading Kimble into a trap. While police await Kimble's arrival in the south end of town, a bulletin reports that they are concentrated in the northwest part of the city.

Kimble is in the back of a truck heading south when it reaches a roadblock. Kimble climbs out and flees, but he is seen and pursued. As the search area is narrowed to one of eight square blocks, the fugitive's capture seems imminent. "Finally, Kimble," Gerard says to no one in particular, "the end game." Lt. Spencer remarks on Gerard's "killer instinct."

Kimble climbs through the window of a house labeled "downstairs for rent," holing up in the unoccupied lower level. He soon finds himself held at gunpoint by Devlin, co-owner of the building for the past 25 years. He knows very well who Kimble is and brings him triumphantly upstairs to his partner, Reed. Devlin and Reed, though inseparable, argue constantly about virtually every subject. During the Kimble trial, Devlin had steadfastly maintained his belief of Kimble's guilt, while Reed had argued in favor of "reasonable doubt." Kimble advises that Reed was right on this one.

Having no phone in the house, Devlin waits for the police to arrive during their house-to-house search. Kimble begins to work on Devlin, applauding him for doing what he thinks is right but pointing out that the discovery of the one-armed man will come too late for Kimble. Reed chimes in that that discovery will prove he was right all along, and that he will spend the next 20 years reminding Devlin "I told you so!" This is too much for Devlin to handle so, by the time the police arrive, he is in on the conspiracy to protect Kimble. Kimble is hidden in the trunk of their vintage car while Reed and Devlin deny having seen the fugitive. With no sign of Kimble anywhere in the search area, the local police begin to disperse the manhunt.

Devlin soon has a change of heart and walks to the roadblock to tell Gerard where Kimble is. Meanwhile, Reed has concocted an escape plan. He and Kimble drive off in the car (which has bad brakes), get on the old hill road, and send the vehicle over the embankment. By the time Gerard gets there, the car is in flames at the bottom of the embankment, and Kimble and Reed are presumed dead. Devlin openly mourns the loss of his companion.

Reed can't resist revealing himself, laughing at Devlin's ignorance and trumpeting his own ingenuity. Kimble is long gone, Reed proudly tells Gerard. Reed will be gone for a while, too, as the result of his abetting a fugitive. He and Devlin argue in the back of the police car all the way to the station.

Act II
The 1964-65 Season

The Fugitive's second season featured 30 more episodes, aired between September 15, 1964, and April 20, 1965.

The show enjoyed its finest Nielsen-ratings year. Competing against CBS's medical drama, *The Doctors and the Nurses*, and NBC's *Bell Telephone Hour*, *The Fugitive* ranked fifth among all prime-time series in 1964-65 (finishing behind the western *Bonanza* and comedies *Bewitched, Gomer Pyle, U.S.M.C.*, and *The Andy Griffith Show*).

David Janssen again appeared as the fugitive on each of the season's episodes and won the Golden Globe Award as Best Male Television Star of the year. Barry Morse portrayed Lt. Philip Gerard in nine episodes: numbers 32, 35, 37, 39, 43, 47, 51, 55, and 60.

Episode #31
MAN IN A CHARIOT
Original Airdate: September 15, 1964

Written by: George Eckstein   Directed by: Robert Butler

Cast: Kathleen Maguire as Nancy Gilman, Ed Begley as Prof. G. Stanley Lazer, Robert Drivas as Lee Gould, Gene Lyons as Art McNeil, Dort Clark as Sgt. Pulaski, Stewart Moss as Judge Charles G. Tyler, Peter Duryea as Paul Mitchell, Walter Brooke as moderator, Harold Gould as Eller, Edward Madden as Dr. Gary.

Kimble is employed as a dishwasher and clean-up man at the Iron Horse, near Lancaster, Pennsylvania (364 miles from Lexington, where he was spotted a few weeks ago). A debate featuring local professor G. Stanley Lazer is being shown on the bar's television set. Kimble's ears prick up when his own name is mentioned among a group of convicted criminals, about whom Lazer claims "I have no doubt that, if I were able to represent these defendants before another jury, I would be able to obtain for each an acquittal or, at worst, a hung jury." After the bartender corroborates Lazer's acumen, Kimble telephones the professor, arranging a meeting on the 8:00 Harrisburg train.

Lazer, who once worked with Darrow, had been a brilliant defense lawyer. A decade ago he had been riding in a car driven by his drunk wife when she lost control and crashed. She was killed and he was crippled. At 70, the wheelchair-confined Lazer is "damned" to what he considers a menial job, professor of law at a college. Lazer is a bitter man, tough on his students and hated by them. Lazer's aide of the past 15 years, Nancy, is always with him and protective of his interests.

Kimble meets with Lazer and Nancy on the train. Lazer says he will have to review the case, seeking grounds for a new appeal. Boasting that he has never lost a capital case, Lazer expresses disinterest in whether or not Kimble is guilty. Afterward, Nancy privately chastises Kimble for putting the professor in danger of disbarment, prosecution, and health problems, in offering "his chance to get back in the arena."

Lazer orders a copy of the Kimble trial transcript and examines it. He becomes convinced that there is enough technical error and reliance on circumstantial evidence to warrant a retrial. He decides to test the case in a classroom exercise: a mock trial with Lazer as the defense attorney. Lazer figures that, if he can win against a bunch of students that hate his guts, he will have no trouble with a real jury. His opponent, representing the State, will be Lee Gould. Gould had idolized Lazer long before his college days and has become his top student. Though bright, Gould is also arrogant and disrespectful at times.

Lazer scolds Gould right off the bat for not taking the "dry run" seriously. Kimble is angry with Lazer for orchestrating this charade, but the professor convinces him to stick around and see how it turns out. Meanwhile, a reporter for the *Herald* has become very interested in the mock trial. The local police had gotten a call from Indiana, wondering why Lazer ordered the transcript, and the reporter's instincts tell him that the professor has Kimble stashed away somewhere. His suspicion mounts when Lazer introduces information that wasn't brought out in the original trial.

At the end of one session, Gould recognizes the man peeking in at the proceedings as Kimble himself and follows him to his hotel. Gould tells Kimble that he has done a lot of research on the case and that he always believed in Kimble's innocence. Kimble is nevertheless troubled that he has been recognized. Kimble tells Lazer that he is leaving, but the professor arranges for a new room — complete with closed-circuit television to watch the proceedings privately — for Kimble.

Things are not going well for Lazer in the courtroom, and he resorts to bullying his way through. He launches a personal attack on Gould, calling him "gutless," and sending him storming out of the room. Kimble meets Gould outside, offering him company, and the two wind up in a bar. Kimble convinces

Gould to return and stand up to Lazer, who chose Gould because he thought he could give him a fight. Besides, Kimble needs Gould to prove whether Lazer is capable of winning. Later, Kimble lectures Lazer about his self-pity, suggesting he concentrate on teaching his students rather than taking his bitterness out on them.

The trial is concluding, and Gould delivers a powerful closing statement. Lazer opens his own with applause for the State's case, then begins an oratory about the defendant: a member of one of the great professions, whose wife was taken in a moment of pointless violence, and who was exiled to a world he hated; a man who asks only compassion, whose memories of mountain-tops blinded him to the beauty of the valley. It soon becomes obvious that Lazer is not talking about Kimble, but issuing his own public apology. Lazer commends the defendant to the jury's mercy.

The police, on the reporter's tip, enter the courtroom in search of Kimble. Gould sees them and approaches the camera man, convincing him to pan the back of the room to get a shot of his girlfriend. Kimble sees the police on the television and hides himself.

The jury returns with a speedy "not guilty" verdict. Lazer is pleased but realizes he couldn't really have won the case. He tells Kimble that some strange chemistry seems to work against the doctor in such a case and that Kimble will have to find his one-armed man after all. The two thank each other, and Kimble takes a bus out of town.

Episode #32
WORLD'S END
Original Airdate: September 22, 1964

Written by: Stuart Jerome **Directed by:** Robert Butler

Cast: Suzanne Pleshette as Eleanor "Ellie" Burnett, Carmen Mathews as Ada Burnett, Dabney Coleman as Sgt. Keith, Henry Beckman as Keller, Woodrow Parfrey as Bill Newlin, Sallie Brophy as Grace Newlin, Paul Birch as Capt. Carpenter, Jess Kirkpatrick as Charlie Watts, Peter Brocco as hotel clerk, Robert Gibbons as inn manager.

Kimble comes across a newspaper ad: "Personal to R.K.—Have information regarding September 17th. Phone me at home. Urgent. E.B." Kimble realizes the message is for him, from the daughter (Ellie) of his late defense attorney, John Burnett. Ellie—who has been secretly in love with Kimble since the trial—had been running the ad for the past week in various cities. Gerard spots the ad about the same time, also realizing who "E.B." is; Ellie and her mother, Ada, are social friends of the Gerards.

Kimble calls Ellie, who tells him about a lead on the one-armed man.

Keller, a private investigator hired by her father, has reported such a man in Missouri as of a few days ago. Ellie asks Kimble to meet her in Kansas City the next day.

Ellie gets to the Missouri Manor hotel in K.C., meeting with Keller. He gives her distressing news: the one-armed man had matched Kimble's description, according to a witness named Newlin, but had burnt to death in a barn-fire on Newlin's property. Ellie breaks the news to Kimble upon his arrival. She is already formulating a plan: if this really was the right man, Richard can stop searching for him and instead run away with her to Brazil.

Gerard meets with Ada, who refuses to betray her daughter. He manages to find out where Ellie went, though, and figures Kimble is with her or on his way to meet her. Gerard contacts the police in Kansas City and is soon on his way there.

Kimble has to make sure that the dead man was *his* one-armed man; if not, he will keep looking as long as it takes. Kimble drives a rented car 30 miles to Springvale to meet with Newlin. Newlin brushes off Kimble's interrogation, advising him to talk to the mortician. Kimble does, learning that the one-armed man did fit the description but that he had been cremated that morning. Kimble is convinced his quarry really is dead.

Keller meets with Newlin's wife, who admits that the dead man, Barney Willis, was the father of her son. She had helped to send him to the Nebraska state prison, which is where he was when Helen Kimble was murdered. He had been blackmailing the Newlin family until his death. Willis obviously could not have been Kimble's one-armed man, and Keller prepares a report to that effect for Ellie.

Gerard arrives in town, meeting with police Sgt. Keith. They stake out Ellie's hotel room for one night but, luckily, the disconsolate Kimble is in another hotel (registered under the name "May"). Gerard and Keith visit Ellie, who insists she is there merely to pursue a lead on the one-armed man and doesn't know where Kimble is. Gerard and Keith leave the room, but wait at the hotel's front desk. When they learn Ellie has placed a call to the Edmund Hotel, they go there in search of Kimble.

Ellie has decided to withhold Keller's report so as not to jeopardize her South American trip. Kimble wonders what was in the report, and Ellie says the one-armed man claimed to have killed a woman two years ago, according to Mrs. Newlin. Ellie tells Kimble that she has arranged a charter plane from a private airport. Kimble agrees to go with Ellie but wants to talk to Mrs. Newlin first.

Gerard and Keith get to the Edmund Hotel, going up on one elevator while Kimble is going down on another. Kimble goes to the Newlin farm, and Mrs. Newlin — wanting to get rid of Kimble with no further questions — concurs with Ellie's lie. He leaves to meet Ellie at the Springvale Inn.

Ada, concerned about what trouble her daughter might be getting into, arrives at Ellie's hotel room. Ellie tells her the whole story, and Mom calls her a liar and a cheat for withholding Keller's information. Ellie leaves, despite pangs of guilt, and Ada, hoping to prevent her daughter's terrible mistake, gets in touch with Gerard. Extracting a promise to keep Ellie's name out of it, Ada tells Gerard that the two of them plan to take off from Tucker Field. Gerard goes there to await Kimble's arrival.

Kimble meets Ellie at the Inn, calling her "something extra-special." They leave for the airport, and Kimble continues to thank Ellie for giving him a new life with new hope. Ellie's conscience can take no more, and she finally shows him the report. Kimble gets out of the car, flags down the Memphis bus, and lovingly kisses Ellie goodbye.

Episode #33
MAN ON A STRING
Original Airdate: September 29, 1964

Written by: Barbara Merlin & Milton Merlin & Harry Kronman
Directed by: Sydney Pollack

Cast: Lois Nettleton as Lucey Russell, John Larch as Deputy George Duncan, Patricia Smith as Amy Adams, Malcolm Atterbury as Sheriff Jake Mead, Cyril Delevanti as old-timer, Russell Collins as Doc Phillips.

Kimble, alias Joe Walker, is dropped off near Overton in the northwestern U.S. at 11:15 on a Tuesday night. He comes across a young woman, Lucey, obviously having car problems. Joe helps get her car started, earning a ride to Overton in return. Lucey, who says she was stood up by her "date," Lark Adams (Joe's look-alike), invites Joe in for coffee, then to spend the night. Her reputation in this town is already soiled beyond repair, she explains; her affair with Lark, a married man, is common knowledge. Joe and Lucey seem to hit it off and kiss goodbye in the morning. Their farewell is interrupted by Deputy George Duncan, with news that Lark was found dead. He had been pushed through the rail of a trestle and hidden in some bushes right near his and Lucey's planned meeting place. Lucey becomes the prime suspect.

Joe vouches that Lucey was with him the night before. George takes Joe to the Overton jail to repeat his story for Sheriff Mead, who had already decided on Lucey's guilt. Mead is unimpressed by the alibi but invites Joe to stick around for a couple of days to testify at the coroner's inquest. George, concerned that Lucey will be railroaded, makes Joe promise to stay. Joe later decides he had better leave. He prepares a signed and notarized deposition with his testimony and delivers it to Lucey at her workplace, the Golden Cage diner. Joe leaves, saying he can't explain why he has to go.

George meets with Lark's widow, Amy, admitting that he killed Lark. Angry at his constant cheating on and physical abuse of Amy, George had followed Lark from a bar, confronted him, and beaten him up. Lark had accidentally gone through the rail and plunged to his death. Amy, who had been the loudest voice in proclaiming Lucey's guilt, is angry — not because George killed her husband but because Lucey didn't. Amy and George have had a secret admiration for one another for some time.

The sheriff, under local pressure to lynch Lucey, disregards the deposition and locks her up. Meanwhile, Joe is given a ride out of town by an old-timer who happens to be a juror for the inquest. The man tells Joe about the deposition being thrown out, and Joe realizes he will have to return to help clear Lucey.

George tells Amy he won't let Lucey take the rap, even if it means confessing his crime. Amy won't hear of such nonsense. George has tracers out on Joe, wondering if he is in some kind of trouble. Joe returns voluntarily, and George warns him not to leave town again.

Joe figures his only chance to clear Lucey without testifying is to reveal the true murderer, whom he suspects is Amy. He pays her a visit, springing his theory on her. Amy, reminding Joe of all the friends she has in town, counters with her own theory: that Joe abetted Lucey in the murder. After Joe leaves, Amy calls George. She tells him to make sure Joe leaves town before the inquest the next day, or she will implicate George herself.

Amy sees Joe is still around shortly before the inquest, and she confronts George about it. George turns on her, saying he will drag her in with him if he is fingered. On Amy's way out of the station, she discovers a partially-hidden Richard Kimble "wanted" poster on the bulletin board and pockets it.

At the inquest Amy sits beside Joe and shows him the poster. He gets the message and goes to leave, but he is stopped by George. Joe is called to take the stand as Lucey's witness, while Amy shows George the poster. Asked his name, Joe balks. Amy speaks up, saying she can help Joe answer the question, but George steals her thunder by coming forward. George dramatically turns in his gun and badge and confesses to manslaughter. In the resultant hubbub, Joe slips away.

Episode #34
WHEN THE BOUGH BREAKS
Original Airdate: October 6, 1964

Story by: James Griffith & George Eckstein   **Teleplay by:** George Eckstein
Directed by: Ralph Senensky

Cast: Diana Hyland as Carol Hollister, Lin McCarthy as Lt. Malleson, Royal Dano as "Preacher," Don Briggs as Whit Pearson, June Vincent as Laura Pearson, Robert Hogan as Sgt. Barrett, Alex Gerry as Dr. Max Eisen, Sue Randall as Ruth Fisher, Marge Redmond as Norma, Jud Taylor as Joey, Eddie Guardino as Eddie, Jo Helton as woman.

With police lurking about the Grand Forks, North Dakota, rail yard, Kimble—alias Pete Broderick—climbs into a freight car. He finds himself in the company of a young lady, Carol, with a five-month-old baby. As the train starts, a hobo chased by a cop tries to make it to the open car. Feeling sorry for the geezer, Kimble puts out his hand and helps "Preacher" aboard.

The train makes an unscheduled stop as two men check the cars. Carol says it may be the police, unnecessarily sent by her father to find her. Kimble turns his sympathy to Carol and offers Preacher $5 to run decoy for them. Preacher jumps out of the car, and while the cops pursue him, Kimble, Carol, and the baby sneak out the other side of the car. They get on a bus to Fargo, where Kimble helps her find a dingy hotel room. Carol says she is reuniting with her husband, Jimmy, in that city. Carol has been under the care of her parents, she says, since being hurt some time ago in an auto accident (that left her with recurrent dizzy spells). Kimble offers to help Carol find Jimmy, and she tells him where his apartment and workplace are.

Kimble finds the apartment abandoned and the building condemned. He checks the workplace and learns a chilling fact: that Carol was the only survivor of the car crash, which claimed her husband and child a year earlier. The deluded widow has kidnapped someone else's child.

Preacher sees a headline in the *Fargo Chronicle*: "Girl Sought in Kidnapping." Hoping for a reward, Preacher goes to the police department and tells them about Carol and her companion. A later edition of the paper will have the subhead, "Boyfriend Also Sought." The Pearsons, Carol's parents, and Mrs. Fisher, mother of the missing child, are soon on their way to Fargo.

Kimble returns to the hotel and asks Carol whose baby she has. Her irrationality surfaces, and she begins calling Kimble "Jimmy." Kimble realizes Carol is not a criminal but a sick girl. He goes out, finds a discarded newspaper, and learns the rest of the story. Kimble anonymously calls the police, telling them where they can find Carol and the baby.

Carol brings the baby to her old apartment as they wait for "Daddy" to come home. She then remembers that he will probably be at the hotel room. Leaving the baby alone in the condemned building, Carol returns to the hotel and is promptly arrested by the waiting police. Carol is brought to Fargo Memorial Hospital and placed under the care of psychiatrist Dr. Eisen. She refuses to reveal where the baby is, saying she will tell only her husband. Dr. Eisen explains that she has transferred her late husband's identity to her freight train companion, and Kimble becomes wanted by the police for a different reason than usual.

Kimble hears the news over the radio and realizes the baby's safety depends on his going to the hospital, although it will mean exposing himself to the police. He goes, introducing himself to Lt. Malleson as "the one you're looking for." He tells of his meeting Carol on the freight, and he is allowed to visit with her. Malleson thinks he has seen Kimble's face before but can't remember where. "It'll come," he assures another officer.

Carol tells "Jimmy" where the baby is, and Lt. Malleson drives him out there. Kimble finds the child and puts it into the car, hoping for a chance to skip out, but Malleson orders him back. He seems to have remembered where he has seen Kimble before but is impressed by the fugitive's decency in putting the infant's safety ahead of his own. Malleson points out that someone hopping freights is likely to be running from a record, and a man on the run is not likely to come forward as he did. If Kimble returns with Malleson, there are bound to be questions asked and photographs taken of him. Malleson stops at a bus depot and suggests that Kimble be on his way.

Dr. Eisen finally allows Carol's parents to see her, warning Mr. Pearson that her delusions center around a deep fear of him. Mr. Pearson warmly embraces his troubled daughter, and she is surely on the road to a complete recovery.

Episode #35
NEMESIS
Original Airdate: October 13, 1964

Written by: Harry Kronman **Directed by:** Jerry Hopper

Cast: Kurt Russell as Philip Gerard, Jr., John Doucette as Sheriff Sam Deebold, Slim Pickens as Hank Corbin, Bing Russell as Matt Davis, Adrienne Marden as Mrs. Deebold, Paul Birch as Capt. Carpenter, Garry Walberg as Jaeger.

Kimble is working at the Evergreen Fish Hatchery in the mountains of Northby, Bardon County, Wisconsin. He drives a Fish Management Division truck loaded with trout to be released in a nearby creek. He notices he is being followed by two men, undoubtedly fishermen hoping to get the jump on this fresh trout supply. Kimble pulls over, as do the men. Sam Deebold, one of the two, advises Kimble to do his job and dump the fish, but Kimble refuses to reveal the drop-spot. Deebold flashes his sheriff's badge, offering an exchange of favors, but no deal is made. Deebold, noting Kimble's reaction to the badge, later checks the "wanted" posters at the station, I.D.'s Kimble, and places a call to Stafford, Indiana.

Lt. Gerard and his son, Phil Jr. are returning home from a midwestern car trip. Gerard promises his son that someday, after Kimble is captured, they will go on a father-son camping trip. During a pit stop, Gerard calls in to his office, learning that Kimble has been identified only some 200 miles from Gerard's present location. Gerard thus changes his travel plans.

Gerard arrives at Deebold's home, and the two officers prepare to go to the hatchery. Phil Jr. wants to accompany the men, but he is instructed to remain with Mrs. Deebold. Under the pretense of getting his precious 1963 Topps football cards, Phil returns to the car and hides under a blanket in the back.

Kimble sees the officers approaching the hatchery, and he sneaks out the side and circles around to the front of the building. Seeing the keys still in Deebold's ignition, Kimble jumps in the car and drives off, speeding through back roads surrounded by mountainous woods. He soon learns he has a passenger: the son of his dreaded pursuer. Kimble decides against releasing the boy, reasoning that he would get hopelessly lost.

Gerard organizes the search effort: the National Guard is sending a helicopter, the forest fire towers are manned, and police from nearby towns are put on the alert. When Gerard realizes that his son stowed away in Deebold's car, the search becomes all the more intense.

Leaving a trail, Phil begins dropping football cards — including his prized "Jim Brown"— out the window. Kimble catches Phil in the act and confiscates the cards, remarking that Phil doesn't have a "John Unitas" card, as every boy ought to.

After Kimble and Phil stop to eat, Kimble discovers the car is out of gas. Before they proceed on foot, Phil leaves his sweater on the ground with the sleeve pointing in the direction they are going. Kimble and Phil bed down for the night and awaken to the sight of Hank Corbin standing over them with a rifle. Phil blurts out Kimble's identity, with Kimble laughing it off as a tall tale. Kimble offers their fishing rod in exchange for breakfast: venison from the buck Hank poached. Kimble remarks on the infraction, and Hank says, "You don't talk about me, and I won't talk about you."

Gerard and Deebold find the abandoned car and recognize Phil's coded message. They head southwest and alert authorities in the area. Game warden Matt Davis visits Hank, asking whether he has seen Kimble and the boy. Hank denies it, while Kimble covers Phil's mouth in the next room. As the warden leaves, Phil knocks over Hank's rifle and it discharges. Matt returns, holds Kimble at gunpoint, and radios in the arrest report. Gerard and Deebold head toward the Corbin cabin but will have to walk the last few thousand yards up the mountain.

Phil shows interest in the warden's radio, examining it. Kimble scolds the boy and takes the radio from him. He suddenly throws the radio at Matt, disorienting him, then knocks out the warden with one punch. Kimble empties Matt's gun and flees into the woods with Phil in pursuit.

Phil gets his foot caught in an animal trap and cries out. Kimble returns to free him and make sure he is all right. Phil can't understand why such a bad person would do that and is beginning to believe in Kimble's innocence. This poses a dilemma for Phil: "You and Dad — you can't both be right." His father is so sure about Kimble's guilt, but Kimble points out that "being sure doesn't make you right." Kimble runs off into the woods, then changes direction. By the time Gerard reunites with his son, Kimble has gotten away again.

Afterward, Kimble mails Phil's football cards back to him (at 934 South Maple Avenue, Stafford). Included in the batch is a "John Unitas" card.

Episode #36
TIGER LEFT, TIGER RIGHT
Original Airdate: October 20, 1964
Written by: William Link & Richard Levinson
Directed by: James Goldstone

Cast: Leslie Nielsen as Harold Cheyney, Carol Rossen as Irene Cheyney, John Lasell as Michael R. Pryor, Jeanne Bal as Laura Pryor, David Sheiner as Lt. Hess, Tim Stafford as Glenn Pryor, James Noah as Doug Warren, Richard Bull as McIntire, Paul Sorensen as radio operator, Robert Cinder as Father Connelly, William Keene as Dr. Garber.

Kimble, alias Frank Jordan, has spent the past two months working as gardener for the Pryors, a wealthy Eugene, Oregon, family. Frank has earned the trust of the family, particularly Laura, and has become something of a father figure to young Glenn. Mike Pryor is too busy becoming wealthier to have time for his son.

Glenn injures his arm and ankle in a fall. Frank drives the boy to the doctor's office in Mike's car. Harold Cheyney, assuming Frank is Mike, follows the car. Cheyney, struck by a Pryor company truck a couple of years ago, had become a paraplegic. He had unwittingly signed a document absolving Pryor of liability in the accident and had then repeatedly written to Pryor asking for employment. His letters, screened by Mike's staff, had gone unanswered. Cheyney's wife, Irene, came up with Plan "B": to kidnap Mike Pryor and hold him for $100,000 ransom.

As Frank returns alone from the doctor's office, he comes across Cheyney posing as a stranded motorist. When Frank checks the car, he is struck from behind and knocked unconscious. When he comes to, he finds himself being held hostage by the Cheyneys in the abandoned Fir Tree Lodge. When the kidnappers realize they have the wrong man, Irene becomes furious. They decide that Frank may still be good for some money — say, $25,000 — or trade-in value on Pryor.

The Pryors, concerned about their missing gardener, ask Lt. Hess to stop by the house. While he is there, Cheyney calls (using a test-phone tapped into a church's phone line) with his ultimatum: $25,000 or Frank dies. Laura shows Lt. Hess a photograph of Frank. The lieutenant, thinking Frank looks familiar, pockets the pic. He soon reports back to the Pryors, telling them who Frank really is.

A special phone is set up in the Pryor home as the kidnapper's next call is awaited. Mike says he will not put up the money to finance a murderer's safe return. Laura privately lambastes her husband, saying that Mike's attitudes turn her stomach and that he is allowing a decent man to die. Mike humbly agrees to cooperate with the police.

Kimble and Irene converse, she hinting that she might just take the money and run, dumping her useless husband (maybe even in favor of Kimble). Cheyney places another call to Mike, and police are able to trace it to the general area. They check around the lodge but come up empty.

The $25,000 is placed in a bookbag along with a concealed radio transmitter. Mike makes the drop, and the Cheyneys and Kimble return to the lodge with the money. Irene gleefully grabs the loot, saying she will bring it to the car while Harold gathers up the rest of the gear. Irene drives off with the money but has a change of heart and returns for Harold.

Police home in on the transmitter's signal. The Cheyneys, having no further use for Kimble, drop him off and continue toward California. They are soon apprehended at a roadblock.

Learning about Cheyney's motive, Mike is sympathetic and vows to help in any way he can.

Episode #37
TUG OF WAR
Original Airdate: October 27, 1964

Written by: Dan Ullman   **Directed by:** Abner Biberman

Cast: Arthur O'Connell as Samuel Cole, Don Gordon as Morgan Fallon, Harry Townes as Art Mallet, Karl Swenson as Axel Nielsen, Katie Sweet as Patty Sorensen, John Harmon as Al, Jon Lormer as pastor.

Kimble, alias Kelly, is a farmhand at Max Henderson's ranch in Cornell, Trinity County, Idaho. With a goat in tow, Kelly stops at the post office to pick up Henderson's mail. A precocious little girl visiting there notices that Kelly matches the Richard Kimble "wanted" poster on the wall and later points this out to Art Mallet. While busybody Axel Nielsen listens in on the party line, Mallet calls the county deputy sheriff, Morgan Fallon, to report the fugitive's sighting. Nielsen jots down the truck's license number and the word "goat" on a notepad mounted by his phone.

Kimble stops at Nielsen's service station for gas, and the proprietor realizes who his customer is. While Nielsen pumps the gas, Kimble goes inside to fetch some water for the goat. He sees the notepad and realizes the owner is somehow on to him. Kimble goes outside, locks Nielsen in the store room, and drives off in the owner's vehicle.

Fallon, formerly a fighter pilot in Korea, searches for the fugitive by helicopter. He locates the Henderson truck at the service station and touches down, rescuing Nielsen. Kimble, meanwhile, ditches Nielsen's car and goes into the wilderness on foot.

Samuel Cole follows the case with unusual interest. He had been county sheriff until resigning some ten years ago, blaming himself for the escape of a murderer who later killed two more people. The murderer had convinced Samuel of his innocence, leading the sheriff to relax his vigilance. This is the opportunity Samuel has been praying for — the chance to make amends with society and with himself by capturing another murderer. Armed with a rifle, he heads off into the wilderness on a mule.

Samuel, whose instincts are still sharp, finds Kimble just where he expected to, and he arrests him. He is not a lawman, he admits, but is doing this for the "satisfaction of seeing justice done."

The sheriff (whom Samuel has little regard for) locates the two from his chopper and lands. Fallon congratulates Samuel and prepares to take Kimble in (and take credit for his capture). Samuel will not allow it, saying Kimble is *his* prisoner and forcing Fallon to relinquish his pistol. Samuel leads what promises to be a long, long walk back to town. They stop at a cabin for the night as a storm hits.

While Samuel and Kimble play chess on a magnetic set, Fallon retrieves his gun and announces that they will be returning to the helicopter. Samuel says that he rigged the chopper's tail rotor so that steering will be impossible, so they will have to continue on foot under Samuel's indispensable guidance.

Fallon, taking his turn in this tug of war, confiscates a vial of nitroglycerin (which Samuel needs for his heart condition) that had fallen out of Samuel's pocket.

The walk is resumed the next day, with a stop to continue the chess match. The game ends in stalemate, impressing Samuel, who rarely fails to win. He tells Kimble his motivation for the arrest, and Kimble says he is sorry for both of them because he is innocent. Samuel, having heard this story before, still plans to bring Kimble to justice.

At another stop the sheriff shackles Kimble to a tree. Kimble manages to free himself and make a run for it. Samuel shoots him down, wounding Kimble in the back of the left thigh. He also gets Fallon's pistol back, discarding it, but the excitement causes his heart to begin acting up. Fallon says he will go up ahead to get help but instead hides behind a tree up the path.

Samuel's heart settles down, and he and Kimble continue onward. Fallon ambushes Samuel and takes his rifle. Samuel pulls a hunting knife on Fallon but collapses before he can use it. Kimble attends to the dying ex-sheriff, too far gone for even the nitro pills. Samuel asks Kimble if he is really innocent, pointing out there is "no need to tell anything but the truth now." Kimble reaffirms his innocence, and Samuel secretly reveals something: he has the rifle bullets in his pocket. At peace with himself, Samuel dies.

Kimble, knowing the rifle is empty, charges and overpowers Fallon. He brings Samuel's body into town on the mule, leaving money with a pastor to pay for the funeral. Kimble is then off and limping again.

68   Act II: The 1964-65 Season

Episode #38
DARK CORNER
Original Airdate: November 10, 1964

Written by: Harry Kronman   **Directed by:** Jerry Hopper

Cast: Tuesday Weld as Mattie Braydon, Elizabeth MacRae as Clara Braydon, Paul Carr as Bob Matthews, Crahan Denton as Sam Braydon, John McLiam as Sheriff Frank Grover, James Seay as Mr. Keeley, Rudy Dolan as Marty, Dave Armstrong as Mike.

Kimble is aboard a bus near Sioux Falls, South Dakota, when it stops for a roadblock. Police are looking not for Kimble but for a man who held up a liquor store, but Kimble doesn't wait to find this out. When two officers enter the bus, Kimble flees out the emergency exit. The police chase him into the night on foot, but he eludes capture (despite suffering a badly hurt left ankle). Kimble takes refuge in a dark, barn-like studio on Braydon Farms, not knowing the room is occupied by sexy Mattie.

The cops ask Sam Braydon and his clan whether they have seen anyone suspicious. Another officer stops by to inform Sheriff Grover that the hold-up man has been apprehended, leaving no further point in pursuing the man who fled. After the police leave, Mattie tells Kimble he can come out. Mattie says she is very glad Kimble — who introduces himself as Jim Russell — is here and invites him to stay in the studio.

Mattie is blind. At age eight, she had tried to push her sister, Clara, over a ledge just past their barn. Mattie had lost her balance and fallen herself, losing her sight (although doctors could find no clinical reason; it is a case of "hysterical blindness"). Although Sam had witnessed the whole thing, he has never let on to knowing how the "accident" happened, nor has Clara accused her. To Clara's chagrin, Sam obviously favors his handicapped daughter, going to great lengths to appease her whims. Clara is engaged to marry Bob, a ranch hand taken in by the Braydons when his parents died 22 years ago, but Mattie is horning in on Bob's affection, too. She had led him into a lewd liaison some four months ago and has been chasing him for more ever since.

Mattie devises a plan to explain Jim. A talented sculptor, Mattie expects her regular shipment of art supplies from Mr. Albers; Jim will help carry them in and claim to be a model sent by Albers. Mattie asks her father to provide Jim with board and employment while she works on the clay bust, and Sam relents as usual. Jim will stay in the studio and be paid $30 per week to do odd jobs around the farm. His first assignment, which he carries out successfully, is to repair a tractor. Meanwhile, curious Clara checks with Mr. Albers, who says he never heard of Jim Russell.

Jim's next job is to see if he can fix the station wagon, which has a bad habit of slipping out of "park." Later, Mattie will demonstrate that Bob taught her how to drive a car, even though she obviously can't. Jim successfully repairs the wagon.

Clara enters the studio and finds her fiancé making out with her sister. An upset Clara runs off with an apologetic Bob in pursuit. He catches her atop the ledge. In her struggle to get away from him, Clara falls down the embankment, suffering a badly twisted back. She is brought to the hospital, where the sheriff joins in the vigil. Mention is made of the Braydon's new hired hand, an oddity in light of the farm's economic problems, and Grover wonders if the new employee is the man he was chasing. He visits Mattie, learning she is doing a bust of the new man. Mattie hears him coming and artfully alters the bust to throw him off the scent.

Sam returns from the hospital, demanding to know what Mattie did to upset her sister. Mattie pleads innocence, so Sam decides to bring Mattie to the hospital for a confrontation. As they prepare to leave, Sam reveals to Mattie that he knows all about her dishonest ways, dating back to the long-ago ledge incident. When Sam gets out of the car to close the garage door, Mattie slips the car into gear and backs over her father, killing him. Mattie mourns the death of her Dad, claiming the gear must have slipped again.

Jim, knowing the car was fine when he left it (and still is), doubts Mattie's story. He confronts her, but she points out it would be his word against the grieving, blind daughter's. Mattie tries coming on to Jim; rebuffed, she phones the sheriff.

Bob brings Clara home, confessing to and apologizing for his past sins with Mattie. She forgives him, and everything will be swell from now on. They get home shortly before Grover arrives and wonder why he is coming. Mattie says Jim is a criminal, while Jim says Sam's death wasn't an accident. Bob can't believe this but Clara, recalling the long-ago day on the ledge, can. Mattie calls Clara a liar, steering the conversation to Bob's infidelity, but Clara already knows all about it. Her best lies and ruses having failed her, Mattie collapses in hysteria and begins to regain her eyesight.

The sheriff screeches in, and Jim admits to Bob and Clara that he is wanted for something he didn't do. Bob allows him to sneak out the back, and Jim later hops a freight out of town.

Grover tells Bob and Clara that Mattie had said there was someone for him to pick up. Gesturing toward Mattie on the floor, Bob says, "There is."

Episode #39
ESCAPE INTO BLACK
Original Airdate: November 17, 1964

Written by: Larry Cohen **Directed by:** Jerry Hopper

Cast: Betty Garrett as Margaret Ruskin, Ivan Dixon as Dr. Towne, Bernard Kates as Sgt. Lascoe, Tom Troupe as Dr. Bloch, Paul Birch as Capt. Carpenter,

Herb Vigran as Marty, Maxine Stuart as Nurse Proctor, Bill Raisch as Fred Johnson, Donald Barry as checker.

Kimble is dropped off in Decatur, Illinois, where a truckdriver had mentioned a one-armed man working in a restaurant. Kimble stops at a diner, asking the counterman about such a character. Their conversation is interrupted by a cry of "fire!" from the kitchen. Kimble goes back there to see if he can help, but the oven explodes in his face. He wakes up in Decatur General Hospital with a subdural hematoma, ruptured eardrums, hand and head injuries, and — television's favorite malady — amnesia.

Most of Kimble's identification gives his name as Frank Barlow (although one lists him as David Merrill). Social services worker Margaret Ruskin is given the task of finding out who Frank Barlow and his next-of-kin are. Meanwhile, neuropsychiatrist Dr. Towne will be monitoring Barlow's condition and progress. Miss Ruskin is a dedicated, compassionate servant, while Dr. Towne is a by-the-book practitioner, often leading them into philosophical disagreements.

While with Miss Ruskin, Barlow faints after seeing a one-armed man in the hospital corridor. Miss Ruskin attaches more significance to this when she learns that Barlow was asking at the diner about a one-armed man. She identifies the eight local eateries which have amputees among their staff and sets out to check each one.

Barlow is in the corridor when a nearby patient goes into a coughing fit. Barlow instinctively goes over, diagnoses that the man is hemorrhaging, and orders a nurse to fetch a half cc of morphine. The nurse is taken aback, especially after a staff doctor arrives with the same diagnosis and prescription. She tells Dr. Towne, who now has a key clue in identifying Barlow: he is apparently a doctor on the run.

Towne confronts Barlow with this deduction, but the patient still can't remember his past. The doctor hypothesizes that Barlow's mind is hiding something (an "escape into blackness") that his conscience can't deal with. Towne licks his chops at the research value of this case, perhaps even leading to a published article. Barlow agrees to submit to Pentothal to stimulate his memory. Under the drug Barlow reveals his real first name, his occupation, and the fact that his wife is dead.

Miss Ruskin meets her eighth and final possibility, dishwasher Fred Johnson—*the* one-armed man. Saying she has an amnesia victim, Miss Ruskin shows the dishwasher a photo of Barlow, but Johnson claims not to recognize him. After she leaves, Johnson anonymously tips the police about Kimble's whereabouts.

By the time Miss Ruskin returns to the hospital, the police have told Dr. Towne who Barlow is and are on their way there. Miss Ruskin realizes that one of the amputees she interviewed must have contacted the cops, offering evidence that Kimble's story is true. Towne advises her to let it go, as they have done their duties, both medically and morally.

Miss Ruskin rushes to Kimble's room, telling him that the police are coming to get him and that he had better leave with her. They sneak out via the fire exit just as the police come. Kimble spends the rest of the morning in the public library, reading up on his own trial and getting a few flashbacks. Meanwhile, Miss Ruskin is rechecking the one-armed men, and learning that Johnson left his job without notice. She is convinced that Kimble is innocent and determined to help him.

Kimble goes to Dr. Towne's house, asking his guidance. Towne advises Kimble to turn himself in, offering false hope that the amnesia could win him a new appeal. Kimble decides to board a train to Stafford and turn himself in to this Lt. Gerard he has been reading about. Towne lends Kimble $20 and drives him to the station.

When Miss Ruskin learns what happened, she rushes to the station in hopes of intercepting Kimble. Meanwhile, Kimble phones Gerard (evidently working late): "I understand you've been looking for me ... my mind really isn't working that properly."

Gerard is incredulous, noting that Kimble has admitted guilt for the first time, but the call is traced to the place Kimble had been spotted. Kimble had said he would be taking the 8:45 train and arriving in Stafford at 11:43, but Gerard doesn't want to wait that long. He drives to Marshfield to meet the train halfway.

Miss Ruskin boards the train and finally finds Kimble. He is having more flashbacks but still thinks he might be guilty of murder. Miss Ruskin tells him he isn't, saying she saw the man who actually killed his wife. Another flashback confirms she is right. Meanwhile, Gerard has had the train stopped just long enough for him and other officers to get aboard.

Kimble sees the police and realizes he has to run again. When he sees Gerard entering his car, Kimble heads for an exit and jumps out of the moving train, a dangerous but successful escape.

Days later, Kimble calls Miss Ruskin to thank her and tell her he is fine. His memory is coming back, and he knows he didn't kill his wife. Miss Ruskin hangs up in tears of joy and Dr. Towne, passing nearby, offers her a handkerchief. She tells him about Kimble, and he offers to buy her coffee.

Episode #40
THE CAGE
Original Airdate: November 24, 1964

Written by: Sheldon Stark   **Directed by:** Walter Grauman

Cast: Brenda Scott as Carla Vardez, Joe DeSantis as Joe Vardez, Tim O'Connor as Dr. Davis, Richard Evans as Miguel, John Kellogg as Officer Chrisman,

Rodolfo Hoyos as Tonino, Richard Angarola as Pete, Joe Dominguez as Pablo, Julian Rivero as old man.

Kimble, alias Jeff Parker, has spent the past month working as a handyman for Joe Vardez Commercial Fishing in Puerto Viejo, southwestern California. Word comes that the "tuna's running," and the Vardez crew breaks into celebration. One festive ritual has the women dance in a circle, passing around a scarf; whoever is holding it when the music stops must select a partner, with whom she has a romantic dance culminated by a kiss. On this occasion, the scarf-holder is Vargez's sexy 15-year-old daughter, Carla. Expected to choose her perennial boyfriend, Miguel, she instead picks Jeff as her partner. Despite the significant age difference, she has developed quite a crush on Jeff, much to the disapproval of her father and boyfriend.

The temperamental Joe breaks up the party at this point, reminding the crew of their busy day tomorrow. While Miguel privately confronts Carla, Joe does the same to Jeff. Joe warns him not to "chase after my Carla," hinting that he knows Jeff has some trouble with the police. Jeff resolves to leave that night.

Carla apologizes to Jeff for any embarrassment or trouble she caused him, all the while subtly leading him on. The two stumble upon Pablo, who has collapsed on the floor of his room. Jeff pronounces Pablo dead, probably of bubonic plague. Jeff urges Joe to call the public health department. Fearing a quarantine that will prevent his fishing expedition, Joe refuses, ordering Jeff out of town.

Putting his integrity ahead of his safety, Jeff calls the Office of Public Health Service. Dr. Davis confirms Jeff's suspicion, and the whole camp is put under quarantine for seven days. Jeff, claiming to have once worked in a hospital, is put to work assisting Dr. Davis. Joe is furious with Jeff, but Carla—who has long romanticized about the medical world—has even more reason to admire him.

Carla tells Jeff she is in love with him. Jeff lectures Carla, advising her to save her love and affection for someone she can share it with and not to experiment with strangers. Rebuffed and upset, she runs off to Miguel. She implies to him that Jeff attacked her, demanding that Miguel prove his manhood by fighting Jeff. Miguel instead tells Joe, who in turn goes to Officer Chrisman at the quarantine roadblock. Joe tells the cop that Jeff hurt his daughter and is probably wanted for something else as well. Jeff's fingerprints are checked and identified. Unfortunately for the police, Kimble cannot be taken into custody until the quarantine is lifted.

Carla is upset that she has led the kindly Kimble to his fatal capture and admits lying about the attack. Dr. Davis is impressed with Kimble's integrity in reporting the plague case in spite of his own safety.

As the quarantine time limit approaches, Carla seems to be feverish. Her temperature is measured at 101.5°, and some blood is taken for analysis. The quarantine must be extended until noon the next day, when the lab report comes back. Carla requests that Dr. Kimble attend to her, and she privately gestures toward some burnt out matches. Kimble realizes she has been faking the fever, and the danger of plague is virtually over.

Kimble, accompanied by Chrisman, goes to check on Carla at 5 A.M. Kimble knocks out the officer from behind and takes his gun. He then flees out the window with Carla, who can help him find a way to safety. She leads him to a motorboat, but he refuses to let her join him.

Joe finds the two and holds Kimble at gunpoint. Carla pleads with her father to let Kimble go. Joe, seeing that she fights and lies for Kimble just as her mother did for Joe at the same age, realizes Carla does love Kimble. He tells Kimble to "take my daughter and get out of here," but Kimble insists on going alone. Carla and Kimble share a juicy farewell kiss, the symbolic conclusion to their earlier dance, and that seems to appease Carla. Kimble motors off into the sunrise.

Episode #41
CRY UNCLE
Original Airdate: December 1, 1964

Written by: Philip Saltzman   **Directed by**: James Goldstone

Cast: Edward Binns as Josh Kovaks, Donald Losby as Sean Thomas, Dianne Ramey as Kathy, Brett Somers as Miss Edmonds, Ronny Howard as Gus, Steve Ihnat as Sgt. Len Hasboro.

Kimble stops at a laundromat, where he meets two youngsters, Gus and Kathy. They are among 20 residents of Valley Village, a children's home in Donnivale and are there on laundry detail. Meanwhile, a nearby market has been held up by three men who wounded an employee and killed a police officer in the process. Police converge on the area, worrying Kimble. He sneaks out of the laundromat and hides in the back of the Valley Village station wagon.

Miss Edmonds, the housemother, returns to the home with Gus and Kathy. The two kids unload the car and discover Kimble. He assures them that he is not one of the robbers, saying he just wants to get away. Kathy agrees to let him, but Gus rushes to tell 12-year-old Sean the news about the stranger who wants to elude the police. Sean, saying "maybe we can use him," follows Kimble and finds him hiding in the bushes as police check the premises. Sean offers Kimble a place to hide, leading him to a storage room. Kimble thanks the lad, who assures Kimble that he will be expected to repay the debt.

Sean is a problem child, always in trouble, always defiant, never vulnerable. His father had been killed, and his uncle, Pat Thomas, had helped raise the boy for a while. When Sean's mother became fatally ill, Uncle Pat split the scene, leaving Sean orphanage-bound. The boy hadn't even been allowed to attend his parents' funerals. The bitter, untrusting Sean has gotten into one scrape after another and is scheduled to go before the discipline committee again on Monday, two days hence. If he shows his usual defiance, he will earn himself a ticket to what the kids refer to as the "Big S": the state mental hospital at Selby. That would be fine with Miss Edmonds, who doesn't want this bad apple spoiling her bunch. Josh Kovaks, the head counselor, has just about given up on Sean, too.

Kimble wants to leave and take his chances, but Sean has another idea: to introduce the stranger as his Uncle Pat here on "visiting day." Uncle Pat has lunch with Edmonds and Kovaks, and the latter takes him aside afterward. Kovaks lambastes Pat for his irresponsibility, having walked out on a grieving child. He says that if Pat doesn't step in to help now, Sean will be at the point of no return in his road to ruin. Pat must retain his undesirable identity, but tries deflecting some of the blame to Kovaks. Kovaks asks Pat to stay for a while, but Pat says he can't.

Sean plans to escape with Gus tonight, with Uncle Pat providing chauffeur service. The two boys plan to steal the station wagon keys from Miss Edmonds's office, knowing they won't be discovered missing until Monday. The police are still floating around, searching for the third hold-up man, so Uncle Pat is pretty much at Sean's mercy.

Gus gets the keys to Sean but is caught by Miss Edmonds before he can escape the office. Gus takes the rap, but she doesn't notice the keys are missing. Sean presents the keys and his escape plan to Uncle Pat, who takes the keys but refuses to assist in such a self-destructive, failure-bound venture. Sean labels Pat a double-crosser, just like every other adult he has encountered. Sean runs to Kovaks, tells him "Uncle Pat" is really a stranger, and flees the premises by scaling the fence. If found off the grounds, Sean's jig will be up.

Pat, deciding to spare Sean from deeper trouble, takes the station wagon and goes after him. Kovaks calls the police to report the mysterious stranger and the car theft.

Pat finds and catches Sean, forcing him into the car. He says he is bringing the boy back to the police-infested Valley Village, but Sean doesn't believe he would dare (Pat has already admitted to being wanted for a murder he didn't commit). Pat decides that, somewhere along the line, somebody will have to prove sincerity and compassion toward Sean; Pat will be the sacrificial lamb for that purpose. They drive through the gate, and Pat is promptly arrested by the police.

Convinced, Sean pleads with the cops, saying Pat really is his uncle. Seeing that the stranger brought back both the boy and the car, Kovaks decides to let Pat off the hook by vouching for him. After the police leave, Kovaks says "I don't know who you are, and I guess I don't want to know ... thanks."

Uncle Pat bids farewell to Kathy, Gus, and Sean, promising to write his "nephew." Sean spontaneously embraces Pat and bursts into tears, a new, mellow version of yesterday's truant. Kovaks gives Pat a ride out of town.

Episode #42
DETOUR ON A ROAD GOING NOWHERE
Original Airdate: December 8, 1964

Story by: Philip Saltzman **Teleplay by:** Philip Saltzman & Wm. D. Gordon
Directed by: Ralph Senensky

Cast: Elizabeth Allen as Louanne Crowell, Lee Bowman as Tod Langner, Don Quine as Sandy Baird, Phyllis Thaxter as Enid Langner, Warren Vanders as Andy, Walter Brooke as Jess Platt, Frank Marth as Sheriff Hornbeck, Barry Cahill as bus driver, Steve Bell as Bob Street, Lana Wood as the doll.

Kimble, alias Stuart Manning, is a clerk at Indian Lake Lodge at Indian Lake, Wyoming. Among the guests there are Louanne (with whom Stu had had an aborted romance) and the Langners, Tod and Enid. The Langners are a middle-aged couple, though Tod (much to his wife's agitation) continually tries to prove his own virility.

Stu catches Sandy Baird looting some cars in the parking lot. He gets a pistol and Louanne's camera before Stu challenges him. Baird pulls a switchblade, while Stu selects a golf iron. Baird takes off after surrendering the camera, which Stu returns to its owner.

Stu is called into manager Platt's office, where he meets with the boss and two police officers. It seems that the resort's safe was robbed last night, during Stu's shift. As procedure, the fingerprints of all employees will be taken for analysis. The results should be back in a matter of hours, and no employees are to leave the premises in the meantime. Stu realizes he will have to break that rule.

Despite a landslide in the area, the regular shuttle bus to Hazelton arrives at 3:00, picking up Louanne, Stu, and the Langners. Stu is soon discovered to be AWOL and becomes the prime suspect in the robbery. By the time Platt finds the money (right where he had left it in his drunken stupor), it is too late to get Stu off the hook: his prints have been identified as those of Richard Kimble.

On the bus Stu and Louanne engage in a bitter repartee. Louanne subtly flirts with Tod, annoying Enid. The bus's path is blocked on the canyon road by a disabled car, whose driver — Baird — bums a ride on the shuttle. He is surprised to find himself in the company of the man who caught him stealing just a little while earlier. Advising Stu to keep quiet, Baird shows him the gun he has concealed in his knapsack. Tod notices the exchange.

Baird makes an unwelcome move on Louanne, but Stu gallantly intervenes.

Louanne sarcastically questions "Galahad" about his motive, and Stu replies that "Maybe I was saving him from you."

The bus runs into a fallen rock zone, screeching to a halt with a broken axle. As the passengers ponder their fates, a bulletin about Kimble comes over the radio. Kimble makes a move for Baird's knapsack and, during the ensuing struggle, Tod grabs the gun. Tod is gratified to be in charge of things.

Kimble is bound, while the driver walks toward a distant emergency phone. Louanne walks up to the defenseless Kimble and slaps his face but later apologizes for both the slap and her starting of the previous night's argument; she had merely been frustrated by her unrequited love. Louanne, sure of his innocence, calls Kimble the gentlest man she has ever met.

Tod knocks down Kimble when he gets too close to the rest of the group and fires a warning shot when he tries to make a break. Should Kimble again attempt to escape, Tod warns, he will be killed. Kimble is confined inside the bus.

Kimble asks Louanne to get Baird into the bus, where perhaps they can make some sort of deal. Louanne has a better plan: to use her feminine wiles on Tod's ego. She announces that she is going into the forest for firewood, whispering an invitation for Tod to follow her. Tod can't resist the prospect of an illicit rendezvous and turns the prisoner and gun over to Baird. Tod leaves in a futile search for the elusive fox.

Baird has ideas of taking advantage of Enid with the others gone. He gives Kimble the gun, urging him to leave them alone. Kimble disarms Baird of his knife and hands the gun to the bewildered Enid. Kimble then makes his escape on foot.

Episode #43
THE IRON MAIDEN
Original Airdate: December 15, 1964

Story by: Peter R. Brooke & Paul Lucey   **Teleplay by:** Paul Lucey & Harry Kronman
Directed by: Walter Grauman

Cast: Nan Martin as Congresswoman Marian Snell, Stephen McNally as Jack G. Glennon, Richard Anderson as Col. Lawrence, Christine White as Susan Lait, Jason Wingreen as Dave Cooley, Paul Lambert as Soloman, John McLiam as Alec Neal, Dennis Cross as Victor, Ed Deemer as crewman, Richard Schuyler as sheriff.

Kimble, alias Parker, is a laborer and first-aid man for a close-knit construction crew in southern Nevada. The crew, managed by Jack Glennon, is preparing a U.S. Air Force missile-launching silo.

Congresswoman Snell, preparing a report on the project for one of her subcommittees, decides she must thoroughly examine the construction site.

This includes a journey down the 200-foot shaft the crew has excavated. Glennon dissuades the politician, saying there is nothing to see down there and, besides, it is no place for a woman. The headstrong Miss Snell, who has had confrontations with Glennon before, insists on going down. Cooley, a photographer for the Interstate News Service, accompanies the group.

Down below, Miss Snell turns her ankle and is attended to by Parker. Cooley eagerly snaps a photo of the fallen congresswoman and her attendant. When Cooley returns to ground level, he accidentally knocks a gas can down the shaft, and it lands beside a blowtorch. The shaft instantly becomes a blazing inferno, trapping the six people — including Parker (who rescues a burning co-worker), Glennon, and Snell — still down below. Two explosions cause a cave-in that kills one laborer and seals off the others. It will take some 20 hours to clear the shaft and rescue them, unless their oxygen runs out first.

The story of the trapped congresswoman is big news. Snell's secretary, Susan, sells her story to Interstate News, while Cooley sends his exclusive photo through a coast-to-coast wire service. Lt. Gerard recognizes Kimble in the photo and thinks he has his fugitive for sure this time. He takes a plane to Nevada.

With the air supply running out, Glennon recalls a conduit running alongside the shaft, and Parker volunteers to search for it. After crawling through debris Parker finds it, tapping on the conduit with a hammer. Workmen above hear the tapping and uncap the conduit, ensuring an ample supply of oxygen. A headphone is sent down so the stranded quintet can communicate with the outside world.

Gerard arrives, meeting with Air Force Col. Lawrence. Gerard tells him who Parker really is, asking Lawrence to keep it quiet. Lawrence introduces Gerard to Susan as a friend of Parker's.

Congresswoman Snell speaks with Susan through the headphone, mentioning Parker as the hero who saved their lives. Susan remarks that Parker's friend, Mr. Gerard, will be delighted to hear about that. Thus, Kimble learns that Gerard is waiting for him "like a cat at a mousehole." Although his cover is blown, Gerard is assured that there is no other way out of the shaft. And, if Kimble won't come up when it is cleared, Gerard will go down after him.

Kimble's cohabitants hear of his plight, and the three crewmen wish they could help. The crane finally breaks through, clearing the shaft for the rescue. Congresswoman Snell is sent up first. Glennon contacts the crane operator and gives him a coded message. He then hollers from below that Kimble has holed himself up in the control room.

Gerard goes down to investigate. When he enters the control room, the door "accidentally" slams shut behind him, and he can't get out. Kimble comes out of hiding to join the crewmen in the next part of the scheme.

The crane lowers its jaws into the shaft, coming up with a load of men. It touches down and the three crewmen scamper out, diverting the attention of the local authorities. The crane then drops the jaws in a secluded place, where Kimble gets out, seen by only Glennon and the congresswoman. She makes a rare not-by-the-book decision, opting not to interfere with his escape. Kimble takes off in a Glennon truck and gets away long before Gerard's rescue.

Episode #44
DEVIL'S CARNIVAL
Original Airdate: December 22, 1964

Written by: William D. Gordon **Directed by:** James Goldstone

Cast: Warren Oates as Hanes McClure, Dee Pollock as Tad Thompson, Strother Martin as Shirky Saulter, Philip Abbott as Constable Charles Edward Shafter, Madeleine Sherwood as Marybeth Thompson, Woodrow Parfrey as Mayor Cleo Potter, Robert Sorrells as Jud Tormey, George Mitchell as John Petri Allsup, Steve Harris as Bead Halleck, David Kent as Little Jim, Ronnie Haran as Sue-Ann Creyton, Matt McCue as cook.

Hanes McClure returns this February to his hometown, Corona, Georgia. He is persona non grata there, having been part of the notorious Schofield gang whose vices included wine, women, and dope. Hanes has moved on to bigger things, having recently been accused of an armed bank robbery in Macon. His imminent return sends panic waves throughout Corona, and Constable Shafter awaits his arrival at the town line.

On his way in, Hanes picks up a hitchhiker: Richard Kimble. After Shafter flags down Hanes, warning him not to bring any trouble into town, Hanes playfully peels out and heads into town with Shafter in pursuit. Hanes nearly runs over pedestrian Tad Thompson, but Kimble grabs the wheel, swerving the vehicle around Tad. Hanes and Kimble wind up in Shirky's Billiards Hall, where they are confronted by the constable. Hanes pulls a gun on Shafter, but Kimble knocks it away from him after two stray shots. Hanes is arrested, as is Kimble — seemingly guilty only of association, but actually recognized by Shafter. The constable regrets having to lock up someone who may have saved both his and Tad's lives, but Kimble is nevertheless incarcerated with Hanes at the Corona Jail.

Shirky turns his establishment into a carnival, trying to capitalize on the historic events that took place there. He jacks up his prices and sells photographs of the bullet holes (pointed out by luscious Sue-Ann, for an extra charge). Shirky is also deputized and takes his turn guarding the prisoners (armed with his bird rifle) while the constable is away at a council meeting. Shirky takes the opportunity to charge a half-dollar to anyone who wants a glimpse of the outlaws.

Tad determines to somehow help the man who saved his life; he can't believe that someone like Kimble could be guilty of murder. Tad's father had been led astray by the likes of Hanes McClure, dying in prison when Tad was nine. His mother has become overprotective of Tad, constantly henpecking and embarrassing him in front of others.

Hanes tries to figure out a way to relieve Shirky of his rifle, and Kimble points out that "If you had any money, he'd sell it to us." Inspired, Hanes and Kimble devise a plan. While Hanes pretends to sleep, Kimble calls Shirky over to the cell. He tells Shirky that Hanes has $50,000 of Schofield money sewn inside the lining of his jacket. Kimble hands the jacket to Shirky, who drops his guard long enough for Hanes to suddenly "awaken" and grab the gun. Just then, Tad enters the jail with his own escape plans for Kimble. The rifle accidentally discharges, alerting the townspeople, who gather outside. Among the group is Jud, who fires his rifle at real and imagined provocation, wounding Sue-Ann in the process.

Tad releases the two prisoners. Hanes tries to sneak out the back door, where he encounters Shafter. A shoot-out ensues, with both men seriously wounded. Hanes staggers back into the jail and dies while Kimble brings Shafter inside.

Tad and Shafter propose an escape plan for Kimble: to take Tad "hostage" at gunpoint, enabling him to bypass the posse and escape in Shafter's car. Kimble and Tad drive off unchallenged. Tad is proud of himself and inclined to continue his flight out of town and away from his mother. Kimble advises Tad to walk out of town, not to run. Tad drops Kimble off and returns to Corona, soon after to leave of his own free will.

Episode #45
BALLAD FOR A GHOST
Original Airdate: December 29, 1964

Story by: Sidney Ellis & George Eckstein   **Teleplay by:** George Eckstein
Directed by: Walter Grauman

Cast: Janis Paige as Hallie Martin, Mark Richman as Johnny Haywood, Paul Fix as Dan Martin, Anne Helm as Nora Martin, Hugh Sanders as Sheriff Frank Larson, Noam Pitlik as Davey.

Kimble, alias Pete Glenn, has worked the past two months at Haywoods Log Cabin (south of Salisbury, Ohio), operating the spotlight and doing odd jobs for the nightclub's owner, Johnny. Hearing that a big star, balladeer Hallie Martin, will be recording an album there the next night (attracting hundreds of people and swarms of media personnel), Pete decides it is time to move on. Johnny is angry with Pete for planning to leave on such short notice and with such a big night coming up. A poster of Hallie is prepared for display, and Pete is astonished: Hallie Martin is the spitting image of Helen Kimble.

Pete has a brief, troubled sleep, dreaming of his wife's murder. He awakens to the guitar and voice of Hallie, rehearsing. Pete gets up to listen at close range and to meet Hallie.

She recognizes Pete as Kimble (she had taken a lot of ribbing for her resemblance to Helen and had followed the trial closely) but doesn't say anything. Hallie asks Pete to remain one more night and operate the spotlight for her, and Pete, unable to resist, agrees. On his way back to his room, Pete discovers Hallie's hypodermic kit. She has been drinking and taking drugs (probably morphine) to combat the pain of an inoperable brain tumor, and she is becoming addicted to them. She wants to keep her fatal illness a secret from her loved ones.

The three people closest to Hallie are her father, Dan, who knows about her condition and worries about how she abuses herself; her younger sister, Nora, who resents Hallie for becoming Dad's pet after their mother's death; and Hallie's ex-husband, Johnny. Hallie had publicly dumped Johnny — who still loves Hallie and still hurts over the break-up — to go out and make it big.

Hallie and Pete rehearse their cues for tonight's performance and begin hitting it off. Pete confronts her about her illness and drug abuse, and Hallie drops the other shoe about his identity. Pete tells her he is innocent, confirming her supposition. "While you're keeping my secret," Hallie says, "I'll be busy keeping yours."

Johnny and Dan look for Hallie, who is scheduled to do a radio interview, and find her in Pete's room. Johnny belts Pete, and Hallie slaps Johnny. After another confrontation with Johnny, Hallie runs off in tears, and Pete follows after her. They drive off together in her car, not to return until a half-hour after her performance is scheduled to start.

While looking for Hallie and Pete, Johnny finds the hypodermic kit in Pete's room. Thinking Pete is a drug addict, Johnny calls Sheriff Larson. Larson arrives at the club, and Johnny asks him to delay arresting Pete until after the performance.

Hallie gives a great performance, during which Dan tells Johnny that the hypodermic kit is Hallie's. Swearing Johnny to secrecy, Dan tells him about Hallie's affliction. Dan and Johnny devise a way to get Pete off the hook.

The sheriff arrests Pete, but Johnny intervenes. Dan tells Larson that the hypodermic kit is his, insulin to treat his diabetes. Johnny then apologizes to Pete.

Hallie prepares to leave, accompanied by Pete. Nora fires off a parting shot at Hallie, blasting her with words she surely will regret later. Johnny says goodbye, not revealing his knowledge, and Hallie drives off.

Hallie lets Pete off at a bus station, and they kiss goodbye. Hallie asks whether the kiss was meant for her (rather than Helen's ghost), and Pete replies "I think so."

Act II: The 1964-65 Season 81

Episode #46
BRASS RING
Original Airdate: January 5, 1965

Written by: Leonard Kantor   **Directed by:** Abner Biberman

Cast: Angie Dickinson as Norma Sessions, Robert Duvall as Leslie Sessions, John Ericson as Lars Morgan, Phillip Pine as Lt. Gavin, Karl Swenson as Mr. Morgan, Buck Young as police sergeant, James Tartan as doctor, Sandra Gregg as girl.

Kimble, alias Ben Horton, looks for work in Santa Monica, California. At the amusement pier he inquires to a man, Lars, who refers him to Norma Sessions at the Beachcomber Gift Shop. Ben approaches the shop as the police accost a purse snatcher nearby. Ben ducks inside, and Norma makes mental note of the behavior. Ben and Norma, age 26, meet and are instantly attracted to each other.

Norma does have a job offer, contingent on the approval of her brother, Leslie. Leslie is an invalid, the result of an auto accident that netted him $100,000 in insurance money. The job would involve acting as a nurse to him for the princely wage of $75 per week. The catch is that Leslie is a rude, bitter man whose nurses rarely last more than a day or so. After interrogating him, Leslie tells Ben that "You got the job, but I'll be watching you!"

Norma has a grand dream, involving the arrival of her knight on a white horse to carry her off and free her of the imprisonment of caring for her brother. The repressed part of the dream is that Leslie will have to be eliminated so that Norma and her knight can live happily ever after with the insurance money. At the moment Lars is the prospective knight, and Ben figures to become an unwitting central figure in their scheme.

Ben exhibits unusual tolerance in breaking through Leslie's bitter facade and proposes exercises designed to help Leslie regain his mobility. Norma — who "hates me," according to Leslie — dissuades the exercise plan, saying it will create undue pain and false hope for Leslie. Norma's disapproval makes Leslie determined to go along with the routine, and he soon is making noticeable progress. During one session Leslie cryptically warns Ben, "Don't let her use you."

Norma tells Lars about the therapy, whose success threatens to ruin their plot. Norma says she will take care of matters in her own way. She goes on a romantic beach-date with Ben, and they wind up making out. Norma later confides in Ben about her dream, hinting that Ben might qualify as the knight. Ben advises her not to confuse dreams with reality. Norma reports to Lars that her plan didn't work, so Lars decides it is time to change the rules.

During an argument with Ben, Leslie spontaneously sits up. It is the big breakthrough that Ben had promised was possible. Pretty soon, Ben has Leslie outside for the first time since his accident, and it seems only a matter of time before he will be walking again. Leslie is extremely grateful, offering Ben all the money he wants, but Ben says seeing Leslie walk will be ample reward for him.

Norma goes out with Ben once more, giving him another chance to take her bait. Her increasingly real-sounding dream cools off Ben's romantic interests, and he goes home. Arriving there, Ben finds Leslie dead and Lars fleeing the building. Lars returns with his father and Norma, accusing Ben of the murder. Lars denies having been in the building, claiming to have been with Norma all evening. Much to Ben's astonishment, Norma vouches for Lars. As Lars goes for the police, Ben gives Norma a long stare before taking off on foot.

Ben can't shake the cops and winds up taking refuge in Norma's room. Ben says that Norma at least owes him the opportunity to hide, after using him as she did. Norma tells Ben that she loves him and that there is still a chance for them to run off together. Ben says he can't, as he is wanted for a murder he didn't commit. Norma realizes she can't have Ben either way, so when the police arrive at her door she turns him in.

As the cops lead Ben downstairs, Norma finally has a change of heart. She admits to the police that Ben is innocent and that she and Lars concocted the murder scheme. As Norma is taken away, she remarks to Ben that she must have meant what she said to him.

Episode #47
THE END IS BUT THE BEGINNING
Original Airdate: January 12, 1965

Story by: George Fass   **Teleplay by:** George Fass & Arthur Weiss
Directed by: Walter Grauman

Cast: Barbara Barrie as Aimee Renick, Andrew Duggan as John Harlan, Frank Maxwell as Lt. Lou Garlock, Robert Yuro as Sam Barlow, Paul Birch as Capt. Carpenter.

Kimble, alias Steve Younger, has spent the past six weeks as a truck driver for the Harlan Fuel Oil Company in Hurley, Pennsylvania. His coworkers are boss John Harlan and bookkeeper Aimee Renick. Harlan is secretly in love with Aimee, some 15 years his junior, but Aimee is attracted to Steve. She offers Steve two tickets to a play and is pleased when Steve invites her to be his companion for the play and dinner as well.

Steve takes the truck on a delivery to Coverton, picking up a hitchhiker (Sam) on the way. Sam tells Steve he has no family and, flashing his dog tags, calls the Army the only home he ever had. At Steiner's Pass they encounter two vehicles blocking the road, and Steve is unable to stop in time. He veers the truck off the road, sending it careening down a mountainside. Steve jumps out near the top, but Sam freezes and goes down with the truck. It explodes at the bottom of the hill, killing Sam and burning his body beyond recognition. While Steve lies in the bushes, unconscious and badly bruised, the body in the truck is presumed to be his.

Lt. Garlock calls Harlan, informing him of the death of his driver. Harlan and Aimee drive to the scene, where they discuss the situation with Garlock. Kimble, having regained consciousness, overhears and gets an idea: if authorities learn that Steve Younger was Richard Kimble, they may stop chasing him.

Kimble hobbles to his motel room and starts a bogus letter to his father, Dr. John Kimble. He is interrupted by Aimee, sent there by Lt. Garlock to gather the deceased's personal effects. Kimble tells her his story, and she feels right about helping him with his plan. She hides Kimble at her place and brings the completed letter (among other items) to Garlock. Convinced that Younger was Kimble, Garlock teletypes the information to Stafford.

Capt. Carpenter brings the report to a very shaken Lt. Gerard. "I hope this ends it," says Carpenter, permitting Gerard a few days in Pennsylvania to wrap up the case.

Gerard flies in, meeting Aimee at Garlock's station. She positively identifies Younger as Kimble, and latent fingerprints gotten from the truck cab (as soon as the fire patrol deems the area safe) will clinch it. Aimee makes a reference to the one-armed man, raising Gerard's suspicion.

Aimee tells the much-improved Kimble about her meeting with Gerard who, according to Kimble, "has a way of sensing things — he's brilliant." Kimble realizes he must somehow retrieve Sam's dog tags from the accident scene or the plan will be ruined.

Gerard pays a visit to Aimee, asking how she knew about the one-armed man story, since it wasn't reported in the local papers. Aimee explains that she subscribes to the newspaper from her hometown of St. Louis and that that one *did* cover the Kimble case thoroughly. Aimee remarks, "You seem to be trying to prove that he's alive," and Gerard replies, "It's a hard habit to break."

Kimble and Aimee visit the crash scene at night, searching for the dog tags. Kimble finds them and announces, "I really think that Gerard's gonna buy our story." They are startled by Harlan's voice: "I think he's going to like my story better, Dr. Kimble!" Harlan holds Kimble at gunpoint and instructs Aimee to leave, but she refuses.

Kimble knocks down Harlan and makes a break to escape. Harlan fires his gun at him, but hits Aimee instead, piercing her subclavian artery. Kimble returns, applying pressure on the artery, and preventing Aimee from bleeding to death. Harlan calls for an ambulance, saying a doctor is at the scene. Lts. Gerard and Garlock learn of the call and rush to the site.

Touched by Kimble's lifesaving effort, Harlan offers him a chance to escape. Kimble shows Harlan how to apply the pressure, and Harlan allows Kimble to take his car to safety. The ambulance arrives, followed shortly after by the lieutenants.

Although Harlan tries to cover for Kimble, Gerard sees that the details don't add up. When he finds Sam's knapsack in Aimee's car, Gerard realizes that Kimble is indeed still alive.

Episode #48
NICEST FELLA YOU'D EVER WANT TO MEET
Original Airdate: January 19, 1965

Written by: Jack Turley **Directed by:** Sutton Roley

Cast: Pat Hingle as Marshal Joe Bob Simms, Dabney Coleman as Floyd Pierce, Mary Murphy as Thelma Hollister, Tom Skerritt as Neely Hollister, Dabbs Greer as Mayor Duncan, Curt Conway as Mr. Hollister, Burt Mustin as Charley, Read Morgan as highway patrolman, Chet Stratton as driver, Kevin Brodie as Johnny.

Popular Joe Bob Simms is marshal in the town of Bixton, Arizona. Simms, who claims Apache ancestry, has donated land at Lookout Point to serve as the site of "Apache Park," sort of a memorial to himself, and enlists the free labor of prisoners to work on the park.

Kimble, alias Richard Clark, is dropped off in Bixton and puts out his thumb for another ride. Simms figures the transient might provide good cheap help and arrests him for hitchhiking. Clark is incarcerated, joining Neely Hollister (arrested for stealing $4) and a drunk.

Simms feels he has the inside track on a job soon opening in the state attorney general's office. This would leave the Bixton marshal's office open, and Simms has hinted to his deputy, Floyd, that the job is as good as his. Floyd is happy, knowing that the extra pay may open the door for him to settle down comfortably with his long-time girlfriend, Thelma (Neely's sister).

Simms puts the three prisoners to work at the park. Clark and the drunk labor under Floyd's supervision, while Simms keeps Neely busy down below. There is bad blood between Simms and Neely, and the marshal has decided to teach Neely a lesson about respect for authority. Neely is instructed to remove rocks from the dirt road, while Simms follows closely behind in his car, taunting and bumping the prisoner. Neely finally fires a rock at Simms's windshield, shattering it. Seething, Simms deliberately runs down Neely, sending him plunging to his death. Simms will report it as an accident, not realizing that Clark witnessed the murder from above.

Mayor Duncan tells Simms that there will be a hearing Tuesday on the "accident" but that Simms can count on the mayor as a character witness.

Duncan mentions that his son, Billy, is having employment problems, and Simms promises to recommend Billy for the marshal's job. Clark, whose sentence has been suspended and who awaits his obligatory ride out of town, overhears the conversation.

Simms escorts Clark to the city limits, advising him not to lose his direction. Clark can't leave without setting the record straight on Neely's death, and he calls the Hollisters to arrange a visit. Clark tells Thelma what he witnessed, and she goes into another room to tell her father. She returns to find Clark gone. Wanting to get him back somehow, so that he can testify at the hearing, Mr. Hollister reports that Clark robbed him of $100.

Simms, suspicious about the report, finds Clark and returns him to jail. The Hollisters come to the station, asking to speak privately with Clark. As Simms listens in on a hidden intercom, Clark tells his story and explains that, being a wanted man, he can't become involved in a public hearing. Simms later does some checking and identifies Clark as Kimble. He figures Kimble's apprehension will clinch Simms's promotion.

Floyd supervises Clark at work in the park. Clark tells a dubious Floyd about Neely's murder. The marshal, informing Floyd about Kimble, arrives to relieve his deputy. Floyd, convinced that Kimble was lying, leaves him and Simms alone at the park.

Thelma goes to the station to withdraw the Hollisters' complaint against Kimble. She tells Floyd she believes Kimble was telling the truth about Neely's death. Worried about what might happen at Apache Park if Kimble *is* telling the truth, Floyd and Thelma head out there.

Simms baits Kimble in much the same way as he did Neely. Kimble momentarily gets behind Simms and knocks the marshal out. Kimble discards Simms's pistol and flees down the hill. Simms regains his senses and pulls his deer rifle out of his car. He tracks Kimble down and misses three shots, just as Floyd and Thelma arrive below.

Simms tells Floyd to leave, but Floyd insists on staying. Kimble tells Floyd about the deal Simms made with the mayor, and Simms reopens fire. Floyd shoots down Simms but is wounded in the crossfire.

Kimble checks on Floyd and decides that he will be all right. Kimble leaves to call an ambulance, then stows away on the back of a departing truck.

Episode #49
FUN AND GAMES AND PARTY FAVORS
Original Airdate: January 26, 1965

Written by: Arthur Weiss   **Directed by:** Abner Biberman

Cast: Katherine Crawford as Joanne "Joansey" Glenn, Mark Goddard as Daniel Harvey Holt, Anthony Call as Phil Andrews, Joan Tompkins as Madge Glenn,

Tom Palmer as Charles Glenn, Peter E. Deuel as Buzzy, Thomas Hasson as Joe, James Davidson as Dave, Gerald Hamer as Warren, Joe Perry as police sergeant.

Kimble, alias Douglas Beckett, works as a chauffeur and gateman for a southern California family, the Glenns. Attractive Joanne is the only daughter of Madge and Charles Glenn, a wealthy couple with the proper social connections. Joanne is in love with Danny, who cleans the family's pool and thus is of inferior social status. Knowing Mrs. Glenn would not approve of such a relationship, the two have had a covert romance for nearly three years. Mrs. Glenn tries to steer her daughter toward Phil Andrews, who has the proper family background. Joanne plans to escape her manipulative mother by running off with Danny.

Joanne hosts a party at the house while her parents go out on an engagement with Senator Barnes. Mother gives Douglas a typed "guest list" (which, much to her consternation, does not include Phil) and leaves him in charge. Joanne plots to elope with the reluctant Danny during the party, a plan Douglas figures out after seeing Joanne pack a suitcase into her car trunk.

Phil tries to crash the party but leaves at Douglas's request. Phil dejectedly returns home and absent-mindedly leafs through his collection of FBI "wanted" posters. When he notices one that matches the Glenns' gateman, he decides to return to the party, armed with the poster as his "invitation" and accompanied by several alcohol-primed friends.

Douglas catches Danny and Joanne preparing to leave. Danny, a premed student who has come to like and respect Douglas, is talked out of going. Danny realizes they would be getting married for the wrong reason and that Joanne is planning his life much the way her mother manipulates her father. Douglas advises Danny to stand up to the Glenns, earning their respect, before planning marriage. Her plan foiled, Joanne storms inside just as Phil returns with his companions. Douglas prepares to evict them, but Joanne insists they stay. After flirting with Phil and some of his friends, Joanne goes upstairs to change her clothes.

The tanked-up gate-crashers create havoc, playing rowdy games that cause property damage and eventually starting a brawl. Douglas, having lost control, tries unsuccessfully to reach the Glenns, and Danny calls the police. Phil then shares his discovery about Kimble with Danny, offering to split the credit for the fugitive's capture. Danny, needing time to ponder the situation, takes the poster and tells Phil to keep quiet. Meanwhile, three of Phil's friends invade Joanne's room with lewd intentions. Her screams bring Danny and Douglas to the rescue.

The police arrive just ahead of the returning Glenns. Danny hands the "wanted" poster to Douglas, giving him the opportunity to escape before Phil blows the whistle on him. Mrs. Glenn plans not to press charges against the vandals, children of some of her influential friends, but her husband overrules her in a rare act of taking charge. Phil, among the arrested, pleads with the police to find Kimble, but Danny convinces the sergeant that Phil's ramblings are alcohol-induced.

Afterward, Danny at last stands up to the Glenns, telling of his and Joanne's marriage plans. Mrs. Glenn is taken aback, but Mr. Glenn seems to approve, admiring Danny for courage he wishes he himself had. Danny vows to try earning the Glenns' blessing.

Episode #50
SCAPEGOAT
Original Airdate: February 2, 1965

Story by: Larry Cohen   **Teleplay by:** William D. Gordon
Directed by: Alexander Singer

Cast: Dianne Foster as Janice Cummings, John Anderson as Justin Briggs, Harry Townes as Bertram Ballinger, Don Quine as Vin Briggs, David Macklin as Roy Briggs, Whit Bissell as Gibson, Tom Reese as Norman, Bill Zuckert as Scales, Doreen McLean as landlady, Russ Bender as timekeeper, R. L. Armstrong as Curry, Ted Gehring and Bill Erwin as bar patrons.

As Kimble (alias Bill Hayes) arrives at work, he is recognized by a man who remembers him as Eddie Frye from Black River (Black River County), South Dakota. The man tells him that Eddie had been presumed dead and that Justin Briggs had been convicted and imprisoned for his murder.

Deciding he must clear up the situation, Eddie leaves his job and takes a bus to Black River. From flashbacks, we learn that Eddie had befriended Janice Cummings, sending Briggs (who had employed Eddie as a handyman) into a jealous rage. Briggs, a widower, had earmarked Janice to be his next wife. With Janice looking on, the drunken Briggs had attacked Eddie with a knife. Eddie had cut his hand trying to hold back the weapon, and Janice had fled when it appeared that Briggs was about to kill Eddie. Eddie had somehow escaped and, knowing it would become a police matter, had not returned. Upon Janice's claim of witnessing a murder, police had arrested Briggs, who was too incoherent to offer a defense. Motive and bloodstains had combined with the testimony of Janice and other townspeople to convict Briggs, with authorities speculating that he dumped the body into one of the nearby bogs. Eddie, of course, had not known about Briggs's arrest or trial until this day.

Black River townspeople, particularly Janice, are shocked at Eddie's return. Eddie learns that Briggs was killed by a posse after escaping from jail. After signing a statement clearing Briggs of murder, Eddie prepares to leave. Janice begs him to stay long enough to talk to Briggs's sons, Roy and Vin.

Vin, a chip off the old block, figures Janice's lie caused his father's death and vows to get even. He gets drunk and takes after Janice with a gun. Eddie talks with the more rational brother, telling him that Janice had really believed she saw his father kill Eddie. Roy is not convinced, wondering why Eddie hadn't spoken up sooner, but he doesn't want Vin to make things worse with a real murder.

Janice is shunned by the townspeople, who feel Vin is justified to avenge his father's death (and feel guilty themselves for having contributed to it). Becoming a scapegoat, Janice loses her job and her apartment. Ballinger, the Briggs's lawyer, gives Eddie the keys to his car and instructs him to leave town with Janice before any bloodshed occurs. Eddie tries to comply, but Vin prevents the departure, opening fire and wounding Eddie in his left leg. Eddie and Janice take refuge in the courthouse.

Ballinger arranges to meet with Vin in an effort to calm him down, but Vin instead goes to the courthouse. The constable had left in resignation, leaving behind his gunbelt, and only Eddie, Janice, and Roy are present when Vin arrives. Vin orders Janice onto the witness stand, where she is forced to repeat her testimony about believing she saw Justin kill Eddie. Roy realizes Janice is telling the truth, but Vin cannot be convinced. When Eddie makes a move for the constable's gun, Vin fires at Eddie and Roy takes the gun. Eddie appeals to Roy, explaining that he had to desert the Briggs family because he, himself, is a wrongly convicted murderer. Vin still insists on vengeance, turning his wrath on Eddie. Roy shoots Vin in the arm to stop him from shooting Eddie.

Hearing the shots, Ballinger breaks into the courthouse. Trying to spare the Briggs children unnecessary legal trouble, Eddie claims to have shot Vin in self-defense.

Realizing that Eddie is a friend to the Briggs family after all, and deducing that Eddie is afraid of the law, Ballinger helps him to leave town without being noticed or hassled further. Meanwhile, townspeople show atonement for the way they had treated Janice.

Episode #51
CORNER OF HELL
Original Airdate: February 9, 1965

Story by: Jo Heims & Zahrini Machadah
Teleplay by: Francis Irby Gwaltney & Jo Heims   **Directed by:** Robert Butler

Cast: R. G. Armstrong as Tully Gage, Bruce Dern as Cody, Sharon Farrell as Elvie Gage, Dabbs Greer as Sheriff Claypool, Sandy Kenyon as Kyle, Edward Faulkner as Roy, James Griffith as dispatcher, Nick Nicholson as truck driver, Paul Birch as Capt. Carpenter.

Lt. Gerard traces Kimble to his present employer, the Inter-South Trucking Co. in Bleeker, Louisiana. He is told Kimble, alias Paul Hunter, is due back soon from a road trip. With the cooperation of the local sheriff, Gerard sets up a roadblock. Kimble rams through it and jumps out of the truck soon after, disappearing into the woods along a side road. The sheriff refuses to risk his life by venturing after him in that "moonshine country," so Gerard decides to go by himself.

Kimble is accosted by one of the bootlegging woodsmen, Cody, and brought to their camp. Cody roughs up Kimble, beating him with a rifle. The two grapple, with Cody suffering a cut artery in his arm, and Kimble managing to get the gun from him. Instead of shooting Cody, for which he has motive and opportunity, Kimble stops Cody's bleeding and patches up his arm. This earns Kimble the group's respect and the nickname "Doc." They permit him to leave.

Gerard arrives at the camp. The moonshiners rough him up, too, taking away his gun while Elvie takes his car out on a joy ride. She stops the car and discovers Gerard's wallet, containing $340 in cash. Cody arrives and roughly wrestles the wallet away from Elvie, throwing her to the ground and knocking her unconscious.

Gerard, having managed to escape from the others, returns to his car just as Cody runs off. The others get there to find Gerard examining Elvie's beaten body and presume him guilty of the assault.

The woodsmen rush Elvie back to camp and send others out to retrieve Doc, hoping he can fix up Elvie just as he did Cody. Kimble and Gerard wind up face to face in an ironic situation: Gerard is a prisoner, Kimble a respected citizen, in this small corner of the world. Further irony is provided by the fact Gerard is accused of assaulting a woman and is being judged guilty because he can't prove his innocence or identify the man he saw leaving the crime scene. Gerard asks Kimble to vouch for him but gets no response. Kimble says Elvie has a severe concussion, and she is brought to her room in an unconscious state.

Cody sneaks into Elvie's room and slips Gerard's wallet under her pillow (after deducting a $40 commission for himself). Gerard escapes again but is recaptured and securely bound, to stand trial in the woodsmen's kangaroo court. Kimble urges them to give Gerard the benefit of the real judicial system, but they reject the idea. Elvie regains consciousness and, protecting her clansman, fingers Gerard for the assault. The lieutenant is sentenced to be hanged.

Elvie finds the wallet and accepts it as Cody's apology. When Kimble helps Elvie discover she has been shortchanged, she becomes enraged. She storms out to the hanging ceremony and demands Cody return the $40. The others now realize Gerard is innocent and set him free, advising him never to return.

Gerard, not a happy camper, leaves without his fugitive. Kimble leaves some time later unchallenged.

Episode #52
MOON CHILD
Original Airdate: February 16, 1965

Written by: Dan Ullman   **Directed by:** Alexander Singer

Cast: Murray Hamilton as Mel Starling, June Harding as Joanne Mercer, David Sheiner as Sheriff Mack, Virginia Christine as Alma Mercer, Dean Stanton as Randy, Mort Mills as George Mangus, Val Avery as Burns, Burt Douglas as Johnny North, Helen Kleeb as Miss Cloud, Charles Thompson as Mr. Duffield, Jim Goodwin as Benny.

Kimble, alias Bill Martin, enters a new town on Friday the 24th and stops at Mangus's Cafe. A patron leaves the establishment, replaced minutes later by a group of male citizens. The cafe is closed, the sheriff is summoned, and Martin is interrogated by the vigilantes. It seems that a serial killer has strangled two town women in recent weeks, making any stranger in town a suspect. Sheriff Mack arrives to question Martin more formally, and Martin flees out the back of the cafe. The sheriff confiscates Martin's eating utensils to check the fingerprints.

Martin sees that the town is roadblocked and takes refuge in a vacant factory building. Mrs. Mercer, searching for her daughter, Joanne, sees Martin and notifies the police. Meanwhile, the fingerprint report comes in: the stranger is wanted for strangling his wife. Townspeople are convinced Kimble is their man, and the sheriff deputizes the vigilantes.

In the building Kimble encounters Joanne, a mildly retarded 19-year-old. She is hiding on a weakly supported loft that appears ready to collapse. Kimble helps her down, earning her trust. The sheriff and his gang arrive outside the building, and someone fires a shot into it. The sheriff chastises the overeager deputy and restores order. Leaving behind her doll, Joanne leads Kimble through a maze. Explaining that the neighborhood basements are all connected, and swearing Kimble to secrecy, Joanne takes him through the "secret tunnel" which leads to her own basement. Kimble stays there as Joanne goes upstairs, where her mother is holding an adult art class. Mrs. Mercer asks Joanne where she has been, and Joanne claims she was in the basement the whole time.

Joanne smuggles some food downstairs but drops it on the floor when Kimble startles her. She gets upset, but Kimble comforts her. Joanne goes back upstairs, promising to return.

Having discovered Joanne's doll, the sheriff arrives at the Mercer house with one of his temporary deputies, Mel Starling. Joanne claims to have left the doll in the building a long time ago, but her mother recalls seeing her with it earlier that day. Noting the discrepancy, and Joanne's other claim of having been in the basement, Mack and Starling decide to check downstairs.

The men find no sign of Kimble, who has escaped through Joanne's secret tunnel. Suspecting that Joanne was harboring him there, Starling concocts an idea to make her talk. He writes a note saying "Goodbye Silly Liar," showing it to Joanne and convincing her that her "friend" wrote it. Upset and angry, Joanne tells the men Kimble is in the vacant building.

Joanne, unable to believe Kimble would do anything to hurt her, has a change of heart. She heads for the building to spare him from the police. The real strangler, flexing a length of clothesline, follows her. Kimble sees the two approaching and tries to overpower the strangler, succeeding only in detaining him while Joanne takes refuge inside. Kimble joins her while the strangler searches around. The men enter the building and find the strangler, shooting him in self-defense. With Joanne now safe, Kimble kisses her on the forehead and steals away.

The men realize that Kimble saved Joanne's life and that they almost killed the wrong man. The sheriff asks them to return to resume the search the next morning (by which time Kimble will be long gone).

Episode #53
THE SURVIVORS
Original Airdate: March 2, 1965

Written by: George Eckstein **Directed by:** Don Medford

Cast: Louise Sorel as Terry Waverley, Ruth White as Edith Waverley, Lloyd Gough as Ed Waverley, Burt Metcalfe as Philip Corbin, Richard Devon as police sergeant, Herb Ellis as Frank, John Newton as Larry. (Note: Diane Brewster also "appears" as the taped voice of Helen Kimble.)

Kimble is just 60 miles from Fairgreen, Indiana (population 10,972), home of the Waverley family: Helen Kimble's parents and younger sister, Terry. He spots a newspaper article about the family's financial crisis and wants to help somehow. He recalls that Helen had an out-of-town bank account containing over $5,000, still unclaimed, and he believes that information about the account can be found among Helen's belongings at the Waverley house. Kimble takes a bus to Fairgreen and phones Terry. He is recognized and chased by a policeman and makes his way to the Waverley home as cops comb the town.

Kimble is not exactly a welcome visitor. Though Terry is certain Kimble is innocent of Helen's murder, Mrs. Waverley (who is not home at the moment) is just as sure of his guilt. Ed Waverley is undecided but leans toward his wife's feelings. Terry is glad to see Kimble, but Ed wants him out of there before the missus returns home. Terry convinces her father to let Kimble hide upstairs, where Mother never goes; after all, he did come to help them, and he can't leave with the police all over town.

Mrs. Waverley returns, very upset by the news that Kimble was spotted in the area. She is accompanied by Phil, an assistant in the district attorney's office who is also Terry's fiancé (although Terry maintains that no commitment has been made). Mrs. Waverley retires to Helen's old room.

Since Helen's death, Mrs. Waverley has suffered from heart trouble and emotional problems, draining the family's savings. Helen's room has remained undisturbed since she moved away some nine years ago, and Mrs. Waverley has turned it into a sort of mausoleum. She closets herself in there, reading old letters from Helen and listening to a recording of her voice over and over.

Kimble and Terry spend hours poring over Helen's things, and Terry acts quite affectionately toward Richard. Ed takes him aside, telling him that Terry has had a crush on him — heightened by his "glamorous" role as a fugitive — since she was 14. This infatuation has prevented her from fully committing herself to Phil or carrying on with her life.

Kimble at last discovers Helen's records of the bank account (written inside a book) and turns the information over to the Waverleys. He insists they keep his share as well as Helen's, and the windfall seems sure to save the family business. Terry helps Ed realize that Kimble has not only immensely helped the family but risked his life in doing so.

Terry enters Helen's room, finding Mother rereading the letters. Terry decries the utter lack of attention and love she gets from her mother in deference to Helen. Terry leaves the room in a rage and spends the next hour crying in her own room. Mrs. Waverley realizes she has indeed been unfair to Terry.

Kimble goes to leave, but the police (on Phil's hunch) are waiting outside to close in on him. Terry runs after Kimble to stop him, then detains the cops as Kimble slips away. With the area boxed in, Kimble can get no farther than the roof of a neighbor's house. Terry and Ed watch from the front lawn as the search intensifies. Kimble is able to return to the Waverley house, entering through the back door and finding himself face-to-face with Mrs. Waverley.

Terry comes inside, pleading with her mother not to turn Kimble in. "I'm asking you for something for the first time," she begs. "I'm asking you for his life." Knowing this might be the first step in re-establishing a relationship with her living daughter, Mrs. Waverley reluctantly agrees.

Upstairs, Terry announces that she plans to leave with Richard. She believes she can earn his love and make him very happy. With calculated cruelty, Kimble says, "Don't flatter yourself." Terry is crushed, and Ed privately thanks Kimble for bursting her bubble.

The police return to the house. Explaining how Kimble had come to be there, of all places, Ed tells them that he broke in. Mrs. Waverley covers for Kimble but allows them to search inside. Kimble hides behind an open linen closet door and is somehow missed by the cops, who assume he escaped their dragnet.

Act II: The 1964-65 Season 93

Phil comes over, and Terry rushes into his arms. The two go out to be alone together for a while. Mrs. Waverley invites them to return for dinner; it is something she wants to do for them. Terry accepts.

After the pressure is off, Ed drives Kimble to an out-of-town bus-stop. Kimble thanks Ed, and he replies, "It's all in the family." The two shake hands and Kimble is on his way to South Bend.

Episode #54
EVERYBODY GETS HIT IN THE MOUTH SOMETIME
Original Airdate: March 9, 1965

Written by: Jack Turley   Directed by: Alexander Singer

Cast: Jack Klugman as Gus Hendrick, Geraldine Brooks as Lucia Mayfield, Michael Constantine as Ernie Svoboda, G. B. Atwater as Cleve Logan, Jimmy Stiles as Jimmy Mayfield, Tracy Statford as Lucy Mayfield, Kathleen O'Malley as receptionist, John Mayo as Mr. Williams, K. L. Smith as Pete, Marlowe Jensen as Sgt. Fountain, James Devine as gas station attendant.

A driver returns late on March 2, 1965, to the Bullet Trucking Company headquarters in southern Colorado. He plans to begin his next assignment immediately, but the dispatcher of a couple of weeks — Kimble, alias Bill Douglas — learns that the driver has reached his daily road-time limit. Adhering to safety regulations, Bill orders the driver to quit for the day.

Lucia stops by to pick up some money and the car keys Gus, the foreman, had left for her with Bill. She tells Bill about the death two years ago of her husband, Kenny, in a truck accident with Gus. In actuality Gus — six hours over his daily limit — had been driving, had fallen asleep at the wheel, and had survived the wreck while Kenny died. Guilt has made Gus promise to "always be there" for Lucia, and Lucia has preyed on that guilt to extort hundreds of dollars from Gus for such things as dance lessons and bicycles for her obnoxious kids, Jimmy and Lucy.

Hot-tempered Gus is irate when Bill ("Hot-Shot") tells him he dismissed the driver. Gus can't make money with the truck parked, so he orders Bill — not a certified driver — to take the load to Colorado Springs. Gus, accompanying Bill, notices they are being followed by Logan, the Trans-Way Insurance Company's road-man. Gus and Bill change places so as not to be caught violating a rule; Gus's company already has a long history of infractions. Gus pulls over and Logan inspects the rig and the drivers' log. Logan interrogates Bill, who gives a phony employment reference which Logan will later expose.

Ernie meets with Gus and offers a money-making scheme. Ernie would "steal" one of Gus's trucks and sell its contents, paying Gus a bonus for the arrangement (while insurance covers Gus's loss). Gus ostensibly rejects the proposal but doesn't forget it.

Lucia returns Gus's car to Bill's apartment. He gives her a lift home and she invites him in. Lamenting her loneliness, she throws a lip-lock on Bill. They are interrupted and taunted by her kids, and Bill returns home.

Trans-Way phones Gus, threatening to cancel his insurance for nonpayment of the $955 premium. Lucia barges in with Jimmy, who has hit his mouth and, according to Lucia, needs at least $300 worth of orthodontic work. Gus tries to turn her down, saying, "Everybody gets hit in the mouth sometimes," but Lucia lays on the guilt trip. Gus finally gives her $300 from the cash register, promising her additional funds soon to, basically, buy her out. Lucia is pleased.

Gus summons Ernie to meet him at a bar. Gus tells him he has a load of electronic parts, insured for $25,000, going to Albuquerque. Gus will leave the truck for Ernie to pick up at the Half Way House Cafe. Ernie gives him $1,000 down-payment, with another $2,000 due after the mission is accomplished.

Lucia boasts to Bill about a $2,000 windfall coming her way, suggesting that she might let him help her spend it. Bill rebuffs her and finds Gus, wondering how he is rich enough to give handouts yet too poor to pay the insurance premium. Gus flashes his bankroll, telling Bill to pay the premium with it. After making a remark which lands him on the floor, Bill agrees to pay the premium — as his final assignment. He smells trouble and wants no part of it.

At the insurance office, Logan sees Bill and calls him into his office, telling him about Gus's history and about discovering Bill's bogus reference. Trans-Way is on to Gus's scheme and planning to sting him. Logan warns Bill that, if he tries to alert Gus, Logan will instigate a thorough police check on Bill.

Logan and police officers camp out at the Half Way House. Ernie calls Bill from there to call off the deal, but Gus, tired and boozed up, has already left. Bill tears out after Gus in another truck, finally catching up with him on a mountain road near the cafe. Before Bill is able to convey the warning, Gus nods off and his truck plunges down the mountain. Bill stops, runs down, and pulls Gus out of the burning rig. Gus tells him the true story about Kenny's death and gives his only possessions — his car keys and $43 — to deliver to Lucia. Gus dies, and Bill gets out of sight of the approaching police.

Bill goes to Lucia's house, telling her Gus is dead and delivering his bequeathment. "That's all?" she complains. Bill leaves after a run-in with Jimmy, taking time to whack the brat on his way out.

Episode #55
MAY GOD HAVE MERCY
Original Airdate: March 16, 1965

Written by: Don Brinkley   **Directed by:** Don Medford

Cast: Telly Savalas as Victor Leonetti, Carol Rossen as Anne Leonetti, Norman Fell as Lt. Cermak, Jud Taylor as Toby Weems, Maggie Pierce as Nurse Stockwell,

Abigail Shelton as Gloria, Noah Keen as Dr. Becker, Mary Jackson as Nurse Oberhansly, Don Eitner as intern.

In April 1965 Kimble, alias Harry Reynolds, works as an orderly in a Selby, Michigan hospital. A nurse asks him to fetch the lab report on Victor Leonetti. Harry recognizes the name: Leonetti was the father of a former patient of Dr. Kimble's. The young patient, Jeannie, had died of heart disease four years earlier. The lab report confirms Leonetti's identity and also shows him to be fatally ill.

Victor's doctor gives him the prognosis: he has ten to twelve months to live. Victor, just 42 and in seemingly excellent health, is flabbergasted. He decides to withhold the information from his wife.

Anne Leonetti comes to pick up her husband and sees Kimble. She tells Victor, who becomes angry. He has always blamed Kimble for Jeannie's death because the doctor was "on vacation" when she had her fatal attack. In reality Kimble had been in New York—at his own expense and on his own time—visiting a leading cardiac specialist and pleading with him to accompany Kimble to Stafford. Kimble had already recommended various open-heart surgeons, all of whom Victor had rejected. Although unaware of Kimble's New York mission, Anne had never blamed Kimble for Jeannie's death (nor, for that matter, for Helen Kimble's). She knows Victor blames Dr. Kimble only to avoid blaming himself.

While Victor calls the police, Anne confronts and warns Kimble. Hearing sirens, Kimble escapes the building and winds up in Anne's car. Feeling guilty about having told Victor that Kimble was there, Anne drives the fugitive to a bus-stop. Leaving the car, Kimble pauses to tell Anne about his trip to New York. The police suddenly recognize and converge upon Kimble, shooting him down as he tries to escape. Kimble is returned to his place of employment as a seriously wounded patient, with tendon and blood vessel damage in his right shoulder. Toby, an intern who fancies himself as the resident Don Juan, delights in the plight of his former co-worker (whom he now calls "Killer").

Anne returns home, "congratulating" Victor for Kimble's capture. She tells Victor about Kimble's New York story, then confirms it with a call to the cardiac specialist. Victor is overcome with remorse and, after a night of soul-searching, visits police Lt. Cermak. Leonetti confesses to the murder of Helen Kimble. He figures the false confession, costing him only the ten months he has left, will square things with Kimble.

Lt. Gerard takes a plane to Michigan. He is surprised to hear about the confession, which Victor repeats for Gerard's benefit. Gerard repeatedly tries to trip him up, but Leonetti is familiar enough with both the murder trial and the Kimble house (which he, as a real estate contractor, had built) to deliver a convincing, unshakable testimony. Victor says he murdered Kimble's wife to make him suffer in grief the way Victor had suffered upon Jeannie's death, but that a "delayed conscience" had led him to finally confess. Cermak is satisfied, but Gerard is still doubtful—as is Kimble, upon hearing about the confession.

Anne, looking for a way to get her husband off the hook, visits Kimble. She is sure Victor's confession is fake and doesn't want him to throw his life away. Kimble tells her to talk to Victor's doctor and the whole scenario will make more sense. She does, and it does.

With the two lieutenants listening in, Anne confers with Victor in a bugged room. She tries to impress upon him his "advantage" in knowing how much time he has left and that those ten months represent the rest of their lifetime together—"please don't throw it away!" Victor retracts his confession.

Kimble has deliberately aggravated his shoulder injury so that he will have to be removed to the less-secure X-ray area, right near an exit door. He congratulates the nurse for something Toby supposedly told him about her (nothing, actually). Mystified, she takes Toby aside to ask him what he's been saying. She leaves, and when Toby reenters the room, Kimble ambushes and knocks out the intern. The nurse returns and is forced into a closet. Kimble then escapes through the exit door, with the police in close pursuit. He stows away in a departing linen service truck, which carries him to safety.

Victor, not yet up to date on the events, tells Gerard he will take care of Kimble's legal expenses. The Leonettis are secretly relieved to learn about Kimble's escape.

Episode #56
MASQUERADE
Original Airdate: March 23, 1965

Written by: Philip Saltzman   **Directed by:** Abner Biberman

Cast: Norma Crane as Mavis Hull, John Milford as Leonard Hull, Edward Asner as Sheriff Cliff Mayhew, H. M. Wynant as Pinto, Rayford Barnes as Bo Jenkins, Wayne Heffley as Grub, Ross Elliott as desk deputy, James Doohan and John Dennis as deputies.

Leonard Hull is an executive for Buddy Blackburn's company. Blackburn faces federal indictment for an unspecified charge, and Hull is in Washington as a secret witness against him. After another witness is bumped off, Hull rents a car and flees to a Clay City, Oklahoma, motel to be with his wife. Both of their lives are now in danger. Clay City police, not wanting their town to be the host of trouble, are on the lookout for Leonard.

Hull's car breaks down and a nearby hitchhiker—Kimble—fixes the fan belt in exchange for a ride. The two stop at a diner, Kimble ordering while

Hull phones his wife. Two police officers, to one of whom Kimble looks familiar, also stop at the restaurant. As Hull hangs up the phone, he notices a hit man examining his car outside. Hull escapes the building undetected.

Kimble, noting that his driver has disappeared and that the cops are eyeing him, nervously leaves the diner. The cops follow and stop Kimble, "returning" Hull's jacket to him. Asked to show identification, Kimble pulls Hull's wallet out of the jacket and offers the driver's license. The police now think they have Leonard Hull, the man they were looking for in the first place. They don't know what Hull looks like, and Kimble doesn't know what they want Hull for. When he finds out at the police station, Kimble retains the Hull identity, deciding it's better to be a wanted witness than a wanted murderer.

Though Kimble wants to be on his way, the police insist on holding him for his own protection. The sheriff decides to escort him to see his "wife." It looks as though Kimble's masquerade will be foiled, but Mrs. Hull fails to expose Kimble. When the police leave the two alone, Mrs. Hull pulls a gun. She thinks Kimble is a hit man sent there by Blackburn and has kept quiet because she wants to propose a deal. Since she and Leonard plan to divorce anyway, she wants to escape this whole mess and "disappear" to start a new life somewhere else.

Mrs. Hull offers Kimble $50,000 to tell Blackburn he has killed her off, leaving her to do the vanishing act. Kimble finally convinces her he is not a hit man, explaining how he came into this situation and why he can't reveal his true identity to the police.

Police pick up the real Leonard Hull trying to sneak into his hotel room, thinking *he* may be a hit man. They bring him downtown, where he at last reveals his identity to the incredulous police. They drive him to Mrs. Hull's motel, with the real hit man still on the trail.

Two policemen guard Mrs. Hull's motel room. She sends one out to get a newspaper; then she and Kimble bind and gag the other at gunpoint. They escape on foot, both hoping to disappear for different reasons. Leonard and the police find the room empty except for the incapacitated guard.

Kimble and Mrs. Hull hide out near a highway intersection, waiting for a bus. The hit man spots them there and opens fire, wounding the lady in the arm. Kimble and Mrs. Hull flee through the countryside into an oil field. They hop onto an open moving truck and disembark just before the hit man catches up. He takes after them on foot and they hide in a building. The hit man pursues them there and misses three shots, before Kimble manages to disarm and overpower the man in a tough struggle. With the situation under control, Kimble leaves Mrs. Hull, urging her to help beat Blackburn through legal avenues.

Mr. and Mrs. Hull are reunited at the police station, reaching some sort of reconciliation. Kimble later stops to look at a newspaper headline: "Blackburn to Face Indictment; Witness Returns to Testify."

Episode #57
RUNNER IN THE DARK
Original Airdate: March 30, 1965

Written by: Robert Guy Barrows **Directed by:** Alexander Singer

Cast: Ed Begley as Dan Brady, Richard Anderson as Barney Vilattic, Diana Van Der Vlis as Claire Whittaker, Vaughn Taylor as Mayor Otis Penfield, Peter Haskell as Bob Sterne, Nellie Burt as Mrs. Ferguson, Bing Russell as Sgt. Eggins, Irene Tedrow as Maude Keller, Don Lamond as TV emcee, Don Ross as officer.

Mrs. Keller calls up Tom Burns, the maintenance man in her Rutledge, Ohio, apartment building, to repair a leaky faucet. While awaiting his arrival she watches the *What's My Name?* television quiz show, whose mystery character this time just happens to be Dr. Richard Kimble. Recognizing Kimble as Tom Burns, she phones the police. When Kimble arrives Mrs. Keller—unable to conceal her panic—drives him away with screams. The town is soon crawling with police and reports on the manhunt go through the airwaves.

Eluding the cops, Kimble vaults a wall and finds himself on the grounds of the Beacon Manor Home for the Blind. Claire, a relative newcomer to the home who depends completely on others, calls for assistance. Kimble responds, and Claire supposes he is a visiting representative of the Good Neighbor Society in Cleveland. Kimble thus adopts that cover, with the new alias of Phil Mead.

Phil meets resident Dan Brady who, unbeknownst to Phil, is the town's former police chief of 38 years. Brady had lost his sight when two hoodlums threw acid in his face, and he was "put out to pasture," as he bitterly refers to it.

Much of his bitterness is directed toward his temporary replacement, Barney Vilattic (a "*college* man"), and the town's front-running mayor, Otis Penfield. Dan, who keeps up to date on the news with his portable radio and earphone, feels his instincts and experience make him still the best man to act as police chief.

A city council meeting to decide on the permanent police chief is scheduled for the next day, and the success of this manhunt figures to be a huge factor in the decision. The mayor, who had endorsed Barney for the job, just doesn't want to look bad. He scolds Barney for not being out with his men as Dan Brady always was. Barney's philosophy is to set the machinery in motion and keep out of the way, and he resents comparisons with Brady.

The fruitless and costly manhunt is hurting the mayor's image. Penfield visits Brady at the home, suggesting that Dan make a television appearance to offer his advice and influence and assure the mayor's constituents that everything is going smoothly. Offended, Brady blows off the mayor, then places a call to the Good Neighbor Society.

Brady introduces Phil to Bob Sterne, a young teacher blinded in a bus accident that claimed the lives of two of the 24 children aboard. Bob had been driving the group back from a football game and made four rescue trips onto the burning bus. Although he was cleared of liability in the accident, Bob punishes himself with guilt. He is a bitter, reclusive inmate who, in truth, is not blind.

Claire, inspired by Phil's efforts to make her less-dependent, descends the building's stairs by herself. She stumbles at the bottom and Bob — watched by Phil — instinctively catches her. Bob asks Phil to come into his room, where he admits his secret. His feelings of guilt are explained by his having had a couple of drinks before driving the bus. When his sight returned, he had maintained the masquerade of blindness as a sort of self-punishment. Phil advises Bob to decide whether he wants to be worshipped or punished; in the latter case, he should come forward with his confession.

Barney comes to the home, wanting to search it, but is rebuffed by Brady. Brady knows who Phil Mead really is — the call to the Good Neighbor Society, plus Phil's professional manner in dealing with Claire and Bob, were more than enough for such trained instincts as Brady's. But with the council meeting about to start, and Brady having delusions of winning back his job, he doesn't want to cooperate with his competitor. After Barney leaves, Brady accosts Bob. Brady had deduced long ago that Bob could see, and he needs Bob's vision to help complete Kimble's capture. Brady gives Bob his gun and the two approach Phil, with Brady revealing his knowledge. Leaving Bob to guard Kimble, Brady makes a dramatic call to police headquarters. He instructs the cops to break up the council meeting with the announcement that Dan Brady has something to say about their decision and that he is bringing Kimble into custody.

The mayor, changing horses in midrace, is abeam with the news. The costly roadblocks are drawn in as they await Brady's arrival. Brady, Bob, and Kimble drive into headquarters, with Kimble at the wheel and Brady in the passenger seat. Kimble offers Bob his final bits of advice and encouragement.

When they arrive, Brady gets out and hands his handcuffs to the driver — whom he thinks is Bob — instructing him to cuff the prisoner to Brady. Dan triumphantly enters the hushed room, handcuffed to Bob, while Kimble makes his escape. Dan finally realizes that he can no longer function as chief.

While the council is making Barney's appointment official, Brady offers his apology and future cooperation to Barney. They shake hands and sit down to talk over coffee.

Episode #58
A.P.B.
Original Airdate: April 6, 1965

Written by: Dan Ullman   **Directed by:** William D. Gordon

Cast: Paul Richards as Neil "Pinky" Pinkerton, Lou Antonio as Matt Mooney, Shirley Knight as Mona, Virginia Gregg as Margaret Ross, Fred Beir as Lt. Pete Peterson, Claudia Bryar as Mrs. Lindstrom, Hugh Sanders as sheriff, Jim Nusser as Smiley, Hal Riddle as dispatcher.

Kimble hops a freight and finds himself in the company of three escaped convicts, one of them dead. They were among eight involved in a breakout at the state penitentiary, the others having been either killed or recaptured. Pinky is a calculating professional killer who suffered a bullet wound in his side during the jailbreak; Mooney is a former middleweight boxing contender who had unintentionally killed a man with his fists, outside the ring. Kimble, identifying himself as Ed Morris, attends to Pinky's wound after making a deal to ensure his safety. Kimble attempts to escape when the train stops, but he is accosted by Mooney as the police, alerted by an A.P.B., search the train. Pinky wants to keep "Doc" around for his medical help and to prevent his alerting the police.

The three, claiming to be stranded motorists, take refuge in Mrs. Ross's home. The owner, who reads a lot, recognizes Kimble. Her widowed daughter, Mona, soon arrives home, seemingly amused by the colorful characters and the evolving intrigue in her own home. Police Lt. Peterson, a suitor of Mona's, drops in at the Ross house to use the telephone. Hiding in another room, the fugitives learn that there are roadblocks being set up all over town.

Mona mentions that Kimble is about the same size as her late husband, a military captain. Pinky devises an escape plan: to dress Kimble in a leftover captain's uniform and pass him off as a friend of Mona's husband who had come to visit her. Pinky and Mooney will hide in the car trunk, with a gun pointing through an opening at the front seat, and they will all drive through the roadblocks and out of town. The sleeping Mrs. Ross, doped up on tranquilizers, seems to pose no danger and will be left behind.

Mooney tries to force himself on Mona, but Kimble intervenes. Mona later tells Kimble she can't believe he killed his wife, and he tells her he didn't. Mooney overhears.

The four depart the house the next morning. Unbeknownst to the others, Pinky has killed Mrs. Ross and plans to do the same to Mona and Kimble after the escape. When Pinky learns that a cleaning lady is on her way to the Ross house, he orders Mona to return home. The housekeeper discovers the body and phones the police, but Pinky arrives and cuts her off. Mooney, realizing that Pinky plans to kill the cleaning lady as well as the others, refuses to turn the gun over to him. Mooney knocks out Pinky and, as the police arrive, Kimble convinces Mooney to surrender.

Kimble, still in the military uniform, escapes suspicion. He tells the police he can be reached at the military post for a statement. Mona lets Kimble use her car, and he drives away unchallenged.

Episode #59
THE OLD MAN PICKED A LEMON
Original Airdate: April 13, 1965

Written by: Jack Turley   Directed by: Alexander Singer

Cast: Celeste Holm as Flo Hagerman, Ben Piazza as Blaine Hagerman, Michael Davis as Paco Flores, Rodolfo Hoyos as Raphael Flores, Jean Hale as Lisa, Jan Shutan as Lois, Armand Alzamora as Ernesto, Rafael Lopez as Pedro, Rico Alaniz as Carlos, Byron Morrow as Leland "Senor Amo" Hagerman, John Clarke as Bill, Lawrence Montaigne as sheriff, Warren Parker as minister, Penny Kunard as Marjorie.

Kimble, alias Jim Wallace, is acting foreman for the Encinas County, California, citrus grove owned by Lee Hagerman. Jim has been there three months, since being discovered (by Paco) hiding in the garage with a bullet wound in his leg. Lee took Jim in, and Jim soon earned the respect of Lee and the "Chicanos," his coworkers.

Lee is pinned under an overturned tractor. The others rush to his side, trying desperately to save "Señor Amo." With his dying words, Lee asks Jim to take care of Lee's soon-to-arrive, troublesome son, Blaine. Heir to the ranch, Blaine is an arrogant, ruthless man, fond of fast cars and women.

Lee's widow, Flo, is the ranch's business manager. She had met Lee eight years earlier in Florida, where she had been employed as a prostitute. After a week together, Lee had proposed, and Flo, truly in love and ready to leave her past behind her, had accepted.

Flo asks Jim to run things amidst the distractions of the next few days. The Chicanos, wanting nothing to do with Blaine, tell Jim they plan to quit after Lee's funeral. A year ago Carlina — Raphael's daughter and Paco's sister — had been killed in a suspicious car accident while with Blaine. She was pregnant at the time.

While Blaine makes a cameo appearance at his father's funeral, Paco slices open the seat of his sports car. Afterward, Jim tells Blaine he will go over the schedules with Blaine, as he used to do with Lee. Blaine has other ideas and tells Jim he will take care of the schedules himself. Flo apologizes for her stepson's attitude.

Blaine zips his car around the groves, getting it stuck in a dirt bank. He soon finds himself surrounded by a group of somber Chicanos, one brandishing a knife. Jim arrives at the scene in a truck, defuses the situation, and drives Jim back to the house, advising him to stay out of the groves. Blaine has no use for Jim's paternal advice or managerial ability and, claiming financial cutbacks, tells Jim his services are no longer required. Flo overrules the firing, also saying she will not stand still for Blaine's plan to turn the ranch into a housing development. Blaine, showing his girlfriend-for-the-day "how the big boys win an argument," goes to Los Angeles. He returns with a detective report on Flo, chronicling her past activities and arrests. Blaine vows to have Flo kicked out of the business on "moral grounds."

Flo confides in Jim with her predicament, hoping he will testify as a character witness. Jim tells her he can't, and she deduces the reason, recalling the circumstances of his arrival coincidental with reports of an escaped fugitive in the area. Blaine suddenly appears, and Jim worries about how much he has overheard. Jim prepares to leave, and Flo pays him with a bonus.

Blaine corners Paco, extorting further information about Jim under threat of physical harm. Blaine then phones the sheriff, who advises him to keep Jim around until he can arrive. Blaine stalls Jim, giving him a false apology and the offer of a permanent position as foreman.

Paco confesses to his father about what he told Blaine. The police arrive, and Raphael tells Paco to warn Jim. Jim knocks down Blaine and escapes out a window. Blaine gets up, grabs a pistol, and is about to fire at the fleeing fugitive when he is fatally stabbed from behind by Raphael. Jim disappears into the groves.

Flo defends Raphael's action for the police. After they leave, Flo invites the Chicanos inside for coffee, calling it "your home, too."

Episode #60
LAST SECOND OF A BIG DREAM
Original Airdate: April 20, 1965

Story by: John Eastman   **Teleplay by:** George Eckstein
Directed by: Robert Butler

Cast: Steve Forrest as Barry Craft, Laurence Naismith as Maj. Alan Fielding, Milton Selzer as Lou Cartwright, Robert Karnes as Sheriff Ralls, Marlowe Jensen as Al, James Sikking as Bert, Don Spruance as desk deputy, Ed Long as bus driver.

Kimble, alias Nick Peters, takes a $50-per-week job feeding animals and cleaning cages at Major Fielding's Jungleland zoo in Morgantown, 55 miles outside of Lincoln, Nebraska (the scenes were actually shot at Jungleland in Thousand Oaks, California). Nick is concerned about the physical condition of a monkey, but Fielding dismisses the worries of an amateur.

Fielding is an eccentric but sensitive man, having a close kinship with his animals, and Barry Craft is his business manager. Craft tells Fielding that, due to Jungleland's financial problems, he has arranged the sale of their prized tiger, Jaipur, to a circus. Fielding is very upset.

Lt. Gerard, acting on a tip, is hot on Kimble's trail and stops at Jungleland on Friday. Learning there is no reward, Craft claims he hasn't seen Kimble. He then has a brainstorm. He thinks that he can orchestrate Kimble's capture into a public relations and financial bonanza at the zoo, much like what occurred at Chicago's Biograph Theater after the shooting of gangster John Dillinger there. After Gerard's departure, Craft calls his newspaper buddy Lou Cartwright, asking him to gather up all the information available on the Kimble case. Craft then tells Fielding his plan: to schedule Kimble's capture at 5:00 the next day, with reporters and photographers (told that "something big" is at hand) there for the show. Fielding disapproves.

Aware now that Nick is a doctor, Fielding takes his worries about the monkey more seriously. He sends Nick to a drugstore to fetch medicine for the animal.

Gerard learns that Cartwright has been inquiring about Kimble and that he is now headed for Jungleland. Suspicious, Gerard returns to the zoo with reinforcements. They arrive shortly after Craft apprises Cartwright of his big dream. Craft again issues a denial, and Gerard goes to question Fielding. The major compares Gerard's job with his own experience as a hunter—both questing to get a "terrified beast into an iron cage." Fielding also denies having seen Kimble, but Gerard is unconvinced.

Nick returns with the medicine, seeing Gerard et al. on the premises. Craft—claiming he "turned in my public spirit years ago"—covers for Nick as he hides. He advises Nick to stay put for his own safety.

Fielding warns Nick that Gerard is "on the scent." Fielding expresses his disdain for the hunter who becomes "an extension of his own weapon" and his belief that a living creature deserves room to die. Telling Fielding that he is innocent, Kimble gives him the monkey's medicine. Fielding suggests an escape route, and Kimble takes off.

Craft lambastes Fielding for allowing the escape. He had canceled the sale of Jaipur, he says, in anticipation of the windfall of his "Biograph" plan; unless Fielding can remember which way Kimble went, he will have to sell the tiger after all. Forced to decide between Jaipur and Kimble, Fielding reveals the fugitive's route.

Craft advises the police to cover the roads and Kimble, finding the area surrounded, is forced to retreat to the zoo. Pretending to assist Kimble, Craft knocks him senseless and imprisons him in a cage. Fielding is disturbed at the sight of a man treated in such a way but has made his decision.

The reporters and photographers arrive at 4:45. Craft whets their appetites and calls the police, while Fielding goes to tend to his animals. Kimble appeals to Fielding's sensitivity, reminding him of his belief in a man's right to dying room. There is no room in the electric chair, Kimble says, and even a beast doesn't suffer the torture of knowing the exact moment of its impending death. This hits home, and Fielding releases the prisoner.

The police roll in and Craft leads the group to his prize. Finding the cage empty, the police launch a search. Their priorities change when Fielding — realizing that Jaipur will now have to be sold — releases the tiger.

The tiger lunges toward the policemen, who shoot it in self-defense. The shots confuse the other cops guarding the perimeter of the zoo, and Kimble dupes the one nearest him by yelling, "Hey Al, over here, we got him!" When the guard leaves his post, Kimble scales the fence and escapes into the darkness.

Craft's dream has gone up in smoke, and Gerard has lost his man once again. Only Fielding gains a measure of satisfaction, in that Kimble escaped and Jaipur had room to die. Inexplicably, neither Fielding nor Craft are arrested.

Act III
The 1965-66 Season

The Fugitive's third season featured another 30 episodes, aired between September 14, 1965, and April 26, 1966. Its competition came from *CBS Reports/News Hour* and the *NBC Tuesday Night Movie*.

Having already shown commercial success, *The Fugitive* now also earned critical acclaim. It received the Emmy Award for "Outstanding Dramatic Series" on May 22, 1966. It also received the Raven Award, as Best Mystery Show, from the Mystery Writers of America.

David Janssen, as usual, appeared as the fugitive on each of the season's episodes. Barry Morse portrayed Lt. Philip Gerard in nine episodes: numbers 64, 69–70, 73, 77, 80, 82, 84, and 87.

Episode #61
WINGS OF AN ANGEL
Original Airdate: September 14, 1965

Story by: Don Brinkley & Otto King **Teleplay by:** Don Brinkley
Directed by: William A. Graham

Cast: Greg Morris as Mickey Deming, Lin McCarthy as Warden Maddox, Lane Bradbury as Janet Kegler, Harold Gould as Dr. Willis, Sue Randall as Nurse Thompson, Ned Glass as Leo Troy, Val Avery as Jerry Kulik, Ted Gehring as Fogarty, Joe Perry as Joe Robbins, Anne Loos as Miss Jay, John Ward as gate guard, Bing Russell and Dave Armstrong as officers.

Kimble, alias George Egan, is aboard a bus when it is stopped by police. They are searching for Joe Robbins, an escapee from the Oklahoma State Prison. Robbins takes passenger Janet Kegler hostage to facilitate his escape and heads for the emergency exit beside Egan's seat. An officer makes his move to rescue Janet, while Egan heroically tries to overpower Robbins. The two scuffle on the ground, and Egan is stabbed in the right side before the police shoot Robbins. The police decide to bring both the outlaw and the hero to the prison hospital. Egan objects, saying he has a job waiting for him and will lose it if he is unnecessarily detained.

The police and patients arrive just as a group of prisoners are returning from laundry detail. The warden orders the prisoners to stand at attention and see what happens to escapees: Robbins is dead on arrival. Meanwhile, two of the prisoners — Jerry and Leo — recognize Egan as "Doc Kimble," with whom they once shared a cell block in an Indiana penitentiary. Mickey Deming, a prisoner entrusted with a job as hospital attendant, wheels Egan into the hospital, expressing disdain toward the "cop-lover."

Jerry and Leo devise a plan to blackmail Kimble and start their own "business." They send a message via Mickey, addressed "Welcome Doc Kimble." Rather than have his identity revealed, Kimble is to deliver morphine and a hypodermic kit to them with the 5:30 laundry load. Kimble admits his identity to Mickey and expresses his aversion to supplying the prisoners with such an evil drug. Mickey advises Kimble to follow instructions but says he can't help. Mickey, regarded as a "model prisoner," has just 18 days remaining until his parole hearing, and he has grand plans for a new life of freedom.

A grateful Janet pays a visit to her rescuer, offering to repay him in any way she can. She is accompanied by the warden, who nearly sees the note from Jerry and Leo.

While Mickey occupies the attention of Nurse Thompson, Egan swipes her keys, opens the medicine closet, and removes the requested items. He deposits them into the laundry sack, which Mickey will momentarily be bringing out, and returns to his room undetected.

Causing an anxious moment, Dr. Willis scolds Egan for the "conspiracy" in which he has partaken. But Willis is just making a dry joke about Egan's repeated requests — supported by the warden and Janet, who don't want him to be "punished" for his heroism by losing his job — for an early release. The doctor gives in, and Egan prepares to leave. The nurse advises Janet, who had offered Egan a ride upon his release.

As Jerry and Leo sort the laundry under an officer's supervision, the cop discovers the morphine kit. He notifies the warden and — since the morphine container's seal is broken — the kit is turned over to Dr. Willis for analysis. The warden, assuming that Mickey smuggled the drugs, calls him on the carpet. Mickey remains mum, only denying his guilt, but finally makes a cryptic statement about protecting someone from the death-house.

An officer offers Egan a ride to the bus terminal. Egan says his goodbyes to the doctor and nurse, learning about Mickey. In good conscience, Egan can't leave without doing something to clear Mickey. Egan stops at the warden's office and is told the warden will be occupied with Mickey for another hour. Egan seals the note from Jerry and Leo in an envelope addressed to the warden, leaving it with the secretary. Egan departs, and the warden leaves his office just a moment later, opening the envelope as he makes his closing remarks to Mickey. The warden reads the note, realizes who Egan really is, and understands what Mickey was talking about.

Egan and the officer are preparing to exit the grounds just as Janet pulls in. The gate guard offers his best wishes to Egan, then has to answer his phone. Correctly guessing that it is the warden calling, Kimble jumps into Janet's car, takes the wheel, and peels out, getting a good head start on the police. He tells Janet who he is and appeals to her promise to repay him. Kimble pulls the car over and gets out, asking Janet to drive to the bus station and tell the police that he bought a ticket there. He then hitches a ride in the back of a pickup truck.

Dr. Willis apprises the warden of the lab analysis result. Dr. Kimble had replaced the morphine with distilled water.

Episode #62
MIDDLE OF THE HEATWAVE
Original Airdate: September 21, 1965

Written by: Robert Hamner **Directed by:** Alexander Singer

Cast: J. D. Cannon as Sheriff Todd Collison, Carol Rossen as Laurel Harper, Sarah Marshall as Sheila Pettie, John Lasell as Frank Pettie, James Doohan as doctor, Mimi Dillard as waitress, Paul Comi and James Johnson as deputies.

Kimble, alias Jim Owen, has completed his job as a highway construction worker in Lake City, New York, which is suffering through a late–June heat wave. Jim takes his girlfriend, Laurel, for dinner and drinks at a roadside inn, where he tells her he will have to end their romance and move on. She becomes irate, and Jim goes outside with her, hoping to give a proper explanation away from the ears of the bar patrons. Laurel refuses to listen, claws Jim's face as she breaks away from him, and drives off, leaving Jim to walk the three miles to his hotel room. It is nearly midnight by the time he returns home.

Three hours later Jim is aroused by a knock at his door. It is Laurel's older sister and brother-in-law, Sheila and Frank, searching for Laurel. Sheila and Frank take Jim to police headquarters to file a missing persons report. Laurel's car is discovered on a dirt road near a wooded area, and the police comb the woods. Laurel is found on the ground, having been physically and sexually assaulted. Jim is at hand when she regains consciousness, and she recoils at the sight of him. She is taken to the local medical center.

Sheila, who hadn't approved of Laurel's relationship with a lowly construction worker, blames Jim for the assault. Despite Frank's pleas to leave matters alone, Sheila convinces Sheriff Collison (a family friend) to lean on Owen. Jim is questioned, and gives an alibi: the hotel clerk saw Jim return home at a time earlier than when Laurel was last seen. Also, Laurel can verify that Jim was not the assailant. Unfortunately for Jim, the hotel clerk has gone shopping for the day and Laurel, claiming an "emotional blackout," can't seem to remember anything. The sheriff has Jim booked, fingerprinted, and incarcerated as a suspect.

Sheila takes Laurel home. Laurel admits that Jim didn't assault her, saying that, in her anger at Jim, she had picked up the first man she found and lost control of the situation. She doesn't mention that the man was Sheila's husband Frank, currently wrestling with his conscience. Sheila breaks a glass and grabs a rag to clean up the mess. She recognizes the rag as the shirt Frank had been wearing the night before and deduces that he was the assailant. Infuriated, Sheila blows off her husband's attempts to explain.

Jim knows it is a race between the return of his witness and the identification of his fingerprints. He talks the sheriff into releasing him so that he can talk to Laurel under police supervision. They arrive and Jim asks to speak to Laurel privately. He is handcuffed to a radiator pipe in her room, but Sheila refuses to leave. Jim admits that he escaped after spending time in jail for a crime he didn't commit, and he needs Laurel's help to get him off the hook before his prints are processed. Unmoved, Laurel says she still can't remember, and the policemen escort him out in cuffs. The sheriff returns inside to take a call: the fingerprints have been identified as those of convicted murderer Richard Kimble. Kimble knocks over the deputy and tries to escape, but finds himself trapped in an estate surrounded by six-foot walls (unable to be scaled by a man whose hands are cuffed behind his back).

Frank tells Sheila he will confess, but she tries to talk him out of it. She wants to avoid scandal and, as she points out, Frank's confession won't help Kimble. Frank is adamant and Sheila theorizes that, if Kimble can get away, Frank might lose his need to confess. She allows Kimble to enter the basement window and hide there. Sheila then goes outside, trying to call off the dogs, and saying she knows Kimble is innocent. The sheriff deduces she knows where Kimble is and finally convinces her to reveal where. They race into the basement, finding only Frank holding a pair of metal-clippers; he has cut off Kimble's cuffs and allowed him to escape out the window and to safety.

Frank is brought into custody, but Laurel vows to testify that she led him on and is thereby partly responsible for her own assault.

Episode #63
CRACK IN A CRYSTAL BALL
Original Airdate: September 28, 1965

Written by: William Link & Richard Levinson **Directed by:** Walter Grauman

Act III: The 1965-66 Season

Cast: Larry Blyden as Sal Mitchell, Joanna Moore as Joan Mitchell, J. Pat O'Malley as Mr. McBride, Nellie Burt as Mrs. Daniels, Frank Maxwell as Lt. David A. Bliss, Walter Brooke as Wilcox, John Crawford as sergeant, Pitt Herbert as motel manager.

Kimble, alias Joe Warren, is a gas station attendant at Arch Garage in a mythical midwestern state. The vicinity has been plagued by robberies recently, troubling the St. Anne Police Department. Sal Mitchell, a newcomer in town, stops at the gas station. A self-professed "clairvoyant," Sal makes a practice of secretly researching his subjects, then amazing them with his knowledge of personal details. Sal figures that offering his "powers" to assist the police would be a good publicity opportunity.

Sal learns who the local police lieutenant is and where he lives, and goes about clandestinely collecting scraps of information about his family. He then pays a visit to Lt. Bliss, offering to help and proving his powers by correctly listing personal facts about this man whom he had never before met (after receiving "emanations" from a fountain pen belonging to the lieutenant). Bliss is impressed, but advises Sal that the robber has already been apprehended. On his way out Sal notices a "wanted" poster on the wall and recognizes Richard Kimble as the local gas station attendant. Plan "B" formulates in Sal's mind.

Sal follows Joe home from work, learning that he resides at Mrs. Daniels's boarding house. Another resident, Mr. McBride, notices Sal taking notes. McBride is an ornery old cuss who recently lost his job to automation and who spends most of his waking hours sitting idly on the porch. Joe tells Mrs. Daniels (who is fond of Joe) he thinks he can get McBride a part-time bookkeeping job at the garage, but he doesn't tell McBride about it just yet.

Sal spends an afternoon researching the Kimble case before returning home to his wife, Joan. He tells her his plan, including her role in the deception. Joan doesn't like the idea of using Kimble or anyone else in such a scheme, but she invariably goes along with her husband.

Sal, promising a big story, gets booked to appear as a guest on KMOL-TV. Meanwhile, Joan leaves a note for Joe with McBride, saying she knows Joe is Kimble and thinks she can help him find the man he is looking for. Joe meets Joan at a restaurant as instructed. She says she followed his case and believed his testimony. Joan tells him she saw a one-armed man working at a souvenir stand at Lincoln State Park 200 miles upstate and offers to drive Joe there that evening. Joe warily agrees to go with her, bids farewell to Mrs. Daniels and Mr. McBride (breaking a date with him), and drives off with Joan.

On television Sal describes his latest "emanations": he felt the presence of Kimble in the area but now senses the fugitive is moving in another direction. Sal visualizes the colors green and blue (perhaps a park overlooking two lakes) and a bearded man with a stone face (a statue, maybe). He describes other cryptic visions that relate to the service station and the boarding house. Sal's "remarkable demonstration" then comes to an end, and a "wanted" poster of Kimble is flashed. Mrs. Daniels and Mr. McBride are watching the show. McBride declares that he knew Joe was no good, but Mrs. Daniels tells McBride that Joe was trying to help find him a job. McBride softens and wants to help Joe somehow.

Kimble interrogates Joan throughout their trip, exasperating her. Kimble can't let go of the possibility that Joan is telling the truth, and she begins to realize he really is innocent of murder. This makes her feel even worse about what she is doing. The two check in at a motor lodge for the night, with plans to go to the nearby park the next morning.

McBride has figured out the Mitchells' scheme and wants to warn Kimble. He does some detective work to find out where Kimble is staying and leaves an urgent message for him to call McBride. The motel manager gives the message to Joan, who destroys it.

The police piece together and translate Sal's cryptic clues to mean that Kimble will appear at Lincoln Park the next day. Spring City sets up a flock of undercover cops near the park's souvenir stand to await Kimble's arrival.

Kimble and Joan check out of the motel, and the manager says, "I hope that message wasn't bad news." Joan peels out with Kimble wondering what he was talking about. She drops him off at the park entrance and tells him she will wait for him there. Kimble, still wary, phones the motel and gets the McBride message. He then calls McBride, learning about the scheme. After Kimble spots an armed park "visitor," and discovers that Joan has left, he realizes McBride is right. Kimble slips away, leaving the police to wait there all day.

Sal feels like a fool, and Joan tells him she will never again cooperate in such a plot. She is glad Kimble escaped, and Sal wonders what makes her think Kimble is innocent. "Maybe I got some emanations," she sneers.

Episode #64
TRIAL BY FIRE
Original Airdate: October 5, 1965

Written by: Philip Saltzman   **Directed by:** Alexander Singer

Cast: Charles Aidman as Capt. James Eckhardt, Frank Aletter as Burton Green, Jacqueline Scott as Donna Taft, Tommy Rettig as J. J. Eckhardt, Marion Ross as Marion Eckhardt, Booth Colman as Les Donaldson, Chris Alcaide as Lt. Horvath, Ed Deemer as Sgt. Rainey, John Durren as Eddie Bragg.

Kimble makes one of his periodic phone calls to his sister, Donna. She tells him of a letter she received from a Chicago man, Capt. Eckhardt, who claims he saw the one-armed man near the Kimble house on the night of the murder. Donna has hired a private investigator to make sure Eckhardt is not just another crackpot. She has also retained Burt Green, the family attorney, to look into reopening the case. Kimble heads for Chicago to talk to Eckhardt.

Lt. Gerard learns that Green has ordered a copy of the Kimble trial transcript, and Gerard wonders what he is up to. He decides to keep an eye on Green.

Kimble visits Capt. Eckhardt, a 43-year-old military hero on disability retirement due to a bad leg that has been operated on several times. He had been visiting his father in Stafford and was on his way to the airport when he found himself behind Kimble's car just as the one-armed man crossed the road. Eckhardt thought little of it and returned to Germany. He did not learn about the Kimble murder until a little over a week ago when he saw a magazine article ("Is Kimble Still Alive?"). He promptly wrote to Donna and two days later received a good job offer. Mrs. Eckhardt says her husband can't afford to miss the job opportunity by taking time out to testify on Kimble's behalf. The captain, now having met Kimble, has new-found sympathy for him and overrules his wife.

At Kimble's request, Green flies to Chicago to examine Eckhardt, finding him to be a "bona fide witness" warranting a new trial. Green then meets Kimble at the Edmund Hotel. Meanwhile, Gerard has tracked Green to the Eckhardt residence and is waiting there when a cab drops him off. Gerard accosts the cabdriver, ordering him to bring Gerard to the place Green just came from. Green sees Gerard and uses the Eckhardts' phone to try and warn Kimble. He gets through just in time. Kimble escapes out a window and down a fire escape as Gerard arrives. Gerard misses a shot and Kimble gets away.

Green returns to Stafford with Eckhardt, filing a writ requesting a new trial. Eckhardt is unshakable at the hearing, which Gerard attends. The judge can make no definite ruling while Kimble is still at large but grants that the new evidence is impressive enough to offer a temporary stay of execution upon Kimble's surrender. Gerard gets a mysterious phone call which seems to please him, making Donna suspect that her brother's case is somehow in jeopardy.

The call came from a prison warden, on behalf of inmate Eddie Bragg. Bragg had seen a news article about the new witness in the Kimble case and recognized Eckhardt as one of his former narcotics customers. Eckhardt had become addicted to morphine during treatment for his bad leg, had kicked the habit, but had had one relapse: Bragg had supplied him with a week's supply of the drug just three days prior to the Kimble murder. Bragg figures his testimony ought to be worth some time off his sentence, while Gerard figures it just may discredit Eckhardt's whole story, preferably after Kimble is in custody.

Donna and Green meet Kimble at a Chicago park. Donna warns her brother about her intuition, but Kimble plans to turn himself in at the Stafford courthouse at noon the next day.

Before leaving for the courthouse, Kimble meets with Eckhardt outside his home. Eckhardt mentions that he lost his job opportunity but opts not to say anything about Bragg. Meanwhile, Green has found out about Bragg and told Donna. Donna reaches Mrs. Eckhardt, asking her to warn Kimble not to come, and mentioning Bragg's name as the reason. Mrs. Eckhardt tells her husband about the call, but Kimble has already left on the Illinois & Indiana bus. Eckhardt gets in his car to chase it.

The bus rolls into Stafford, where many anxious people await, but Kimble does not get off. He has finally been intercepted by Eckhardt, who tells Kimble about Bragg. Eckhardt is still willing to testify, but Kimble decides it is just not worth the risk.

At the courthouse, Green asks Gerard how he feels about Kimble now that he has heard Eckhardt's story. "Take the word of a junkie?" asks Gerard. "You're not serious." Donna remarks to Green that Gerard can't really believe what he just said. "He has to," Green replies.

Episode #65
CONSPIRACY OF SILENCE
Original Airdate: October 12, 1965

Written by: William D. Gordon   **Directed by:** Jerry Hopper

Cast: Donald Harron as Maj. Christopher Beck, Malachi Throne as David Jones, Bill Gunn as Dr. Avery, Wesley Addy as Homer Price, Robert Cornthwaite as Pickett, Mort Mills as Murchison, Byron Morrow as Gen. Ormand Fredricks, Lawrence Montaigne as section leader, Dick Wilson as Berger.

Fred Tate works as an attendant at the High Desert Inn, a secluded lodge and golf club 62 miles from Reeseburg, Arizona. Unbeknownst to Tate, the resort is about to go under military jurisdiction for a clandestine operation. Military personnel, in cooperation with David Jones's chemical company, will be testing an air pollutant developed by an adversary nation and a detergent designed to neutralize it. The pollutant is lethal to all animal life, and attackers could administer it to wipe out a city's population, then neutralize the pollutant and take over the city unchallenged. If word gets out about this testing, though, the U.S. may come out looking like the "bad guys" who developed the horrid weapon. Maj. Beck, who is in charge of military security during the operation, will engage in a power struggle with Jones throughout it.

Beck and Jones check into the inn posing as tourists, with Tate attending to their luggage. The two then meet with others (posing as inn employees) involved in the operation. Tate eventually is the only genuine employee with no knowledge about the operation and is checked out. He overhears a receptionist telling a caller the place is booked up until Friday even though it is actually almost empty. Tate wonders if the mysterious behavior involves a heavily insured gem collection on the premises. When Tate returns to his room, he notices it has been entered and examined by someone else. Smelling trouble, he packs up to leave. Tate is stopped outside and brought into custody, and his fingerprints are checked through military records. They show him to be Richard Kimble, a former medic in Korea. With a false identity and references, and an attempt to leave, Kimble is suspected to be a spy, and his prints are sent to the FBI.

As Kimble is being led away by Pickett, the land is rocked by a huge explosion two miles out in the fields. The tank of pollutant has exploded, releasing toxic gas into the air and injuring five of Jones's employees. Pickett is distracted, giving Kimble the opportunity to overpower him and flee. Kimble inexplicably heads toward the explosion site and is overcome by fumes. Two guards arrest him and return him to the inn. Meanwhile, the neutralizing detergent has been released above the explosion site and appears to be working.

Despite Jones's objections, Beck tells Kimble the truth about the operation, figuring that is better than having him make dangerous guesses. Kimble, made to realize his life may be in danger due to the pollutant, is treated by Avery, a military doctor.

Beck gets the FBI report and learns that Kimble is not a spy but a doctor wanted for murder. Kimble tells Beck he will try to escape but first must assist Avery. Avery takes ill, and Kimble is forced to take charge of the medical situation.

Jones would just as soon cover up the whole mishap and eliminate Kimble, especially with a group of snoopy military VIPs due in from Washington that evening. Jones suggests to Beck that a "missile accident" be arranged to knock off Kimble, who could endanger national security (not to mention Beck's and Jones's jobs) if he talked. Beck, a solid military man, rejects the idea on moral grounds.

Beck is impressed with Kimble's medical assistance and his affirmation of innocence. Despite his growing trust in and appreciation of Kimble, Beck will be obliged to hold him until the arrival of Gen. Fredricks, who will then turn Kimble over to the military police. Kimble is imprisoned in his room and handcuffed to a bedpost.

Jones decides he will take matters into his own hands, allowing Kimble to "escape," then shooting him in the act. He knocks out the guard at Kimble's door and cuts off the handcuffs, explaining that he is grateful for Kimble's helping his injured employees. They escape out a window and onto the grounds, just as the VIPs are rolling in. Jones pulls a gun and is about to fire at Kimble when he is caught from behind by Beck. Beck overpowers Jones and gets the gun but is wounded in the process. Kimble starts to leave, but Beck warns him that he will have to shoot if Kimble doesn't return with him voluntarily. Kimble says he will not allow himself to be executed for something he didn't do and that Beck will have to shoot him in the back. Kimble turns and walks to freedom, and Beck can't bring himself to fire.

Beck explains what happened to the general, who indicates that no discipline will be forthcoming, under the circumstances. Jones is taken into custody for assaulting an officer, among other things.

Episode #66
THREE CHEERS FOR LITTLE BOY BLUE
Original Airdate: October 19, 1965

Story by: Chester Krumholz   **Teleplay by:** Chester Krumholz & Harry Kronman
Directed by: Walter Grauman

Cast: Richard Anderson as George Forster, Edward Asner as Roy Malinek, Fay Spain as Nora Keel, Woodrow Parfrey as Mort Graham, Milton Selzer as Ben Willoughby, Doris Singleton as Janet Willoughby, DeForest Kelley as Charlie, Amy Douglass as aunt, Jason Wingreen as Jack, Byron Foulger as Colby, Vaughn Taylor as Arvin.

Kimble, alias Tom Nash, serves as chauffeur for George Forster. George is from the small midwestern town of Ardmore, which he escaped some 15 years ago. He had left behind his girlfriend, Nora (whose father forbade their marriage), and his good friend, Roy (whose pro football prospects were derailed by an accidental leg injury). George, penniless when he left Ardmore, has become a very successful businessman since. Six weeks ago he had discovered Tom sleeping in his garage and burning up with fever. Suspecting Tom had trouble with the police, but not prying about it, George had hired him as his driver.

Tom drives George to Ardmore, where he plans to build a factory, and where he returns as a local hero. Banners announcing his return hang everywhere, a party in his honor is slated for that evening (at Roy's hotel), and a celebratory parade will be held the next day. Beneath this facade, however, many townspeople have feelings ranging from jealousy to resentment toward this "big important man." Tom overhears an anonymous phone call from someone threatening to kill George the next day.

Tom meets many of the townspeople: Mort Graham, the police chief; George's aunt, who advises Tom to "take him away before this town breaks his heart"; Nora, who has become a bitter lush; Roy, who hints that George was partly responsible for his accident, but insists that the two are best of friends; and Ben, whose sultry wife, Janet, constantly belittles him in comparison to George.

Tom tells about what he heard, but George dismisses it as a crank call, and Roy assures him nobody would want to hurt George. Tom takes the car out and is nearly killed when the steering and brakes fail. He tells Graham about his experiences, and the chief gives Tom a gun so he can act as George's bodyguard. As procedure, Tom must be fingerprinted to gain possession of the weapon. Tom reluctantly submits, figuring he will be long gone before the report comes back but not realizing the police will expedite the process and get the report back in mere hours. Tom tells George what happened, and George realizes the fingerprints may lead to trouble for Tom. He offers Tom a chance to leave, but Tom turns it down.

At the party, Janet flirts with George but he rebuffs her. Nora shows up with Charlie, both tanked up, and makes a scene. Tom stops Charlie from assaulting George, and the party is over almost before it starts. Roy suggests that he, George, and Tom celebrate by themselves, then goes to his office to load a concealed revolver.

The police get the print report back and calls George. George covers for his chauffeur, saying he doesn't know where Tom is, and the police say they are on their way there. George gives Tom an opportunity to hide in the building while the police make a cursory search. Meanwhile, Roy invites George to accompany him on a walk. Tom passes through Roy's office, finds some bullets lying out, and deduces that Roy is George's prospective killer. Tom becomes more concerned about George's safety than his own.

Roy confronts George at the scene of Roy's accident. He tries a football move on George but is pushed aside. He then pulls the gun. With Nora close behind, Tom arrives just in time to rescue George, but the gun discharges, alerting the police. George asks Nora to give Tom a ride out of town and covers for Roy, saying the gun went off accidentally during a demonstration. George escorts the remorseful Roy away while Nora takes Tom to a busstop.

Episode #67
ALL THE SCARED RABBITS
Original Airdate: October 26, 1965

Story by: William Bast   **Teleplay by:** William Bast & Norman Lessing
Directed by: Robert Butler

Cast: Suzanne Pleshette as Peggy Franklin, Liam Sullivan as Dr. Dean Franklin, Debi Storm as Nancy Franklin, R. G. Armstrong as Marshal Matt Peters, Nancy Rennick as Ann Franklin, Robert Sorrells as Hank, Meg Wyllie as Mrs. White, Garry Walberg as Lt. Wilson, Edward Faulkner as Sheriff Frank Brill, Steven Bell as mechanic, Susan Davis as Mona, Hal Lynch as sergeant.

Peggy Franklin advertises for a driver to take her from Iowa to California, and her ad is answered by Kimble, alias Joe Taft. Peggy is an attractive divorcée whose ex-husband, Dean, is a successful research pathologist. He has remarried and obtained custody of his and Peggy's young daughter, Nancy, but Peggy has full visitation rights. She has arranged to take Nancy for the weekend but secretly plans to kidnap her daughter and take her to California to live.

Peggy had voluntarily relinquished custody of Nancy so that she could devote full attention to her elderly father. Peggy had enjoyed playing nursemaid to "Papa," after a car accident while she was driving had injured him. Papa's death a few months later had sent Peggy into a nervous breakdown and left her with feelings of guilt and desolation. An emotional block has left her unable to drive a car since then. Peggy wants to fill her emptiness by reclaiming her daughter and has arranged to stay with her aunt in San Diego.

Before Nancy leaves for the "weekend," she sneaks into her father's lab and removes a rabbit from a cage, concealing it in her luggage. She has no idea the rabbit is part of an experiment and has been injected with advanced tularemic meningitis bacteria. By the time Dean realizes Nancy has taken the rabbit, she is long gone. Dean, hoping to avert a tragedy, arranges for an A.P.B. and press release.

When Peggy sees the rabbit, Nancy claims that Dad "gave him to me ... for Easter." Joe stops at a Council Bluffs pet store to buy a cage. The trio checks in at a hotel for the night, and Peggy and Joe share a drink at the bar. Peggy spills her guts, except about the kidnapping scheme, and offers a toast "to all the scared rabbits on the run." She and Joe kiss good night.

After a stop in Dalhart, Texas, the travelers begin experiencing mechanical problems with the 1953 jalopy. A mechanic advises that it will require at least a couple of days to fix but offers them a working vehicle for $100 plus the jalopy. Peggy accepts, but the new wheels throw the pursuing police off the scent for a while.

Nancy admits that her father didn't really give her the bunny, worrying Peggy. Shortly after, the rabbit is dead and Nancy is burning up with fever and complaining of head and neck pain. She soon lapses into a coma. Apprised of the facts, Joe diagnoses Nancy's illness and speeds in search of a hospital. He stops near Dos Palos, New Mexico, at a home with the sign "Alfred M. White, M.D.," and brings Nancy inside. He is told that the doctor is out on a call to an Indian reservation, where he can't be reached and won't be back for several hours. Furthermore, there is no other doctor within 100 miles. Joe, knowing he can't get the necessary medication without a prescription, drives off and breaks into Hawkins' Pharmacy nine miles away. While he removes the medicines, police recognize his car as the one they are searching for and arrest him as he leaves the pharmacy. The marshal recognizes Joe as someone he has seen on a "wanted" poster, but he accompanies Joe to Dr. White's house. The marshal calls Albuquerque police to run a make on Joe. Joe must reveal his medical knowledge—providing another clue to his identity—in order to save Nancy. Joe administers the medicine, bringing Nancy out of danger. The marshal, who has kids of his own, is touched by Joe's lifesaving efforts and compassionate manner toward Nancy. He decides not to follow up on the police check and allows Peggy to accompany Joe to the bus stop. Peggy and Joe kiss goodbye, and Peggy drives off by herself for the first time since her father's death. Encouraged by Joe, she is now determined to earn back custody of Nancy through legal means.

Episode #68
AN APPLE A DAY
Original Airdate: November 2, 1965

Written by: Dan Ullman   **Directed by:** Ralph Senensky

Cast: Arthur O'Connell as Josephus Harrison Adams, Sheree North as Marianne Adams, Kim Darby as Sharon Wolfe, Amzie Strickland as Mildred Crandall, Walter Baldwin as Mr. Weaver, Bill Quinn as Dr. Olney, Gene Darfler as Sheriff Olsen, Marlowe Jensen as officer.

Kimble is pursued by a sheriff's posse in Bradley, Briar County, Colorado. During his flight he trips and rolls uncontrollably down a long, steep hill, landing at the bottom with a badly-sprained left ankle. Two passing motorists, the Crandalls, see the injured man near the roadside and take him to the home of "Doctor" Josephus Adams. Josephus attends to Kimble, who gives his name as Ed Curtis.

Josephus, never having made it through medical school, had worked as an orderly in a hospital. There, he met a nurse named Marianne, who became his wife. Encouraged by Marianne, Josephus earned a certificate from the American Natural Medicine Institute in 1938 and started a lucrative practice. Scoffing at drugs and hospitals, Josephus has combined natural remedies like honey and horseradish with an endearing bedside manner to win over the town. His practice became so successful that it drove away the area's conventional physician, Dr. Olney, to become the county coroner ("as a doctor," Olney says of Adams, "he's a great bee-keeper"). The Adamses market their "medicines" through their store and a national mail-order operation.

Ed notices that Mrs. Crandall has a bad cough, suggestive of congestive heart disease, and wonders if she has sought medical attention. Josephus keeps her supplied with honey-laced cough medicine and warns Ed to keep his medical opinions to himself. Ed encounters the same attitudes from Marianne and Sharon, the Adams's nieces, whenever he broaches his medical philosophies. Sharon tells Ed that her father died in a hospital, proof that such places are bad. Ed is very disturbed by the Adams family values.

Ed is invited to stay with the Adamses while he recuperates. Mrs. Adams reads a newspaper article: "Countywide Search for Fugitive — Believed to Be Dr. Richard Kimble." She deduces Ed is Kimble but decides to keep this information to herself until it can be used to best advantage. She burns the paper and, later, tells a policeman making his rounds that she has seen no sign of the fugitive.

Mr. Weaver, a customer at the store, extols the prowess of Josephus, who "saved" him during a bout with pneumonia. Ed continues to appeal for more sensible attitudes toward medicine, making Sharon very upset with him.

Mrs. Crandall takes a turn for the worse and is rushed to the Adams house. She is dead on arrival. Ed storms out in disgust, shattering Mrs. Crandall's cough medicine bottle. Sharon has newfound interest in Ed's ideas, wondering if Mrs. Crandall's death could indeed have been postponed by early detection and hospital treatment, as Ed had said. Josephus is riddled with guilt, knowing that Ed is right and that other people have died earlier than necessary because of him.

Fearing that Mrs. Crandall's death might set back public trust in Dr. Adams, especially with Ed around preaching, Marianne tells Josephus about Ed's identity. He dissuades her from calling the police, and they go off to Mrs. Crandall's funeral. Ed prepares to leave.

As Ed waits at the bus station, he runs across Mr. Weaver. Weaver tells Ed about the funeral and how Sharon repeatedly yelled, "She didn't have to die," and then collapsed. Ed is troubled by this; just about to board the bus, he changes his mind and hitches a ride with Weaver back to the Adams house.

The Adamses return from the funeral, with Marianne chastising Sharon for "disgracing your uncle in front of the whole town." Sharon runs into the bee-keeping area and collapses again, unconscious. Ed diagnoses that Sharon is in a diabetic coma and could be dead within a few hours if she is not hospitalized. He carries her to the truck. Marianne, more concerned with her reputation than her niece's health, tries unsuccessfully to stop Ed. Fearing that they will be "laughed out of this county" if their own kin resorts to hospitalization rather than home cures, Marianne coerces Josephus into calling the police. He does but says only that he wants the truck stopped because a man took it.

The sheriff pulls Ed over, and Ed explains he must take Sharon to the Greeley hospital. Josephus arrives moments later, telling police he wanted the truck stopped only because he didn't think it was safe. Josephus drives Sharon to the hospital with a police escort, while Ed heads for the bus stop.

Josephus meets Ed at the station afterward, telling Ed that his diagnosis was correct, and that Sharon is out of danger. He also promises to abandon his practice: "You were my last patient." The two shake hands, and Ed boards yet another bus.

Episodes #69-70
LANDSCAPE WITH RUNNING FIGURES (Parts I & II)
Original Airdates: November 16 & 23, 1965

Written by: Anthony Wilson   Directed by: Walter Grauman

Act III: The 1965-66 Season

Cast: Barbara Rush as Marie Lindsay Gerard, Herschel Bernardi as Capt. Arthur Ames, Jud Taylor as Detective Sgt. Rainey, Arthur Franz as bus driver, Noam Pitlik as salesman, Rodolfo Hoyos as Luis Bota, Bill Zuckert as sergeant, Ronnie Dapo as oldest boy, Sy Prescott as officer, Stuart Nisbet as desk clerk, John Clarke as Arthur Jarvis, Stephen Coit as ticket seller, Don Ross as policeman, Adam Williams as truck driver, Robert Doyle as Tommy, Judith Morton as Joannie, Robert Biheller as Beavo, James Devine as intern.

Kimble, alias Steve Carver, is a kitchen helper at K's Diner, about 150 miles west of Joplin, Missouri. He works the 2–11 A.M. shift with Luis. On April 23 Steve makes a grievous slip-up, listing his name as "Richard Kimble" in the sign-out book. Checks are made, and the police await his arrival at work the next night. Luis warns Steve as he approaches the rear entrance, and Steve is able to make a getaway.

Capt. Ames leads the local search effort, while Lt. Gerard is called away from his vacation. He and his wife, Marie, arrive later that morning and check into a hotel. Marie is not at all happy about the abruptly ended vacation, just the latest in the continuing saga of her husband's obsession with Kimble. She pleads with him to "let go," but he leaves to meet with the local police force, promising to call Marie at 11:00 sharp.

Gerard gets caught up in the search efforts, instructing and criticizing members of the local force. Kimble takes refuge in a laundry building, where he meets three young boys. The oldest brother offers him a foolproof hideout, for a price, and locks Kimble in a cell-like side room. Gerard enters, asking the boys whether they have seen anyone. They say "no" but Gerard is suspicious. He tries to cajole information from the youngest boy with the price of a candy bar. The ploy appears success-bound until the candy machine jams. Gerard leaves and the boys set Kimble free. Meanwhile, Gerard has forgotten all about calling Marie.

Marie becomes fed up, especially when practically everything she hears or reads contains Kimble's name. She leaves shortly before her husband finally tries to call and boards an east-bound bus at 2:10, using her maiden name, Marie Lindsay. At the station a local cop recognizes Marie from a previous meeting.

Kimble hitches a ride with an obnoxious truck driver. They approach a roadblock and the nervous Kimble snaps at the driver. He orders Kimble out. At that moment the Joplin-bound bus pulls up to the roadblock. The threat of a flood has blocked off many roads in the Temple County area, and bus passengers are given the opportunity to disembark here. Most do, giving Kimble the chance to board the already-checked bus in the confusion, thus bypassing the roadblock. He joins a handful of other passengers, including Marie, whom he has never before met.

A loud-mouthed salesman tries to liven things up, distracting the driver just as they pass a "road closed ahead" sign. Seconds later the bus crashes into a construction truck parked across the road. Marie is the only one seriously injured, knocked unconscious with a head injury and probable concussion. She is brought out of the bus, while Kimble starts to walk away. He is drawn back by the woman's screams; she has regained consciousness and discovered herself temporarily blind.

Kimble calms Marie somewhat, then brings her to the truck. He plans to drive her to the nearest town to seek medical attention. The two head for Tilden and Marie says, "Whoever you are, you're very kind." Meanwhile, Lt. Gerard has learned that his wife boarded the bus and is trying to track her down, as long as it doesn't interfere with the Kimble manhunt.

A young lady flags down Kimble. When he stops her two male companions appear, stealing the truck's spare tire, harassing Marie, and beating Kimble with a tire iron, before driving off.

The truck runs out of gas just as Kimble and Marie arrive in Tilden. They discover the town has been evacuated by order of the Flood Control Authority, and there is no telephone or electric service.

Kimble breaks into the Valley Telephone Exchange, hoping to use the switchboard to find a phone line out. Hearing a car pull in, Kimble sets Marie up on the switchboard and goes out to investigate. He finds that the vehicle he heard belongs to the three hoodlums, who are in a bar looting the liquor cabinet. Kimble asks for their help, saying that Marie could slip into shock and die if she is not promptly brought to a hospital. They reply with sarcasm.

Marie gets through to the Fredonia operator and calls for an ambulance. She then calls her husband, asking him to come and get her, but not telling him of her condition or whereabouts. He hedges, thinking Marie is just testing him by making him choose between her and Kimble. "If you have to think about it," she says, "don't come." As she hangs up, one of the hoods enters and begins terrorizing Marie. Her screams bring Kimble to the rescue as the truants depart.

Lt. Gerard has Marie's call traced and begins the two-hour journey to find her. Kimble comforts Marie, the two taking refuge in the bar as they await the ambulance. They share cheese, crackers and wine, and Marie rambles on with a stream of personal questions to keep the conversation going. Kimble combs through the "dust and dead leaves" of his memory to recall details of his prefugitive life.

Time stands still for a while as the two strangers share anecdotes and details about their lives. Kimble talks about his marriage and honeymoon, his service hitch in Korea, and his first house; Marie relates how she lost her husband to a will-o'-the-wisp that drifts into and out of their lives, twisting them around. They find that they have a common bond in that each lived in a small town, not realizing they are both describing Stafford, Indiana. Kimble repeats a local joke about his town having one-and-a-half newspapers, since the *Coral-Dispatch* comes out only twice a week. Marie then realizes she is with Kimble

Act III: The 1965-66 Season   121

and tries to devise a way to hold on to him so that he can be brought to justice, breaking the "triangle" in her marriage. "Promise me you won't leave," she says.

The two return to the switchboard. Lt. Gerard calls and Marie answers. Kimble starts to get suspicious of the conversation and walks toward Marie. She abruptly cuts off the call and tries a new ploy, telling Kimble she is very attracted to him. The phone rings again and Kimble answers. "This is Lt. Gerard," the caller says. "I'd like to talk to my wife again."

Kimble now knows what is going on, and he prepares to leave. Marie tries vainly to pursue him and works herself into such a frenzy that she passes out in Kimble's arms. Just then the ambulance finally arrives. Kimble answers a few questions, then slips away seconds before Lt. Gerard gets there. Marie is brought to a hospital.

Lt. Gerard visits with Marie, telling her that Kimble somehow got through their dragnet. Gerard admits Kimble is "stuck in my throat and I can't swallow him," but he is grateful that Marie is the one part of his life that Kimble can't get to.

Episode #71
SET FIRE TO A STRAW MAN
Original Airdate: November 30, 1965

Written by: Jack Turley   **Directed by:** Don Medford

Cast: Diana Hyland as Stella Savano, Edward Binns as George Savano, Joseph Campanella as Jesse Stansel, Clint Howard as Johnny Stansel, Kelly Thordsen as Sgt. Kelly, Shelley Morrison as Ginny Stansel, Lewis Charles as Max, Barbara Baldwin as Mickey, Wally Shannon as waiter.

Kimble, alias Chris Benson, works in the warehouse and drives a truck for the George Savano Auto Parts Company in Tractor, New Jersey. Jesse, his co-worker, is being mugged by arrangement of George's brother Stella. The police approach the scene and the muggers flee, one jumping into the back of the truck Chris is driving. The police follow the truck to the warehouse, where the mugger leaves Chris's vehicle and hops aboard a departing truck. Chris is arrested as a suspect until Jesse clears him. George wonders why Chris was so uncomfortable, and Chris admits to some previous trouble with the police.

Chris pays a service call, inspecting Stella's flat tire. Stella flirts with Chris to the disapproval of Max, whose job seems to be keeping an eye on Stella for her brother. Max calls George to tell him, then puts Chris on the line. George asks Chris to meet him at the Gatewood Inn for a drink. There George warns Chris to stay away from Stella, saying she is engaged and that her flirting shouldn't be misinterpreted. Chris says he appreciates the "big brother act" and that George need not worry.

At work the next day, Jesse also warns Chris to keep away from Stella, then invites Chris to his home for dinner. Chris meets Jesse's five-year-old boy, Johnny. The boy tells Chris about his secret friend, "Mr. Straw," who gives him candy and toys. The secret benefactor is Stella, who regularly leaves the gifts hidden around the scarecrow across the road and atop the hill from the Stansels' house.

Chris finds an anonymous note on his boarding house door, inviting him to the inn. He arrives to find Stella waiting for him. She starts coming on to Chris, making him nervous, so he leaves with her. Max sees them depart together. Stella drives Chris home, but he rebuffs her attempt to invite herself in. Angered, she pulls a pistol on the startled Chris, then laughingly demonstrates the gun is a music-playing toy. Chris, not amused, says "good night."

Johnny is dropped off at the warehouse the next day, and he playfully pulls a gun on Chris. Chris recognizes it as the same one Stella had the night before, and deduces she is "Mr. Straw." Chris confronts Jesse about it, and Jesse flies into a rage. Meanwhile, Stella comes to the warehouse, undoubtedly to see Chris, and George evicts her. On her way out she encounters Johnny and asks him if he knows who she is. Stella embraces him uncontrollably, frightening the lad. He breaks away, saying "I don't like you!" In tears, Stella speeds away in her car.

Stella drives to Chris's boarding house, throwing an embrace on him and asking for his help. Chris learns that Stella is Johnny's mother and that she is under the delusion Chris is her long-lost boyfriend, Owen. Stella wants him to help her get her son back. Realizing that Stella is emotionally ill (amazingly like the character portrayed by Diana Hyland in episode #34), he humors her, instructing her to wait for him at home.

Johnny visits Mr. Straw for today's goodies. Stella suddenly appears, beckoning Johnny to come along with her. Stella takes him home, locking him in her basement and leaving to find "Owen."

Chris meets with George, who is angered by Chris's repeated visits with Stella. Chris tells George that Stella needs professional help, but George does not want to hear about it. George tells Chris that he drummed Owen (a warehouse employee who got Stella pregnant) out of town and arranged for the baby's adoption by the Stansels, thinking that would solve the whole problem. Now, he is drumming Chris out of town: he instructs his receptionist to call the police in one hour, telling them Chris has stolen some merchandise and that he is probably wanted for something else as well. George then calls Max to see to it that Chris leaves on schedule.

Chris goes to his room to pack, and Stella comes knocking at his door. She says she is ready to go and that Johnny is waiting for them. Chris tries to find out what she has done with Johnny. Meanwhile, Max reports to George that Stella is in Chris's room.

George heads for the boarding house. Finding the two of them, he holds

Chris at gunpoint, while Stella pretends she knows nothing about going away with "Owen" or hiding Johnny. Chris, knowing how her mind works, says that if he isn't Owen, then Johnny couldn't be their child. This breaks her facade and sends her into hysterics, convincing George that Chris was right and was trying to help her. The police arrive, and George allows Chris to hide in the closet. He tells police Chris has already left. Chris hops a freight out of town.

George takes Stella to a hospital, where she presumably will get proper care. He then brings Johnny home, apologetically hoping for the opportunity to establish a relationship with the Stansel family. Jesse will allow that, with the proviso that Johnny "doesn't need any more straw men."

Episode #72

STRANGER IN THE MIRROR

Original Airdate: December 7, 1965

Written by: Don Brinkley   Directed by: Joseph Sargent

Cast: William Shatner as Tony Burrell, Julie Sommars as Carole Burrell, Norman Fell as Lt. Ed Green, Tony Face as Benny Bichek, Paul Bryar as Sgt. McKay, Jeff Burton as Berger, Kyle Johnson as Chuck.

Kimble, alias John Evans, is hired as the underpaid custodian of the Saturday Morning Club, a recreational gathering place for young boys in Sona Falls, Washington. Tony and Carole Burrell run the camp. Tony had been a good police officer until recently, when he failed his physical — supposedly because of a heart murmur, but actually because he was pronounced "psychologically unstable" and he refused help. When Tony was eight, his father — also a cop — had shot and killed his mother. After a year in jail, Tony's father was killed by a policeman during a prison riot. Tony grew up in foster homes.

When he learns that Tony was a cop, John tells Carole he may have to leave at the drop of a hat because of a job opportunity "back east." John keeps his bag packed so he can leave quickly, if necessary.

Lt. Green questions Tony about the murder of a police officer last night. Hal Brubaker, whom Tony had visited with earlier, had been killed in the same way as another local officer, Joe Hogan, not long before: his head was bashed in by a rock and his badge was ripped off his uniform. Green asks for Tony's help.

The key suspect is an 18-year-old, cop-hating gangster, Benny. Benny does not deny killing the cop, knowing that suspicion of such a crime will make him a hero among his group. Tony examines the hoodlum and tells the police he doesn't think Benny is guilty.

In his room, John hears footsteps, then a clanking noise. He finds a locked humidor on the floor. Just then Sgt. McKay enters the room, asking John questions. John tells him he heard a prowler, so McKay goes outside to investigate. McKay is ambushed and slain by the serial killer: Tony Burrell.

The next day Tony stays home, not feeling well, so John volunteers to play ball with the kids. John shows the humidor to Carole, who recognizes it as one that had belonged to Tony's father and which she had discarded years ago. Puzzled, she is determined to find out what is inside the box. She returns home and asks Tony if he knows how the box got there and whether he has the key. He gives a double-negative.

John hits some balls to the boys. A stray hit into the weeds finds McKay's body. John calls the police, then Tony. As the cops arrive, John tries to slip away. Green sees this and sends an officer to check on John. Finding his bag packed, the police deem him suspicious. Green asks John to write down the names and addresses of his most recent employers, then confiscates the pencil to have the fingerprints checked.

Carole tries some of Tony's keys on the humidor and finds one that works. She opens the box to find the badges of officers Hogan and Brubaker. Carole wonders if Tony was involved in the murders, but he can't or won't remember any such thing. He decides to question John and heads for the club.

Carole picks up a pair of Tony's soiled slacks, and McKay's badge falls out of a pocket. She realizes he is indeed involved in the murders and goes to the camp to confront him.

Tony finds John preparing to leave, but he detains John and accompanies him inside. All but accusing John of the crimes, Tony pulls out his old police revolver and holds John at gunpoint. Carole arrives with the evidence, and Tony tries to defend himself, becoming irrational. Carole and John piece together the psychological factors which have led Tony to this state of mind.

The police get the fingerprint report on John and speed to the club. Tony wonders why the cops are there, and John tells him they are after the man who killed those officers. Tony breaks a window and fires at officer Berger, wounding him. John knocks the gun away from him, telling Carole to pick it up. John leads Tony to the window to see what he did. Almost hysterical, Tony knocks John down and picks up a dumb-bell. He is about to bash in John's head with it when Carole, pleading with Tony to stop, shoots him in the chest. Tony's last words are "Don't be sore at me, Mommy."

John sneaks out the back of the building but sees backup police units surrounding the place. He turns back and an officer orders him to stop, asking him what he is doing. "I heard some shooting in there," John stammers. The cops assure John they will take care of it, and order him away. Of course, he complies.

Carole philosophizes to Lt. Green: "All those murders ... there was only one man Tony wanted to kill, and I had to do it for him."

Act III: The 1965-66 Season   125

Episode #73
THE GOOD GUYS AND THE BAD GUYS
Original Airdate: December 14, 1965

Written by: Don Brinkley   **Directed by:** Alexander Singer

Cast: Earl Holliman as Charles T. Judd, Collin Wilcox as Laura McElvey, Bruce Dern as Hank, Michael Witney as Roy, Erik Holland as Wally.

Kimble, alias Bill Watkins, is recognized in Drover City (12 miles from Acorn Falls), Montana. Lt. Gerard is notified, and police await Bill's arrival at work in the stockyards the next morning. Bill sees the cops and flees, and Gerard arrives a couple of hours later.

It happens to be the occasion of Drover City's annual "Vigilante Round-Up," July 18–20. Anyone in town not dressed in western-style clothing is considered an "outlaw" and subject to arrest by any of the locals. Whoever gathers up the most outlaws is crowned "chief vigilante," entitling him to privileges such as free meals and tickets. The local high school cafeteria serves as the vigilante headquarters and stockade.

Bill is walking through town when he is accosted by Hank, who happens to be Marshal Charley Judd's deputy. Bill is not aware of the local festival and thinks he is really being arrested. He makes a run for it but is lassoed by Roy and Wally. Charley drives up and is asked to settle the dispute over credit for the arrest. He solicits contributions to his "pension fund" and awards the arrest to the most generous donor. A protesting Bill is then brought to the stockade to be locked up until 6:00.

Hank escorts Gerard to the cafeteria in search of Charley. Bill sees Gerard coming and slips into an office. Roy tries to arrest Gerard, who is not amused. Gerard is given a cowboy hat to avoid further harassment, and he leaves.

Gerard finally finds Charley and shows him Kimble's picture. Charley says Kimble looks familiar, but he can't remember where he has seen him before. Gerard soon becomes annoyed with Charley's lax treatment of the manhunt and his general attitude of putting the situation ahead of the law. Charley has equal disdain for Gerard's gung-ho spirit.

Charley visits the stockade to reexamine the outlaw. Charley toys with him, letting him know he is on to Kimble's identity, and asks about Gerard. He handcuffs Kimble to a pipe in the office and schemes with Laura, his perennial fiancée, on the next step. He convinces Laura that the big reward (which surely accompanies Kimble's capture) will finance their long-awaited wedding. First they must get rid of Gerard, so Charley can claim the entire reward. Laura appeals against the scheme, but Charley is calling the shots.

Laura hates Drover City and its silly customs. She knows Charley is no good but figures she could do no better at this stage of her life. Her "engagement" to

Charley is the subject of constant snickering among the locals, who know he is just stringing her along.

Laura must hide Kimble so Charley won't get caught in the conspiracy. Under pretense of helping him escape, she unlocks Kimble's cuffs and sneaks him out the back door. She takes him to the marshal's office and forces him into historic "Jack Slade's Cell" at gunpoint. Meanwhile, Charley calls the state police with a bogus report of a Kimble sighting. He also asks them to check on the amount of Kimble's reward.

Gerard shows the photo to Hank, who recognizes Kimble as the man Charley sent to the stockade. Gerard now knows Charley has lied to him, and he hurries to the cafeteria. He finds only an empty room and heads for the marshal's office.

Kimble talks with Laura, pointing out that Charley gambled with her life by leaving her in charge of a convicted murderer. He tells Laura she deserves better than Charley, advising her not to sell herself short. Kimble also tells her he is innocent and that there is no reward for his capture.

Gerard arrives at the office but doesn't see Kimble. He tells Laura that Charley faces charges of impeding justice and dispensing false information and won't have his badge much longer. After Gerard leaves, Laura realizes that he would have no case without Kimble as a witness.

Gerard finds and confronts Charley, who tries to bargain with Gerard on the distribution of the reward money. Gerard threatens Charley and orders him to take Gerard to Kimble. They head back to the marshal's office.

The state police call the office and tell Laura that Kimble's capture carries no reward. At this, Laura releases the prisoner. As they exit the building Charley and Gerard pull in, and Laura quickly hides Kimble in the back seat of her car.

When Charley sees that Kimble is gone he slaps Laura, calling her a "used-up old maid." Laura tearfully explains that she released Kimble to protect Charley, and he becomes apologetic. Gerard arrests Charley, but Charley smugly points out that Gerard has no witnesses. Laura dramatically announces that she will testify against Charley. Charley is locked up, with Hank left in charge.

With Kimble still in the car, Laura drives off, bringing him to safety. "I guess maybe we both just escaped," she remarks.

Episode #74
END OF THE LINE
Original Airdate: December 21, 1965

Written by: James Menzies   **Directed by:** William A. Graham

Cast: Andrew Prine as Neil Hollis, Barbara Dana as Betty Jo Unger, Crahan Denton as Roy T. Unger, Richard Roat as Glenn, Len Wayland as Chief Bill Kress,

James Hong as Edward Hee, James McCallion as Sammy, Eddie Firestone as taxi driver, Jon Lormer as conductor, Ted Gehring as truck driver.

Kimble, alias Bob Mossman, hitches a ride on Route 23. When the dozing Bob realizes the truck is entering the Florida State Prison grounds in Raiford, he hurriedly disembarks, leaving behind his wallet. He hops on a train at the nearby station, finding himself in a car full of policemen going home from work. When the conductor comes to collect the $2.25 fare, Bob realizes his wallet is gone. He goes into the men's room, hoping to find an exit or a way to avoid a scene amidst the cops. Passenger Roy T. Unger is there, having left his jacket hanging outside the stall he occupies. Bob, desperate, removes Roy's wallet from the jacket and heads back to his seat to pay the fare. He finds that the monogrammed wallet contains four $20 bills.

Having overcome one crisis, Bob tries to find a way to return the man's wallet with a promise to repay what he "borrowed." He can't very well do it on the train, so he tries to approach Roy after they get off at the first stop, Fort Scott. Roy is greeted by a policeman there, however, foiling Bob's plan. Roy doesn't realize his wallet is missing until he gets home. He remembers the man approaching him after they got off the train, and figures Bob stole his wallet. Roy reports the theft, describing Bob to the police.

Bob takes a $1.25 per hour job as a dishwasher at Hee's Rice Bowl, a Cantonese restaurant. He works four hours, earning enough to replenish the money he spent. He then begins a search for the wallet's owner, armed with Roy's description and initials. A cabdriver gives Bob directions to Roy's home.

Bob goes to the Unger house, encountering Roy's pregnant daughter, Betty Jo. Her boyfriend, Neil, is to be released from prison today, and Betty Jo hopes the two can now get married and raise their child. Bob returns the wallet to a suspicious Betty Jo and leaves. After a telephone argument with her father, Betty Jo decides to pocket the money and take off with Neil, contrary to her father's wishes.

Neil comes to town and calls Roy. Roy offers Neil $1,000 to get out of his daughter's life, and Neil agrees to meet Roy at the Fort Scott Dairy, which Roy owns.

Hee puts Bob back to work, asking him to deliver empty milk bottles back to the dairy across the street. As Bob walks there, he notices Betty Jo disembarking from a cab at the nearby train station and paying the driver out of her father's wallet. He stops to talk to her, wanting to make sure she returns the wallet to her father. Bob admits he can't go to the police to report her. Betty Jo deduces he is in trouble with the law and stores that fact for future reference. She enters the station and Bob continues to the dairy.

Roy gives Neil a dairy stationery envelope containing $500, promising the other $500 after the baby is born. Neil doesn't like this deal so he cracks Roy over the head with a milk bottle. Bob enters, unseen by Neil, just in time to witness the murder, then rushes to the station to tell Betty Jo her father is dead.

She runs into the dairy to find Neil dragging away the body. Neil claims he killed her father in self-defense. He tells Betty Jo he will have to hide out, but that everything will work out just fine if she covers for him.

A cop recognizes Bob as matching the wallet thief's description and takes Bob in for questioning. After an escape attempt, Bob is handcuffed. After Roy's body is discovered, the police chief goes to the Unger house, finding Neil wearing milk-stained pants and Roy's sweater. Neil is brought in to be booked.

On Tuesday, June 9, Betty Jo bursts into police headquarters, claiming she murdered her father in a moment of rage. She is protecting Neil, knowing that a pregnant orphan will get off a lot easier than an ex-con. She also wants to get the only witness out of there and tells police that Bob returned the wallet.

Bob asks to speak to Betty Jo alone and is granted five minutes. He tries to convince her that she is foolish to protect Neil and that her baby deserves to be born out of jail. Betty Jo refuses his advice, warning "Sam" that she will "make so much noise" to the police if he tries to interfere. Bob and Neil are both released, but a deputy is sent to keep an eye on Neil.

Bob goes to the Unger house, finding Neil stashing away the money envelope. A fistfight ensues, and Bob gets the envelope away from Neil just as the deputy arrives. Bob turns the evidence over to the deputy, who then drops Bob off at the train station and brings Neil back into custody. Betty Jo, realizing Neil would have taken the money and vanished, slaps Neil in the face and asks the deputy for a ride home.

Episode #75
WHEN THE WIND BLOWS
Original Airdate: December 28, 1965

Written by: Betty Langdon **Directed by:** Ralph Senensky

Cast: Johnny Jensen as Kenny Carter, Georgann Johnson as Lois Carter, Harry Townes as Russ Atkinson, Larry Ward as Steve Jackson, Don Hanmer as Jake Wilkins, Gregory Mullavy as Carl Ritter, George Brenlin as Will, E. A. Nicholson as Wally, Elmer Modlin as postman, Don Saroyan as officer.

Kimble, alias Jim McGuire, eats at a Smallgroves, Wyoming, cafe (eggs, toast and coffee for 61 cents), when the postman delivers a package there for constable Jake Wilkins. It is a "wanted" poster on Kimble, distributed countywide after rumors the fugitive had been spotted in Casper. Jim departs, hitching a ride with trucker Carl Ritter, just moments before Jake opens the package and sees a picture of his last customer. Jake calls the county sheriff's office at Taggert City but is told the sheriff is out. Jake decides to forget the sheriff and pursue Kimble on his own, perhaps earning a promotion for the fugitive's capture.

Carl drops Jim off about ten miles east of the cafe. Jim notices a "help wanted" sign at a nearby motel and inquires about the job. Lois Carter offers him $20 per week plus meals and board to work as a temporary handyman, helping to get the motel ready for the season.

Jim meets Lois's son Kenny, an unusual child. Kenny describes eggs as "ideas for birds," and laments how the wind keeps blowing down the bird's nest. Jim promises to help Kenny build a birdhouse. Kenny, who rarely gets close to anyone, takes a liking to Jim, telling his mother "Mr. McGuire is my friend."

Kenny and Lois return from a teacher's conference. Jim asks Lois why she seems upset, and she relates her continual difficulties with Kenny. Kenny is labeled a "problem child," and Lois doesn't know how to communicate or deal with him. The two have moved from place to place, encountering the same problems wherever they go. Jim comforts Lois by saying he finds Kenny bright and alert.

Russ, the sheriff's deputy, questions Jake about his encounter with Kimble. Jake says he was mistaken in recognizing the fugitive, but it is decided to run Kimble's picture in the *Smallgroves Clarion*, with the front-page headline "Murderer Sought in County."

After Jim and Kenny put up the birdhouse on Saturday, Kenny invites Jim into his special place, a small cave. Kenny had never invited even his mother into the hideaway. Kenny shows Jim his "dead things": toys and clothing that have outlived their usefulness.

Steve Jackson, Lois's suitor, drops by the motel. He brings Kenny a fishing rod and invites the lad to go fishing with him. They go, but Kenny is upset by the ritual. Kenny, describing how he "felt the fish scream" and saw it "drowning in the air," throws a fish back into the water. Steve brings Kenny home, telling Lois the boy is not normal. Lois angrily sends Steve away.

Lois recognizes Jim's picture in the paper about the same time as Carl does. Carl tells Russ and Jake where he let Kimble off, and the lawmen head out there. When Lois sees them coming she tells Kenny to warn Jim to hide; otherwise the men will hurt him. Kenny takes Jim to his cave while Lois tells Russ and Jake she hasn't seen Kimble. Their search of the premises turns up nothing, and they leave.

Lois finds Jim and explains why she protected him: he is a children's doctor whom her son seems to need and respond to. Jim invites Lois into the cave to see Kenny's private world. He advises her to stop worrying about his difference, stop running, ask questions, and encourage Kenny to abandon his hideaway. Jim points out that Kenny is "an original" and just might wind up becoming someone very special.

Jim goes to leave, hitching a ride with a trucker stopped at a gas station. Kenny sees him leaving and, not ready for him to go, climbs into the back of the truck. When Jim gets off, Kenny jumps out to join him. Jim takes Kenny into a vacant building, trying to explain why Kenny can't stay with him.

Steve, in the cafe with Russ and Jake, recognizes the newspaper picture. The three rush to the motel to find Lois alone. Steve stays with Lois, Jake leaves, and Russ, suspicious, waits in his car nearby. Jim calls Lois, telling her where he and Kenny are. Lois convinces Steve to help her cover for Kimble.

Lois drives off in the wrong direction, with Russ in pursuit. While she decoys Russ, Steve drives to the building to pick up Kenny. As Steve drives Kenny home, he tries to be more understanding of the child, and the two begin to establish a relationship. Meanwhile, Kimble is presumably well on his way to safety.

Episode #76
NOT WITH A WHIMPER
Original Airdate: January 4, 1966

Written by: Norman Lessing   **Directed by:** Alexander Singer

Cast: Laurence Naismith as Dr. Andrew Emmett "Mack" McCallister, Lee Meriwether as Willis Hempstead, Audrey Christie as Nurse Murdock, Jimmy Stiles as Joey Anderson, Jack Dodson as lieutenant, Joseph Perry as counterman, Garrison True as Pete, Marcelle Hebert as teacher.

Kimble is dropped off at Hempstead Mills, West Virginia, home of his mentor, Dr. McCallister. Mack, who taught Kimble at medical school and gave him a job, is hospitalized with a fatal heart condition. Kimble reads a newspaper article about Mack's condition and gets directions to the hospital from a diner employee. The man recognizes Kimble's face from one of his magazines and later finds his picture in a copy of *Fighting Crime*. He calls police to tell them Kimble is visiting McCallister at the hospital.

Kimble is greeted by Murdock, Mack's long-time personal nurse. Murdock feels Kimble's visit will agitate Mack's condition, but Kimble insists. The two doctors have deep admiration for one another.

McCallister has devoted much of his life trying to prove the deadliness of smog. He moved eight years ago to this industrial town rife with it. The main offender, and target of Mack's most energetic crusades, is a plant operated by George Hempstead. Ironically, George's daughter Willis is Mack's most avid disciple, fighting for her beliefs in spite of family interests. However, McCallister has begun to "lose it" mentally, a side-effect of his physical condition, and his crusades have become less rational.

The police arrive and Murdock warns Kimble. He hides while Mack tells them that Kimble called but did not visit. The cops leave and Willis drops by. Mack introduces Kimble as Dr. Richard Spalding and asks Willis to drive the doctor to Mack's home. He also asks her to deliver a decoratively-wrapped "present" — supposedly an "accurate smog-measuring device" but actually a time-bomb — to the lab of Hempstead's plant. The bomb is set to detonate at noon the next day, Saturday. Mack wants to deliver a powerful message but at a time when no people are liable to be injured.

Willis and Kimble stop at the factory to drop off the package. Willis mentions that she is escorting a fifth grade class on a field trip, which will take them to the factory at 11 A.M. tomorrow.

McCallister returns home Saturday morning. A cop stops to ask whether he has heard any more from Kimble, who hadn't passed through the roadblocks and thus must still be in town. Mack denies it.

Mack philosophizes to Kimble about public fear of an atomic bomb that may never come, while pollution quietly kills millions. Quoting T. S. Eliot, he says, "This is the way the world ends: not with a bang, but a whimper." Kimble mentions the field trip, and Mack is aghast. His heart begins acting up, bringing Murdock to his aid. Murdock has learned about the bomb and wants to call the police, but Mack overrules her. Murdock tells Kimble about the bomb and instructs him to evacuate the building and retrieve it.

Kimble takes Murdock's car and arrives at the factory at 11:22 A.M. Without explaining why, he forces Willis to evacuate the building. One child is unaccounted for. Joey, an inquisitive and undisciplined boy, wanders around the plant inspecting anything that looks appealing. He has found the attractive package and intends to take it home. When Kimble realizes the package is missing, he figures he will not have time to find the bomb and bring it back to Mack. He phones the doctor for instructions to dismantle the bomb. Mack warns Kimble that, in the final minutes before noon, even a vibration or loud noise could bring the contact wires together, causing detonation. Murdock drives Mack to the scene and calls the police at 11:44.

Kimble finally finds Joey, but the boy — thinking he will be in trouble — won't let Kimble near him. Kimble finally corners him in the lab and gets him to leave the package on a table. Joey flees the room, locking it behind him with the fire bar at 11:53.

Kimble tries to unwrap the package so he can get at the bomb. Mack takes to the building's P.A. system, telling Kimble to get out of the building before it is too late. Kimble finds that he is locked in and has one minute to save himself somehow. He drops the package into a full barrel of oil, defusing the bomb.

Kimble opens the door with a coat hanger just as the police arrive en masse. They suspect the man in the building is Kimble. Kimble takes some lab apparatus, including an egg-timer and some beakers of chemicals, to craft a phony bomb. He leaves the building carrying the contraption, which Mack claims is the bomb he made, and ordering the police to keep away from him.

Kimble instructs Willis to drive him away, and the police have no choice but to let them go.

As Kimble is brought to safety he is about to discard the bogus bomb, but Willis stops him. She wants to bring it back with her to prove that neither McCallister nor Kimble is really that dangerous.

Episode #77
WIFE KILLER
Original Airdate: January 11, 1966

Written by: Dan Ullman **Directed by:** Richard Donner

Cast: Janice Rule as Barbara Webb, Kevin McCarthy as Herb Malone, Lloyd Haynes as Ed Warren, Bill Raisch as Fred Johnson, Stephen Roberts as Chief Blaney, Charles McDaniel as Nurse Cassidy, Steve Wolfson and John Luce as reporters.

Barbara Webb arrives at Baker City, Michigan. She had formerly worked as a reporter for the *Baker City Herald* but was fired three years earlier by her boss and lover, Herb Malone. He disapproved of her methods, which sometimes crossed the lines of professional ethics, but he never lost his personal affection toward Barbara. She now works for a wire service in Dayton and is here to cover the murder of a congressman's wife. Barbara and Herb greet each other warmly.

The two walk past police headquarters. Chief Blaney is so fanatical about apprehending even the most minor offenders that his prisoner population has far outgrown the prison. It has become necessary to fence in the station's parking lot to accommodate all the law-breakers, one of whom happens to be the one-armed murderer of Helen Kimble. Barbara sees him and her reporter's instincts take over; she photographs the man and sends the shot through the wires. Thursday's newspapers show the picture, with captions such as "Kimble's One-Armed Man?" Kimble and Lt. Gerard are drawn to Baker City from different directions.

Kimble arrives and scopes out the prison grounds. The one-armed man is shocked to see Kimble and flees inside the station, from which he is about to be released anyway. Kimble waits near the entrance to catch the man on his way out, but he instead returns outside and scales the fence to escape. With Kimble chasing on foot, the man finds a car with keys in the ignition and drives off. Barbara is nearby and recognizes Kimble. Quickly sizing up the situation, she runs to her car, calling Kimble to accompany her. The two take off after the one-armed man, much to Herb's disapproval.

Barbara chases the man through winding mountain roads, which she knows well. Unnerved by the pursuit, the one-armed man loses control of his car and plunges down the mountainside. The car flips over and the driver is thrown clear. Barbara parks, and she and Kimble rush down to check on the unconscious man. Kimble determines he is in shock and has a concussion, along with possible internal injuries. Janice drives them to an abandoned girls' camp with cots and first-aid supplies, so Kimble can attend to him.

Barbara takes more than thirty photos as Kimble administers aid to the man. Checking his effects, Kimble at last learns the name of his quarry: Fred Johnson, age 47. Kimble convinces Barbara to get him some necessary medical supplies. She is afraid he will leave and she will lose her exclusive story, but Kimble points out the story will be better if Johnson survives.

Gerard has arrived in town and talked with Herb and the police. Gerard suspects Barbara is the mysterious woman who drove off with the man he assumes to be Kimble, but Herb protects his old flame by refusing to corroborate this fact. Officer Warren reports that Barbara was seen returning to her hotel, and he and Gerard head there to keep an eye on her. The two follow Barbara as she drives to Herb's office. She tells him she is onto the "biggest story of my life" but is being followed. She arranges to switch cars with Herb. He drives off, followed by Warren and Gerard; then she returns to the camp unpursued.

Johnson, on an I.V., regains consciousness, and he and Kimble are face-to-face (without the protection of glass or amnesia) for the first time. Kimble, vowing to do all he can to save Johnson, asks for the truth: "Did you kill my wife?" Johnson nods slowly but emphatically, with Barbara witnessing, and Kimble slumps into a cot, drained. He has not slept in the two days since he saw the newspaper article.

Barbara convinces Kimble to nap while she watches Johnson, unconscious again. While Kimble dozes, Barbara types out a confession for Johnson to sign. Johnson awakens and tries to get away, but collapses on the floor. Barbara asks if he will sign the confession, and he nods but, just as he is about to sign, faints. Barbara finds no pulse and is terrified she has lost a great story. She decides to forge Johnson's signature, copying it from his blood donor card. She practices on scrap paper before signing Johnson's name on the confession. She then wakes Kimble, telling him that Johnson is dead but that he signed the confession. Johnson's groan belies her diagnosis.

Gerard confronts Herb, who is not intimidated. He warns Herb that Barbara will be in serious trouble if she is abetting Kimble. Herb wonders why Gerard would be drawn in by a one-armed man, if he believes Kimble's story is false. Gerard says psychiatrists have advised him that Kimble may have come to believe his delusion as the "only way he can live with his own conscience."

Kimble has Barbara call for medical help on the C.B. radio. He knows the police will follow, but is willing to turn himself in with Johnson in custody, too. Kimble then discovers Barbara's forgery practice-sheet and realizes the confession is worthless. He leaves, saying he will get in touch with Gerard later. He hides nearby as the camp is stormed by Gerard, Herb, police, and an ambulance. Herb takes the camera away from Barbara, furtively removing the film. Gerard arrests Barbara but will have no case against her.

Johnson, in remarkably good shape, escapes the hospital after overpowering his attendant. Kimble calls Gerard, learning he is just as much a fugitive as ever.

Episode #78
THIS'LL KILL YOU
Original Airdate: January 18, 1966

Written by: George Eckstein **Directed by:** Alex March

Cast: Mickey Rooney as Henry Aldridge A.K.A. Charlie Paris, Nita Talbot as Paula Jellison, Phillip Pine as Pete Ragan, George Tyne as Sgt. Thorpe, Henry Scott as Harrison, Naomi Stevens as gypsy, William Wintersole as desk clerk, Allen Joseph as enforcer, Richard Gilden as Bracken, Don Ross as driver, Carol Allen as Mrs. Belson, Dani Nolan as woman.

Kimble, alias Nick Phillips, has worked at Charlie Paris's Priority Laundromat in New York for the past five weeks. Charlie, a former night-club comedian with a joke for every occasion, considers Nick his good luck charm: since Nick arrived business has been good, Charlie has kept away from gamblers and jail, and he is about to reunite with his long-lost girlfriend, Paula. Nick is equally fond of Charlie.

Sgt. Thorpe makes his periodic visit to the laundromat, checking whether Charlie has resumed any illegal activities. Thorpe thinks Nick looks familiar and later confirms it with the station's "wanted" posters.

Paula is due at the Maxwell Hotel, and Charlie sends Nick to leave a gift for her. Nick stops at the hotel bar and is hit on by an attractive woman. Nick brushes her off, not realizing the woman is Paula.

Charlie is nervous about his big reunion with Paula, to whom he plans to propose. Paula drives in, but she is followed by Pete Ragan, a syndicate man. Charlie had once been called in as a witness by the New York Crime Commission, and his testimony—about overheard conversations involving the syndicate—was enough to put a price on his head. Ragan is there to locate Charlie and set up the hit.

Charlie sends Nick out to decoy Ragan. Nick gets in Paula's car and they drive off. Paula flirts some more with Nick, who is disgusted with the behavior of someone who means so much to Charlie. After Nick leaves, Ragan visits Paula's room, offering her $5,000 if she can tell him where Charlie is. Paula rebuffs Ragan but makes a note of his room number.

Charlie finally meets Paula the next day. He had led Paula to believe he was wealthy but now confesses he is broke. Disheartened, she says she is, too.

Charlie suggests they shake Ragan and go to California together. Later, Paula approaches Ragan with a counteroffer: she will sell out Charlie for $7,500. Ragan figures the raise entitles him to some liberties with Paula, and he bruises her in the process.

Thorpe returns to the laundromat, asking Charlie where Nick is. Charlie covers for Nick, saying he took off. Thorpe says he will return tomorrow. Nick returns from a delivery, and Charlie tells him about the visit. Nick will have to leave, but Charlie asks him one last favor: to deliver an envelope, containing $100, to Paula. Nick goes to the hotel and sees Paula sitting at a bar table with Ragan. He realizes what is going on and returns to Charlie's hotel to warn him. Charlie refuses to believe Nick and throws him out. On his way out Nick runs into Paula. "I hope you got a good price," he remarks, leading Paula to slap Nick and to develop some feelings of guilt.

Charlie confronts Paula with Nick's accusation. Paula denies it, showing her bruises as proof that Nick tried to force himself on her. Enraged, Charlie phones Thorpe, advising him that Nick is on his way to the laundromat. Moments later, Charlie discovers the payoff money in Paula's purse and realizes Nick was telling the truth. He races off to try and protect Nick from the police. Ragan and his enforcer follow.

Nick is packing in his room above the laundromat when Thorpe and another officer come and cover the exits. Charlie pulls up and heads for the entrance. Ragan's man then guns down Charlie in the street, bringing the cops out of the building. Paula pulls up in a cab and runs to her dying ex-beau. His last words are, "I can't think of anything funny." In the excitement, Nick slips away to safety. Nick later hitches a ride with a trucker and hears over the radio that Charlie's assailants were apprehended.

Episode #79
ECHO OF A NIGHTMARE
Original Airdate: January 25, 1966

Story by: Robert Lewin **Teleplay by:** John Kneubuhl
Directed by: James Sheldon

Cast: Shirley Knight as Jane Washburn, Ford Rainey as Lt. C. Wynn, Arch Johnson as Mitch Jackson, Elizabeth Fraser as Millie Jackson, John Lasell as Mr. Cramer, Dennis Joel Olivieri as Wes Cramer, Kevin O'Neal as Perry Jackson, Harry Millard as Harry, Paul Lukather as Barney, Hugh Sanders as Al, Marc Winters as Marc.

Kimble is being paid by his employer at the Sugar Bowl, a teenager hangout in the southwestern U.S. Four teens see Kimble receiving the wad of bills and get an idea. They follow Kimble in their car, stop, and rob him. Two police officers, Harry and Jane, witness the mugging. Harry rushes to the scene, getting just the car's plate number, while Jane, in plain clothes, is suspicious when she sees Kimble sneaking away. She follows him into a restaurant and confronts him, saying she is a concerned citizen upset about the mugging. Kimble, giving the name Richard Taylor, says he lost only $12 in the robbery and has to catch the 2:00 plane to Denver, where a job awaits him. Jane calls headquarters to learn that the thugs have been apprehended and that their take was $112; she also knows there is no 2:00 flight to Denver. Kimble goes to leave, but Jane offers him a ride to the airport.

In the car, Jane furtively slips handcuffs on Kimble, physically joining the two. A struggle causes her to lose control of her car, which screeches to a halt and won't restart. Jane throws the handcuff key into a creek and intends to walk Kimble to headquarters. Kimble has other ideas and begins towing Jane through the countryside. Meanwhile, one of the muggers has identified Kimble from a mug-shot book.

Kimble and Jane approach a passing freight train; Kimble throws her over his shoulder and jumps aboard. They remain on the train for some time, during which Jane dozes and has a nightmare. As they near Redlands, Kimble leads a jump out of the train, with Jane breaking her ankle in the process. As Kimble attends to her, Jane realizes he is the doctor wanted for murder she saw in a recent state-wide bulletin. Kimble gags Jane and carries her to the next stop.

The two approach the Jackson home, whose residents are on their way to a boxing event. Kimble finds an old hacksaw in the barn and finally succeeds in cutting the chain linking the handcuffs (rhetorical question: why didn't he just cut his own cuff?). He carries Jane to the house, breaking into it. Jane remarks that "You don't have to be a murderer to kill somebody," and Kimble tells her he didn't kill anybody.

Kimble cuts the phone lines and carries Jane to a bed, making a splint for her ankle. Jane, figuring she will never again see Kimble, decides this is a good time to unburden herself of something that has tortured her conscience for many years. At age 15, she says, she was kidnapped and violated by a man. She managed to get hold of a hammer and beat the man over and over with it. Her widowed father, a cop, found them in the barn. Not wanting his beloved daughter to face any consequences, the father took the blame for the killing. He was dismissed from the police force and, heartbroken, died some time later.

The Jacksons have had a family argument and left the boxing event almost as soon as it started. Kimble, unprepared for their early return, looks for a way to escape. Jane tries to follow him but collapses, unconscious. Kimble brings her back to the bed, where he is discovered by the Jacksons. Mr. Jackson sees the cut phone lines and handcuffs and deduces these are the fugitive and policewoman they heard about on the car radio. A fistfight between Jackson and Kimble ensues, until Mrs. Jackson pulls a shotgun. Mr. Jackson takes the gun and instructs his wife and son to go to a nearby farm and call the police. Having ideas of taking justice into his own hands, Mr. Jackson orders Kimble outside. Jane intervenes, grabbing the gun as Kimble pushes down Jackson, knocking him out. Jane holds the gun on Kimble, but he gambles that she won't shoot him. He walks out to safety and hops another freight, filing off his cuff during the ride.

Jane turns in her badge, confessing not only her failure to stop Kimble but also her long-ago murder. Her lieutenant refuses her resignation, telling her to take a week off before making any decision.

Episode #80
STROKE OF GENIUS
Original Airdate: February 1, 1966

Written by: John Kneubuhl   Directed by: Robert Butler

Cast: Telly Savalas as S. Keller, Beau Bridges as Gary Keller, Malcolm Atterbury as Sheriff Harry Bilson, Gene Iglesias as George, Ellen Corby as Mrs. Barlow, Argentina Brunetti as Mexican woman, Olan Soule as Chet Carter, Don Eitner as officer, Martin Priest as guard, George Savalas as prisoner.

Kimble, alias Frank Whistler, meets the elderly Rev. Barlow at a Santa Elena, New Mexico, diner. Barlow had stopped there to borrow Chet's jeep for a fishing excursion. Kimble hitches a ride with Barlow, who offers him a job fixing up his fishing cabin on High Peak Road. Barlow gives Kimble a key to the cabin.

Gary Keller absent-mindedly aims his rifle at hypothetical targets. He accidentally pulls the trigger as he points at a passing jeep, striking the driver, his dear friend Rev. Barlow. The jeep goes out of control, flipping over and throwing the passengers. Barlow is dead, Kimble injured with a torn muscle in his right arm. Gary and his father rush to the scene, while Kimble limps away after getting a glimpse of the two. Kimble stops to instruct a woman to call the police, then continues on foot to the fishing cabin. Along the way he encounters a group of prisoners on work duty and a disabled school bus full of deaf children.

Chet tells the police about Barlow's companion and identifies Kimble from a "wanted" poster. The cops theorize that Kimble murdered Barlow, and they call Lt. Gerard in nearby Mayersburg, where Kimble had recently been spotted.

Mr. Keller has great plans for his artistically talented young son, and does not want them derailed by a manslaughter arrest. He orders Gary not to confess, but Gary is having a hard time with his conscience. The sheriff calls Keller in for a few questions, then deputizes him to help in the manhunt. Keller worries that Kimble will be able to identify him and his son and leaves (armed with a rifle) to search for Kimble.

Gerard arrives. He can't believe Kimble killed Barlow and realizes he will have a difficult time extraditing Kimble if he is accused of this murder. Gerard notices there is no cabin key among Barlow's personal effects and decides to go to the cabin.

Kimble gets to the cabin, followed shortly after by Keller. Keller holds Kimble at gunpoint, questioning him about what he saw after the accident. Kimble says he saw a man and boy, perhaps involved in the shooting. Keller blurts out that it was a freak accident, the boy didn't mean to shoot, and that Keller doesn't want the boy to get into trouble. He wants Kimble to get away, but Gerard arrives, so Keller must pretend Kimble is his prisoner. He warns Kimble that if he says anything about "a man and a boy," Keller will kill both Kimble and Gerard. Kimble gives Gerard an abridged version of what happened.

Gary visits Mrs. Barlow, who tells him how much the Reverend liked and admired Gary. She tells him her husband had secretly applied, on Gary's behalf, for a $5,000 grant to study art in Europe. The acceptance letter had arrived minutes after the Reverend left on his fatal trip. Gary, overcome with remorse, breaks down.

Gerard, Keller, and Kimble walk toward Gerard's car. As Gerard calls in to headquarters on his car radio, Keller points the rifle at Gerard and is about to fire. Kimble pushes Keller to the ground as his rifle goes off, wounding Gerard. Kimble scampers away through the mountains as Gerard recovers and pulls his pistol, holding Keller. Just then a dispatch comes over the radio: Gary has confessed to the shooting.

At headquarters, Gary apologizes to his father, who doesn't blame his son. The sheriff remarks that Gary will get off a lot easier than his father.

Episode #81
SHADOW OF THE SWAN
Original Airdate: February 8, 1966

Written by: Anthony Lawrence   **Directed by:** James Sheldon

Cast: Joanna Pettet as Tina Andresen, Andrew Duggan as Harry Andresen, David Sheiner as Lt. Lou Jacobs, Don Quine as carny, Ken Lynch as Lenny, Monroe Arnold as Dr. Motter, Carole Kane as carny's wife, Shirley O'Hara as landlady, William Woodson as carnival barker, Robert Dornan as doctor.

Twenty-two-year-old Tina visits a neighborhood carnival and is hit on by a sleazy carny. They flirt until the concession owner breaks it up. Tina walks to a nearby lake, where she feeds the ducks and admires the swan. Kimble, alias Paul Keller, also goes to the lake, releasing a goldfish he had won at the carnival. They meet, and Tina is immediately attracted to Paul (as she is to 'most anything in pants). He mentions he is looking for work, and she tells him about a job opening at the veterinary hospital where she works. Tina escorts Paul to the hospital, where Dr. Motter offers him the $50-per-week job of kennel man. He accepts, replacing Jerry, who was fired for stealing (a crime Tina actually committed).

After work, Tina and Paul return to the carnival. The carny hits on Tina again and drags her into a tent. Her screams bring Paul to the rescue, and a fistfight ensues. Tina brings Paul home to get first aid.

Tina lives with her uncle Harry, a former cop. He has raised Tina since she was ten, when her parents died in a fire. Harry, a suspicious and over-protective guardian, scolds Tina for getting involved in yet another incident. One such affair had cost Harry his job after he nearly killed the man who had troubled his niece. After Paul leaves, Harry contacts Lou, his friend on the police force. He reports the incident and, having a hunch about Paul, arranges to check the mug-shot files the next morning. Lou is skeptical about Harry's hunch, knowing his history of overreaction involving Tina and of interference with police business.

Harry finds Kimble's mug-shot, and he and Lou rush to the hospital. Paul sees them coming and departs, asking Tina to cover for him. Tina says Paul isn't Kimble, and Lou is inclined to believe her.

Tina goes to Paul's boarding house, finding him packing to leave. She asks Paul to take her with him, saying she thinks she is in love with him. Paul tells Tina to go home, enraging her. She tells her uncle where Paul is, and Harry calls Lou. Told to forget his delusion, Harry takes matters into his own hands, much to Tina's delight. Harry loads his revolver and leaves.

Paul is about to leave when his phone rings. It is Tina, stalling him to give her uncle time to get there. She tells Paul she plans to run off with the carny tonight, then hangs up when she hears a knock at Paul's door. The visitor is Paul's landlady, who tells Paul the bus will arrive in five minutes and that it does go by the carnival. Paul wants to stop there to save Tina from a life-ruining mistake. Harry arrives seconds after Paul boards the bus, and the landlady tells Harry that Paul is bound for the carnival.

Tina visits the carny in his trailer. The two make out until the carny's wife appears, breaking it up. While the couple argues, Tina knocks over a gas stove, setting fire to the trailer, and locks the door behind her. Police are called to the scene and the couple is rescued. Paul finds out that Tina committed the arson, and goes to look for her.

Paul finds Tina at the lake. Tina embraces Paul just as Harry arrives. Harry holds Paul at gunpoint, telling Tina to get Lou. Paul tells Harry the police are looking for Tina because she started the fire; she denies it, saying she saw Paul start it. Harry, knowing Paul was still home at the time the fire started, realizes Tina is lying. He suddenly recalls the fire that killed Tina's parents and tells his niece, "I'm taking you in." She resists and the two fall into the lake, with Harry's gun discharging. Paul rushes to help, but Tina has been mortally wounded. She dies in Harry's arms, and he is too preoccupied to notice Paul slip away. Police, alerted by the shot, rush to the scene, ignoring Paul, whom they have no reason to suspect. Paul hops a freight and escapes.

Episode #82
RUNNING SCARED
Original Airdate: February 22, 1966

Written by: Don Brinkley   **Directed by:** James Sheldon

Cast: Jacqueline Scott as Donna Kimble Taft, Lin McCarthy as Leonard Taft, Joanne Linville as Harriet Ballinger, James Daly as Michael Ballinger, Wright King as Joe Penny, Frank Maxwell as Det.-Sgt. Burns, Tommy Alexander as bellhop, Ira Barmak as airline clerk, Arch Whiting as Reynolds.

Kimble learns that his father, Dr. John Kimble, has died. He had suffered his first heart attack right after his son's trial and had deteriorated ever since. Kimble calls his sister, Donna, whose house is being staked out by "Gerard's watchdogs." The siblings are anxious to see each other and arrange to meet at the Harwood Hotel in Ft. Wayne, Indiana, where Donna and her husband, Len, will register as the Townsends.

Donna and Len manage to shake Gerard's men through convoluted travel plans. At the Indianapolis Airport, Donna is recognized by Harriet Ballinger. Her husband, Mike, was the prosecuting attorney in the Kimble trial, and his victory had launched his political career. Mike, aided by campaign manager Joe, is now running for governor. Harriet despises what politics have done to her husband, turning him into a pill-popping, self-centered, obsessive man. Harriet points out Donna to her husband. Joe, noting that she is traveling under an assumed name, theorizes that Donna is meeting her brother. Joe reasons that Kimble's capture, with Mike visibly involved, would virtually clinch the election. Harriet strongly disapproves, and is sorry she pointed out Donna. Joe phones Gerard.

Donna and Len arrive separately at the hotel. Sgt. Burns listens in as Kimble phones his sister there, saying he will meet her at 7:00. Gerard arrives, and he and Burns set up a dragnet at the hotel. Harriet also arrives there, sees what is going on, and delivers a note to Donna: "Police are watching—be careful." Len intends to intercept Kimble, but Burns follows Len outside and suggests that he return in.

Kimble walks toward the hotel and sees the cop talking to Len. Kimble slips into an alley, where Harriet drives up and calls to him. She offers her help, and he skeptically goes with her. Harriet takes him to her hotel room, explaining her motivation: she does not want Mike to become governor because his political career is ruining their marriage. Kimble remarks that "harboring a fugitive, in some circles, is considered a much worse crime than being governor." Kimble says he is not leaving until he sees Donna, who Harriet says appears thin and drawn as a result of her brother's ordeal. Harriet promises to arrange a meeting.

Harriet goes to Donna's hotel, leaving Kimble in hers. Harriet makes airline reservations under the Townsend name, a red herring for Gerard, and arranges a meeting at the coliseum, where a basketball game will occupy everyone else's attention. Harriet and the Tafts leave, with the cops tailing Harriet's car.

Mike has learned his wife is in Ft. Wayne and angrily goes there to find her. He finds Kimble in her room and overpowers him just as Harriet returns. Harriet explains that she did this for Mike because she wants a husband, not a basket case, and doesn't want to share him with everyone else. Meanwhile, Kimble slips away en route to the coliseum. Mike calls Gerard, who considers bringing charges against Harriet. Mike tells Harriet he is dropping out of the race, although it meant more to him than anything else in the world, and that their marriage is virtually over. Harriet, desperate to salvage something, tells her husband where Kimble is meeting his sister, and Mike calls Gerard back to tell him.

Kimble finally meets with Donna, who is a wreck. He tells her he needs her to be strong, not to fall to pieces. The short visit does her a world of good, and Kimble goes to leave the stadium. Gerard arrives and sees Kimble leaving. A race up ramps and escalators ensues, but Kimble manages to escape once again.

Episode #83
THE CHINESE SUNSET
Original Airdate: March 1, 1966

Written by: Leonard Kantor   **Directed by:** James Sheldon

Cast: Laura Devon as Penelope Dufour, Paul Richards as Edward Slade, Wayne Rogers as Sgt. Fred Bragin, Ned Glass as Sam Vogle, Sandra Warner as Frankie Topps, Sheldon Allman as Orin, Connie Sawyer as Alice Ball, Mary Gregory as Rita, Karl Held as Buddy, Val Avery as Gordie Schiller, Melville Ruick as Woody, Robert Brubaker as Cooper, Jhean Burton as waitress, James Oliver as cab driver, Robert Yuro as Saul.

Kimble, alias Jack Fickett, is a "factotum" at the Chinese Sunset Motel, located on the Sunset Strip between Los Angeles and Beverly Hills, California. Among the residents there are scam artist Eddie Slade, "king of the bookmakers," and his "secretary," Penelope. A 23-year-old bimbo with a fourth-grade education, her motto is "a girl with looks don't need books." Eddie sizes up the rest of the motel's tenants as "penny-ante hustlers."

Penelope strikes up a conversation with Jack, but their differences in education and values create tension. Penelope lists her material possessions as evidence of success: 27 pairs of shoes, two mink coats, and 3½ carat diamond earrings. She hopes to marry Eddie, her benefactor, before she loses her looks.

Eddie meets a former accomplice, Gordie, who is hospitalized with injuries. He hopes Gordie can repay a favor by offering some financing, but Gordie wants nothing to do with Eddie. In fact, he doesn't want Eddie even in the same town; police know the two have worked together, and any link between them now might screw up Gordie's operations in progress. He gives Eddie two weeks to make whatever score he can and leave L.A.

Sgt. Bragin, working undercover, checks into the Chinese Sunset. He is there to keep an eye on Eddie and anyone in his company. During his two weeks there, Bragin becomes suspicious of Jack, who seems to have too much class for the job he has.

Penelope approaches Jack with a proposal: she will pay him to give her a crash-course in reading, grammar, and manners to help make her more desirable for Eddie. Jack reluctantly agrees to help, without pay, and proceeds to tutor Penelope while doing his mundane chores. At one point she comes on to him, but he does not respond. Jack says he enjoys watching Penelope learn and fostering her "drive to grow."

Eddie returns from an unsuccessful trip to raise money from old friends. Penelope tells him how Jack has helped her, showing off her improved skills. Eddie is not at all pleased, preferring Penelope's "beautiful innocence of mind." He confronts Jack, accusing him of fooling around with Penelope, and warning him to stay away from her.

Penelope tells Eddie that the other motel residents aren't hustlers, according to Jack. Eddie says he will prove both of them wrong by suckering the guests out of $50,000 that night, his last before Gordie's time-limit elapses. Eddie tips off Sam, an old Hollywood agent, to a big deal he is on to, paying off $20 per dollar invested. Eddie says he has the final $50,000 he needs coming tomorrow, but if Sam can raise the money before then, Eddie will cut him in. Sam is willing to risk his life savings of $11,000 and goes off to convince some of his friends to join him in this "once-in-a-lifetime" opportunity.

At a motel party, a guest takes a picture of Jack. Bragin sees Jack stuffing away the photo and becomes more suspicious. Bragin fishes the negative out of a trash can and brings it to the station to have another print made. The police match it up with a "wanted" poster of Kimble and head to the motel.

Penelope tells Jack about Eddie's scheme, and Jack holds a meeting to warn the potential investors. They don't believe Jack until Penelope vouches for him. Jack applauds her newfound integrity. Meanwhile, Gordie's men come to make sure Eddie leaves on time. A fight ensues, and Eddie winds up sailing through a window. The police arrive, sirens blaring, and Jack slips away. He eludes capture and takes a bus out of town. Bragin questions Penelope, who seems to be a new woman as the result of Jack's tutelage.

Episode #84
ILL WIND
Original Airdate: March 8, 1966

Written by: Al C. Ward **Directed by:** Joseph Sargent

Cast: Bonnie Beecher as Katherine "Kate" Kelly, John McIntire as Lester Kelly, Tim McIntire as Jonesie, Jeanette Nolan as Naomi Kelly, Lonny Chapman as Jock Sims, Lew Brown as sheriff, Renata Vanni as Mrs. Herrera, Silvia Marino as Josephina Herrera, Mel Gallagher and Laurence Aten as deputies.

Kimble, alias Mike Johnson, is a farm worker at Crawford Farms, 20 miles north of the Gulf of Mexico. He had been found there some time ago, sick and delirious and apparently on the run. He soon became a well-liked and respected co-worker of the Kelly family—Lester, Naomi, and Kate—and the other migrant laborers. A newspaper wire story on the national "farm labor shortage" happens to include a photo of these laborers, including Mike. Gerard sees it and heads south.

Mike decides it is time to move on and bids his farewells. The most difficult is with Kate, who has grown quite fond of Mike. Mike heads off to the packing shed, from where he should be able to hitch on with a freight train. A storm is brewing.

Gerard and local policemen arrive shortly after Mike leaves and question Lester and the others. They say Mike left a week ago, but Gerard is suspicious. He warns Lester he could face a year in jail if he is covering for the fugitive, imposing great hardship on the Kelly clan. Intimidated, Lester tells Gerard where Mike is, to the hysterical disapproval of Kate.

Gerard gets to the shed just ahead of the train and arrests Mike. As they drive to San Martin, a radio bulletin informs the police that a hurricane is on the way. The local cops will have to go to Junction Center for several hours to attend to the evacuation of some 40 residents of the rest home there. Gerard doesn't have time for this and asks if he can be dropped off somewhere with his prisoner. The most convenient place happens to be Crawford Farms.

The laborers seek shelter at the Crawford Farms headquarters, but Jock, the foreman, charges $2 a head for the privilege—and refuses it entirely when he learns the Herrera baby shows symptoms of typhoid fever. Jock forces the workers to take refuge in the none-too-sturdy stable.

Gerard arrives with Mike, but Jock refuses to let Gerard use his truck.

The laborers are glad to see Mike, hoping he can help the baby, but are hostile toward Gerard. A remorseful Lester apologizes to Mike for squealing on him, but Mike is understanding. Mike attends to the baby with a first aid kit wheedled from Jock and tells the others that if the fever breaks it is not typhoid.

Gerard cuffs himself to Mike as they retire for the night, sleeping against hay bales. Mike awakens to see Kate throwing a pitchfork toward the sleeping lieutenant's head and pulls Gerard out of its path just in time. Mike later makes Kate promise not to try any such thing again.

Throughout the episode, Jonesie and his guitar ad lib a running ballad, a "sad, sad song" about the outlaw (Mike), the sheriff (Gerard), and the girl (Kate).

Everyone is relieved when the baby's fever breaks. Their joy is short-lived as the storm wreaks havoc on their shelter. Falling debris knocks Gerard down, lacerating his forehead and severing an artery in his arm. Mike goes to his aid, a source of puzzlement to the Kelly family. Mike tells Jock the baby does not have typhoid and the group must come inside; Jock tries to resist but is soon outnumbered and gives in. Gerard is impressed with the fugitive's selflessness but affirms that it "doesn't change anything."

Mike tells the others that Gerard will die if he doesn't get a blood transfusion and asks for a type-B donor. Not wanting to help someone intent on sending Mike to his execution, no one volunteers. Kate finally approaches Mike, asking him to explain his motivation. Mike says that, "For a doctor, every life is worth saving." Kate still doesn't understand but, willing to do anything to please Mike, admits she has the correct blood type. Mike sets up the transfusion, saving Gerard's life yet again.

The storm is about over and the roads are clear, so the police will be there soon. Lester and his crew break open some of Jock's whiskey to celebrate surviving the ordeal. Mike makes sure Gerard is O.K., then goes to leave. Gerard pulls his pistol, threatening to shoot Mike, but Lester and the others block his path. Gerard is too weak to pursue Mike, who reaches the highway and hitches a ride on a truck.

The police arrive at Crawford Farms. Gerard tells them there is no point in bringing charges against the workers — there were too many involved, it would tie Gerard up for too long, and it would give Kimble too much of a head start.

Episode #85
WITH STRINGS ATTACHED
Original Airdate: March 15, 1966

Written by: John Kneubuhl **Directed by:** Leonard Horn

Act III: The 1965-66 Season

Cast: Rex Thompson as Geoffrey Tilston Martin, Donald Pleasence as Max Pfeiffer, Carol Rossen as Ellen Harned, Bill Quinn as Sgt. Lyman, Jason Johnson as watchman, Paul Pepper as stage manager, Jim Raymond as officer.

On September 30 Kimble, alias Frank Carter, applies for a job as chauffeur and companion to Geoffrey Martin. Geoffrey is billed as a 15-year-old concert violinist, although he is actually almost 18. His coach, manager, and guardian is Max, whose own musical career was curtailed by alcoholism. Max had recognized Geoffrey's talent when the boy was only nine and signed a contract with Geoffrey's parents. Max is a slave-driver who denies pleasures, emphasizing the "burden of genius" Geoffrey must bear. They are preparing for an important concert in two days.

Geoffrey tells Ellen, a live-in employee, that his canary (whom Max supposedly disliked) has died. Max is in the process of rejecting Carter for the job, but Geoffrey interjects his approval, and Carter is hired. A day later, Geoffrey sees that the neck of his Stradivarius (which Geoffrey prefers over the fiddle Max has supplied) has been broken. Max's jacket button is found in the canary's cage, and Carter and Ellen suspect Max of killing the bird and vandalizing the instrument. In actuality, Geoffrey had staged both incidents.

Ellen encourages Carter to drive Geoffrey into town to pick out a new canary. Carter obliges, against Max's orders. Geoffrey tells Carter that his contract with Max ends this month, when Geoffrey turns eighteen, and that he looks forward to his freedom. Carter and Geoffrey return home to an angry Max, who releases the new bird outside and privately scolds Geoffrey for his indulgence. Geoffrey returns holding his hand in apparent pain, claiming that Max hit him with a paperweight. Carter sees that the skin is not broken, and that no swelling develops, and he deduces that Geoffrey has lied about not only this but also the other incidents. Carter correctly surmises that Geoffrey is building a case against Max, portraying him as a cruel tyrant, but Carter can't figure out why, since the lad will be free of Max in a few weeks anyway.

Ellen, upset by Max's series of apparently cruel acts, calls the police to come. Sgt. Lyman arrives, questioning Ellen, Carter, and Geoffrey. Geoffrey, playing the role of the loyal subject, defends Max, while Carter is uncomfortable and evasive. Lyman has a hunch about Carter and will check on it at the station.

On concert night, Geoffrey gives Carter a $50 bill, encouraging him to take Ellen out on the town afterward. Carter figures that Geoffrey is trying to get rid of them and shares his suspicions with Ellen. Ellen thinks Geoffrey's contract runs until age 21, not 18, which would explain why Geoffrey can't seem to wait for his freedom. Carter and Ellen go to the house to check the contract, confirming Ellen's belief and also discovering that Max's revolver is missing. Sizing up the situation, they rush back toward the concert hall.

Just before Geoffrey is due on stage, a present—including a bottle of liquor — arrives for Max, presumably from management but actually arranged by Geoffrey. Geoffrey can't very well insult the management by returning the bottle, so he leaves it in the dressing room — even pouring a glass before he leaves. The temptation is too much for Max, and he leaps off the wagon. By the time Geoffrey's performance is over, Max is violently drunk. Geoffrey and Max skip their reception with the British consul and return home. Carter arrives to an empty room and an empty bottle and is told that Geoffrey left.

Geoffrey fills Max with more booze at the house. Sgt. Lyman arrives, seeing Max's condition and asking where Carter is. A cab drops Carter at the house, and he sees the police car. Hiding in the bushes, he hears Lyman say "if Carter is Kimble …" and sees the cops pull the car around back. Despite his opportunity to escape, Carter feels he must avert the crime in progress, and he slips inside the house.

Carter finds Geoffrey holding Max at gunpoint upstairs. Geoffrey has things all figured out: he will shoot Max, gaining his freedom, and everyone will believe the act was in self-defense. Now that Carter is a witness, he will have to be shot, too. Carter points out that Geoffrey will have a difficult time explaining a second shooting, but Geoffrey says he will claim Max shot Carter. Carter tells Geoffrey he is a wanted criminal and that killing him would make Max a hero; besides, Ellen knows about the plot, too. His scheme falling apart, Geoffrey breaks down. Police are alerted by the sound of six shots and rush inside. They find that Geoffrey has shot up his own violin. Meanwhile, Carter slips away and escapes.

Geoffrey will undergo psychiatric evaluation while Max remains by his side. Ellen asks Lyman whether Kimble is really that dangerous. Lyman replies, "He's desperate — that makes a man dangerous."

Episode #86

THE WHITE KNIGHT

Original Airdate: March 22, 1966

Written by: Dan Ullman **Directed by:** Robert Gist

Cast: Steven Hill as Glenn Madison, Jessica Walter as Pat Haynes, James Callahan as Russ Haynes, Nancy Wickwire as Claire Madison, Ted Knight as Lt. Al Mooney, Robert Do Qui as Evers, Peter Marko as dispatcher.

Kimble, alias Dan Gordon, is driving a van for Hogue's Tri-City Delivery Service in the Phoenix, Arizona, area. He witnesses the crash of a private plane and rushes to the scene, rescuing Glenn Madison and Pat Haynes from the burning craft just before it explodes. Glenn has suffered a broken leg, but Pat is merely shaken up. Dan leaves to call an ambulance and does not return, fearing publicity. Pat waits for the ambulance, then leaves; she, a married woman, had no business being with Glenn, a married man.

Glenn is a politician with designs to run for the Senate. His wife, Claire, is a long-suffering lush, aware of his extramarital affairs and manipulative nature. Glenn's loyal aide is Russ, who also happens to be Pat's husband. Neither Russ nor Claire is aware of this particular affair between their spouses.

Glenn is treated and released to his luxurious home, where a hospital-style bed is set up. Under Russ's direction, the media crusades to find the "mysterious Samaritan" who saved Glenn's life. Evers, a police artist, uses Glenn's reluctant help to put together a composite of the rescuer. The finished product goes into the newspapers, and Evers is sure he has seen that face elsewhere — perhaps on a mug-shot.

Dan returns to work the next day to find Pat waiting for him (she had remembered the company name on his van). She wants to ensure he won't tell anyone about her being on the plane, and he assures her he won't: "You have your reasons for avoiding publicity. I have mine." Pat then reports to Glenn, telling him Dan isn't even interested in any reward. Glenn worries that Dan has an ulterior motive and might come back to haunt Glenn at an inopportune time. Meanwhile, Dan's co-worker recognizes the man depicted in the sketch as Dan and contacts Russ. Russ finds the reluctant hero and drives him to meet Glenn. On the way, Russ uses Glenn's car phone to tell Lt. Mooney that Evers's sketch paid off and that the Samaritan is on his way to Glenn's home. Evers tells Mooney about his suspicion, and mug-shots are checked.

Dan and Glenn meet over a drink, with Glenn offering to help Dan in some way. Russ interrupts the meeting with news that police, thinking Dan is Richard Kimble, are on their way there. Glenn offers to hide Kimble out as repayment for saving his life. While Kimble hides in another room, Glenn tells the cops that the fugitive has already left. Glenn's drunken wife sees Kimble and figures out what is going on. After the police leave, Claire visits Kimble's room and "welcomes" him. She threatens to call the police back if Kimble doesn't tell her who was on the plane with Glenn, but he keeps mum.

Pat arrives at the house, supposedly returning from a trip to San Diego. Talking privately with Glenn, she reaffirms what she had said before the accident: their relationship is over. Pat then visits Kimble, and he learns who she is. She explains her affair with Glenn and how she happened to be on the plane with him; Claire walks in, having overheard enough to know what is going on.

Claire confronts Glenn, announcing that she is leaving him. He doesn't take her seriously, but she vows to tell the world about Glenn's seedy side. Glenn calls Claire "an over-the-hill, self-pitying drunk." She slaps him, and he grabs her and throws her to the floor, apparently breaking her neck. Claire is dead (although a shoddy film edit reveals a split-second of her turning her head and opening her eyes).

Glenn hobbles from his bed and drags Claire's body to her room. He then goes to Kimble's room, giving Kimble his car keys and instructing him to drive north and drop off the car 90 miles away at Navajo Point. After Kimble leaves, Glenn stages signs of a struggle in his room and calls Russ to come. Glenn tells Russ that Kimble roughed him up and stole his car and there's no telling what he might have done to Claire. Russ finds Claire's body and assumes that Kimble did it. Glenn points out that, if they called the police, their harboring of a fugitive would be revealed. He manipulates Russ into chasing Kimble with a gun.

Pat sees Russ leaving and asks Glenn why; Glenn tells her, saying he would have stopped Russ if only he could have gotten out of his rig. Pat sees a stain on the bottom of Glenn's foot, realizes he is lying, and deduces the rest. She calls Kimble on the car phone to warn him.

Russ has nearly caught up with Kimble in a highway chase. Kimble veers to a stop. Russ comes at Kimble with the gun, but Kimble gets him to talk to Pat, still on the phone. She tells Russ everything.

Russ accompanies Kimble to a bus station. Kimble recommends that Russ stick with Pat and says to tell her that they are even now. Russ wishes Kimble luck and sends him on his way.

Episode #87
THE 2130
Original Airdate: March 29, 1966

Written by: Dan Ullman **Directed by:** Leonard Horn

Cast: Melvyn Douglas as Dr. Mark Ryder, Susan Albert as Laurie Ryder, Jason Wingreen as Doug Bassett, Hampton Francher as Marty "Homer" Macklin, William Bramley as Tim Oates, June Dayton as Millie Oates, Kevin Burchett as Alan Oates, Don Mitchell as laborer, Harlan Warde as detective, Lillian Adams as store owner, Jon Kowal as police captain, Stuart Nisbet as Richardson, Bob Duggan as driver, Peter Canon and Paul Hahn as officers, Pat Riley, Clay Tanner, and Mark Russell as deputies.

Kimble, alias Jack Davis, is a chauffeur for Dr. Ryder and his daughter, Laurie, in the Denver, Colorado, area. Late one winter night, Laurie knocks frantically at Jack's door. She has been involved in yet another fender-bender in her sports car and is afraid of what her father will say and do. She pleads with Jack to take the rap for her just this one time, and he reluctantly does—not aware that the dent resulted from a hit-and-run accident that put a man in the hospital.

After Laurie leaves for school the next morning, police arrive at the Ryder house, inquiring about the accident. Jack speeds off in the family car, ditching it at a gas station and trading in his uniform at a used clothing store. Due to his suspicious behavior, and his admitted involvement in the accident, Jack's prints are taken from objects in his room. They reveal his true identity.

Act III: The 1965-66 Season 149

Dr. Ryder, angered by his employee's betrayal, has a brainstorm: he will utilize the digital "2130" computer at the Medical Research Center to aid in tracking Kimble. Ryder leaves word for Gerard to come and bring Kimble's files. After the skeptical lieutenant arrives, Ryder demonstrates the system and begins inputting data supplied by Gerard.

While hitchhiking, Kimble meets a resting motorist, Tim Oates. Oates introduces Kimble — now Bob Grant — to his family. They are headed for California to work in the walnut groves and offer to give Bob a lift if he will share in the driving. They are soon all working together at Richardson's Walnut Groves.

The 2130 gives preliminary findings on Kimble: "movement of subject random — no discernible pattern." This surprises Ryder but not Gerard. Ryder fine-tunes the input and finally gets some definite probabilities: #1 is that Kimble is harvesting citrus in Florida, #2 is that he is in California's walnut groves. Police are sent to the likely locales, including Richardson's, with Kimble's "wanted" poster. Alan, the oldest Oates boy, runs ahead to warn Mr. Grant, and Kimble escapes on foot. Nevertheless, the computer's value in tracking him has been proven. Reporter Doug Bassett asks Ryder what he and Gerard are up to, and Ryder promises Bassett an exclusive story when the time is right.

Kimble hops a freight bound for Portland, Oregon, joining "Homer," a writer/artist who is actually a wanted cop-killer. Homer writes about his new companion ("Jack") in his notebook, sketching a picture of him while Kimble dozes. Meanwhile, the 2130 has predicted Kimble's next stop as either Salt Lake City or Portland, and police are set up at both train stations. As the freight pulls in, Homer sees the cops and assumes they are after him. He makes a break and is chased and killed in a shoot-out. Kimble slips away in the confusion, and joins the nearby Multnomah County Flood Control gang with his fourth alias of the episode, William Smith. Police find Homer's sketch and realize they were on the right track.

Ryder pores through Kimble's files and determines that, except for the murder charge and the hit-and-run accident, Kimble has always been a good and decent man. He inputs data on convicted criminals, trying to determine the probability of a man like Kimble committing murder; the result is 98 percent negative ("the remaining two percent is enough for me," harrumphs Gerard). Ryder confronts Laurie about the accident and she admits Kimble took the rap for her. Both Ryders are remorseful about the manhunt they have set in motion and which no longer can be stopped. There is one thing the doctor *can* do, however: leak the story about the computer pursuit in hopes that Kimble will be forewarned. Ryder calls Bassett with the scoop.

Kimble is among a cartload of laborers en route to the flood area, with Gerard (alerted by the 2130's latest prediction) awaiting a few miles down the road. Kimble notices an article ("Man vs. Machine — Computer Tracks Fugitive to Oregon") on the back of a laborer's newspaper. Kimble pays a dime for the paper, scans the article, and jumps out of the truck. Not wanting his pattern to be predictable, Kimble travels cross-country to get a job as a cranberry picker for Royal Crest Foods in cold New England. Told about the near-miss, and the ten-cent investment, Gerard remarks, "He'll never get a better bargain than that."

Gerard, knowing that Kimble will now defy predictability, doesn't have time to stick around and fool with the computer any longer. After Gerard leaves, Ryder decides to try a reverse-pattern request on the 2130. Its second probability reads "cranberry bogs, New England."

Episode #88
A TASTE OF TOMORROW
Original Airdate: April 12, 1966

Story by: Mann Rubin   Teleplay by: John Kneubuhl   Directed by: Leonard Horn

Cast: Fritz Weaver as Joseph Tucker, Michael Constantine as Lt. Ben Wyckoff, Brenda Scott as Sarah Tucker, Dabbs Greer as Charles A. Fletcher, Robert Ivers as Dave, Mary Jackson as Carolyn Fletcher, Paul Sorensen as Shep, Paul Sheriff as officer.

In Boise, Idaho, police are hot on the trail of Joe Tucker, a fugitive who has been at large for four years. Kimble, alias Alan Mitchell, sees the cops and thinks they are after him. He takes refuge in a seemingly abandoned camp snack bar, but finds himself held at gunpoint by Joe. Kimble assures Joe he has nothing to fear from him and becomes concerned about Joe's physical condition. Joe is suffering from "mountain fever," similar to typhoid.

Joe was wrongly convicted (a source of empathy to Kimble) of embezzling $200,000 from Andy Fletcher's farm machinery company, and Andy's son Charlie had delivered the most damaging testimony. Joe has returned to Boise to kill Charlie, whom Joe thinks committed the crime. In reality Andy himself had embezzled the money and coerced his son to lie, as revealed in Andy's deathbed confession just days ago. Unbeknownst to Joe, police are now looking not to imprison him, but to tell him he looks to be in the clear.

Joe lets Kimble borrow his truck so he can go into town for medication. There Kimble is stopped by the police after they recognize the truck. When Kimble can't satisfactorily explain how he came into possession of the vehicle, he is booked, fingerprinted, and locked up for auto theft.

Kimble refuses to admit knowing where Joe is, even after hearing about the confession. Joe's daughter Sarah visits and tearfully appeals to Kimble, convincing him it is not a trick to lure Joe back. Kimble finally admits he knows where Joe is and that he needs medical attention. He says he will take Sarah to Joe if he is released, without police accompaniment, and the cops reluctantly let him go. The fingerprint report comes back just at that instant, and Kimble escapes in the truck. Roadblocks are set up immediately, and Kimble cuts in front of a produce truck to take a side road toward the camp. The driver reports the incident at the roadblock, and police move in after Kimble.

Kimble drives across a creek to get to the camp and bring the medicine to Joe. Kimble tells Joe about the confession, but Joe can't believe that the benevolent Andy, who gave Joe his job and put him through school, could have done such a thing. He thinks it is another trick being perpetrated by Lt. Wyckoff and that perhaps Kimble is in on the scheme.

Kimble gives the shuddering Charlie his jacket and at last talks him into returning to town. Kimble waits in the truck for him as the police, unable to cross the creek by car, approach the camp on foot. Seeing a man in Kimble's jacket leave the building, they order him to stop and a shoot-out ensues. Joe dives into the truck and he and Kimble speed away. Joe, thinking Kimble double-crossed him, holds him at gunpoint and orders him to drive to Charlie's house.

Joe passes out, and Kimble stops the truck at a service station, removing the key. Kimble calls Wyckoff to tell him where Joe is, but Joe has regained consciousness and set out on foot for Charlie's house. When Kimble discovers Joe gone, he looks up Charlie's address in a phone book and heads there. When the police find the empty truck, they too head for Charlie's house.

Joe, brandishing the gun, arrives first. Charlie tells Joe he turned over all the records corroborating his father's embezzlement to the police today, and that he faces a charge of perjury. Kimble shows up, explaining why the police were after him, not Joe, and the Fletchers' newspaper confirms this. Joe, finally convinced, puts down the gun.

The police roll in with Sarah, and Kimble hides upstairs. Charlie tells Wyckoff that Joe came alone. Joe reunites with his daughter and they all leave. Kimble makes his escape after the roadblocks are called in.

Episode #89
IN A PLAIN PAPER WRAPPER
Original Airdate: April 19, 1966

Story by: Jackson Gillis & Glen A. Larson **Teleplay by:** John Kneubuhl
Directed by: Richard Donner

Cast: Lois Nettleton as Susan Cartwright, Michael Strong as Mr. Shaw, Pat Cardi as Gary Reed, Kurt Russell as Eddie, Michael Shea as Richard, Wolfe Barzell as Mr. Hoffman, Bing Russell as officer, Arthur Malet as Swanzie, Mark Dymally as Joe, Kay Riehl as landlady.

Kimble, alias Robert "Bob" Stoddard, has been a bartender at the Little Vienna Restaurant in New York state for the past couple of months. His co-worker and romantic interest is Susan, a waitress. Susan has just been given temporary custody of her 12-year-old nephew, Gary. Gary's parents had died in an auto accident, and his foster parents had been deemed unfit by the child welfare bureau. Gary was thus turned over to his nearest blood relative, his mother's sister, whom he had never before met.

Three youths, Eddie, Rick, and Joe, are plotting to buy a .303 carbine rifle from a mail-order outfit. Anyone with the required capital can order the weapon, and the boys lack just $2.75 of the purchase price. They are excited about their impending acquisition, although they have no specific plans for the gun's use. Gary wanders by, and Eddie invites him to join the group — provided he can come up with the $2.75 "initiation fee." Gary, eager to make friends in his new neighborhood, runs off to hit up Aunt Susan for the money. She can't be bothered at work and tells him to leave. Gary grabs a handful of quarters (from a stack the boss had left next to the cash register) on his way out. Bob yells after Gary, who recognizes the bartender as Dr. Kimble, the escaped murderer who had helped coach Little League where Gary used to live. Bob — not wanting Gary and Susan to start off on the wrong foot — replaces the $3 the boy stole.

Gary tells the boys about Kimble, but they don't believe him until he goes to the library and copies a newspaper article about Kimble's arrest. The boys now have a plan for the rifle: to capture a murderer. Eddie swears Gary to secrecy and sends him to mail the rifle order. The gun should arrive in two weeks.

Bob goes to Susan's house for dinner and officially meets Gary. Gary seems terrified and refuses to shake hands with Bob. Susan, puzzled, scolds Gary for his rudeness. Bob leaves, suggesting that he take Gary to a movie Saturday in hopes of breaking the ice between the two.

Mr. Shaw, a representative of the welfare bureau, visits Susan. His duty is to recommend whether Susan will serve as a fit parent on a permanent basis. Shaw shares an "area of concern": the lack of a male parental figure in the household. He inquires about Susan's relationship with Bob, who conceivably could become the next-closest person to the boy. Susan does want to keep Gary, and he seems content there.

The rifle arrives, covered in a plain paper wrapper. The boys are triumphant. At a burger joint, they trick old Swanzie into getting them some bullets, and they are all set. They plan to make their move this evening, when Kimble returns to his rooming house.

Shaw stops at the restaurant to question Bob. Bob is forced to lie, but he realizes Shaw will check on his answers. This may lead to his identity being revealed or at least endanger Susan's chances of getting custody of Gary. Bob decides to leave town, figuring that Shaw will then discontinue his check. Bob tells Susan he must talk to her privately and they go to her apartment. Gary eavesdrops from another room.

Susan tells Bob she has fallen in love with him and deserves an explanation for his leaving. Bob reluctantly tells his story, explains he is leaving to get her off the hook, and tells Susan he didn't kill his wife. Gary rushes to his friends, hoping to cancel their plan. They blow him off and Gary speeds back home to warn Bob, but he has already left. Gary dashes off again, hoping to avert the confrontation.

The cocky boys wait in the bushes near Kimble's place, and Eddie orders Kimble to put up his hands. Gary arrives and tries to wrestle the gun away from Eddie. It goes off, wounding Gary in the arm, and the boys are suddenly not so brave any more. Kimble attends to Gary and the landlady calls the police.

As the cops arrive, Gary strikes a deal: Gary won't say how he got shot if the others will keep quiet about Kimble. An officer scolds the kids, ordering them brought to the station, and remarks "there ought to be a law" (gun control, today's moral message). Kimble slips away and takes a bus out of town.

Relative to the incident, Mr. Shaw meets with Gary and Susan, who tells Shaw that Bob has left. Seeing that Susan and Gary are developing a warm relationship, Shaw advises that "I wouldn't worry about what I'll be putting in my report."

Episode #90
CORALEE
Original Airdate: April 26, 1966

Written by: Joy Dexter **Directed by:** Jerry Hopper

Cast: Antoinette Bower as Coralee Reynolds, Murray Hamilton as Joe Steelman, Patricia Smith as Lucille Steelman, Dabney Coleman as George Graham, James Frawley as Pete, Joe Maross as Milt Carr, Rusty Lane as Frank Reynolds, Harry Ellerbe as minister, Peter Madsen as patrolman.

Kimble, alias Tony Carter, works as the intercom operator on Joe Steelman's derrick barge, used for salvage diving and mooring service off the California coast. Johnny is under water when the seal on his helmet is broken by falling debris, and he drowns before he can be hauled up. Tony inspects the helmet, whose safety catch appears corroded. Joe, seeing this, grabs the helmet and throws it overboard.

The barge returns to port, where Lucille (Joe's wife and Johnny's sister) and Coralee (who dated Johnny a few times) await. Lucille, very upset, censures Coralee: "You should have stayed away from him!" Coralee leaves disconsolately and Tony, concerned, follows her. He learns that Coralee is considered a jinx, having been close to two other men who met with tragedy. Tony tells her he doesn't believe in jinxes and offers his shoulder but is told to mind his own business. Coralee later visits Tony in the rooming house both live in, apologizing for her rudeness and asking about Johnny's death.

Lucille is very concerned about the accident, recalling a similar one six years earlier: a negligence suit had closed up Joe's operation for a while, leaving the Steelmans deeply in debt. This time they could lose everything. Joe assures her it was simply an accident and that the harbor police were satisfied with his report. Secretly, however, Joe is worried, particularly about what Tony might say to authorities. After Johnny's funeral Joe learns that officials have been "snooping around." Later comes a letter, informing Joe that a formal hearing on the accident will be held Monday, with all barge employees required to attend.

Coralee works at her Uncle Frank's restaurant. One loyal customer is George, a harbor policeman. Others, especially Joe, have refused to be served by the "Jonah," and business has slowed down. The cafe is all Frank has, and, though he doesn't necessarily believe the talk, he asks his niece to leave at the end of the week. Meanwhile, Coralee and Tony are becoming drawn to one another. She sees him sitting out in the terrace and goes out for "air." The two lock into a passionate kiss, starting a short-lived romance.

Joe and Pete, a simple-minded barge hand, have beers at the restaurant. Joe eggs Pete on, saying Tony is "trouble," supposedly having questioned Pete's role in the accident — "Who knows what he'll say at the hearing?" Coralee and Tony enter, and Pete, encouraged by the beer and Joe's goading, harasses them at their table. When Tony tries to ease him away, Pete belts him. George breaks it up, and Coralee administers first aid with the cafe's kit. Afterward, Tony tells her he will have to leave at the end of the week. Coralee wonders if he has become a "believer" in the jinx, but Tony admits he is in trouble with the police.

After he gets the letter about the hearing, Joe goes on a drinking binge. He returns home, babbling to Lucille about the danger of losing everything, saying, "Tony is going to blow the whistle, and I can't let him do it." Appalled by the thought of what Joe might do, Lucille visits Coralee. Suggesting that Coralee "stop some trouble for a change," Lucille advises her to keep Tony from going to work the next day. Coralee passes on the warning, but Tony dismisses it — he can't imagine Joe trying anything with so many people around, and he wants to convince Coralee she isn't a jinx. They both go to work.

At the cafe Coralee asks George to rescue Tony from the barge. George can't do that without reason, so Coralee gives him one: having no idea of the seriousness of Tony's trouble, she tells George he is wanted. George asks for a sample of Tony's fingerprints, and Coralee gives him the first aid kit. George soon returns with the report, then heads out on the port police boat.

Joe orders Tony on a diving mission, even though he is not qualified. Coralee calls the barge through the marine operator, warning Tony, and arranging to meet him at sea. Tony — dressed in scuba gear with a one-hour tank — goes under shortly before the police arrive, cuts himself loose, attaches something to the tow-line, and starts swimming underwater toward the agreed-upon meeting place.

The police arrive and George orders Tony hauled up. The only thing that surfaces is a helmet — Johnny's. Pete blurts out what it is, and the police confiscate the evidence.

Tony reaches the motorboat Coralee waits in, and the two speed off. Coralee brings Tony to her car, gives him an opportunity to change his clothes, and drives him to a bus station. Tony points out that his problems are not her fault, and the "jinx" is broken. He boards a northbound bus to his next destination.

Act IV
The 1966-67 Season

The Fugitive's fourth and final season featured 28 episodes, aired between September 13, 1966, and April 11, 1967. Its competition again came from the *CBS News Hour* and the *NBC Tuesday Night Movie*.

The fourth season was produced by Wilton Schiller and was the only one shown in color.

David Janssen once again portrayed the fugitive in each of the season's episodes. He received his third Emmy nomination for Best Actor in a Dramatic Series and was named Actor of the Year by *Photoplay Magazine*. Barry Morse appeared as Lt. Philip Gerard in just six episodes: numbers 94–95, 100, 104, 111, and 116.

Episode #91
THE LAST OASIS
Original Airdate: September 13, 1966

Written by: Barry Oringer Directed by: Gerald Mayer

Cast: Hope Lange as Annie Johnson, Mark Richman as James Steel, Arch Johnson as Sheriff Prycer, John McLiam as Deputy Kelton, Lew Brown as Danny O'Hara, Jamie Sanchez as Sam, Vincent Arias as Roger, Silvia Marino as Nellie, Don Ross and Eugene Iglesias as border guards.

Sheriff Prycer and Deputy Steel are hot on Kimble's trail in Puma County, southwestern Arizona. Steel wounds Kimble just above the left knee, but Kimble manages to get away in a car. The lawmen find the car parked beside the railroad tracks, and it looks as if Kimble has hopped the freight bound for Lawler. Prycer is content to admit defeat and turn things over to Lawler authorities, but Steel — a man with uncanny instincts — is sure Kimble is still in the area. Steel's late father, a marshal, had once let a murderer slip away, and four more people were subsequently killed by the man. Steel is determined to avenge Dad's failure by capturing Kimble. Prycer is annoyed by his deputy's insubordination and obsessiveness in this matter.

Kimble sacks out under a discarded mattress, where he is discovered by a Mexican man. Seeing he is hurt, the man drives him to the nearby Indian school taught by Annie Johnson, a tough, self-sufficient gal. Annie tends to Kimble, who gives his name as David Morrow, and manages to extract the bullet. David is enlisted to help in teaching the orphans and to weave hats for them. Over the next ten days, he becomes well-liked by the kids and their teacher, who is determined to break David's mysterious habit of running.

Steel, still on the scent, discovers a set of keys Kimble had dropped near the mattress. The fingerprints confirm Steel's hunch and suggest Kimble may still be in the area. Meanwhile, Deputy O'Hara happens to be in the local ice cream parlor when the schoolkids make a pilgrimage there. Admiring the new hat worn by young Roger, the deputy asks him about it. Roger tells him about the new man at the school and trades him the hat for a pocket-knife. When O'Hara mentions the transaction at work the next morning, Steel formulates another correct hypothesis: that Kimble is the new man at Annie's school.

David realizes his cover may be blown when Roger tells him about the swap. Above Annie's objections, David leaves around 9 P.M. Steel comes looking for him nine hours later, and they are met by a less-than-enthusiastic Prycer. Annie has little use for policemen in general, but, stunned by the news, she volunteers that David headed north on foot. The police go to Kittyville to await his arrival. Annie has second thoughts and goes out to head off David herself, armed with a rifle and provisions.

Annie finds David and, assured he is innocent of murder, drives him toward the Mexican border. The car overheats, forcing the two to complete the journey on foot. Annie recommends the longer route through the mountains, where they will have better cover than in an eight-mile stretch of desert. She plans to have David cross the border at the Santurras River, then meet a friend of hers in Mexico. As night falls, the two camp out in a cave and share at least a kiss.

After Steel discovers Annie's car, he again deduces Kimble's moves. Prycer gives Steel the O.K. to join a helicopter search the next morning, but he is only to report Kimble's position, not go after him.

David awakens and goes out to gather firewood. The helicopter passes overhead, and Steel spots him. Defying Prycer's order, Steel demands the pilot land and let him out. Steel orders Kimble out of the cave and he exits, making a break for it. Steel fires, knocking Kimble off his feet. As Kimble lies helplessly, Steel raises his gun to fire. Suddenly Annie comes up behind Steel and, pointing her own rifle, orders Steel to drop his. She reminds him that there is a law against murdering an unarmed man who is not even resisting arrest; Steel counters that there is also a law against holding a gun on a lawman. "There's a worse law for shooting one," says Annie, "but I will if I have to." Steel, folding like a beaten poker player, puts down the gun. Kimble limps off, crosses the border under the river bridge, and takes refuge in Mexico for a while.

Afterward, Steel thanks Annie for stopping him and asks if she really would have shot him. She ignores the question and changes the subject.

Episode #92
DEATH IS THE DOOR PRIZE
Original Airdate: September 20, 1966

Written by: Oliver Crawford **Directed by:** Don Medford

Cast: Lois Nettleton as Marcia Stone, Howard DaSilva as Pete Dawes, Ossie Davis as Johnny Gaines, Kevin O'Neal as Gary Lee, John Lasell as Victor Lee, June Vincent as Martha Lee, Len Wayland as Jim Boles, Jess Kirkpatrick as Ben Gilbert, Wolfe Barzell as Ed, John Harmon as Mr. Patterson, Harlan Warde as Anderson, John Ward as Dan, Bill Erwin as man.

Kimble, alias Ed Sanders, gets off a bus and sees what appears to be a one-armed man entering the grounds of a west coast hotel, where an international electronics show is being held. Kimble rushes after the man and bumps into Marcia. Kimble helps pick up her things and hurries off before discovering he has taken Marcia's wallet (containing two weeks' pay) by mistake. He pockets it with the intent to relocate Marcia later. A man witnesses the whole scene and reports a pickpocket to the nearest security guard, Pete Dawes.

Kimble finds that the man he saw is not *his* man and sets off to return the purse. A badge in it identifies the owner as a representative of ABF Electronics, which has a table set up in the hotel. Kimble finds it and returns Marcia's wallet, to her great relief. Marcia demonstrates her company's home video tape recorder, taking some footage of Kimble before he stops her. Kimble goes to leave the grounds when he is stopped by Dawes, who recognizes him as the alleged pickpocket and chases him back toward the hotel. Kimble ducks into a basement storeroom full of electronics, ripping his jacket sleeve and cutting his left hand on the door's broken window. He finds himself in the company of Stuart and Gary, two youths burglarizing the place. Dawes enters seconds later, ordering the kids to freeze. Stuart makes a move toward his back pocket and Dawes, a retired cop, shoots and kills the lad. In the confusion, Kimble slips out and tries again to escape but is forced to hide out when an alert on him is broadcast over the public address system.

Dawes is in a sticky situation when no weapon is found on Stuart, and Gary isn't talking. Unless Dawes can produce a witness before the coroner's inquest, chances are he will face a manslaughter charge. Dawes checks through police files in hopes his potential witness, the already-cleared "pickpocket," has a previous record. Dawes recognizes Richard Kimble's mug-shot but keeps quiet, knowing how desperately he needs Kimble's testimony. Dawes questions Marcia and views the videotape of Sanders, confirming he is Kimble. It is known that Kimble is still on the grounds and has a cut hand and ripped jacket.

After another unsuccessful attempt to leave, Kimble heads for Marcia's table. Grateful for his return of her wallet (and attracted to him, too), she hides Kimble in her nearby room and lies to guards about whether she has seen him. While Kimble sacks out, Marcia takes his jacket to a tailor shop for repair.

Dawes asks around town if anyone has seen Kimble. He stops at the tailor shop and spots the jacket. Told that Marcia brought it in, and is due back to pick it up at any time, Dawes waits outside the shop for her. When Marcia picks up the jacket, Dawes surreptitiously follows her back to her room.

Marcia brings Kimble back his jacket, and he tells her he has to leave and that she is better off not knowing why he is on the run. Marcia leaves her room and is accosted by Dawes, who tries to force his way in. Marcia's yells alert Kimble, who slips out the window.

Dawes calls up Boles, the site detective, asking him to detain Kimble. Boles does and Dawes at last confronts the fugitive. Dawes warns Kimble he will be in deep trouble unless he testifies on Dawes's behalf. He tones down the blackmail angle when Kimble sympathizes with the wrongly accused man. Dawes promises that if Kimble testifies, Dawes will let him walk.

At the inquest, Kimble verifies Dawes's version of the shooting. If Gary will corroborate Kimble's testimony, Dawes will be off the hook. After prodding from his father, Gary finally admits that Stuart did make a threatening move. The hearing is over, but Chief Gaines thinks Kimble looks familiar.

Kimble goes to leave and finds Marcia waiting for him. Gaines suddenly orders Kimble to stop while he checks the police files. Kimble thinks Dawes has double-crossed him, especially when Gaines returns with a "wanted" poster. It turns out that Kimble resembles a crook named Frank Finlay, except he is too tall and too young. Gaines apologizes and Kimble is on his way. Marcia drops him off at the terminal, the two embrace, and Kimble boards another bus.

Episode #93
A CLEAN AND QUIET TOWN
Original Airdate: September 27, 1966

Written by: Howard Browne   **Directed by:** Mark Rydell

Cast: Michael Strong as Oliver Enright, Bill Johnson as Fred Johnson A.K.A. Steve Cramer, Carol Rossen as Cora, Eduardo Cianelli as Victor Luchek, Ed Deemer as Ralph, Bill Bramley as Lynch, George Brenlin as cabdriver, Peter Brocco as dry-cleaning man, Susan Davis as Miss Morretti, Ted Gehring as Sgt. Weber, Alan Emerson as A. L. Hamp, Lloyd Haynes as Bill, Robert Karnes as John Abbott, Orville Sherman as hotel clerk.

Victor Luchek, a notorious organized crime figure presumed dead many years ago, oversees a tidy operation in little Clark City, Kentucky. Right-hand man Oliver Enright runs the organization (with the full cooperation of the paid-off police force) from his Enright Investments Company. An employee there is none other than Kimble's one-armed man, Fred Johnson, alias Steve Cramer, who had once saved Enright from a knife-wielding thug in a Detroit bar. Kimble, alias Paul Miller, has tracked Johnson to Clark City and is walking the streets in search of him.

Cramer learns that Kimble is in the area and pays two cops to run him out of town, supposedly on Enright's orders. The cops obligingly accost Kimble, whom they suppose to be an out-of-town gambler, and administer a brutal beating with the suggestion that he leave town. Cora, a girlfriend of one of the cops, witnesses the assault and half-heartedly offers aid to Kimble. Saying she doesn't want to get too involved, she helps Kimble to her apartment and attends to his wounds, charging $10 for her services and sending him on his way. Kimble suspects Cramer arranged for the beating, but he can't very well complain to the police.

Kimble asks around and, with the help of another $10 donation, learns of Enright's influence with the local police. Kimble goes to Enright's office and is granted three minutes to state his business. He tells Enright about the beating (showing his bruised chest as proof) and asks him to help ensure he isn't bothered any more. Enright, who doesn't like incidents like these disrupting his smooth-running operation, promptly calls Chief Abbott to investigate the matter. No officer admits to the beating, so Enright appeals to Kimble to get to the bottom of it. He hires Kimble to tend bar at a strip joint, serving as "bait" for the assailants.

Cramer sees Kimble at the bar and appeals to the two cops to help him out again, but they decline. Cramer then visits Hamp, the local funeral director/hit man, paying him $500 (supposedly on Enright's orders) to bump off Kimble. Hamp misses a shot through Kimble's hotel window. Kimble heads straight for Cora's place, suspecting she knows who is behind the attacks. She is uncooperative, but Kimble warns her that Enright will want the same answers from her.

Cora meets with Cramer, and they plan to set up Kimble. Cora meets Kimble at the bar, telling him she has a lead on where to find the one-armed man. They leave together and Cramer ambushes Kimble, but Kimble manages to overpower him in the ensuing struggle. Kimble brings Cramer to police headquarters, identifying himself and his prisoner, and instructing the police to contact Lt. Gerard.

The cops instead contact their local activity-directors, Enright and Luchek, and bring Kimble and Cramer to Luchek's mansion, where Enright awaits them. Luchek appears, scolding first Cramer for threatening his operation, then Enright for hiring Cramer in the first place. Luchek advises Kimble that they don't need *his* kind of trouble, either, and turns the whole matter over to Enright.

Act IV: The 1966-67 Season   161

In repayment for the Detroit debt, Enright gives Cramer two weeks' severance pay and a 24-hour head start on Kimble. Cramer happily drives off, north on Route 30, in a company car. Enright asks for Kimble's word that he won't leave before noon the next day, warning that he will call the police if Kimble crosses him. Kimble promises and leaves, immediately stealing an Enright car and heading in pursuit of Cramer. He figures this rare chance to catch up with the one-armed man is worth the gamble. An Enright employee sees Kimble leave and reports to Enright, who instructs the state police to intercept the car thief.

Kimble has almost overtaken Cramer when he is stopped. The cops return him to Enright, who advises Kimble to get out of town and stay out. By now Cramer has an ample lead and the chase is over.

Episode #94
THE SHARP EDGE OF CHIVALRY
Original Airdate: October 4, 1966

Written by: Sam Ross   **Directed by:** Gerald Mayer

Cast: Robert Drivas as Roger Rolande, Madlyn Rhue as Elizabeth Rolande, Eduard Franz as Edward Rolande, Rosemary Murphy as Mrs. Turney, Richard Anderson as Lt. Sloan, Ellen Corby as Mrs. Murdock, Judee Morton as Millie Brandt, Walter Gregg as boyfriend, Ralph Montgomery as fingerprint man, Peter Madsen as sergeant, Bobby Johnson as man, Kay Riehl as woman, Sy Prescott as plainclothesman; Henry Scott, Bob Duggan, and Paul Kent as policemen.

Kimble, alias Carl Baker, is superintendent of three adjacent tenement houses in a large city. Among the residents within his domain are Edward Rolande and his grown children Liz and Roger. Edward is a blue-blooded lawyer who obsesses about the family's royal heritage and whose apartment has become a museum of artifacts from the chivalric age. Liz is a humorless gal with eyes for Carl, while Roger is a deeply troubled young man, resentful of his father's fixation. Roger even dyes his hair black to free himself of the fair mane associated with his regal bloodline.

Roger hides out in the stairwell, spying on Millie (with whom he is infatuated) and her boyfriend as they make out in the hall. They catch and ridicule Roger, sending him running off all upset. Carl later invites Roger to his room for a chess game. From there, Roger can see the window of Millie's room, where she is undressing for bed. This agitates him even more. Roger tries to confide his troubles to Carl, with cryptic statements like "I feel like I have something big to do" and "my father's a loser ... it's up to me now." Their conversation and game are interrupted by a call from Mrs. Murdock, a kindly old lady fond of Carl. She has a short circuit in her ceiling lamp, so Carl goes to attend to it, asking Roger to wait for him.

After Carl leaves Roger removes Millie's key from the superintendent's rack, entering her room and startling her. He tells Millie he loves her and just wants to talk and be with her, but she loudly resists his advances. Frightened and upset Roger struggles to keep Millie quiet and finally bludgeons her with a paperweight. Mrs. Turney, a neighbor alerted by the screams, opens her door and sees the back of the assailant as he flees the locked room. The hallway is soon full of tenants abuzz about the murder.

Roger returns to Carl's room, stuffing the weapon behind a desk and returning the key to the rack, and Carl returns a moment later. The police come, and Carl supplies them with Millie's key. Police find a lock of black-dyed hair clutched in Millie's hand and speculate that she either knew and let in the assailant or that he had a key. The black-haired Carl, having known Millie *and* having had a key, appears to be a legitimate suspect. Lt. Sloan questions him and tells him not to leave the premises. Carl returns to his room and discovers the murder weapon. Deducing that Roger is the murderer, he hides the weapon. Meanwhile, Mrs. Turney is giving police her description of the assailant: black hair, six feet, and thirtyish.

Lt. Gerard hears a telecast about the murder, noting that the suspect's description and M.O. fit Kimble's. Gerard takes the next flight out there and arrives within hours.

Carl visits the Rolandes, telling Edward and Liz his suspicion about Roger. Edward won't tolerate such slander and suggests that Carl is the murderer, threatening to call the police. Carl leaves, going out a hall window to the fire escape, from which he sees Gerard. Desperate, Carl wends his way to Mrs. Murdock's room and knocks on her window. Mystified, but aware that Carl was with her at the time of the murder, she lets him in. Carl explains that the police think he killed Millie and that "some other kind of trouble" precludes his going to the police even with her as his alibi.

Gerard grills Mrs. Turney, showing her Kimble's "wanted" poster and asking if he was the man she saw leaving the murder scene. Under pressure from Gerard and Sloan, the confused woman identifies Kimble as Millie's killer. Fingerprints in the super's room verify his identity, and the murder weapon is discovered. "It looks like we've both got our man," remarks Sloan to Gerard.

Kimble goes to hide out in the basement, where Mrs. Turney is finishing her laundry. Roger, fearful that she might expose him as the murderer, suddenly grabs the lady from behind. Kimble rescues her, but Roger gets away. Kimble goes to check on Mrs. Turney, but she goes into hysterics and scares him off.

Roger goes home to his concerned family, saying, "I didn't do anything ... everybody's after me." Kimble then arrives, appealing to Roger to give himself up and telling the others that Roger is sick and needs help. Edward pulls a loaded antique pistol on Kimble and calls the police, saying Millie's murderer is in his apartment. Kimble breaks Roger down, and it becomes painfully obvious that Roger is the killer. Liz pleads with her father to let Kimble hide and to turn Roger in before he kills someone else. When the cops arrive, Edward tells them that his son is the killer.

Kimble hides out in Mrs. Murdock's place until the police, figuring that Kimble somehow slipped through, pull out. The local police have got their killer, but Gerard must leave without his.

Episode #95
TEN THOUSAND PIECES OF SILVER
Original Airdate: October 11, 1966

Story by: E. Arthur Kean   Teleplay by: E. Arthur Kean & Wilton Schiller
Directed by: James Nielson

Cast: June Harding as Cathy Lawrence, Joe Maross as Sheriff Mel Bailey, Lin McCarthy as Jacob Lawrence, Paul Mantee as Jack Burmas, Bonnie Beecher as Ella Lawrence, Ford Rainey as Oliver Nelson Corman, Simon Scott as Martin Pierce, James Sikking as Deputy Marsh.

Kimble, alias Dave Livingston, is a hand at Jacob Lawrence's Monroe County farm. In his couple of weeks there, he has become well-liked by Jacob and his two grown daughters, Ella and Cathy. Cathy is a mentally challenged young lady (similar to the character portrayed by June Harding in episode #52), and Dave spends a good deal of time teaching her to read in her "special place" (a hidden cave in the mountain).

Sheriff Bailey shows the Lawrences a poster of Jack Burmas, an escaped murderer believed to be in the area. Bailey remarks that Dave's face looks familiar, and he searches his memory to place it.

Lt. Gerard reads an editorial in the *Stafford Daily Chronicle*: "How to Murder Your Wife and Get Away with It." Gerard is not amused and tells editor Pierce so. Gerard feels Pierce is grinding an ax with the local police, who recently arrested Pierce's son for "borrowing" someone else's car. But Pierce backs up his editorial with a $10,000 reward, and newspapers around the country will soon accompany Kimble's picture with headlines such as "Reward: $10,000 Offered by Indiana News Chain."

The newspapers arrive at Corman's general store, and the owner recognizes the wanted fugitive as the Lawrences' farm hand. Deciding to go for the reward, Corman hides all the newspapers (later telling the sheriff they didn't come) and calls the *Stafford Chronicle*, leaving a message for Pierce to call him back.

As Dave drives Jacob's pickup on an errand, Burmas jumps into the back of the truck. He smashes the back window and orders Dave to take a side road to avoid the roadblocks. They come to a washed-out bridge, and Dave is unable to stop in time. Burmas jumps out, but Dave and the truck plunge into the creek. Cathy has a feeling "Uncle Dave" is in some kind of trouble, and Jacob relays her worries to the sheriff. Bailey searches for and finds the truck, rescuing Dave. Bailey again insists he has met Dave before, perhaps in a hospital in Korea. Dave is worried the sheriff will soon remember where he "knows" Dave from.

Jacob asks Dave why he spends so much time with Cathy. Dave says that he believes Cathy is capable of learning more things and ought to be brought to a clinic. Jacob becomes defensive, saying Cathy has been checked by doctors before, and Dave's meddling will only frustrate her.

Dave announces he is leaving, upsetting both Lawrence girls. Meanwhile, Pierce calls Corman, who says he can lead Indiana police to Kimble. The sheriff overhears the conversation and demands an explanation. Corman figures his claim has already been staked, so he shows Bailey the newspaper. The sheriff is livid with Corman and heads to the Lawrences' farm to find Kimble. Dave has already left.

Lt. Gerard arrives, and Bailey tells him the bad news (that the suspect is gone) and the good (that it definitely is Kimble, and that he is boxed in by the Burmas search efforts). The manhunt for Kimble begins. Burmas, figuring the hunt is for him, finds Kimble hiding in the bushes and holds him at gunpoint. He orders Kimble (his "ticket out of here") to bring him to a safe place, and Kimble takes him to Cathy's cave.

Gerard questions Jacob, who figures the $10,000 might come in handy for the farm's needs. He suggests that Cathy might know where Dave would be, and he might be able to trick her into telling where. "You'd turn in a friend for a mess of chicken coops," scolds Ella. Jacob tells Cathy that Dave is hiding, like a game, and she must help find him. Ella tells Cathy the truth. Cathy, upset, later heads for the cave alone.

Cathy gets to the cave, where she is grabbed by Burmas. Burmas tells Kimble to leave the cave and run interference for him, or he will harm Cathy. Kimble obliges, and the police spot him running through the mountain woods. They chase him toward the lake. Burmas takes Cathy and inexplicably also heads toward the lake, arriving there seconds after Kimble. The police see Cathy struggling with Burmas, whom they assume to be Kimble, and head toward them. Burmas shoots at the cops, and Kimble jumps into the lake. After Kimble convinces Cathy to jump in with him, she breaks free and dives in. Burmas, now without a hostage, makes a desperate dash with his gun blazing but is shot down. The police rush to the scene, and Gerard makes the grim discovery that the man is not Kimble.

Dave and Cathy somehow get back to the cave, while the men continue their fruitless search. Cathy asks Dave why they are trying to hurt him, and he explains that they think he did something wrong. Cathy figures that if she runs off, the police will chase her instead. She does and they do. When the time is right, Kimble will make his escape.

Act IV: The 1966-67 Season 165

Episode #96
JOSHUA'S KINGDOM
Original Airdate: October 18, 1966

Written by: Lee Loeb Directed by: Gerd Oswald

Cast: Kim Darby as Ruth Simmons, Harry Townes as Joshua Simmons, Tom Skerritt as Pete Edwards, Walter Burke as Doc Martin, John Milford as Sheriff E. Tate, Vaughn Taylor as Feeney, Mark Russell as Jay.

Kimble, alias Jim Corbin, stops at a Utah drugstore to ask about work. The owner tells him that the local veterinarian, old Doc Martin, may need help. At the store, Pete makes unwelcome advances on 17-year-old Ruth, and Jim asks what is going on. Pete takes umbrage at Jim's meddling and challenges the stranger. Jim, noticing Pete's deputy's badge, backs off. He later learns that Pete is an *ex*-deputy (having been bounced from the force for carousing), who continues wearing the badge as part of his ego trip.

Jim visits Doc and is hired on the spot. Doc likes Jim right off and is impressed when he straightens Doc's cluttered office in a matter of minutes. Jim accompanies Doc on a house-call to attend to Joshua Simmons's ailing horse. Josh, a widower, happens to be Ruth's father.

Doc and Jim go inside to collect the fee, meeting Ruth and her sick infant, Billy. The boy had been born out of wedlock, fathered by an army recruit who subsequently died. Jim notices the child has a high fever and recommends he be seen by a doctor. Josh righteously objects to Jim's suggestion, saying he doesn't believe in medicine because God is the Healer (reminiscent of the philosophy of the guardian of Kim Darby's character in episode #68). A worried Ruth privately asks Jim to return tomorrow, to examine the child while her father works in the fields. Jim agrees, driving off with Doc under the watchful eye of Pete. Inside, Josh accuses Ruth of flirting with the stranger and decries her sinful and disgraceful ways.

Jim asks Doc to prescribe some antibiotics so Jim can care for the baby. Doc reluctantly agrees, warning Jim not to stick his neck out too far. At the drugstore Jim encounters Pete, who remarks that Jim is a little old for Ruth and reminds him that she is "kinda my girl." Jim visits Ruth with the antibiotics, showing her how to administer them. Josh walks in and becomes enraged, smashing the bottle and preaching about the Lord's will. Jim asks Josh what kind of religion permits him to seek medical help for his horse but not his grandson. Josh orders Jim to keep away from them and slaps Ruth for her latest sin.

Jim again runs into Pete, who notes that Jim is not like any other drifter he has seen. Pete theorizes he is on the run and vows to check into it. Jim begins packing to leave. Ruth barges in with Billy, who is in shock, and Jim diagnoses the problem as critical anemia, requiring a blood transfusion. Since the only local M.D. is out of town, Jim and Doc must do the procedure. Jim, being type O-negative, will be the donor.

Josh finds his house empty and sets out after Ruth and Jim with a rifle. Doc sees him coming and permits Ruth, Jim, and Billy to hide out back, in his motor boat. Josh can't find them and heads for the sheriff's office. Jim takes Doc's car to drop Ruth and the baby off at their house.

Pete hangs around the sheriff's office, once again being refused for reinstatement. The sheriff makes it clear he doesn't want Pete around. Josh barges in, making a complaint about Jim. Pete finds this amusing and leafs through some "wanted" posters while Josh and the sheriff talk. Pete comes across Kimble's poster, with a notice about the $10,000 reward. He pockets the document and heads off on his own personal manhunt. Pete checks at Doc's place and takes an article of clothing from Jim's partially packed suitcase. This will give Pete's hound dogs the scent they need to pursue Jim.

Ruth detains Jim from leaving, and Josh gets there before he can depart. Holding Jim at gunpoint, Josh calls the sheriff's office. Referring to Jim's medical applications, Josh says that if the baby dies Jim is guilty of murder. Jim observes that Josh twists the Bible to justify his hatred for the child, a symbol of his daughter's "sin." If Josh had sought medical help in the first place, Jim points out, the baby would be OK by now — therefore, if it dies, *Josh* is the one guilty of murder. Ruth announces that the baby appears to be dead. Jim rushes over, revives the child and says the fever has broken. Appealing to Josh's convoluted beliefs, Jim suggests that maybe he was "sent" to save the baby. Ruth convinces her father to let Jim go.

Pete comes with his hounds. Josh exchanges jackets with Jim and heads out back into the mountain brush. The dogs follow the scent into the mountains, finally catching Josh, while Jim hides inside. Jim makes his escape moments before the sheriff arrives.

At the sheriff's office Pete tells his story, saying Josh abetted Kimble's escape. Josh denies ever seeing the man on the poster. Although the sheriff senses Josh is covering for Kimble, he takes the opportunity to throw Pete out on his ear, with the warning that the next time he comes around the station he will be jailed for loitering. After Pete leaves, the sheriff asks Josh why he let Jim escape after calling the police to apprehend him. Josh denies blame for the escape, saying it was God's will.

Episode #97
SECOND SIGHT
Original Airdate: October 25, 1966

Written by: Dan Ullman   **Directed by:** Robert Douglas

Cast: Tim Considine as Howie Keever, William Sargent as Sgt. Wally Denny, Sidney Clute as Sid, Stuart Lancaster as Wingo, Ted Knight as Dr. Rains,

Act IV: The 1966-67 Season 167

Richard O'Brien as Macklin, Ned Glass as Albert, Crahan Denton as George, James Noah as Detective Campbell, Janet MacLachlan as nurse, Byron Keith as foreman, Victor Millan as Officer Garcia, Nancy Jeris as policewoman, Angela Greene as floor nurse, Bill Raisch as Fred Johnson A.K.A. Walters.

Kimble, alias Jack Anderson, works this October for Apex Film Service in Pennsylvania. He develops Howie Keever's photograph, depicting a happy couple (Macklin and someone other than his wife), with a man — the one-armed man — in the background. Kimble resolves to personally deliver this order. He knocks at Howie's door but gets an answer from a neighbor: Wingo, Howie's meddling uncle and landlord. For the price of a bottle of booze, Wingo directs Kimble to the bar in which he is likely to find Howie.

Kimble enters the bar to find Howie being beaten by Macklin, from whom Howie had been trying to extort blackmail money. Kimble pulls them apart, appeasing Macklin with a copy of the photo. Kimble helps Howie up and accompanies him home, where he tells Howie what he is looking for. For $10, Howie advises Kimble that Fred Johnson, alias Walters, hangs out at the same bar they just came from.

Kimble returns to the bar around midnight, learning that Walters has just left for his job as night watchman at the chemical warehouse. Meanwhile, Howie visits Walters there, unsuccessfully trying to sell him some "valuable information." Kimble arrives shortly after, peeking in the window, and he and Johnson see each other. Kimble goes inside as Johnson plays hide-and-seek. When Johnson gets cornered upstairs, he pushes over a stack of crates of chemicals, causing an explosion. Kimble is blinded and knocked unconscious, while Johnson is slightly injured. With the warehouse ablaze, Howie takes pictures which he will peddle to the local newspaper. Kimble and Johnson are brought to Allegheny General Hospital.

Dr. Rains examines Kimble, saying there appears to be no tissue damage in the eyes and that, in cases like these, a patient's sight sometimes returns without treatment. Kimble is brought downstairs to the X-ray area, unknowingly passing Johnson in the hall. Johnson immediately makes an anonymous phone call, telling Sgt. Denny that Kimble is the injured man on the third floor. Johnson then unofficially checks out.

Denny calls Officer Garcia at the hospital lobby, telling him to make sure Kimble doesn't leave. Garcia heads for the third floor and Kimble, who has overheard the conversation, heads for the exit. Kimble wanders aimlessly down the street and is out of sight by the time the police figure out what has happened. Kimble spends the night in a power company shed.

Kimble is awakened by the sounds of workmen and he staggers into a high-voltage transformer area. The foreman orders Kimble to halt before he electrocutes himself. Apprised of Kimble's handicap, he offers to have him driven to the bus station, from which he can be transported to Howie's apartment.

Sgt. Denny, wondering how Howie happened to be at the scene of the fire, visits the photographer. He gives Howie a "wanted" poster of Kimble, asking Howie to call if he sees the fugitive. The ever-present Wingo, frothing at the thought of the $10,000 reward, comes in after the cop leaves.

The bus drops off Kimble, and a lady offers to help him up to Howie's apartment. Kimble does not realize she is a cop until Howie tells him afterward. They realize she will soon get the A.P.B. on Kimble and direct her boss to Howie's. Kimble, affirming his innocence, asks Howie to hide him and find Johnson, offering Howie the chance to collect the reward after Johnson's capture. Howie agrees to hide Kimble, but they are stopped by Wingo. The police then arrive to arrest Kimble, and Wingo figures the $10,000 is his.

Kimble tells Denny that Howie was responsible for his capture and ought to get the reward money. The sergeant relays this to Howie, who has stopped to say good-bye to Kimble. Howie tells Kimble that he did not turn him in and that he believes he is innocent. Kimble's eyesight suddenly begins to return, and Howie realizes this before he leaves. Howie, armed with his camera, waits outside on his motorcycle.

It is time to go to Indiana, and Kimble is handcuffed and helped outside by a single officer, who assumes Kimble is still blind. Howie asks the officer to turn around for a picture, and he obliges. Kimble knocks out the officer from behind, unlocks the cuffs, and flees with Howie on the motorcycle.

Howie drops Kimble off at a bus station, returning the $10 Kimble had paid him earlier, and declaring them even. He warns Kimble, though, that next time he will go for the reward money.

Episode #98
WINE IS A TRAITOR
Original Airdate: November 1, 1966

Written by: Arthur Dales   **Directed by:** Gerd Oswald

Cast: Roy Thinnes as Carl Crandall, Pilar Seurat as Elena Morales, James Gregory as Pete Crandall, Carlos Romero as Mr. Morales, Dabbs Greer as Thomas, Robert Wilke as Johnny, Warren Kemmerling as Nick, Chet Stratton as tour guide, William Challe as Jim, Richard O'Brien as Sam, Martin Garralaga as Felipe, Jason Johnson as Mann, Grandon Rhodes as physician, Roy Jenson and Arch Whiting as deputies, Rodolfo Acosta and Victor Millan as Mexicans.

Felipe and Morales are among a number of laborers, mostly Mexican-American, who work in Pete Crandall's vineyards in the southwestern United States. The night before, Felipe had proposed a strike during a union meeting and, despite Morales's objections, the proposal had met with favor. Word filters to Carl Crandall, Pete's son and partner, and Carl decides that Felipe's death will avert the strike. Morales is the logical fall guy, and Carl gets hold of Morales's rifle and prepares to shoot Felipe as he drives by.

Kimble, alias Taylor, hitches a ride with Felipe and Morales. Their trip is interrupted by rifle shots, fatally wounding Felipe and nicking Kimble's right shoulder. Kimble gets a glimpse of the sniper's bright red and white shirt. Men scatter as the police are on the scene almost instantaneously. They stop Kimble and, figuring a fleeing man with a bullet wound generally makes for a good suspect, bring him to the station.

The police, having recovered the murder weapon, declare Morales is the prime suspect, and release Kimble (who wasn't introduced to Morales in the truck). Kimble goes to a restaurant to eat. Elena, a waitress, tells Kimble she needs to speak to him privately. They go to her apartment, where Elena tells him Morales, her father, did not kill Felipe. Kimble says he can't identify who did or didn't kill him. Elena assumes Kimble has been paid off by the Crandall family, who own most of the town, and she leaves angrily. Kimble then sees a picture of Elena's father and recognizes him as the third man in the truck.

Kimble goes to the police station to report the new information but changes his mind when he sees a man (Carl) there wearing that red and white shirt. He realizes it will be a stranger's word against that of a high-status local and decides to instead write a letter apprising the district attorney of the facts. He goes to the hotel/post office (another Crandall property) to get a stamp for the letter. The manager/postmaster becomes suspicious about Kimble's mysterious missive and alerts a Crandall trustee. Two thugs, Johnny and Nick, mug Kimble and swipe the letter, and Kimble's intentions are soon known among Crandall's men. Assuming Kimble's story to be true, they are less worried about Carl's potential confrontation with the law than that with his own father. Pete is an honest, well-liked boss, and nobody wants to see him get hurt.

Pete tells Carl he doesn't like the smell of what happened to Felipe and wonders if Carl was involved. Meanwhile, Kimble encounters hostility from various townspeople intent on keeping him in town. Kimble walks outside and is nearly run down (on Carl's instructions) by Johnny and Nick. Kimble takes refuge in Elena's apartment, explaining his predicament. She allows him to spend the night there, with plans to stow away on a truck bound for "Tent City" the next day. In the morning Kimble jumps from Elena's window into the already-searched truck and gets a free ride to the laborers' camp.

Police are hovering around the camp, and Kimble ducks into a trailer. Morales is also hiding there. Kimble tells his story, explaining that he can't go to the police but will sign a statement if Morales and his friends can help him get out of town. Kimble is concealed on the laborers' wagon, bound for the vineyards. As the wagon passes through town, it is stopped by Carl's men. Kimble jumps out and flees into the nearest building, Crandall's winery, with Carl, Johnny, and Nick in close pursuit. Kimble joins a tour in progress.

Kimble slips away from the group but, unable to get to an exit, hides out behind some barrels. He is eventually discovered by Carl and his thugs, who lead him away with deadly intentions. Pete, wondering what is going on, enters the winery. Kimble gives his version, which Pete finds more credible than his son's. Johnny and Nick see the jig is up and refuse to cover for Carl. Carl then admits to the murder, defending his action as being in the best interests of the family business. He points out that Kimble's testimony would put Carl on death row; therefore, Pete must choose between the life of his son and that of a "two-bit drifter."

Kimble makes a break, and Carl chases after him with a gun, missing two shots. He corners Kimble and is about to fire again, but Pete intervenes. He guns down his own son to save Kimble.

Morales is cleared of Felipe's murder. Kimble, who says he is heading for Arizona, is driven out of town by the laborers, who invite him to come back and work with them sometime.

Episode #99
APPROACH WITH CARE
Original Airdate: November 15, 1966

Written by: Lee Loeb   **Directed by:** William Hale

Cast: Denny Miller as Willie Turner, Collin Wilcox as Mary Turner, Malcolm Atterbury as Sheriff, Dabney Coleman as Steve Edwards, Michael Conrad as Hogan, Nick Colasanto as Matt, Art Lewis as Speiler, E. J. Andre as old man, Marcelle Fortier as woman, Phil Chambers as carny, Mark Allen as wrecker, Jimmy Stiles as Joey, Paul Lukather, Marlowe Jensen, and Don Ross as deputies, Rory Stevens and Marc Winters as boys.

Kimble, alias Pete Allen, works for a traveling carnival, which is setting up shop for a June 1–6 engagement at Longdale. He stays in a trailer, his home for the past couple of weeks.

Willie is a 27-year-old muscle-man with the mind of a child. After years of baby-sitting him, his sister Mary had finally convinced their dying father to have Willie institutionalized. Mary cherishes her newfound freedom and is engaged to marry Steve next week. Willie had rebelled against the idea of being "locked up," and had run away. He has been wandering around, avoiding authorities, since March.

Willie barges into a boys' football game, just wanting to play, and accidentally injures Joey. The boy's mother runs to the scene, and the police happen by at that moment, scaring Willie away. Joey's mother says that Willie almost killed her boy, giving police even more reason to pick up Willie.

Willie wanders into the carnival grounds, striking up a conversation with Pete. Pete soon sizes up his handicap and befriends the lad. Willie then goes on a mischievous romp and soon is being chased by a bunch of workers. Pete stops them from harming Willie, who continues to hang around, helping Pete drive in tent stakes. Matt, the boss, is impressed by Willie's strength and offers him a job as a roustabout.

The sheriff, looking for Willie, enters the grounds. Willie hides out until he leaves. Afterward, Willie explains to Pete how the boy got hurt and tells of his plan to someday return to live with his sister. Pete drives Willie to Mary's house, thinking she might help straighten things out.

Willie reunites with his sister, then is sent outside while Mary tells Pete about Willie's situation. Pete returns to work as Steve comes to call on Mary. Willie is jealous and angry at the idea of sharing Mary with anyone and thinks she no longer loves him. He seeks out his next-favorite person, Pete.

The police — accompanied by Mary, Steve, and Hogan, a nurse from the state institution — go to the carnival. Mary and Pete convince Willie that institutionalization is the best thing for him. Hogan doesn't yet remember where he knows Pete from: they once worked together at Fairgreen Memorial Hospital.

Hogan talks with Willie, then suddenly remembers Pete's true identity. Hogan says he will have to tell the sheriff about the escaped murderer. Willie, worried that Hogan will bring trouble to his friend, beats him up and runs to the truck Pete is in. Willie tells Pete about Hogan's ravings, and they drive off together.

Hogan identifies Kimble for the sheriff. When Pete encounters a roadblock, he makes a U-turn, with the police in pursuit. Pete manages to lose them and to bring the old heap into a junkyard. Pete and Willie hide out in the abandoned office building.

Over Willie's objections Pete decides to leave at nightfall. Pete calls Mary, asking her to pick up Willie. Pete points out that, were he really a killer, he would have eliminated Willie long ago. Mary goes to the junkyard under the watchful eyes of the police. They approach the building, calling for the fugitives to surrender. Pete tries to stop Willie from making a desperate rush on the cops, but Willie knocks him aside and goes into the next room. The police enter the building there and Willie begins hurling heavy objects at them. One officer fires in self-defense, mortally wounding Willie, while Pete slips out a window. The cops find the other room empty, but if they learn that Kimble just left it, they won't have much trouble tracking him down.

The sheriff asks the prostrate Willie where his friend, Pete, is. Willie's dying words are "He's not *my* friend — he went away a long, long time ago and left me here all alone."

Mary corroborates her brother's story, saying Pete called her from out of town to tell her where her brother was. Figuring that Kimble is long gone, the police will undoubtedly call off the search.

Episode #100

NOBODY LOSES ALL THE TIME

Original Airdate: November 22, 1966

Written by: E. Arthur Kean   Directed by: Lawrence Dobkin

Cast: Joanna Moore as Ruth Bianchi, Barbara Baxley as Maggie Tippet, Phillip E. Pine as Lt. Rowan, Ben Wright as Mr. Ferguson, Bill Raisch as Fred Johnson, Don Dubbins as McCaffey, Herb Ellis as Hallet, Nora Marlowe as woman in hotel, Laurence Aten as workman; Patrick Riley, Guy Remsen, Pat O'Hara, and Robert Munk as police officers.

Kimble is tending bar at the HMS Bounty in Burlington (western United States). The television set behind him reports on the major factory fire nearby. Kimble turns his attention to the set as the camera pans the rubberneckers, one of whom happens to be Fred Johnson. Kimble immediately leaves work to rush to the scene of the fire. He spots Johnson, who is quarreling with his girlfriend, Maggie. When Johnson sees Kimble, he pushes Maggie aside and flees. Maggie chases after him and is struck by a car. His Hippocratic Oath getting the better of him, Kimble gives up on Johnson and attends to the injured woman.

Not wanting to lose his link to Johnson, Kimble says he is a physician — Dr. Harry Robinson — and accompanies Maggie in an ambulance. The fire emergency has depleted the hospital staff, so Dr. Robinson is put to work. Maggie is not yet up to answering questions, so Robinson pilfers her hotel key and visits the room, searching for clues to Johnson's whereabouts. He pockets a photo of Johnson and Maggie together.

Robinson returns to the hospital the next morning, assigning Maggie to a private room and keeping an eye out for any visitors. He has coffee with nurse Ruth Bianchi, who is attracted to him. Robinson indicates that friendship must be the extent of their relationship, so Ruth offers, "If you ever need a friend …"

After four days, Robinson finally gets Maggie alone for questioning. He tells her he is looking for her boyfriend and that the reason involves the police. Though Maggie is angry with Fred, and sympathetic toward the man who has taken such good care of her, she feels Fred is about the best she can do, romance-wise, and is reluctant to expose him to any trouble. After Robinson leaves, Maggie calls Fred, who orders her to blow the whistle on the doctor. Lt. Rowan brings in a "wanted" poster, and Maggie confirms that Kimble is the mysterious doctor. Rowan orders the hospital staked out and has a call put in to Lt. Gerard.

Kimble is spotted entering the hospital, and some 15 officers converge on him. Kimble ducks into the ascending main elevator, trades his jacket for a surgeon's smock lying in a laundry bin, then takes the emergency elevator down as the cops concentrate on the main one. He steals an ambulance and drives off, with the police in pursuit. Kimble abandons the car and hops a departing freight as the cops miss four shots. Kimble jumps off soon after, determined to somehow return to the hospital and preserve his link to Johnson.

Gerard arrives and is apprised of the facts. He figures Maggie is somehow responsible for Kimble's being in the hospital, a high-risk place for a doctor on the run. Kimble's jacket is found and Gerard sees the photo in the pocket. He now knows the connection between Kimble and Maggie and realizes Kimble will be back. Gerard advises Rowan to prepare a battalion of trained officers in anticipation of Kimble's return. Rowan reluctantly deploys 20 plainclothesmen, planted throughout the hospital.

Kimble hitches a ride and goes to Ruth's apartment, reminding her of her promise of friendship. After being told the reason for Kimble's mission, Ruth agrees to help him get back to the hospital but warns him that there are more policemen than interns there. She hides him in the back of her station wagon and drives him to the hospital, managing to smuggle him into an unguarded door leading to a therapy room.

Ruth tells Maggie it is time for her "therapy." The two women have become friends, and Maggie senses what Ruth is up to. Hallet, the officer entrusted with guarding Maggie, is confused by this unplanned appointment. Hallet follows them downstairs to the therapy room, but Ruth asks him to wait outside, saying she has to undress Maggie and put her under the heat lamp. Ruth then entices him to join her for coffee while Maggie undergoes "treatment." This gives Kimble the opportunity to confer privately with Maggie.

Maggie sympathizes with Kimble but still refuses to reveal Johnson's whereabouts. Gerard learns that Maggie is not in her room and deduces that she is with Kimble somewhere. He leads a search for the correct therapy room. Warned by Ruth, Kimble ducks out the back door just before Gerard barges into the room. Both Maggie and Ruth detain Gerard as he races for the exit, and Kimble is able to leave the building and hide outside. Gerard goes out and sees a departing hearse, which he figures Kimble is aboard. He orders the police to pursue the hearse, clearing up the hospital grounds for Kimble to slip away on foot.

Maggie is discharged and bids farewell to Ruth, observing that the nurse seemed to have a "thing" for Kimble. "It's all one big roll of the dice," Ruth replies, "and nobody loses all the time."

Episode #101
RIGHT IN THE MIDDLE OF THE SEASON
Original Airdate: November 29, 1966

Written by: Sam Ross **Directed by:** Christian Nyby

Cast: Dean Jagger as Tony Donovan, Nancy Malone as Nedda Donovan, James Callahan as Joe Donovan, James Seay as G. Morgan, Douglas Henderson as Lt. R. Irwin, Charles Wagenheim as fisherman, Ron Stokes as boatswain's mate, John Mayo as fingerprint man, James Johnson as crewman, Greg Benedict and Robert Kline as policemen.

Kimble, alias Eddie Carter, works on Tony Donovan's fishing boat off the Texas coast. The *Tillicum* has been out to sea for two weeks, and now it returns (with over six tons of albacore tuna) to the island on which Tony lives. Tony, from a long line of fishermen, has paternal affection for Eddie and would like to pair him up with his daughter, Nedda. There have been some romantic sparks between the two.

The island dock is crowded with picketing strikers bent on preventing the boat from being unloaded. Ironically, the leader of the striking association is Joe, Tony's son. Tony had heard rumors of the strike but chose to ignore them in the midst of such a successful expedition.

Tony is greeted by Joe and Nedda. Joe warns Dad that there will be trouble if he tries to unload his catch, but Tony is not about to let a $2,000 haul go to waste, even if the price is too low. Morgan, the local packing company owner eager to do business with Tony, calls the police to come in anticipation of trouble.

Tony, assisted by the loyal Eddie, begins unloading the boat, touching off a dock-fight between the strikers and the two-man crew. The cops arrive and arrest them all, booking and fingerprinting the brawlers. Morgan bails out Tony—who slaps Joe—and Eddie, who realizes his identity will soon be revealed. Joe threatens Eddie with bodily harm should he aid his father in any more trouble-bound ventures.

Nedda prepares dinner for Eddie and her father, but Eddie announces he has to leave. Tony is angered by Eddie's abandonment of loyalty. Eddie attempts to cross the bridge linking the island to Texas but is stopped by a policeman. Coastal merchants have complained about vandalism caused by returning fishermen, so the cops want to keep the trouble boxed up on the island. Eddie avoids some menacing strikers and makes his way back to the Donovans' house, where the police have already looked for him.

Tony and Nedda, now knowing why Eddie had to go, and believing him innocent, are sympathetic. Tony offers a deal: he will take Eddie to the safety of foreign soil the next morning if Eddie will help him haul in another catch on the way there. Nedda, worrying about her father's heart condition, disapproves.

Joe tries to talk his father out of the Mexican trip, warning him of possible legal consequences. Police Lt. Irwin arrives to search the *Tillicum* while Eddie hides in a nearby boat. Joe wonders why they are looking for Eddie, but Tony—still miffed at his son—ignores Joe. The police leave and Joe starts to.

Eddie comes out of hiding and helps the *Tillicum* to shove off. Joe sees this, as does a man on the harbor. The man gets word to Irwin, who doubles back, while Joe tries to stop Eddie. A vicious fight ensues, with Eddie finally knocking out Joe. In the confusion, Nedda stows away on the boat. Tony at last gets the vessel going just before the police arrive. The U.S. Coast Guard is called, and they take off after the *Tillicum* in a cutter. They almost catch up but lose the boat in a fog-bank as their radar fails.

The *Tillicum* reaches Mexican waters and they drop anchor a mile from shore to begin hauling up fish. Tony collapses with heart failure, and Eddie rushes to his aid. He tells Nedda to call the Coast Guard so Tony can be rushed to a hospital. Eddie revives Tony and stays with him until the last possible moment, diving overboard as the Coast Guard seaplane arrives. Eddie treads water on the far side of the boat, while Nedda tells the authorities that he swam ashore an hour ago. Joe, who came along to aid in the search, privately confers with Nedda, who tells him what Eddie did for their father. Joe tells the men to stop worrying about Kimble and to get Tony to a hospital. The officers and Nedda fly off with Tony, while Joe takes the boat back and Eddie swims toward the Mexican shore.

The day after Tony is discharged from the hospital, he is back on his boat. He invites a reluctant Joe to join him, and the two leave on their first father-son fishing trip in many years.

Episode #102
THE DEVIL'S DISCIPLES
Original Airdate: December 6, 1966

Story by: Robert Dillon & Steven W. Carabatsos
Teleplay by: Jeri Emmett & Steven W. Carabatsos   **Directed by:** Jud Taylor

Cast: Bruce Dern as Hutch, Lou Antonio as Don, Diana Hyland as Penny, Robert Viharo as Chino, Robert Sorrells as Curley, Crahan Denton as Mr. Benson, Frank Marth as Deputy Hendricks, Hal Lynch as Andy, Harry Ellerbe as Dr. Crossland, William Wintersole as Billy.

The Disciples are a motorcycle gang of about 20, led by Hutch, whose "turf" is near Twin Forks Junction in the western U.S. The police force there is hot on Kimble's trail. A sheriff's helicopter has tracked Kimble through the desert mountain trails, reporting his position to the ground force before turning for home due to a fuel shortage. Four police cars race toward the scene.

Hutch, Penny, and Don come across Kimble. Always eager to hinder the police, they offer Kimble escape with them. Having little choice, Kimble hops on the back of Don's bike and they all ride off, leaving the cops in the dust. They stop at the Hob Nob restaurant, the gang's hideout. Kimble prepares to leave, but Hutch stops him, reminding Kimble that he owes them. They are soon joined by the rest of the gang.

Hutch announces that the Disciples are going to pay a visit to Mr. Benson's place to avenge the death of former Disciple Tommy Joe. Tommy, Hutch, and Don had been involved in an armed robbery together, and Benson had turned Tommy in to the police. Adhering to the gang's code of ethics, Tommy had taken the rap for all three. He had told his father the truth, but Dad did not believe him. Faced with a choice between jail and service in Vietnam, Tommy had chosen the latter. Tommy was killed in action and, the way Hutch figures it, Benson is thus responsible for his death. This crime cannot go unpunished.

The police arrive at the Hob Nob, and Don hides Kimble in the men's room. The cops ask about Kimble, but nobody volunteers any information. Meanwhile, Kimble encourages Don to challenge Hutch's authority. Hutch is aiming the group toward serious trouble, and even intimidates Don into avoiding the girl (Penny) he is attracted to. Don becomes enraged, but Kimble's words will eventually sink in.

Having learned of Kimble's record, Hutch decides Kimble will repay his debt by killing Benson. The other Disciples are not too keen on partaking in a murder, but they won't challenge their leader.

Penny asks Kimble why he is working Don against Hutch, and Kimble says that Don will have to stand up to Hutch sometime, or be led into deep trouble. That night, as the Disciples sleep, Penny unties Kimble and allows him to escape, instructing him to contact the police and avert the trouble at Benson's.

Kimble finds a phone booth on the highway and calls the sheriff's office, but the deputy doesn't take the anonymous tip seriously and puts Kimble on "hold."

Meanwhile, Penny has been accused of setting Kimble free. Irate, Hutch slaps Penny and hurls her against a motorcycle, seriously injuring her. The gang finds Kimble at the phone booth and brings him back.

Kimble says that Penny may have a ruptured spleen, requiring immediate medical attention. Hutch is all for dumping her as they depart for Benson's, but Don says he will take Penny to a doctor and catch up with the gang later. Hutch is not pleased with this insubordination, but the gang goes off without Don.

At the doctor's office, Penny tells Don the true story of what happened the night of the robbery. Hutch had literally begged, tears and all, for Tommy to take the rap for him. Hutch's plan to kill Benson is his way of cleansing his own conscience by making a sacrifice, and he is dragging the rest of the gang in with him. Don kisses Penny and heads after the gang, while Penny warns the police about the trouble brewing.

The Disciples arrive at Benson's and make their intentions known. Benson seems to feel he deserves whatever they do to him. Kimble talks to him and learns that Tommy Joe was Benson's own son.

Benson is brought outside and terrorized by the gangsters. Hutch approaches him with a shovel, but Kimble grabs another shovel and engages Hutch in a bizarre fencing match.

Don arrives and, over Hutch's protests, tells the Disciples Penny's story. Chino announces that he is leaving, and the others follow suit, leaving just Hutch, Don, Kimble, and Benson. Hutch goes after Don with his shovel, but Kimble drops Hutch from behind. The police arrive, and Don hides Kimble in the garage as Hutch drives off.

Kimble encourages Don to stick with Penny, saying he would be a fool to let her go. Benson thanks Don for revealing the truth about the robbery, verifying Tommy Joe's version and proving his son was not such a bad kid after all. Don drives Kimble to safety on a back road.

Episode #103

THE BLESSINGS OF LIBERTY

Original Airdate: December 20, 1966

Written by: Dan Ullman   Directed by: Joseph Pevney

Cast: Ludwig Donath as Dr. Josef Korak, Julie Sommars as Carla Korak, Noam Pitlik as Jim Macklin, Tony Musante as Bolin A.K.A. Billy Karnes, Jan Merlin as Jan Korak, Arlene Martel as Magda Korak, George Tyne as Sgt. Charney, Edwin Max as Stark, Nolan Leary as judge, Chuck Courtney as detective, Bruce Manning as attendant, Calvin Brown as cop.

Kimble, alias Ben Russell, takes a $2-per-hour job as a furniture upholsterer for Elco Corporation. Among his coworkers is a family of Hungarian immigrants, the Koraks: Josef; his grown children, Carla and Jan; and Jan's wife, Magda. Carla has been dating another employee, Billy, who is actually a wanted killer.

The police come to Elco, making both Ben and Josef nervous. They are after Billy, who makes a break, knocking over a couple of cops and escaping. Because of Carla's relationship with Billy, the police will keep their eyes on the Koraks, even posting a stakeout across the road from their apartment building.

The Koraks invite Ben over for dinner and then ask him to spend the night at their place. The kids speak of their hopes to become naturalized U.S. citizens, hopes that have been often thwarted by their frequent moves. Josef, obviously troubled, leaves the room. Ben later discovers Hungarian medical books in the guest room and deduces that Josef was a doctor. Indeed, Josef had been a surgeon in Budapest for 25 years before immigrating. During his internship in America, something had shaken up his life. He had been falsely charged with performing an illegal abortion which had resulted in the patient's death — legally tantamount to murder. Josef, fearing imprisonment and deportation, had fled before the hearing and has had his family on the run ever since.

Macklin, an undercover cop, is assigned to infiltrate Elco as a custodian. While there, he pockets a coffee cup used by Ben, who looks suspiciously familiar to him. Macklin later has the fingerprints checked.

The Korak kids ask Ben's advice about their father's predicament. Josef, angry at being betrayed by his offspring and wanting to "disappear" without dragging his family down with him, packs and leaves the next day. They assume Pop is just on his usual Saturday morning walk, but Ben notices that Josef's books and other personal items are gone. Volunteering for a grocery errand, Ben leaves to search for Josef.

Billy, boxed in by the manhunt, breaks into the Koraks' building and takes refuge in the basement. Carla goes there to do laundry, but Billy forces her back upstairs at gunpoint. He enters the apartment, draws the shades, and holds the Koraks with the gun. Macklin, meanwhile, has gotten Kimble's print report.

Ben finds Josef at the bus station. Ben tries to talk him out of leaving, saying he is depriving his children of the opportunity to become Americans and the world of his medical knowledge. Besides, his flight will make police (thinking he is abetting Billy) issue an A.P.B. on Josef. Ben, hinting that he has his own similar problems, encourages Josef to face his accusers and finally convinces him to return to his family. Ben and Josef pick up the groceries and head for home.

Macklin visits the Koraks, telling them Ben's real identity, but quickly finding himself at the other end of Billy's gun. Macklin throws a vase toward Billy and is shot in the chest. Billy heads downstairs, encounters the other stakeout cop, guns him down, and continues to the basement. Josef and Ben hear the shot and rush inside.

Josef diagnoses Macklin's wound, and Ben realizes it will take both of them to save the cop. The two perform "kitchen surgery," successfully stabilizing Macklin's condition and preparing him for hospital treatment. The two fugitive doctors bid each other farewell, and Ben slips away.

Sgt. Charney arrives at the scene, finds Billy, and winds up killing him in a shoot-out. Charney goes to the apartment and sees the handiwork done on Macklin. He suspects that Kimble assisted Josef, but the Koraks say Ben left some time ago. Josef tells Charney that he wants to go to the station and make a statement about a problem he needs help with. His family is elated that Pop is finally going to come clean.

Josef is arrested at work, starting the wheels in motion to clear up the old charge. Charney wonders why the rest of the family is not there, and Josef tells him they are becoming citizens today.

Episode #104
THE EVIL MEN DO
Original Airdate: December 27, 1966
Written by: Walter Brough   Directed by: Jesse Hibbs

Cast: James Daly as Arthur Brame, Elizabeth Allen as Sharon, David Sheiner as Robinson, James McCallion as Jim Delaney, Bill Zuckert as Clark, Barry Russo as Sgt. Endicot, Tom Signorelli as mechanic, Jhean Burton as waitress.

Kimble, alias Russell Jordan, works for Brame Farms in the Pocono Mountains of Pennsylvania. The proprietor owns a stately manor on the premises, and a string of enterprises throughout the country under the umbrella of Arthur Brame Industries. Brame's businesses, superficially legitimate, are funded by the syndicate. His personal background includes stints as a racketeer and hit man.

Robinson, a Pennsylvania State Police officer, is 90 percent sure he recognized Kimble driving a station wagon with commercial plates in the area recently. Robinson was unable to match the face with the name until later. He contacts Gerard, who comes to Pennsylvania, and they begin a needle-in-the-haystack search.

Workers are having difficulty controlling the farm's new thoroughbred stallion, so Brame himself attends to matters. He enters the horse's corral but is quickly knocked down and cornered by the beast. It looks as if Brame will be trampled to death, until Russell rushes to the scene and pulls the horse away. "You're one up on me," declares a grateful Brame. "Now, I've got to square things with you." Russell is invited into the mansion, where he is offered a permanent job, a new wardrobe, cash, anything he wants. "One way or another I'll pay you," says Brame. "I don't like to owe anybody anything." Russell will settle for a month's severance pay, but Brame isn't satisfied to give such a small reward for such a great deed. On the way out, Sharon — Brame's woman — advises Russell to push for whatever he can get now, since Brame will soon be leaving on an overseas business trip. Russell indicates he is not out to extort any special reward, making Sharon suspicious. She thinks "Honest Sam" is too cool and is pulling some sort of con.

Robinson and Gerard arrive at Brame Farms. As Brame watches, Russell sneaks out the back and jumps into a departing horse van. Gerard questions Brame and Sharon and is told that Kimble was working there but was reassigned to Brame headquarters in Pittsburgh. Brame figures this false lead will give Kimble several hours' head-start in the other direction. After the cops leave, Arthur has a Brame-storm: he will knock off the persistent Gerard, thus repaying his debt to Kimble. Brame sends his yes-man, Clark, after Kimble to give him his "severance pay" and to tell him he won't have to worry about Gerard any more.

Clark finds Kimble and delivers an envelope containing $1,000. The message disturbs Kimble, and he pumps Clark for more details. Clark says a contract has been taken out on Gerard, and that Brame is about to leave on his London trip. For $200, Clark gives Kimble his car keys and lets him speed off to the airport in hopes of catching Brame.

Kimble gets there and is told that Brame's private plane has just taken off. Brame has actually stayed behind, planning to carry out his secret mission before his trip. Kimble runs into Sharon, who doesn't know about Brame's plan. When Sharon sees Brame getting into a car, she realizes something is awry. She and Kimble agree to share their knowledge: Kimble's of the planned hit, Sharon's of the place Gerard was sent. Both wanting to avert Brame's plan, they drive off to the processing plant in Pittsburgh.

Brame's number-one man tells Gerard he has never seen Kimble before. Gerard doesn't believe him and begins wandering around the plant in aimless search. Brame has arrived, taken a sniper's position, and assembled his rifle. He sees Gerard and takes aim just as Kimble and Sharon enter the building. Kimble yells, startling Brame, and pushes Gerard out of the line of fire just as Brame shoots. Kimble gets hold of Gerard's pistol and the two huddle, awaiting Brame's next move. Noting that Kimble has saved him from a killer, but is now holding a gun on him, Gerard remarks that Kimble has his "own unique system of justice." Kimble retorts, "We'll talk about justice later." Gerard instructs Kimble to shoot out the light, figuring they will have a better chance in the dark. Kimble does, but Gerard knocks his arm and retrieves the pistol.

Sharon tries to stop Brame, pointing out that Kimble doesn't want him to carry out the hit. Brame is determined to complete his mission regardless, and Sharon realizes out loud: "You're not doing this for him ... you've missed killing! Why, you get some kind of kick out of it!"

Kimble flees as Gerard and Brame prepare for the showdown. Gerard kills Brame in a shoot-out while Kimble escapes. The upset Sharon wonders why Gerard chose to go after Brame, rather than the other killer. Gerard explains that Brame was a bred killer, posing an immediate danger, while Kimble is "no real menace to anyone but himself."

Episode #105
RUN THE MAN DOWN
Original Airdate: January 3, 1967

Story by: Fred Freiberger   **Teleplay by:** Barry Oringer
Directed by: James Sheldon

Cast: Georgann Johnson as Laura Craig, James Broderick as Sheriff Owen Troupe, Edward Asner as Joe Bantam, Robert Doyle as Larry, Val Avery as Jim Ross, Sam Melville as Lee Runnels, John Davis Chandler as Kenny, Roy Engle as Lt. Hodges, Stuart Nisbet as Ossie.

Act IV: The 1966-67 Season

Kimble drives a truck on a highway, with Sheriff Owen Troupe and a battalion of state policemen hot in pursuit. Kimble pulls into a pine forest and takes off on foot. As nightfall approaches, the prospect of locating one man in thousands of acres of woods is overwhelming. The state cops decide to search anyway, but the sheriff and his deputy, Lee, return to the station. Owen becomes worried about his ex-girlfriend, Laura, when he learns that she rented the old Tyler cabin (with no telephone) deep in the forest.

Kimble comes across Kenny, down with a serious bullet wound. Kenny, along with Joe, Larry, and Jim, was involved in a big armored car robbery in Flatsboro yesterday. Kenny, after instructing the others to meet him at the presumably abandoned Tyler cabin, had been shot by a guard but had gotten away. Attempting to hop a freight, Kenny had deposited the loot into an empty boxcar but was unable to jump in with it. The $100,000 had rolled away aboard the Kansas City-bound train.

Seeing that Kimble is also on the run, Kenny offers a deal: if Kimble will help him, Kenny will lead him to a place safe from the police. Kimble, realizing Kenny is in rough shape, agrees. They make their way to the cabin, telling Laura that Kenny was involved in a hunting accident. Laura doesn't believe it but takes them in anyway. Kenny is placed in a room in the back of the cabin, while Kimble (giving his name as Tom Anderson) chats with Laura. Kimble conks out and, the next thing he knows, Laura is fixing him breakfast.

Joe, Larry, and Jim arrive at the cabin, looking for Kenny but telling Laura they are hunters whose car broke down. Larry hears moans and sneaks around to the back, finding Kenny and Kimble. The men drop their cover and take over the cabin. Joe and Larry interrogate Kenny about the whereabouts of their loot and don't believe the answer. They rough him up until he passes out, and Kimble returns to his aid.

With no sign of Kimble found, Owen deduces that he is between Strawberry Mountain and the Louisburg Plateau — right about where the Tyler cabin is. He and Lee drive to a point near the cabin and walk the rest of the way. Joe sees them coming and ushers Kimble and Larry into Kenny's room.

Owen shows Kimble's picture to Laura, Joe, and Jim, the men claiming to be stranded motorists. They say they haven't seen Kimble. Before Owen leaves, Laura asks him to deliver a message to Mr. Tyler. Owen realizes this is a coded distress signal, since Tyler is dead. Unfortunately, Joe realizes it, too. By the time Owen surreptitiously doubles back, the men are ready for him. Larry guns down Lee and knocks down Owen. The men get Owen's gun and are again in control. Kimble is cuffed to Kenny's bed, Larry is left to guard Laura, and Joe and Jim take Owen into town to get parts for their disabled car. While Larry makes a move on Laura, Kenny gets away. Larry goes out after him, and Kimble affirms his innocence to Laura.

Joe, Jim, and Owen return, while Larry brings Kenny back. The escape attempt has caused the bullet to work itself in deeper, putting Kenny in grave danger. Figuring they will never see the loot if Kenny dies, Joe makes a deal with Dr. Kimble: "You fix up Kenny and you get turned loose." Kimble asks that the sheriff assist him and that everyone else clear out of the room. Kenny dies, and Kimble realizes that the others will have no further reason to keep any of them alive. Owen devises a plan: to pretend that Kenny revealed the location of the treasure before he died and use the bogus information as bargaining power.

Kimble tells the others Kenny talked about the money's location, babbling about "lightning hitting a pine tree." Owen says he knows what that means and will take them there as long as they guarantee his, Laura's, and Kimble's safety. They agree, and Owen leads them on a winding journey into the forest. The crooks don't realize Owen is bringing them in a circle. At last, Owen points to a lightning-scarred pine atop a ridge and runs ahead, disappearing over the ridge. On the other side is Owen's car, with his rifle inside it. Owen arms himself and the outlaws realize they've been had. A shoot-out ensues, with Owen shooting all three with the help of Kimble's distractions. Kimble runs into the woods.

Owen aims to fire at Kimble, but Laura reminds Owen that he saved their lives. Owen puts down his gun and Kimble escapes into the wilderness. The state police will soon abandon their search, and Owen will say nothing to dissuade them. Meanwhile, it is obvious that he and Laura have reconciled.

Episode #106
THE OTHER SIDE OF THE COIN
Original Airdate: January 10, 1967

Written by: Sam Ross **Directed by:** Lewis Allen

Cast: John Larch as Sheriff Ben Corby, Beau Bridges as Larry Corby, Joseph Campanella as Harry Banner, Melinda Plowman as Ellen, Parley Baer as Al Cooney, Claudia Bryar as Mrs. Blake, Pitt Herbert as Mr. Sears, Buck Young as officer, Glenn Sipes, Don Eitner, Jim Raymond, and George Sims as deputies.

Kimble, alias Jim Parker, has worked the past week in a liquor store in Ocean Grove, California. He works with the owner, Al Cooney, and Sheriff Ben Corby's son, Larry. Ben is not too happy with Larry, who hasn't been home in three days, and who never seems to measure up to his father's expectations. Larry secretly plans to elope tomorrow with his pregnant girlfriend, Ellen.

As Jim counts up the day's receipts, a masked gunman enters the market through the unlocked back door. Cooney sees the holdup from his back room and phones the sheriff. After the robber departs, Cooney chases after him with a pistol and fires, wounding the villain in the stomach. The robber manages to escape in a stolen car. The sheriff arrives seconds later, and Cooney sends him on a chase. The robber loses control and flips the car. Ben gets out to examine the driver and is shocked to discover it is his own son.

Ben prepares to rush his son to the hospital, but Larry pleads with him. Pointing out that his gun wasn't loaded and the money was recovered, Larry begs, "Please don't be a cop now.... Please help me." Ben takes Larry home.

Officer Harry Banner, suspecting Jim was an accomplice, questions him about the holdup. Not satisfied with the answers, Banner has Jim taken to the station and fingerprinted. Banner calls the sheriff to inform him about the arrest, and Ben tells him the gunman got away.

Larry tells his father Jim had nothing to do with the holdup and asks him to get Jim off the hook. The sheriff goes to the station and questions Jim, interested mostly in whether Jim can identify the gunman. Ben convinces Banner to release Jim. Minutes after he does, the fingerprint report comes back, revealing Jim's true identity. Banner informs Ben, who has been busy raiding the supply room for medical supplies.

Ben goes to Kimble's boarding house, finding him packed and ready to leave. A struggle ensues, spilling out into the front lawn, where Ben at last gets the upper hand. A neighbor sees the fight and reports the disturbance to the police. Ben cuffs Kimble and takes him to his house (Larry, after all, needs a doctor).

Offering freedom in exchange, Ben demands that Kimble attend to Larry, who is sinking fast. Kimble objects, saying Larry needs hospitalization, but Ben refuses to expose his and Larry's guilt. Ben says he would instead try to dig the bullet out himself, so Kimble agrees to do his best.

Kimble extracts the bullet in the wee hours of the morning, saying he has done all he can but that Larry is still in grave danger. Ellen, worried when Larry failed to show up for their engagement, comes to the Corby house. She and Ben take turns blaming each other for leading Larry into criminal behavior. Larry says that he pulled the robbery to be able to provide for his new wife and child (Ellen, fearful of what Ben would do when he found out, had wanted to have an abortion). Ellen pleads with Ben to take Larry to a hospital, and Larry tells his father to do what she says. Larry slips into a coma, and Kimble says he will die if he isn't hospitalized. Ben finally calls for an ambulance.

Ben and Ellen follow the ambulance in Ben's car, with Kimble concealed in the trunk. The sheriff's identity enables him to bypass the roadblocks before releasing Kimble. Ben apologizes to Ellen for his attitude toward her and offers to "take Larry's place" in seeing her through the birth of the baby.

Larry recovers to get a five-year suspended sentence. Ben resigns from the police force, admitting his guilt in abetting Larry. Banner, who had grown increasingly suspicious about Ben's connection with Kimble, notes that the hospital staff had called Larry's first aid a "professional job." Ben replies that he has acknowledged guilt of harboring a fugitive—what difference does it make how many he harbored?

Episode #107

THE ONE THAT GOT AWAY

Original Airdate: January 17, 1967

Written by: Philip Saltzman & Harry Kronman   **Directed by:** Leo Penn

Cast: Charles Bronson as Ralph Schuyler, Anne Francis as Felice Greer, Charles Drake as Oliver Green A.K.A. George Barber, Harlan Warde as Lt. E. J. "Mitch" Mitchell, David Renard as Guillermo, Pepe Callahan as Lt. Felipe Calderon, Vince Howard as Brooks, Thordis Brandt as Patty Stockwell, David Fresco as Hodges, Rico Alaniz as Perez.

Kimble, alias Bill March, has spent the past week in California as deck hand for Gus Hargas's boat. It has been chartered for the next five days by Felice Greer, who plans a trip to the small coastal Mexican town of Tanango. There she will secretly reunite with her husband, Ollie, who fled after embezzling some $275,000 (mostly in negotiable securities) from his company. The securities have never been recovered, and police suspect that Mrs. Greer has cashed them in or will at least lead the cops to her husband. Officer Ralph Schuyler is assigned to work undercover and replace Gus as skipper on this trip. Ralph thinks the deck hand ought to be checked, too, in case he has some connection to this whole affair.

Ralph, Bill, and Mrs. Greer set off. Ralph pockets a cigarette pack handled by Bill, with plans to deliver it for a fingerprint check. While Mrs. Greer prepares lunch, Ralph checks her room for clues. He comes up empty, not knowing she has converted the securities into a change purse full of rare coins. She had reasoned that anyone looking for a quarter-million dollars wouldn't bother checking her loose change.

The K5 boat experiences a power failure (actually, a ruse arranged by Ralph so that he could go ashore and drop off the fingerprint sample). They stop to get a replacement fuse, and Ralph calls Lt. Mitchell to tell him the prints are waiting for him. The trio shoves off again.

A gas can tips near the boat's electrical box, setting a fire below deck. Ralph goes down to battle the raging blaze but gets badly burned and passes out. Bill rushes to the rescue, saving Ralph and somehow extinguishing the fire. The boat reaches Tanango, and Bill goes to seek medical help for Ralph. Felice, who has come to like and trust Bill, asks him to deliver a letter addressed to George Barber at the Hotel Flores. She admits that George is really Ollie (whom Bill had read about in the newspapers) but says he is innocent.

Bill goes to the hotel, asking the clerk to call a doctor for Ralph. The clerk gives Bill a telegram from Mitchell for Ralph: "Bill March prints match those of Richard Kimble. You want help?" Bill hands the envelope for George Barber to the clerk, who in turn gives it to "Senora Barber" just passing by. She is actually Ollie's secretary and playmate, Patty, and Bill has no trouble figuring out what is going on.

Ralph calls Mitchell on the ship radio, learning about Kimble. Bill returns to the boat and attends to Ralph's burns, explaining that he acquired first aid skills in the service. Ralph retorts, "The only thing I got in the service was three years older." Ralph finally pulls a gun on Kimble and says, "The doctor I want is already here." Kimble shows Ralph the telegram, and Ralph realizes Kimble could have just left him there.

Ollie and Felice reunite on the dock, and she tells him about her clever conversion of the securities. Ralph, having overheard, comes off the ship and holds the Greers, along with Kimble, at gunpoint. He explains that he is a police officer and that Kimble is a convicted murderer. Ollie remarks to Felice, "You picked a great bunch of shipmates."

Ralph, who is in no condition to be up, collapses. Felice grabs his gun, and Ollie asks her for the coins. "Give him that purse," Kimble warns, "and that's the last you'll see of it or him." He describes the "other" Mrs. Barber, and Felice realizes who it is. Enraged, she holds the gun on Ollie and begins throwing the coins into the water. Among them are an 1894-S Liberty Head dime, worth $12,500 (a specimen sold in 1990 for $275,000) and an 1875 proof $3 gold piece, worth $19,000 (1995 price: $110,000).

Mexican police, alerted by Lt. Mitchell, rush toward the boat in search of Kimble. Felice allows Kimble to hide under the dock and tells the cops that Ollie is Kimble. Ollie tries to make a break but is wounded and arrested. Meanwhile, Kimble makes his escape. Later, Lt. Calderon apologizes to Ralph for not getting Kimble. "All I lost was a dividend," says Ralph, ordering the Greers to be locked up.

Episode #108
CONCRETE EVIDENCE
Original Airdate: January 24, 1967

Story by: Jack Turley **Teleplay by:** Jack Turley & Jeri Emmett
Directed by: Murray Golden

Cast: Celeste Holm as Pearl Saunders Patton, Jack Warden as Alex "Pat" Patton, Harold Gould as Thomas Crailer, Jason Wingreen as Nebbs, Larry Blake as Charlie, Billy Snyder as Pete, Ray Kellogg as sheriff, Jim Crowell as deputy, E. A. Nicholson as roughneck, Jane Barclay and Ed Garrett as townspeople.

Kimble, alias Steve Dexter, applies to work for Alex Patton Construction Company, which is building a superhighway in northern Nebraska. Pat, the owner, recognizes Dexter from a "wanted" poster recently left there by police and secretly decides to keep Kimble around as his private physician. Pat's wife and partner, Pearl, dismisses Dexter for lack of experience, but Pat overrules her and hires him on the spot.

While Pat and Pearl remain partners on paper, they have lived apart for a decade. Ten years ago, a theater Patton had built — barely within legal safety limits — had collapsed in Pat's hometown of Coleman, killing three children and crippling several others. The Pattons' daughter had escaped physical harm but had been emotionally devastated. At 21, she still occupies a "school" for the mentally disturbed. While Pat had been cleared of manslaughter, he has been unable to clear himself of the wrath of the townspeople or of his own conscience. The only thread holding him and Pearl together is the benefit of doubt she allows him and her desire to be there when he finally betrays his guilt. Pat, in declining physical condition, privately plans an apologetic gift to Coleman: a top-of-the-line children's hospital. Not wanting his plan (which he views as a "signed confession") to be revealed, Pat has the building — supposedly a motel — erected by the phantom "Fairplay Construction Company."

Dexter is "promoted" to work in the field office as an assistant to Pat. Pearl views this as just another move designed to undermine her authority. She talks privately with Dexter, telling him the theater story, and trying to talk him into leaving for another job she can line up for him. Dexter, feeling allegiance to Pat, declines.

Tom Crailer, Coleman's town manager, learns that Fairplay is being funded by Patton, and word gets around town. Crailer advises Pat to abandon his project, employing various frustration tactics. The punch line is a "stop work" order, citing Patton for 22 nebulous violations of codes (some dating back to 1897). Pat counters by producing a copy of a check, from the owner of the First-Rate Construction Company to Crailer, dated just a week before First-Rate was granted a contract for Coleman's new civic auditorium. The blackmail works, and Crailer slinks away with his tail between his legs.

Dexter helps Pat through an attack of angina pectoris, with Pat's ever-ready first aid kit. Pat tells Dexter he knows his true identity and lays the ground rules: if Kimble stays around to monitor his health, his secret is safe, but if not, Pat will alert the police.

In Coleman townspeople repeatedly demonstrate against and vandalize the "motel." Pat and Dexter examine the damage, and Dexter remarks that the building resembles a hospital. Pat tells Dexter the truth, asking him to keep Pat on his feet for one more month so he can complete the project.

Pearl has decided to walk out. While Pat oversees the motel construction, she types a farewell note in Pat's office, where she happens across the "wanted" poster. Changing her mind, Pearl calls Dexter into the office, giving him one hour to get out of town. If he tries to contact Pat, Dexter will forfeit the hour. Pearl sees Dexter head toward the motel in a company truck, so she calls the sheriff and heads out after him.

Pat, battling a blaze set by a fire-bomb, feels his heart failing and staggers into a shelter. Kimble finds him and administers Pat's portable oxygen mask, but it is too late. Pearl arrives, and Pat extracts a promise to complete

Act IV: The 1966-67 Season 187

the hospital, then expires. Kimble explains the project to the grief-stricken Pearl.

Sirens alert the approach of the police, and Kimble hides in the hospital. The cops go in looking for him. Pearl orders one of the construction workers to take her car and speed off after a doctor for Pat. She knows the police will chase after the car, thinking it is Kimble making his getaway. They do, and Kimble leaves on foot, stopping only to remind Pearl of her promise to Pat. Kimble catches a bus to his next destination.

Pearl soon takes charge of things and lifts the veil of secrecy, and it is "all systems go" for the new hospital.

Episode #109

THE BREAKING OF THE HABIT

Original Airdate: January 31, 1967

Written by: John Meredyth Lucas   Directed by: John Meredyth Lucas

Cast: Eileen Heckart as Sister Veronica, Antoinette Bower as Sister Angelica, Linden Chiles as Father Taylor, Heather North as Marie Dorland, Adrienne Hayes as Victoria, Kelly Thordsen as Tarleton policeman, Clay Tanner as Officer Landers, Bill Erwin as counterman, Peter Marko as attendant, Pat Patterson as intersection policeman, Dallas Mitchell and Paul Hahn as highway policemen.

Kimble had saved enough money to purchase the services of an informant to help in finding Fred Johnson. The informant had sent Kimble to Tarleton, California (population 40,627), where Johnson reportedly was a numbers-runner working out of a cafe. A photograph shows Johnson there, with most of the establishment's sign ("—UDSON'S") visible. When Kimble approaches Tarleton, he finds the police waiting for him (the informant had sold him out).

Kimble manages to escape, suffering a bullet wound in his right thigh. He hops into a passing truck and eventually gets to Sacramento, some 100 miles away.

Kimble looks up his old friend Sister Veronica (from episodes #22–23), who is now principal of the St. Mary Magdalene School in Sacramento. He visits her there, reminiscing about their previous "enchanted voyage," and reminding her of her three-year-old promise to help him if ever she could.

Kimble asks the Sister to go to Tarleton, find and positively identify Johnson, and have the police arrest him for numbers-running. Once Johnson is in custody, Kimble will contact Gerard and turn himself in. Sister Veronica says she is very busy (particularly with problem students like Vicky and Marie) but will try to help. She sets Kimble up in the janitor's room, passing him off as new custodian Tom Marlowe.

Marie visits Kimble's room, explaining that she used to visit the previous janitor. Sister Veronica shoos her away. Marie sees a newspaper, on the front page of which is a picture of Kimble and a story of his escape in Tarleton. She decides to go to the police.

Veronica prepares to leave for Tarleton but learns that Vicky has run away again. Vicky is a bright but misguided young lady, and Veronica feels personally responsible for setting her on the right path. She decides to look for Vicky rather than do the Tarleton thing and spends the whole day in a futile search. Meanwhile, Marie leads the cops to the school, and Kimble sees them coming. He escapes out the window and spends the day eluding them, kept going by the belief that Veronica is taking care of the Johnson matter.

Sister Veronica returns at nightfall. Father Taylor tries to comfort her, reminding her of the many girls she *is* helping. He mentions the manhunt for their janitor, and she confesses to harboring Kimble. She tells the Father about their previous encounter, when Kimble restored her faith and persuaded her not to renounce her vows. Father Taylor points out that Kimble, then, has given her all the time she has left and is justified to ask for some of it back.

Kimble finds Sister Veronica and is upset to learn she didn't even try to find Johnson. She promises to do it tomorrow, but Kimble says that he will have been positively identified from fingerprints by then. Kimble notices there is something wrong with the Sister's health, and she admits she has an inoperable brain tumor and very little time left on this Earth.

Sister Veronica hides Kimble in the trunk of her car and takes off for Tarleton. She runs over a curb on the way out, breaking the exhaust pipe. The Sister gets to a roadblock and is asked if she is alone. "My religion teaches me that we are never alone," she glibly responds, and the officer sends her on her way. Kimble beats at the trunk door, and Veronica pulls over. He is almost overcome by exhaust fumes by the time she rescues him. He spends the rest of the ride in the front seat, wearing Father Taylor's jacket.

The two get to Tarleton and Kimble, scanning a local phone book, narrows the possibilities down to two. Hudson's doesn't seem to be the right place, so they head to Knudson's Cafe (after being detained by a close call with a traffic cop). Sister Veronica checks there and is told Johnson "embezzled" a stash of loot and left that morning. The Sister gives Kimble the bad news, bidding him farewell and saying "we won't be seeing each other again." Kimble finds his way to a rail yard and hops a freight out of town.

Sister Veronica returns to the school, lamenting her failure to help both Kimble and Vicky. She learns that Vicky has returned voluntarily and realizes that "Someone Else" is watching over her sheep. Referring to Kimble, the Sister remarks that "God always seems to send him to me in my hours of crisis."

Episode #110
THERE GOES THE BALL GAME
Original Airdate: February 7, 1967

Written by: Oliver Crawford Directed by: Gerald Mayer

Cast: Martin Balsam as Andy Newmark, Gabriel Dell as Chester, Lynda Day as Nadine Newmark, Vincent Gardenia as Capt. Bill Gibbs, Jonathan Lippe as Phil, Susan Seaforth as Vicky Walton, Joan Tompkins as Rose Newmark, Sidney Clute as Joe, John Ward as Jerry, Barbara Dodd as Aggie, Jon Kowal as Al, Michael Harris as guard.

Kimble, alias Gene Tyler, takes in a Saturday afternoon baseball game. He occupies the seat next to 22-year-old Nadine, who awaits her companion, Vicky. The ladies meet at the park each week, always taking the same seats, but this time Vicky is detained by a mysteriously empty gas tank. A man, Chester, approaches Nadine, saying she has a phone call from Vicky and leading her away.

Chester is a professional kidnapper, hired by Nadine's jilted lover, Phil, in an act of revenge. Nadine had dumped Phil about the same time as a sore arm derailed his major league pitching prospects. Chester takes her to a secluded country house, where she will remain hostage of the two men until her father — wealthy publisher Andy Newmark — can come up with a large sum of money (to be split evenly between Chester and Phil). Chester calls Andy to tell him his daughter has been kidnapped.

Vicky asks Tyler if he has seen Nadine, and he says she left with a man (whom he would know if he saw again) a half hour earlier. Vicky is paged to report to the stadium security office. Moments later, a guard asks Tyler to accompany him to the same office. Tyler meets Andy, who calls him the sole witness to the kidnapping. Newmark leaves Tyler no choice but to accompany him home to help get Nadine back.

Newmark has his staff begin a check of former employees and servants and, while they are at it, they might as well check out Tyler, too. Newmark gets another call from Chester, instructing him to round up $200,000 in small bills without publicizing the kidnapping or contacting the police. Unfortunately for Newmark, the news has already been leaked to and published by a rival newspaper. And, unfortunately for Tyler, the story mentions a man who can describe the abductor. When Chester reads about this, he decides to somehow silence the mysterious witness. When Capt. Gibbs reads about it, he pays a visit to his friend, Andy. Gibbs thinks Tyler looks familiar and resolves to check mug-shots upon his return to the station.

Chester calls Newmark again, instructing him to have the witness deliver the money, alone, at the old power plant at 8:00 that evening. Tyler refuses to do the delivery, knowing it is a suicide mission, but Newmark reveals that he knows who Tyler really is (having found the answer in his own newspaper morgue). If Kimble doesn't deliver the money, Newmark warns, he will turn him over to the police.

Kimble prepares to leave with the suitcase full of money but is stopped by Gibbs, who has a warrant for his arrest. Newmark begs Gibbs to let Kimble go through with the delivery before he arrests him, and Gibbs—figuring he can get two birds with one stone—finally agrees. Kimble, equipped with a miniature homing device concealed in a pack of cigarettes, is sent off to make the drop.

Kimble delivers the money to Chester, then warns him that the bills are marked. Kimble explains the warning by saying he wants a piece of the action. Chester suspects a trap, but Kimble advises him that he is a wanted murderer and thus has no reason to help the police. Satisfied, Chester drives Kimble back to the country house. The police, accompanied by Newmark and armed with their homing device receiver, follow closely behind. Following the cops are Vicky and a Newmark aide, driving in Newmark's limousine.

Chester, Kimble, Phil, and Nadine are in the house when it is surrounded by the police. Kimble grabs Nadine and flees the building, taking cover behind a car. A shoot-out between police and Chester ensues, and Kimble slips into the woods in the confusion. Chester is gunned down by Gibbs, Phil is arrested, and Nadine is safely reunited with her father.

Kimble is ordered into a passing car—Newmark's limo. He is driven to safety and given an envelope, presumably filled with cash, courtesy of Newmark. The police ask Newmark what he knows about Kimble's disappearance, coinciding with the spectacle of his limo speeding off at 70 MPH. Newmark wryly reports the theft of his car.

Episode #111
THE IVY MAZE
Original Airdate: February 21, 1967

Written by: Edward C. Hume **Directed by:** John Meredyth Lucas

Cast: William Windom as Prof. Fritz Simpson, Geraldine Brooks as Caroline Simpson, Bill Raisch as Fred Johnson A.K.A. Carl Stoker, Lorri Scott as Sally, Bill Quinn as Chief Henry Terry, Don Mitchell as Ken, Dani Nolan as Mrs. Thayer, Mark Russell as Bill, James Farley as Al, Carl Reindel as assistant, Victor Brandt as volunteer, Perry Cook as bus driver; Jill Janssen and Iris Ratner as coeds.

Prof. Fritz Simpson, Kimble's old fraternity brother, conducts dream research in the psychology department of Wellington College (founded 1856). Fritz had been engaged to Helen before Dick had taken her away from him; still, the two men had remained close friends. On the rebound, Fritz had taken up with Helen's best friend, Caroline, and wound up marrying her. Fritz had never really fallen out of love with Helen, a source of envy for Caroline. When Helen was murdered, Fritz had believed in Dick's innocence while Caroline had been sure of his guilt.

By fantastic coincidence Fred Johnson, alias Carl Stoker, has a $75-per-week job in Wellington's maintenance department. Simpson had connected Stoker with Kimble's description of the one-armed man and had contacted Dick's sister who, in turn, had gotten hold of Dick. Kimble reunites with Simpson, then identifies Stoker from a window overlooking the grounds. Kimble is ready to have Stoker picked up right away, but Simpson has a grander plan. He will lure Stoker into volunteering for his "dream withdrawal" experiment, in which the subject is monitored for four days and during which he is allowed to sleep but prevented from dreaming. A console measures the subject's vital signs; when it indicates the subject is beginning to dream, he is promptly awakened by one of the 'round-the-clock student lab assistants. Gradually, the subject's defenses erode, and his deep, dark secrets — normally released through dreaming — come spilling out. Simpson is sure he can evoke a full confession (or at least incriminating details) from Stoker, to be picked up by a hidden microphone and transmitted to a tape recorder in Simpson's office.

Simpson posts a handbill on the employees' bulletin board, offering cash for human guinea pigs. Those accepting will get $10 for the first day, $20 for the second, $30 for the third, and $100 for the fourth, in addition to their normal wages. Stoker jumps at the chance to make $160 for sleeping. He is wired to the console and sent to bed; his progress (or regress) will be observed through the one-way glass in his room.

Three days later, Kimble — introduced as medical writer Jerry Sinclair — departs the graduate house at which Simpson has had him put up. Caroline, driving by, sees Kimble and is horrified. She calls Fritz but is told he is unavailable. She then places an anonymous long-distance call to Lt. Gerard, telling him Kimble is on the Wellington campus. Gerard, of course, is soon on his way to Wellington (population: 5,000).

Caroline goes to the college to confront her husband and sees Kimble near his office. At home the Simpsons argue about the arrangement. Fritz explains his experiment, and Caroline tells him she has called Gerard. She believes Fritz is going to all this trouble not for Dick but for Helen's ghost. Fritz gets Dick away from the campus just as Gerard arrives. Much to Caroline's disapproval, Fritz hides Kimble out in their home. She softens noticeably after they talk about old times, and Kimble reaffirms his innocence. Meanwhile, Gerard leads police on a futile campus manhunt and begins to wonder if the tip was a hoax.

After more than four days Stoker cracks, revealing more and more about his sordid past. Seeing that he is close to pay dirt, Simpson summons Kimble to the lab to identify parts of the confession that only the murderer could know. Shortly after Kimble arrives, Gerard pays a second visit to Simpson, whom he has begun to suspect. Gerard sees the one-armed man in the lab, validating his hunch. Caroline calls Gerard there, confessing that she was the tipster, but saying Fritz doesn't know Kimble is in town. She directs Gerard to the dorm in search of Kimble, buying Fritz a few precious minutes to conclude the experiment.

Simpson grills the zombie-like Johnson, extracting the clinching details of Helen's murder. Kimble enters, getting Johnson to identify him as the man whose wife he killed. Johnson regains full consciousness and is told that his confession is all on tape.

Kimble holds down Johnson, while Simpson goes to his office to meet the returning Gerard. Simpson begins playing the incriminating tape, but Gerard is interested only in locating Kimble. He barges into the lab, finding Kimble and Johnson. Kimble hurls Johnson at his pursuer, saying, "Here's your man, Gerard," as he flees the room. Johnson knocks over Gerard, Simpson, and Kimble in turn, then takes the tape and runs. Johnson drops the tape into a container of sulfuric acid and escapes. Kimble climbs out a window and makes his way to the departing Wellington Dukes' football team bus, climbing into its luggage compartment. He gets out at a stop sign and disappears into the country.

At the conclusion, Fritz seems finally to have exorcised Helen's ghost from his life and is ready to devote more attention to his flesh-and-blood wife.

Episode #112

GOOD-BYE MY LOVE

Original Airdate: February 28, 1967

Written by: Lee Loeb   Directed by: Lewis Allen

Cast: Jack Lord as Alan Bartlett, Marlyn Mason as Gayle Marten, Patricia Smith as Norma Bartlett, James Lanphier as Paul, Jack Raine as Charles, Ivan Bonar as detective, Hal Riddle as policeman.

Gayle Marten is a professional musician who had a hit record a couple of years ago but is now reduced to singing and playing piano in the bar of a country club. A shrewd, manipulative, and beautiful woman, she has her sights on club patron Alan Bartlett — or, rather, on the $10 million estate controlled by Alan's wheelchair-bound wife, Norma. Gayle has been carrying on a covert romance with Alan but sees no likelihood of his leaving Norma for her (even if he did, Gayle would lose her link to the fortune). Enter club parking attendant Bill Garrison, whom Gayle recognizes as wanted murderer Richard Kimble. An intricate plan forms in Gayle's mind, and its first step calls for her romantic involvement with Bill.

Bill and Gayle seem very attracted to each other and spend more and more time together. Alan asks Gayle what is going on between them, and Gayle replies that it is none of his business. Unless she can become Mrs. Bartlett, she says, their relationship is over.

Gayle visits Norma, telling her that she and Alan are in love and have been having an affair for months. Gayle suggests that Norma agree to a divorce. Norma later confronts Alan, who begs forgiveness and promises repentance. Furious with Gayle, Alan pays her a visit. He finds a news clipping Gayle had planted for him, showing a picture of Kimble and telling about the reward for his capture.

Alan gets the brainstorm Gayle had hoped he would: he will murder Norma and set up Kimble as the fall guy. That way, Alan and Gayle can have each other and the $10 million, too.

Alan offers Bill a job as chauffeur and handyman, paying $600 a month — considerably more than Bill makes at the club. Gayle encourages Bill to accept, and he does. Gayle begins dropping hints to the bartender, depicting Bill as a manipulator who had designs on such a job from the beginning.

Gayle will go to work as usual while Alan orchestrates the plot all by himself. Alan provides theater tickets to his other servants, ensuring that they will be out of the house until midnight. He will kill both Norma and Bill, claiming that Bill killed Norma during a burglary and Alan nailed Bill trying to escape.

Norma learns that Alan is not where he said he would be and guesses he is with Gayle. She rummages through his desk in search of Gayle's telephone number and finds the Kimble clipping. Norma is horrified to think she is alone in the house with a murderer and figures Alan hired Kimble to kill her.

Norma arms herself with a pistol and tries to phone the police. Kimble overhears and goes toward her, seeing the clipping. He cuts off the call and Norma pulls the gun on him. Kimble denies being hired to kill her and says that if her life is in danger it is not from him. Kimble figures out Alan's plan and reasons that he wouldn't have left Norma with access to a loaded gun. Kimble proves himself right, and Norma realizes he is telling the truth.

Kimble tries to call the police but finds the phone lines dead (Alan had cut them outside). Kimble tries to take the car out, but it, too, is dead. He returns inside and advises Norma to lock herself in her room. Alan enters the house through her window, foiling that plan. Kimble knocks at Norma's door, and Norma warns him to get away. Alan chases Kimble downstairs, but Kimble shuts off the main circuit breaker, darkening the house. Kimble jumps Alan and a struggle ensues. Alan returns to his feet and is about to proceed with his plan, but Norma hurls her wheelchair down the stairs, breaking Alan's leg. He passes out, and Kimble leaves to call the police and then keeps going.

Police arrest Gayle at the club, and she feigns ignorance to the plot, saying that she knows Alan only casually. The police inform her that Alan has signed a confession, indicating that the murder scheme was all Gayle's idea.

Episode #113
PASSAGE TO HELENA
Original Airdate: March 7, 1967

Written by: Barry Oringer   Directed by: Richard Benedict

Cast: James Farentino as Ray Carter, Percy Rodriguez as Chief Deputy Emory Dalton, Phyllis Love as Laura Benson, Russ Conway as Sheriff Matt Thornton, J. Pat O'Malley as Joseph McGinnis, Garry Walberg as Web Webster, Gene Kirkwood as Lockett, Michael Mikler as Kline, Orville Sherman as Prewit, Marc Winters as Tom Benson.

Kimble, alias Thomas Barrett, is in Wyler City in northern Montana. He buys a one-way bus ticket to Helena, but the bus doesn't leave until tomorrow. Leaving the depot, Kimble is ordered by two policemen to stop. They think he matches the description of an auto thief. Kimble runs but is caught by the cops. He punches out one officer but is arrested by the other.

Kimble is cleared of the theft, but there still are the matters of resisting arrest and assaulting an officer. Besides, Chief Deputy Dalton has a "feeling" about Dalton and doesn't want to release him just yet. Kimble is placed in a cell adjoining one occupied by Frank Carter, a local boy accused of two murders and guilty of two others as well. Carter, a reader of detective magazines, recognizes Kimble.

Dalton decides to drive Carter and Kimble to Helena the next morning, accompanied only by another deputy, Lockett. The sheriff warns Dalton that it is a treacherous ride, through "Carter's country": Carter has a slew of friends and relatives, none too fond of policemen, along the route. One punctures the police wagon's gas tank even before they leave. The officers take off with the two prisoners handcuffed in the back. Shortly into the journey, two men fire at the wagon from above the road. Both officers are wounded, Lockett fatally. A shoot-out between Dalton and the snipers ensues, with Dalton eventually gunning the two down. Meanwhile, Carter and Kimble try to leave on foot. Somehow, Dalton catches up and brings them back. Kimble, who says he was a medic in Korea, patches up Dalton's wounded leg.

The truck is inoperable, and Dalton announces that the three are going to walk the remaining 40 miles to Helena. Kimble warns him that he will wind up losing his leg if he attempts such a trek, and Carter warns that he will wind up losing his life trying to traverse "Carter's country" on foot. Among his other attributes, Carter is a racist, creating additional friction between him and the African-American deputy.

Dalton follows the two prisoners, chained together, for many miles. They spend the night in the backwoods home of a widow, Laura, and her two kids, then push on again the next morning.

Kimble scolds Carter for his verbal abuse of Dalton. Miffed, Carter tells

Dalton who Kimble is; he wants to make sure Kimble is on his side when an escape opportunity comes. Kimble is agreeable, as long as their cooperation is limited to escaping, but Carter has other ideas. Dalton, who has lost a lot of blood and not slept in two days, begins to nod off. The prisoners jump him, disarming the officer and freeing themselves. Kimble starts off into the woods, but Carter chases Dalton with the deputy's own rifle and pistol. Carter has Dalton cornered and is about to shoot, when Kimble delivers a flying tackle. As Kimble and Carter struggle, Dalton gets his rifle back. Carter grabs the pistol, and Dalton shoots him in self-defense.

Dalton tells Kimble he will have to take him in but promises to testify that Kimble saved his life. Kimble says he is innocent and that no testimony of Dalton's is going to help him. Kimble prepares to leave, and Dalton warns that he will fire. "If shooting me makes you somebody," Kimble says, "that's what you're gonna have to do." Kimble turns his back and walks away, and Dalton can't bring himself to shoot.

At the Wyler County Sheriff's Station, Dalton turns in his report and his badge. The sheriff asks why he is resigning, and Dalton says it is because of what is in the report: he let a murderer go. The sheriff says he interprets the report differently: "Under conditions of extreme duress, with your own life in danger, one of your two prisoners got away." He refuses to accept the resignation of "the best man I know."

Episode #114
THE SAVAGE STREET
Original Airdate: March 14, 1967

Story by: Mario Alcalde **Teleplay by:** Jeri Emmett & Mario Alcalde
Directed by: Gerald Mayer

Cast: Gilbert Roland as Jose Anza, Tom Nardini as Jimmy "Chico" Anza, Michael Ansara as Miguel Anza, Ross Hagen as Harve Benton, Barney Phillips as Sgt. Harrigan, David Macklin as Banks, Miriam Colon as Mercedes Anza, Bobby Diamond as Ollie, Kevin Coughlin as Cotton, Frank Puglia as compadre, Ralph Montgomery as policeman.

Jose Anza, a renowned cigar maker, is an immigrant living in a big U.S. city with his wife and teenage son, Jimmy. Kimble, alias Tony Maxwell, is a temporary employee of J. Anza Cigars and has become a trusted friend of the family.

Jose wants the best for his son and thinks Jimmy might become a world-class violinist, so Jimmy reluctantly takes daily lessons. He walks home carrying his case and is surrounded by three neighborhood toughs, who figure a violinist can't possibly be cool. They rough Jimmy up and play catch with his violin until Tony happens by and breaks it up. When Jose hears about the incident he is furious and calls his brother, Miguel, a police officer. Miguel comes, promising to have a few words with the youthful trio, but encourages Jose to let the kids work things out for themselves. Miguel's partner thinks Tony looks familiar and resolves to check the "wanted" posters at the station. Jose asks Tony if he thinks Jose was wrong to call the police, and Tony replies, "You do what you have to do."

The bullies surround Jimmy again the next day, but Jimmy ducks into the basement window of a rooming house. Meanwhile, the police approach Anza's store in search of Kimble, who sees them coming and flees. He takes a bullet above his left knee but gets away, winding up in the same basement as Jimmy. Tony tells Jimmy he didn't kill anyone. Jimmy, calling Tony his only friend, promises to help. Forgetting his violin, Jimmy takes Tony to his secret hiding place on the rooftop: a hole in a brick wall, concealed by boards and debris, which leads to a den-like area. Tony asks Jimmy to bring him first-aid supplies.

The police have the whole block barricaded and conduct a house-to-house search for Kimble. Sgt. Harrigan and Miguel question the Anzas; Harrigan thinks Miguel warned Kimble so as to spare his brother a delicate situation. Mrs. Anza sees Jimmy lurking around the medicine cabinet and gets suspicious. She asks the cops what would happen to someone aiding the fugitive and is told such a person would be imprisoned.

The bullies search the basement they had seen Jimmy enter. They find his violin and a few drops of blood, putting two and two together, and deciding to wait there. When Jimmy returns to retrieve his violin, they will rough him up some more and find out where he is hiding Kimble.

Jimmy brings the supplies to Kimble, who extracts the bullet. Jimmy returns to the basement and encounters the toughs. They threaten him, and Jimmy offers to take them on one at a time. Jimmy is overmatched, but he doesn't back down and does get in some good licks, finally earning their respect. Now that they are all friends, Jimmy lets the others in on his secret and brings them up to meet Kimble.

Kimble affirms his innocence to the newcomers, and they agree to protect him. Jose, searching for his son, knows and checks Jimmy's hiding places. He finds the quintet in the den and orders his son home. Jimmy, finally taking a stand with his father, refuses to go. He introduces his new friends and tells his father Kimble is innocent. Proud of his son's manliness, Jose agrees to help them get Kimble to safety.

With Jimmy accompanying him, Jose sneaks Kimble into the back of his delivery truck. They drive toward the barricade and, just as they are stopped by the police, the three youths throw bottles at the cigar store window. The cops are distracted, and all but Miguel go after the kids. Miguel orders Jose to open the back door of the truck. Jose asks if Miguel would want his own brother and nephew to go to jail for helping an honorable, innocent man.

Apparently unmoved, Miguel repeats his order. Jose opens the door, but Miguel closes it without looking inside (so he can truthfully say the door was opened and he didn't see Kimble). They go through the barricade and Kimble is on his way to safety.

Afterward, Miguel chastises Jose for making him choose between betraying his badge or his family. Jose paraphrases Kimble's quote: "We all do what we have to do." He figures that is what they did.

Episode #115
DEATH OF A VERY SMALL KILLER
Original Airdate: March 21, 1967

Written by: Barry Oringer   Directed by: John Meredyth Lucas

Cast: Arthur Hill as Dr. Howell, Carol Lawrence as Dr. Reina Morales, Carlos Romero as Sgt. Manuel Rodriguez, Valentin de Vargas as Capt. Pablo Gomez, Rodolfo Hoyos as Sancho, Stella Garcia as nurse, Roberto Contreras as Diego, Sam Gilman as Capt. Mulvaney, Bard Stevens as Lanny, Mike Abelar as Arturo, Robert Hernandez as man, Natividad Vacio as delivery man, Raoul Perez as Officer Arenas, George Lymburn as officer.

Kimble is in coastal Texas, battling pneumonia and trying to elude the police. A sailor sees Kimble hiding and, on a whim, offers him an escape plan: to board the departing fishing boat, the *Prowler*, and tell the captain Lanny sent him. Kimble does, offering the captain $100 and free labor, while Lanny decoys the cops. A three-day journey brings Kimble to Puerto Vinales, Mexico. Taking the alias Thomas Barrett, he checks into a motel but collapses on the way to his room. He is rushed to the Clinica Central, coming under the care of Drs. Howell and Morales. They diagnose his illness and measure his temperature at 104.4°.

Howell is an American who had interned in Mexico. As a young girl, Reina Morales had seen her family wiped out by an earthquake and had been adopted by Dr. and Mrs. Howell. After Mrs. Howell had died of a strain of meningitis peculiar to this region, Dr. Howell had devoted his life to finding a cure for the deadly disease. He works obsessively on his research while also administering to the locals, who are grateful to have him there. Reina had grown up, attended college, and joined her adoptive father at the clinic.

Sgt. Rodriguez is Mexico's answer to Lt. Gerard. Since hearing about the American stranger who straggled into town, Rodriguez has fished around on the hunch that Barrett is an outlaw. He confiscates the motel key Barrett had handled, so the fingerprints can be checked (a lengthy process in this neck of the woods). Capt. Gomez has little patience for the sergeant's dogged pursuit of a hunch while there is so much else to do. Besides, now that Barrett is in the care of the community's good friend, Gomez doesn't want Rodriguez to trouble Dr. Howell unnecessarily. Rodriguez continues his checking nonetheless.

Howell recognizes Barrett as Dr. Kimble and offers a deal: if Kimble will help him run the clinic (so Howell can concentrate on his research), Howell will not blow the whistle on him. Kimble agrees and spends several weeks attending to patients and building his own reputation as a skillful doctor. Along the way, Kimble and Reina fall in love.

Dr. Howell makes a breakthrough: a combination, including the experimental drug soperidone, produces a favorable response in three-fourths of the lab animals tested. The drug is potentially fatal in large doses and particularly dangerous to heart patients; nevertheless, Howell is ready to start administering it to many of his 42 meningitis patients. Kimble has serious misgivings about experimenting on humans and says he will have to leave. Howell tells Kimble that he needs him more than ever, as he himself has meningitis.

Kimble learns that half of the patients are getting no medication at all, per Howell's orders. Howell claims they are out of soperidone, but Kimble turns up a whole case of it in the supply room. He realizes Howell is sacrificing some of his patients in the quest to prove his cure (which, Howell reasons, could save thousands of lives, as compared to the handful at stake here). Kimble cannot deal with this violation of ethics. Despite Howell's threat to turn him in, Kimble administers the medication to the rest of the patients.

Dr. Howell collapses and is brought to his death bed. Having once had a coronary attack, Howell was unable to use his own miracle cure on himself without risking instant death. Howell warns Kimble to get away while he can. He is concerned not only with Kimble, who has Rodriguez hot on his tail, but with Reina, who oughtn't to hold on to this doomed relationship. He suggests she take Kimble to San Pablo, where he will be able to board any departing boat by simply dropping Howell's name. Reina and Kimble leave.

Moments later, Rodriguez and Gomez arrive. The prints have been identified as Kimble's, and a "wanted" poster of him has been delivered. Rodriguez declares that the poster depicts Barrett, and he needs only Howell's corroboration. Howell says Barrett is gone, and he didn't look anything like Kimble. The doctor's dying words are good enough for Gomez, and he orders Rodriguez to drop the matter.

Kimble reluctantly leaves his lover and heads back to the U.S.

Episode #116
DOSSIER ON A DIPLOMAT
Original Airdate: March 28, 1967

Story by: J. T. Gollard   Teleplay by: J. T. Gollard & Jeri Emmett
Directed by: Gerald Mayer

Act IV: The 1966-67 Season

Cast: Ivan Dixon as Ambassador Unawa, Diana Sands as Davala Unawa, Diana Hyland as Alison Priestley, Lloyd Gough as Frank Hobart, K. L. Smith as cabby, Vince Howard as policeman, Don Kennedy as mover, Jonathan Hawke as police lieutenant, Marlowe Jensen and William Hudson as detectives.

Kimble, alias Charlie Farrell, reads the book *Unjustly Convicted*, by D.C. lawyer Frank Hobart. The book includes a section devoted to the Kimble case: how Hobart believes he could get Kimble — unnecessarily convicted on circumstantial evidence — acquitted in a new trial. Kimble travels to Washington, arranges a meeting with the author, and searches for a place to stay.

Kimble rushes to the aid of a man who has collapsed to the ground, helping him to his feet and assisting him across the road. The grateful man is Ambassador Unawa, whose nature is to trust all people. Unawa invites Kimble to come for dinner and even stay at the embassy as his guest. Kimble meets Mrs. Unawa (who complements her husband's trust with her own habitual suspicion) and Alison, an aide to the couple who is immediately attracted to the new guest.

Mrs. Unawa notices the Hobart book in Kimble's jacket pocket. After Kimble says he is in town on a "legal matter," she asks her aide to pick up a copy of the book for her (Alison winds up buying out the bookstore's entire stock). Mrs. Unawa reads it and learns the true identity of the mysterious guest. She confronts Kimble, warning him to make an excuse to leave that evening. Alison, having overheard, apprises the ambassador of the situation. Unawa, who can't believe his friend is guilty, resolves to stand by him.

At dinner, Kimble announces he has to leave because of a phone call he received. The ambassador wryly says that the person had called again, saying the problem was solved; therefore, Kimble is welcome to stay. The Unawas then have a private discussion about his harboring a fugitive. This action stands to not only ruin the ambassador's political career, but jeopardize relations between his country and the U.S. The ambassador responds, "Can a man serve his country, who does not even serve his own conscience?"

The ambassador meets with Kimble, who affirms his innocence over a game of chess. The next day, Unawa's driver takes Kimble to Hobart's office. As soon as they leave, Mrs. Unawa calls the police.

Hobart tells Kimble he is sure he can get him off, and he already has two investigators packing for Indiana. He tells Kimble it may take months for things to fall in place and strongly advises he stay in the embassy — which, technically, is foreign soil and is thus out of the jurisdiction of the U.S. police. Kimble takes a bus back and eludes the swarm of cops just long enough to get back on the embassy grounds.

Mrs. Unawa visits with Kimble, saying she sympathizes with his predicament, yet she is determined to get rid of him. She is worried about not only her husband's political life but his physical one: he has an inoperable brain tumor. She thinks the ambassador is unaware of his condition; ironically, he does know about it and thinks *she* is uninformed. Each thinks he/she is protecting the other from the horrible news.

Lt. Gerard arrives at the embassy to claim "my prisoner." Unawa corrects him: "a guest of the embassy, but no man's prisoner." Gerard and Unawa trade trash-talk about such issues as diplomatic immunity and extradition treaties. After Gerard leaves, Kimble tells Unawa of the three goals that have kept him going for four years: "to avoid capture, to find the man that killed my wife, and to secure a new trial." Unawa is impressed by Kimble's unshakable faith in the U.S. legal system.

Mrs. Unawa decides that, since she can't get Kimble away from the embassy, she will get *it* away from *him*. She contacts movers, saying that the Unawas will be leaving by 5:30 the next day. Gerard and the local cops have the go-ahead to move in at that time. Mrs. Unawa goes to inform her husband but finds him unconscious. The prescribed medication will keep him that way until after the move is completed.

Hobart advises Kimble to turn himself in; if he flees, he is again a fugitive, and Hobart will be unable to help him. Kimble decides to run anyway, and Alison devises an escape plan. The moving van drives off with a load of large boxes. Alison goes to the gate, where Gerard and other cops stand guard, lamenting that the van was not supposed to leave just yet. She says that she believes everybody is gone from the embassy. Gerard concludes that Kimble is aboard the van and orders it followed. As police chase the vehicle, Kimble slips out the unguarded rear exit of the embassy and boards a bus out of town.

Episode #117
THE WALLS OF NIGHT
Original Airdate: April 4, 1967

Written by: Lawrence Louis Goldman   **Directed by:** John Meredyth Lucas

Cast: Janice Rule as Barbara Wells, Steve Ihnat as Art Meredith, Tige Andrews as Buck Leonard, Sheree North as Willy, Martin Brooks as Lt. Gould, Marcelle Fortier as landlady, Jeane Wood as manager.

Kimble, alias Stan Dyson, drives a truck for Leonard Freight in the Portland, Oregon, area. He has become romantically interested in Barbara, who works in Leonard's dispatcher's office. Stan doesn't know that Barbara is in the work-release program of the Women's Correctional Center, to which she must return nights and weekends. Trying to help out a boyfriend, she had been locked up for small-time embezzlement.

Stan returns from a Friday run with a figurine and two tickets to that

Act IV: The 1966-67 Season   201

evening's ball game, but Barbara has to decline (much to her regret). Her parole officer, Art, checks in, telling her that the board failed to review her case and won't meet again for another six months. Barbara's frustration mounts.

Buck, the boss, asks Barbara to deliver Stan's next assignment to him: to bring a load to Seattle tonight, stay the weekend, and bring back a load from Vancouver on Monday. Stan invites Barbara to spend the weekend with him; he knows a nice, out-of-the-way place at Lake Shohalis. She again reluctantly declines without explanation. Stan leaves for Seattle, and Art drops Barbara off at the Correctional Center. Instead of entering, she rebelliously takes a bus out of town. She has decided to take Stan up on his offer.

Stan checks into the Lake Shohalis Inn. He meets Willy, a waitress there, who invites Stan to join her for a drink. He politely refuses and retires to his room. There he finds the figurine he had given Barbara — and a note: "Room 10." He and Barbara are reunited and spend a romantic weekend together.

Art informs Buck that Barbara didn't show up at the Correctional Center. Buck tries to track her down, suspecting she has gone to meet Stan. Buck locates the place Stan had talked about staying at and calls. Willy answers and later tells Stan about the call. Stan calls Buck on the C.B. radio, learning the truth about Barbara and promising to bring her back. Meanwhile, Art has discovered that Stan's references don't check out; he gains entrance to Stan's apartment and confiscates a fingerprint sample.

Stan and Barbara drive off, and she pleads with him to take her to Canada rather than back to jail. She finally tells Stan the whole story and says that if he doesn't take her north of the border she will go by herself. To appease her, Stan agrees to take her to Canada, where they will be free to continue their relationship. Kimble stops to pick up a few groceries. While he is out of the truck, a call comes over the C.B., warning Barbara she is in the company of a convicted killer.

The police have Buck continually call in to the truck, hoping to get a fix on its location. Kimble becomes suspicious, figuring they are after him rather than Barbara. The cops track him to a point 80 miles south of Seattle and 10 miles east of Route 99. Once on the highway, Kimble can head either north toward Vancouver (236 miles) or south toward Portland (97 miles). The police decide to set up roadblocks north of the intersection; if the truck doesn't show up there, they will await his arrival in Portland so as not to jeopardize Barbara's safety.

Barbara falls asleep, and Kimble heads south on 99. When she awakens, she discovers they are just six miles from Portland. Barbara admits she knows who Kimble is and warns him he is driving into a trap. Kimble tells Barbara he didn't kill his wife, and his problems with the police are the reason he could not take Barbara with him. Kimble stops the truck, kisses Barbara good-bye and, seeing the police waiting nearby, tells Barbara to drive off. The cops chase the truck as Kimble slips away on foot.

At the Correctional Center, Art coaches the disconsolate Barbara on what to say to minimize the possible consequences of her weekend escapade.

Episode #118
THE SHATTERED SILENCE
Original Airdate: April 11, 1967

Story by: Ralph Goodman   **Teleplay by:** Barry Oringer
Directed by: Barry Morse

Cast: Laurence Naismith as John Mallory, Antoinette Bower as Andrea Crutch, Paul Mantee as Deputy Robert Howe, Dabbs Greer as Sam Jensen, James McCallion as Kugler, Jack DeMave as deputy.

Kimble, alias Ben Lewis, is pursued by the police in the northwestern U.S. After hopping a freight, Ben stops at a grocery store, where he meets a customer named Andrea. A divorcée, Andrea seems smitten by Ben. She offers him $10 per day plus food and board to do some work around her Pinedale, Washington, house. Ben reluctantly agrees. Deputy Howe stops by the house to speak to Andrea, in whom he has romantic interest.

Andrea hears a radio bulletin about Kimble and realizes who Ben is. She confronts him, and he affirms his innocence. Andrea offers her car to Ben, suggesting he run it off the mountain road and make his escape while the cops follow the car. Ben drives off but encounters Howe, who also realizes who Ben is. Howe fires, wounding Ben in the left arm, then pursues him by car. Ben ditches the vehicle as planned and escapes into the woods on the side of the road. He collapses and seems destined to bleed to death.

Ben is discovered by John Mallory and his two dogs. Mallory has lived alone in the woods for 14 years, shunning civilization. He helps Ben to his cabin and attends to his wound. While Ben recuperates, he and Mallory play chess and exchange philosophies. Mallory won't admit he has missed companionship.

Ben prepares to go on his way, but the dogs will not permit it, and Mallory claims he can't overrule them. Mallory goes off hunting and instructs Ben to stay. Ben tries to leave, but Mallory and his dogs track him down and return him to the cabin.

Mallory takes ill with a pulmonary infection, and Ben tells him he will die if he doesn't get medicine. Mallory thinks it is a bluff to permit Ben's escape, even after Ben admits he is a doctor wanted for murder. Ben manages to get away, finding his way to Andrea's house. Andrea informs Ben there is no doctor within 100 miles but drives him to Kugler's Pharmacy.

Kugler — reluctant and suspicious — turns over some prescription antibiotics to Ben and Andrea, then contacts the police. Andrea drops Ben off to return to Mallory's cabin. Meanwhile, Mallory has discovered Ben's absence and gone out to retrieve him again. When he sees Ben he thinks he has caught him leaving and is about to turn his dogs loose as punishment. Ben tells Mallory he is returning from town, but Mallory doesn't believe it. Ben tosses Mallory the medicine, and the hermit realizes Ben has been honest with him all along. They return to the cabin, where Ben administers the antibiotics and prepares to leave unchallenged.

Howe and another deputy, accompanied by Andrea, set off for Mallory's house. They arrive just as Ben is about to leave. Mallory detains the cops just long enough for Ben to escape through the back of the cabin. The deputies search the building and conclude Ben is long gone. They set out on the 100-mile drive to fetch a doctor for Mallory, while Andrea remains with him. Mallory ostensibly objects to her staying, but seems pleased when she does.

Epilog
The Series Finale

The Fugitive ended its four-year run in historic fashion: a two-part series finale that uniquely purported to resolve the conflict that had sustained its existence. Aired in color on August 22 and 29, 1967, the final shows were produced by Wilton Schiller.

The final episode was seen by more viewers than any previous single episode of a regular series. Its 72 percent viewer share remained a regular series record until the notorious "Who Shot J.R.?" episode of *Dallas* on November 21, 1980. *The Fugitive* was replaced in ABC's lineup by the short-lived musical-comedy series *That's Life*.

Reruns of *The Fugitive* were shown by ABC on weekday afternoons between April 1967 and March 1968. Thereafter, the show seemingly disappeared for two decades, until the A&E cable network revived it between 1990–93. *TV Guide*, in its 1993 fortieth anniversary poll, named *The Fugitive* "Best Drama of the 1960s."

A major motion picture based on the series was released in August 1993. Starring Harrison Ford, *The Fugitive* became the blockbuster movie of the season.

Episodes #119-120
THE JUDGEMENT (Parts I & II)
Original Airdates: August 22 & 29, 1967

Written by: George Eckstein & Michael Zagor   **Directed by:** Don Medford

Cast: Diane Baker as Jean Carlisle, Jacqueline Scott as Donna Kimble Taft, Richard Anderson as Leonard Taft, J. D. Cannon as Lloyd L. Chandler, Louise Latham as Betsy "Princess" Chandler, Joseph Campanella as Capt. Ralph W. Lee, Michael Constantine as Arthur Howe, Bill Raisch as Fred Johnson A.K.A. Carson, Skip Ward as Nat Harris, Johnny Jensen as Bobby Taft, Lloyd Haynes as Detective Frank, James Nolan as driver, Don Lamond as newscaster, Seymour Cassell as cab driver, Perry Cook as attendant, Mark Allen as trucker, Paul Comi, Paul Hahn, Arch Whiting, and Michael Harris as police officers, Tom Palmer, John Ward (Uncredited: Diane Brewster as Helen Kimble).

Epilog: The Series Finale

Kimble, alias Frank Davis, spots a newspaper article: "Only One Arm — Wrecks L.A. Bar." He recognizes the suspect as Fred Johnson, his elusive one-armed man. Davis quits his job as driver for Tri-State Trucking and hitches a ride with a company truck bound from Tucson to Los Angeles.

Jean Carlisle is a court stenographer who works closely with the L.A. Police Department. Originally from Stafford, Indiana, Jean is the daughter of a former golfing partner of Kimble's. She is also friends with Kimble's sister, Donna Taft.

Lt. Gerard arrives in L.A., knowing Kimble will come there when he reads the trumped-up wire story about Johnson. Gerard works with Capt. Lee to set up a dragnet for Kimble. Jean recognizes Gerard and learns what is going on. She telephones Donna, suggesting she warn Dick if she can. Donna calls Tri-State Trucking, then calls Jean back to tell her Dick is on his way there. Jean sets up a watch for the Tri-State truck so she can intercept Kimble before he walks into the trap. Jean catches up with Dick at a produce market in an area swarming with police. Jean convinces him to accompany her. Kimble carries a box of apples to shield himself and gets in Jean's car. He is recognized by a cop at that point, but he and Jean drive off and elude capture.

Gerard questions Johnson about his whereabouts on September 19, 1961, the night of Helen Kimble's murder. Gerard has learned that, as Gus Evans, Johnson had been fired from an Indianapolis plant just two weeks prior to the killing. Johnson denies involvement in the murder, but Gerard catches him in some lies. He is beginning to suspect that there may be something to this "one-armed man" story after all.

Kimble takes refuge in Jean's apartment. Gerard appeals through the media for Kimble to give himself up, promising to fully investigate Kimble's accusation of Johnson. Kimble asks Jean to make sure they really have Johnson in custody before he turns himself in. Jean confirms it, calling Kimble, who takes a taxi bound for police headquarters. Jean returns to the department to tell Gerard Kimble is coming but finds Johnson being bailed out. Howe, a bail bondsman, turns over the $3,000, refusing to name his client. Police have no choice but to let Johnson go, but they send two officers to tail his and Howe's taxi. Jean rushes out to intercept Kimble coming out of his cab. She tells him what has happened, and they hop into her car to follow Johnson. Jean is becoming more and more involved and realizes she is falling in love with Dick.

The cab lets Johnson and Howe out at the zoo. Howe tells Johnson his client has not only put up the $3,000 but entrusted him with another $1,000 for Johnson to jump bail. Howe suggests that if they combine their knowledge — Howe's of the client's name, Johnson's of his reason for putting up the money — they can extort, say, $50,000 more, to be split evenly between the two. Meanwhile, Kimble is unable to approach Howe because of the two cops. Johnson and Howe leave for Howe's office to talk business.

Johnson gives Howe his story: he witnessed Helen Kimble's murder while burglarizing the house, and the client must be the true murderer. Howe reveals the client's name: Leonard Taft, Kimble's brother-in-law. Johnson, having no further use for Howe, beats him to death. Jean enters the bondsman's office building, letting Kimble in through a service door. They discover the victim and search his office for clues. They find a note, written in speed-writing (which Jean translates), naming Taft as the man who put up the bail money. Jean is recognized by two officers who see her enter and leave the building. When Gerard hears about this, and learns she is from Stafford, he puts two and two together. He decides to pay Jean a visit.

Jean makes a convincing denial as Kimble hides in her bedroom. Gerard leaves but notices the box from the produce market in Jean's car and realizes his hunch is right. Kimble suggests that Donna drive off, so the police will follow her while he gets away. The cops do follow her, but Gerard stays behind and hides. Kimble calls a cab, but when he goes outside to board it, Gerard arrests him. The two get on a train bound for Stafford, with the chase apparently over at last. Meanwhile, Johnson is already on *his* way to Indiana, having hopped a freight. He is eager to meet Leonard Taft.

Kimble waives extradition and, at his request, Gerard delays the press release of his capture. Kimble pleads for a little more time to prove his case. Gerard finally grants him about 15 hours, ending at noon the next day. They get off at South Bend to avoid being spotted at the Stafford station.

Lloyd Chandler drops the Tafts' son, Billy, off at their house. Lloyd, the city planning commissioner, regularly supervises several youngsters as they learn to shoot a gun. Lloyd is regarded as a war hero, having earned a silver star in military service. It was he who had posted Johnson's bail, using Taft's name. Donna mentions a "crank call" she got earlier that day: for Leonard to meet someone (Johnson) at Mitchell Stables at 7:30 that evening. Lloyd realizes the message is actually for him.

Kimble and Gerard arrive at the Tafts' house. Leonard denies having posted the bail, and Kimble and Gerard realize it was someone else using Len's name. Meanwhile, Lloyd — armed with a pistol — arrives at the stables. Johnson ambushes him, taking his gun. He instructs Lloyd to bring $50,000 to the abandoned amusement park at noon the next day. Johnson dumps out Lloyd's bullets and leaves. Donna tells Dick about the "crank call," and he and Gerard rush to the stables, where they find one of the bullets on the ground. Gerard is coming to believe Kimble's story.

Lloyd tries unsuccessfully to raise money from creditors and friends. The next day he puts his house up for sale and makes sure his life insurance and will are up to date. This all befuddles and upsets his wife, Betsy. Lloyd is very protective of his emotionally unstable wife, whom he calls "Princess." She finally pries out his confession: Lloyd was in the Kimble house the night of the murder. Helen, intoxicated and upset, had phoned him after her argument with Dick. She had wanted him to come right over to convince her that adoption was a positive thing, as he had testified two nights earlier. Lloyd had walked over to the house and found Helen in her bedroom. They had heard a noise below, and Helen had rushed downstairs to find the one-armed man burglarizing the house. Helen had fought with the man, crying for Lloyd's help. Lloyd had sat cowering in the stairs as Johnson beat Helen over the head with a lamp base. Johnson had taken a long look at Lloyd, then left. Lloyd had fled through the back way before Dick returned home.

Lloyd had kept quiet, figuring the one-armed man would be caught. He did not want to risk his reputation as a hero or subject "Princess" to a scandal. Betsy urges him to come clean now, to save Kimble's life. Lloyd has other ideas and leaves for the amusement park armed with a rifle.

Jean comes to the Taft house to tell Donna she saw Dick, unaware that he has been apprehended and is in the same house. Dick spends his last free moments with her as Gerard's deadline approaches. As Gerard and Kimble prepare to leave, Donna — preparing Billy's room for Jean — discovers a bullet in his drawer. Gerard sees that it matches the one found at the stable. When Donna theorizes Billy got the bullet from Lloyd, and recalls that she had mentioned the "crank call" to Lloyd, they all realize that Lloyd is the one who put up the bail. Gerard and Kimble rush to the Chandlers' house. Betsy repeats her husband's story and tells them he is on his way to the amusement park to hunt down Johnson.

Lloyd opens fire on Johnson, and a shoot-out ensues as Gerard and Kimble race to the scene. Gerard disarms Lloyd but is wounded by a stray shot from Johnson. Disabled, Gerard hands his pistol to Kimble and urges him to pursue Johnson. Gerard tries to extract Lloyd's confession, to no avail.

Kimble finds Johnson and orders him to drop his gun. Johnson fires his last bullet but misses. He runs off and climbs a tower, part of one of the park's rides. Kimble chases him, catching him at the top. Johnson knows Kimble needs him alive and won't shoot. They circle around and begin to grapple, with the gun getting loose. Kimble gets the upper hand and pounds a confession out of Johnson. Drained, Kimble gets up and turns away, enabling Johnson to get the gun. Johnson is about to shoot Kimble when Gerard fires Lloyd's rifle from below. Johnson plunges to the ground, dead.

Kimble descends the tower and tells Gerard about the confession, which Gerard deems worthless. Lloyd finally speaks up, promising to testify to clear Kimble.

The show ends with Kimble leaving the courthouse, a free man at last. He walks toward the road, encountering Gerard. In a dramatic moment, the two solemnly face each other and shake hands. As Dick, accompanied by Jean, reaches the road, a police car pulls up beside them. Kimble reflexively tightens, but Jean snaps him out of it and they laugh it off.

The narrator speaks his last: "Tuesday, August 29th — the day the running stopped."

Appendices: The Show

Appendix 1: Writers

Writers' names followed by episode numbers of shows. Cowriters denoted with an asterisk *.

ALCAIDE, Mario 114*
BARROWS, Robert Guy 57
BAST, William 67*
BLACK, John D. F. 7
BLEECKER, Perry 17*
BRINKLEY, Don 55, 61*, 72, 73, 82
BROOKE, Peter R. 43
BROUGH, Walter 104
BROWNE, Howard 93
CAILLOU, Alan 3*
CARABATSOS, Steven W. 102*
COHEN, Larry 39, 50*
CRAWFORD, Oliver 9, 92, 110
DALES, Arthur 98
DENNIS, Robert C. 12*, 26
DEXTER, Joy 90
DILLON, Robert 102*
EASTMAN, John 60*
ECKSTEIN, George 8, 29, 31, 34*, 45*, 53, 60*, 78, 119–120*
ELLIS, Sidney 45*
EMMETT, Jeri 102*, 108*, 114*, 116*
FASS, George 47*
FREIBERGER, Fred 105*
GERARD, Merwin 25
GERMANO, Peter 13*, 28
GILLIS, Jackson 89*
GOLDMAN, Lawrence Louis 117
GOLLARD, J. T. 116*
GOODMAN, Ralph 118*
GORDON, William D. 2, 42*, 44, 50*, 65
GRIFFITH, James 34*
GWALTNEY, Francis Irby 51*
HAMNER, Robert 62
HAWKINS, John 20*
HEIMS, Jo 51*
HUME, Edward C. 111

JEROME, Stuart 11, 19, 32
KANTOR, Leonard 46, 83
KEAN, E. Arthur 95*, 100
KING, Otto 61*
KNEUBUHL, John 79*, 80, 85, 88*, 89*
KRONMAN, Harry 3*, 13*, 18, 20*, 25*, 33*, 35, 38, 43*, 66*, 107*
KRUMHOLZ, Chester 66*
LANGDON, Betty 75
LARSON, Glen A. 89*
LAWRENCE, Anthony 81
LESSING, Norman 67*, 76
LEVINSON, Richard 36*, 63*
LEWIN, Robert 79*
LINK, William 36*, 63*
LOEB, Lee 96, 99, 112
LUCAS, John Meredyth 109
LUCEY, Paul 43*
MACHADAH, Zahrini 51*
MENZIES, James 74
MERLIN, Barbara 33*
MERLIN, Milton 33*
MORWOOD, William 21*
ORINGER, Barry 91, 105*, 113, 115, 118*
PIROSH, Robert 10
ROSS, Sam 94, 101, 106
RUBIN, Mann 88*
SALTZMAN, Philip 24, 41, 42*, 56, 64, 107*
SCHILLER, Wilton 95*
SEARLS, Hank 4–5
STARK, Sheldon 16, 21*, 27, 40
TRIVERS, Barry 12*
TURLEY, Jack 48, 54, 59, 71, 108*
ULLMAN, Dan 37, 52, 58, 68, 77, 86, 87, 97, 103
WARD, Al C. 22–23, 84
WEISS, Arthur 6, 15, 47*, 49

209

WHITMORE, Stanford 1, 14, 17*, 30
WILSON, Anthony 69–70

WOOD, William 21*
ZAGOR, Michael 119–120*

Appendix 2: Directors

Directors' names followed by episode numbers of shows directed.

ALLEN, Lewis 106, 112
BENEDEK, Laslo 17
BENEDICT, Richard 113
BIBERMAN, Abner 37, 46, 49, 56
BUTLER, Robert 31, 32, 51, 60, 67, 80
COHEN, Larry 50
DOBKIN, Lawrence 100
DONNER, Richard 77, 89
DOUGLAS, Robert 97
ERMAN, John 20
GIST, Robert 86
GOLDEN, Murray 108
GOLDSTONE, James 36, 41, 44
GORDON, William D. 58
GRAHAM, William A. 4–5, 25, 27, 29, 61, 74
GRAUMAN, Walter 1, 22–23, 40, 43, 45, 47, 63, 66, 69–70
GUZMAN, Claudio 7
HALE, William 99
HIBBS, Jesse 104
HOPPER, Jerry 9, 13, 15, 19, 21, 24, 26, 28, 30, 35, 38, 39, 65, 90
HORN, Leonard 85, 87, 88

LUCAS, John Meredyth 109, 111, 115, 117
LUPINO, Ida 10, 12, 16
McCULLOUGH, Andrew 2, 8
McEVEETY, Vincent 14
MARCH, Alex 78
MAYER, Gerald 91, 94, 110, 114, 116
MEDFORD, Don 53, 55, 71, 92, 119–120
MILLER, Robert Ellis 6
MORSE, Barry 118
NIELSON, James 95
NYBY, Christian (Chris) 11, 101
OSWALD, Gerd 96, 98
PENN, Leo 107
PEVNEY, Joseph 103
POLLACK, Sydney 33
ROLEY, Sutton 48
RYDELL, Mark 93
SARGENT, Joseph 72, 84
SENENSKY, Ralph 34, 42, 68, 75
SHELDON, James 3, 18, 79, 81, 82, 83, 105
SINGER, Alexander 52, 54, 57, 59, 62, 64, 73, 76
TAYLOR, Jud 102

Appendix 3: Guest Stars and Support Players

Actors' names followed by episode numbers of shows appeared in; uncredited spots in parentheses. Recurring roles denoted with an asterisk (*). Birch played Captain Carpenter in 13 episodes; Heckart played Sister Veronica in 3; Raisch played Fred Johnson (alias Steve Cramer, Walters, Carl Stoker, Fred Carson) in 10; Scott played Donna Kimble Taft in 5.

ABBOTT, Philip 44
ABELAR, Mike 115
ACOSTA, Rodolfo 98
ADAMS, Lillian 87
ADDY, Wesley 65
ADLER, Jay 12
AIDMAN, Charles 64
AKINS, Claude 27
ALANIZ, Rico 59, 107
ALBERT, Susan 87
ALCAIDE, Chris 64
ALETTER, Frank 64

ALEXANDER, Tommy 82
ALLEN, Carol 78
ALLEN, Elizabeth 13, 42, 104
ALLEN, Mark 99, 119
ALLMAN, Sheldon 83
ALZAMORA, Armand 59
AMES, Rachel 4
ANDERSON, John 17, 50
ANDERSON, Richard 43, 57, 66, 94, 119–120
ANDRE, E. J. 99
ANDREWS, Tige 117
ANGAROLA, Richard 40

Appendix 3: Guest Stars and Support Players 211

ANSARA, Michael 114
ANTONIO, Lou 8, 58, 102
ARIAS, Vincent 91
ARMSTRONG, Dave 38, 61
ARMSTRONG, R. G. 3, 51, 67
ARMSTRONG, R. L. 50
ARNOLD, Monroe 81
ASNER, Edward 56, 66, 105
ATEN, Laurence 84, 100
ATTERBURY, Malcolm 33, 80, 99
ATWATER, G. B. 54
AVERY, Val 52, 61, 83, 105
BAER, Parley 20, 106
BAKER, Diane 119–120
BAL, Jeanne 36
BALDWIN, Barbara 71
BALDWIN, Walter 68
BALSAM, Martin 110
BARCLAY, Jane 27, 108
BARMAK, Ira 82
BARNES, Rayford 56
BARRIE, Barbara 47
BARRY, Donald 39
BARTELL, Harry 4
BARTLETT, Martine 30
BARTON, Dan 20
BARZELL, Wolfe 89, 92
BATANIDES, Arthur 19
BAXLEY, Barbara 100
BAXTER, Alan 26
BECKMAN, Henry 4, 10, 32
BEECHER, Bonnie 84, 95
BEGLEY, Ed 31, 57
BEIR, Fred 58
BELL, Steven (Steve) 42, 67
BENDER, Russ 50
BENEDICT, Greg 101
BENSINGER, Ted 30
BERNARDI, Herschel 69–70
BEST, James 13
BIHELLER, Robert 70
BINNS, Edward 12, 41, 71
BIRCH, Paul (1), 3, 4, (7), 10, 11, 15, 26, 32, 35, 39, 47, 51*
BISSELL, Whit 50
BLAKE, Larry 108
BLYDEN, Larry 63
BONAR, Ivan 112
BOONE, Randy 17
BOURBON, Diana 5
BOWER, Antoinette 90, 109, 118
BOWMAN, Lee 42
BRADBURY, Lane 61
BRADFORD, Lane 23
BRADLEY, Stewart (Stuart) 7, 21
BRAMLEY, William (Bill) 87, 93
BRANDT, Thordis 107

BRANDT, Victor 111
BRENLIN, George 75, 93
BREWSTER, Diane 14, (120)
BRIDGES, Beau 80, 106
BRIGGS, Don 34
BRINCKERHOFF, Burt 10
BROCCO, Peter 32, 93
BRODERICK, James 105
BRODIE, Kevin 48
BRONSON, Charles 107
BROOKE, Walter 31, 42, 63
BROOKS, Geraldine 9, 54, 111
BROOKS, Martin 117
BROPHY, Sallie 32
BROWN, Calvin 103
BROWN, Lew 20, 84, 91
BRUBAKER, Robert 83
BRUNETTI, Argentina 80
BRYAR, Claudia 2, 58, 106
BRYAR, Paul 72
BULL, Richard 36
BURCHETT, Kevin 87
BURKE, Walter 96
BURT, Nellie 57, 63
BURTON, Jeff 72
BURTON, Jhean 83, 104
CAHILL, Barry 42
CALL, Anthony 49
CALLAHAN, James 86, 101
CALLAHAN, Pepe 107
CAMPANELLA, Joseph 30, 71, 106, 119
CANNON, J. D. 62, 120
CANON, Peter 87
CARDI, Pat 89
CARLSON, Richard 28
CARR, Paul 11, 38
CASSELL, Seymour 119
CHALLE, William 98
CHAMBERS, Phil 99
CHAMBERS, Richard 30
CHANDLER, John Davis 3, 105
CHAPMAN, Lonny 84
CHARLES, Lewis 19, 71
CHILES, Linden 109
CHRISTIE, Audrey 76
CHRISTINE, Virginia 17, 52
CIANELLI, Eduardo 93
CINDER, Robert 36
CLARK, Dort 12, 31
CLARKE, John 59, 69
CLUTE, Sidney 97, 110
COE, Peter 26
COIT, Stephen 69
COLASANTO, Nick 99
COLEMAN, Dabney 32, 48, 90, 99
COLLINS, Russell 17, 33
COLMAN, Booth 64

COLON, Miriam 114
COMI, Paul 27, 62, 119
CONNELLY, Christopher 30
CONRAD, Michael 99
CONSIDINE, John 20
CONSIDINE, Tim 97
CONSTANTINE, Michael 54, 88, 119
CONTRERAS, Roberto (Robert) 7, 115
CONWAY, Curt 48
CONWAY, Russ 113
COOK, Elisha 2
COOK, Perry 111, 119
CORBY, Ellen 80, 94
CORNTHWAITE, Robert 65
COUGHLIN, Kevin 114
COURTNEY, Chuck 103
CRANE, Norma 56
CRAWFORD, John 63
CRAWFORD, Katherine 49
CROSS, Dennis 19, 43
CROWELL, Jim 108
CROWLEY, Patricia 2
DALY, James 82, 104
DANA, Barbara 74
DANO, Royal 34
DAPO, Ronnie 69
DARBY, Kim 68, 96
DARFLER, Gene 68
DaSILVA, Howard 92
DAVIDSON, James 49
DAVIS, Michael 59
DAVIS, Ossie 92
DAVIS, Susan 67, 93
DAY, Johnny 3
DAY, Lynda 110
DAYTON, June 9, 14, 87
DEE, Ruby 6
DEEMER, Ed 43, 64, 93
DELEVANTI, Cyril 33
DELL, Gabriel 110
DeMAVE, Jack 118
DENNIS, John 56
DENNIS, Sandy 3
DENTON, Crahan 2, 38, 74, 97, 102
DERN, Bruce 3, 17, 51, 73, 102
DeSANTIS, Joe 40
DEUEL, Peter E. 49
de VARGAS, Valentin 115
DEVINE, James 54, 70
DEVON, Laura 83
DEVON, Richard 53
DIAMOND, Bobby 114
DICKINSON, Angie 46
DILLARD, Mimi 62
DIXON, Ivan 39, 116
DODD, Barbara 110
DODSON, Jack 76

DOLAN, Rudy 14, 38
DOMINGUEZ, Joe 40
DONATH, Ludwig 103
DOOHAN, James 56, 62
Do QUI, Robert 86
DORNAN, Robert 81
DOUCETTE, John 35
DOUGLAS, Burt 22, 52
DOUGLAS, Melvyn 87
DOUGLASS, Amy 66
DOYLE, Robert 17, 70, 105
DRAKE, Charles 107
DRIVAS, Robert 31, 94
DUBBINS, Don 24
DUGGAN, Andrew 47, 81
DUGGAN, Bob 87, 94
DUKE, John 24
DUNCAN, Craig 29
DUNN, James 6
DURREN, John 23, 64
DURYEA, Peter 31
DUVALL, Robert 4–5, 46
DYMALLY, Mark 89
EDWARDS, James 6
EITNER, Don 55, 80, 106
ELLERBE, Harry 90, 102
ELLIOTT, Ross 56
ELLIS, Herb 53, 100
EMERSON, Alan 93
ENGLE, Roy 105
ERICSON, John 46
ERWIN, Bill 50, 92, 109
EVANS, Richard 40
FACE, Tony 72
FARENTINO, James 113
FARLEY, James 111
FARRELL, Glenda 10
FARRELL, Sharon 51
FARRELL, Tommy 21
FAULKNER, Edward (Ed) 7, 51, 67
FELL, Norman 55, 72
FIEDLER, John 30
FIRESTONE, Eddie 74
FIX, Paul 45
FORREST, Steve 60
FORTIER, Marcelle 99, 117
FORTIER, Robert 29
FOSTER, Dianne 50
FOULGER, Byron 66
FRANCHER, Hampton 87
FRANCIS, Anne 107
FRANK, Joanna 18
FRANZ, Arthur 69
FRANZ, Edward 94
FRASER, Elizabeth 79
FRAWLEY, James 90
FRESCO, David 107

Appendix 3: Guest Stars and Support Players

FRYE, Gil 30
GALLAGHER, Mel 84
GARCIA, Stella 115
GARDENIA, Vincent 110
GARLAND, Beverly 7
GARRALAGA, Martin 30, 98
GARRETT, Betty 39
GARRETT, Ed 108
GEHRING, Ted 50, 61, 74, 93
GERRY, Alex 34
GIBBONS, Robert 32
GILCHRIST, Connie 18
GILDEN, Richard 78
GILLESPIE, Gina 2
GILMAN, Sam 115
GLASS, Ned 61, 83, 97
GODDARD, Mark 49
GOODWIN, Jim 52
GORDON, Don 37
GORDON, Gerald 21
GOUGH, Lloyd 53, 116
GOULD, Harold 31, 61, 108
GRAHAME, Gloria 28
GRANT, Lee 25
GREENE, Angela 97
GREER, Dabbs (1), 48, 51, 88, 98, 118
GREGG, Sandra 46
GREGG, Virginia 58
GREGG, Walter 94
GREGORY, James 98
GREGORY, Mary 83
GRIFFITH, James 28, 51
GUARDINO, Eddie 34
GUNN, Bill 65
HAGEN, Ross 114
HAHN, Paul 87, 109, 119
HALE, Jean 59
HALOP, Billy 13
HAMER, Gerald 49
HAMILTON, Murray 52, 90
HANMER, Don 75
HARAN, Ronnie 44
HARDING, June 52, 95
HARMON, John 17, 37, 92
HARRIS, Michael 110, 119
HARRIS, Steve 44
HARRON, Donald 65
HASKELL, Peter 57
HASSON, Thomas 23, 49
HAWKE, Jonathan 116
HAWKINS, Jimmy 8
HAYES, Adrienne 109
HAYNES, Lloyd 77, 93, 119
HEARN, Chick 30
HEBERT, Marcelle 76
HECKART, Eileen 22–23, 109*
HEFFLEY, Wayne 56
HELD, Karl 83
HELM, Anne 45
HELM, Peter 7
HELTON, Jo 34
HELTON, Percy 22
HENDERSON, Douglas 101
HERBERT, Charles 11
HERBERT, Pitt 63, 106
HERN, Pepe 7
HERNANDEZ, Robert 115
HICKOX, Harry 11
HILL, Arthur 115
HILL, Steven 86
HILLS, Beverly 18
HINGLE, Pat 19, 48
HOGAN, Robert 34
HOLLAND, Erik 73
HOLLIMAN, Earl 73
HOLM, Celeste 59, 108
HOLMES, Ed 4
HONG, James 74
HOWARD, Clint 15, 71
HOWARD, Ronny 41
HOWARD, Vince 107, 116
HOYOS, Rodolfo 22, 40, 59, 69, 115
HUDSON, William 116
HYLAND, Diana 34, 71, 102, 116
IGLESIAS, Eugene (Gene) 80, 91
IHNAT, Steve 41, 117
IVERS, Robert 88
JACKSON, Mary 28, 55, 88
JAGGER, Dean 101
JANSSEN, Jill 111
JENSEN, Johnny 75, 120
JENSEN, Marlowe 54, 60, 68, 99, 116
JENSON, Roy 98
JERIS, Nancy 97
JOHNSON, Arch 2, 79, 91
JOHNSON, Bobby 94
JOHNSON, Georgann 75, 105
JOHNSON, James 62, 101
JOHNSON, Jason 27, 85, 98
JOHNSON, Kyle 72
JOLLEY, L. Stanford 19
JOSEPH, Allen 78
KANE, Carole 81
KARNES, Robert 60, 93
KATES, Bernard 14, 39
KEEFER, Don 18
KEEN, Noah 55
KEENE, William 36
KEITH, Brian 1
KEITH, Byron 97
KEITH, Robert 15
KELLEY, Barry 7
KELLEY, DeForest 66
KELLOGG, John 40

KELLOGG, Ray 27, 108
KEMMER, Edward 6
KEMMERLING, Warren 98
KENNEDY, Don 116
KENT, David 44
KENT, Paul 94
KENYON, Sandy 22–23, 51
KING, Walter Woolf 28
KING, Wright 27, 82
KIRKPATRICK, Jess 32, 92
KIRKWOOD, Gene 113
KLEEB, Helen 52
KLINE, Robert 101
KLUGMAN, Jack 13, 54
KNIGHT, Shirley 28, 58, 79
KNIGHT, Ted 86, 97
KOBE, Gail 9
KOWAL, Jon 87, 110
KRIEGER, Lee 30
KULUVA, Will 4
KUNARD, Penny 59
LADD, Diane 17
LAMBERT, Paul 43
LAMOND, Don 57, 119
LANCASTER, Stuart 97
LANE, Rusty 90
LANE, Scott 11
LANG, Doreen 11
LANGE, Hope 91
LANGTON, Paul 10
LANPHIER, James 112
LARCH, John 33, 106
LARKIN, John 9
LASELL, John 36, 62, 79, 92
LATHAM, Louise 120
LAWRENCE, Carol 115
LEARY, Nolan 103
LEE, Ruta 23
LESLIE, Bethel 29
LEWIS, Art 99
LINVILLE, Joanne 82
LIPPE, Jonathan 110
LONG, Ed 60
LOOS, Anne 61
LOPEZ, Rafael 59
LORD, Jack 112
LORMER, Jon 37, 74
LOSBY, Donald (1), 41
LOVE, Phyllis 113
LUCE, John 77
LUKATHER, Paul 79, 99
LYMBURN, George 115
LYNCH, Hal 67, 102
LYNCH, Ken 22–23, 81
LYONS, Gene 9, 31
McCALLION, James 74, 104, 118
McCARTHY, Kevin 77
McCARTHY, Lin 34, 61, 82, 95
McCAY, Peggy 16
McCUE, Matt 44
McDANIEL, Charles 77
McGIVENEY, Maura 26
McGIVER, John 30
McINTIRE, Carl 27
MACKLIN, David 50, 114
MacLACHLAN, Janet 97
McLEAN, David 17
McLEAN, Doreen 13, 50
McLIAM, John 17, 38, 43, 91
McNALLY, Stephen 43
MacRAE, Elizabeth 38
McVEY, Patrick 27
MADDEN, Edward 31
MADISON, Ellen 24
MADSEN, Peter 90, 94
MAGUIRE, Kathleen 31
MALET, Arthur 89
MALONE, Nancy 20, 101
MAMAKOS, Peter 26
MANNING, Bruce 103
MANTEE, Paul 95, 118
MARDEN, Adrienne 35
MARGOLIN, Stuart 30
MARINO, Silvia 84, 91
MARK, Flip 25
MARKO, Peter 86, 109
MARLOWE, Nora 100
MAROSS, Joe 90, 95
MARSHALL, Sarah 62
MARSHALL, Shary 22
MARTEL, Arlene 103
MARTH, Frank 42, 102
MARTIN, Nan 19, 43
MARTIN, Strother 44
MASON, Marlyn 112
MATHESON, Murray 9
MATHEWS, Carmen 32
MAX, Edwin 103
MAXWELL, Frank 47, 63, 82
MAYO, John 21, 54, 101
McINTIRE, John 84
McINTIRE, Tim 84
MELVILLE, Sam 105
MENARD, Tina 5
MERIWETHER, Lee 76
MERLIN, Jan 103
METCALFE, Burt 53
MIKLER, Michael 113
MILES, Vera 1
MILFORD, John 7, 56, 96
MILLAN, Victor 97, 98
MILLAR, Robert 26
MILLARD, Harry 79
MILLER, Denny 99

Appendix 3: Guest Stars and Support Players 215

MILLS, Mort 7, 52, 65
MITCHELL, Dallas 109
MITCHELL, Don 87, 111
MITCHELL, George 2, 44
MODLIN, Elmer 75
MONTAIGNE, Lawrence 59, 65
MONTGOMERY, Ralph 94, 114
MOORE, Joanna 27, 63, 100
MORGAN, Read 48
MORRIS, Greg 61
MORRISON, Shelley 71
MORROW, Byron 59, 65
MORTON, Judith (Judee) 70, 94
MOSS, Stewart 31
MULLAVY, Gregory 75
MUMY, Billy 15
MUNK, Robert 100
MURPHY, Mary 48
MURPHY, Rosemary 94
MUSANTE, Tony 103
MUSTIN, Burt 48
NAISMITH, Laurence 60, 76, 118
NARDINI, Tom 114
NELSON, Ed 14, 24
NETTLETON, Lois 33, 89, 92
NEWELL, William 14
NEWTON, John 53
NICHOLSON, E. A. 75, 108
NICHOLSON, Nick 25, 51
NIELSEN, Leslie 12, 36
NISBET, Stuart 69–70, 87, 105
NOAH, James 36, 97
NOLAN, Dani 78, 111
NOLAN, James 15, 119
NOLAN, Jeanette 84
NORTH, Heather 109
NORTH, Sheree 68, 117
NUSSER, Jim 58
OATES, Warren 21, 44
O'BRIEN, Richard 97, 98
O'CONNELL, Arthur 37, 68
O'CONNOR, Carroll 24
O'CONNOR, Tim 9, 25, 40
O'HARA, Pat 100
O'HARA, Shirley 81
OLIVER, James 83
OLIVER, Susan 4–5
OLIVIERI, Dennis Joel 79
O'MALLEY, J. Pat 8, 63, 113
O'MALLEY, Kathleen 24, 54
O'NEAL, Kevin 79, 92
OVERTON, Frank 11
PACKARD, Ruth 21
PAIGE, Janis 45
PALMER, Tom 12, 49, 119
PARFREY, Woodrow 32, 44, 66
PARIS, Jerry 14
PARKE, Lawrence 5
PARKER, Warren 12, 59
PATRICK, Dennis 29
PATTERSON, Pat 109
PELLICER, Pina 7
PEPPER, Barbara 11
PEPPER, Paul 85
PEREZ, Raoul 115
PERRY, Barbara 21
PERRY, Joseph (Joe) 49, 61, 76
PETIT, Michel 27
PETTET, Joanna 81
PHILIPS, Lee 4–5
PHILLIPS, Barney (1), 114
PIAZZA, Ben 59
PICERNI, Paul 19
PICKENS, Slim 35
PIERCE, Maggie 55
PINE, Phillip E. 46, 78, 100
PITLIK, Noam 25, 45, 69, 103
PLEASENCE, Donald 85
PLESHETTE, Suzanne 32, 67
PLOWMAN, Melinda 8, 106
POLLOCK, Dee 44
PRATT, Judson 17
PRESCOTT, Sy 69–70, 94
PRIEST, Martin 80
PRINE, Andrew 15, 74
PUGLIA, Frank 114
QUARRY, Robert 12
QUINE, Don 42, 50, 81
QUINN, Bill 68, 85, 111
RAINE, Jack 112
RAINEY, Ford 79, 95
RAISCH, Bill (14, 19), 39, 77, 93, 97, 100, 111, 119–120*
RAMEY, Dianne 41
RANDALL, Sue 11, 34, 61
RATNER, Iris 111
RAYMOND, Jim 85, 106
REDMOND, Marge 34
REESE, Tom 50
REINDEL, Carl 111
REMSEN, Bert 5
REMSEN, Guy 100
RENARD, David 107
RENNICK, Nancy 67
RETTIG, Tommy 64
REY, Alejandro 7
RHODES, Grandon 98
RHODES, Hari 6
RHUE, Madlyn 26, 94
RICHARDS, Addison 19
RICHARDS, Paul 58, 83
RICHMAN, Mark 45, 91
RIDDLE, Hal 58, 112
RIEHL, Kay 89, 94

RILEY, Patrick (Pat) 87, 100
RIVERO, Julian 40
ROAT, Richard 74
ROBERTS, Stephen 77
ROBINSON, Chris 8
RODRIGUEZ, Percy 113
ROGERS, Wayne 83
ROLAND, Gilbert 26, 114
ROMERO, Carlos 98, 115
ROONEY, Mickey 78
ROSS, Don 57, 69–70, 78, 91, 99
ROSS, Marion 64
ROSSEN, Carol 36, 55, 62, 85, 93
ROSSON, Eddie 28
RUICK, Melville 83
RULE, Janice 77, 117
RUSH, Barbara 69–70
RUSSELL, Bing 14, 35, 57, 61, 89
RUSSELL, Kurt 35, 89
RUSSELL, Mark 87, 96, 111
RUSSO, Barry 104
SALMI, Albert 22–23
SANCHEZ, Jamie 91
SANDERS, Hugh 3, 45, 58, 79
SANDS, Diana 116
SARGENT, William 97
SAROYAN, Don 75
SAVALAS, George 80
SAVALAS, Telly 18, 55, 80
SAWYER, Connie 83
SCHUYLER, Richard 43
SCOTT, Brenda 40, 88
SCOTT, Henry 78, 94
SCOTT, Jacqueline 15, 64, 82, 119–120*
SCOTT, Lorri 111
SCOTT, Pippa 16
SCOTT, Simon 95
SEAFORTH, Susan 110
SEAY, James 7, 38, 101
SELZER, Milton 60, 66
SEURAT, Pilar 98
SHANNON, Wally 71
SHATNER, William 72
SHEA, Michael 89
SHEINER, David 36, 52, 81, 104
SHELTON, Abigail (1), 55
SHERIFF, Paul 88
SHERMAN, Orville 93, 113
SHERWOOD, Madeleine 2, 44
SHUTAN, Jan 59
SIGNORELLI, Tom 104
SIKKING, James 15, 60, 95
SIMON, Robert F. 6
SIMS, George 106
SINGLETON, Doris 66
SIPES, Glenn 106
SKERRITT, Tom 48, 96

SMITH, K. L. 54, 116
SMITH, Patricia 33, 90, 112
SNYDER, Billy 108
SOLARI, Rudy 24
SOMERS, Brett 41
SOMMARS, Julie 72, 103
SOREL, Louise 53
SORENSEN, Paul 36, 88
SORRELLS, Robert 44, 67, 102
SOULE, Olan 80
SPAIN, Fay 66
SPRUANCE, Don 60
STAFFORD, Tim 36
STANTON, Dean 52
STATFORD, Tracy 54
STEVENS, Bard 115
STEVENS, Naomi 78
STEVENS, Rory 99
STEWART, Peggy 27
STILES, Jimmy 54, 76, 99
STOKES, Ron 101
STORM, Debi 67
STRATTON, Chet 98
STRICKLAND, Amzie 68
STRONG, Michael 89, 93
STUART, Maxine 18, 39
SULLIVAN, Liam 67
SUTTON, Frank 3
SWEET, Katie 37
SWENSON, Karl 37, 46
SWOGER, Harry 6
TALBOT, Nita 78
TANNER, Clay 29, 87, 109
TARTAN, James 46
TAYLOR, Buck 13
TAYLOR, Jud 12, 34, 55, 69–70
TAYLOR, Vaughn 10, 57, 66, 96
TEAL, Ray 2
TEDROW, Irene 57
THAXTER, Phyllis 42
THINNES, Roy 98
THOMPSON, Charles 52
THOMPSON, Rex 85
THORDSEN, Kelly 71, 109
THRONE, Malachi 21, 65
TIFFIN, Pamela 14
TOMPKINS, Joan 49, 110
TOWNES, Harry 1, 37, 50, 75, 96
TRIKONIS, Gus 26
TROUPE, Tom 39
TRUE, Garrison 76
TYNE, George 78, 103
VACCARO, Brenda 8
VACIO, Natividad 115
VANDERS, Warren 28, 42
VAN der VLIS, Diana 12, 57
VAN HORN, Maya 27

Appendix 3: Guest Stars and Support Players

VANNI, Renata 84
VERNON, Glen 21
VIGRAN, Herb 39
VIHARO, Robert 102
VINCENT, June 34, 92
VINCENT, Russ 13
VINCENT, Virginia 21
VOSKOVEC, George 20
WAGENHEIM, Charles 101
WALBERG, Garry 10, 35, 67, 113
WALTER, Jessica 86
WARD, John 61, 92, 110, 119
WARD, Larry 75
WARD, Skip 119
WARDE, Harlan 87, 92, 107
WARDEN, Jack 108
WARNER, Sandra 83
WATSON, Bobs 11
WAYLAND, Len 74, 92
WEAVER, Fritz 88
WEBB, Richard 13
WEBBER, Robert 16
WELD, Tuesday 38
WESSELL, Richard 13
WESTON, Jack 10
WHITE, Christine 43
WHITE, David 9
WHITE, Ruth 3, 53
WHITING, Arch 82, 98, 119
WICKWIRE, Nancy 11, 86
WILCOX, Collin 73, 99
WILKE, Robert 98
WILKERSON, Guy 24
WILLIAMS, Adam 69
WILSON, Dick 65
WINDOM, William 111
WINGREEN, Jason (8), 22, 43, 66, 87, 108
WINTERS, Marc 79, 99, 113
WINTERSOLE, William 78, 102
WITNEY, Michael 73
WOLFE, Ian 11
WOLFSON, Steve 77
WOOD, Jeane 117
WOOD, Lana 42
WOODSON, William 81
WRIGHT, Ben 100
WYLLIE, Meg 67
WYNANT, H. M. 56
YOUNG, Buck 7, 27, 46, 106
YURO, Robert 47, 83
ZAREMBA, John 25
ZUCKERT, William S. (Bill) 22, 50, 69–70, 104

Appendices: The Character

Appendix 4: Places Visited or Lived In

Following is a partial list of places visited or lived in by Dr. Richard Kimble during his flight from justice. Fictional places are denoted with an asterisk (*), and corresponding episode numbers are shown in parentheses.

ALASKA
  Ketchikan (9)

ARIZONA
  Bixton* (48)
  Flagstaff, Coconino County (8)
  Phoenix, Maricopa County (86)
  Puma County*—southwestern, between Kittyville* & Mexico (91)
  Tucson, Pima County (1, 119)
  Unknown—62 mi. from Reeseburg* (65)

CALIFORNIA
  Encinas County* (59)
  Hidalgo Grove*, San Diego County (7)
  Hollywood, Los Angeles County (8)
  Los Angeles, Los Angeles County (4, 6, 83, 119)
  Ocean Grove* (106)
  Puerto Viejo*—southwestern (40)
  Sacramento, Sacramento County (23, 109)
  San Francisco, San Francisco County (14)
  Santa Barbara, Santa Barbara County (4–5)
  Santa Monica, Los Angeles County (46)
  Tarleton*—pop. 40,627 (109)
  Unknown—southern (49, 98)
  Unknown (87, 90, 107)

COLORADO
  Bradley*, Briar County*—near Greeley (68)
  Denver, Denver County (87)
  Unknown—southern (54)

CONNECTICUT
  Westborne* (16)

FLORIDA
  Fort Scott* (74)
  Key Blanca* (29)
  Raiford* (74)
  Weber's Landing* (29)

GEORGIA
  Corona* (44)
  Unknown—southeastern (28)

IDAHO
  Boise, Ada County (88)
  Cornell*, Trinity County* (37)

ILLINOIS
  Chicago, Cook County (19, 64)
  Decatur, Macon County (39)

INDIANA
  Fairgreen*—pop. 10,972 (52)
  Fort Wayne, Allen County (82)
  South Bend, St. Joseph County (120)
  Stafford*, Stafford County*—75 mi. from Indianapolis (15, 120)

IOWA
  Sioux City, Woodbury County (12)
  Unknown (67)

KANSAS
  Temple County*—150 mi. west of Joplin, MO (69)
  Tilden*, Wilson County (70)

KENTUCKY
  Clark City* (93)
  Ellsmore* (10)

Appendix 4: Places Visited or Lived In

LOUISIANA
Bleeker* (51)

MICHIGAN
Baker City* (77)
Meadville* (24)
Selby* (55)

MISSOURI
Hainesville* (2)
Kansas City, Jackson County (32)
Springvale*—30 mi. from Kansas City (32)

MONTANA
Drover City*—12 mi. from Acorn Falls* (73)
Wyler City*—northern, 40 mi. from Helena (113)

NEBRASKA
Black Moccasin*, Tyler County* (17)
Coleman*—northern (108)
Morgantown*—55 mi. from Lincoln (60)

NEVADA
Lincoln City* (22)
Ravenna* (22)
Reno, Washoe County (18)
Unknown—southern (43)

NEW HAMPSHIRE
Northoak*, Oak County* (11)

NEW JERSEY
Tractor* (71)

NEW MEXICO
Bellinda* (27)
Dos Palos* (67)
Santa Elena*—near Marisburg* (80)
Sierra Point*—pop. 562 (8)
Tucumcari, Quay County (67)

NEW YORK
Lake City* (62)
Unknown (78, 89)

NORTH DAKOTA
Fargo, Cass County (34)
Grand Forks, Grand Forks County (34)

OHIO
Rutledge* (57)
Unknown—south of Salisbury* (45)

OKLAHOMA
Clay City* (56)
Unknown (61)

OREGON
Eugene, Lane County (36)
Portland, Multnomah County (87, 117)

PENNSYLVANIA
Hurley* (47)
Pittsburgh, Allegheny County (104)
Unknown (31, 97)

SOUTH DAKOTA
Black River*, Black River County* (50)
Sioux Falls, Minnehaha County (38)

TEXAS
Dalhart, Dallam County (67)
Unknown (101, 115)

UTAH
Highpoint*, Salt Lake County (13)
Unknown (96)

VIRGINIA
Unknown (20)

WASHINGTON
Lake Shohalis* (117)
Pinedale*—100 mi. from Bellman* (118)
Seattle, King County (9)
Sona Falls* (72)

WEST VIRGINIA
Hempstead Mills* (76)
Unknown—northern, near Blueville* & Clarksburg* (3)

WISCONSIN
Northby*, Bardon County*—western, near LaCrosse, Melrose* & Wilson* (35)

WYOMING
Indian Lake* (42)
Smallgroves*, Freed County*—central (75)

DISTRICT OF COLUMBIA
Washington (116)

MEXICO
Puerto Vinales*—eastern (115)
Tanango*—western (107)

TOWNS IN UNIDENTIFIED STATES
Ardmore (66)
Burlington (100)
Donnivale (41)
Lark County* (23)
Longdale (99)
Marshfield* (39)

Monroe County (95)
Overton, Overton County (33)
Pikesville — pop. 963 (10)
St. Anne (63)
Wellington — pop. 5,000 (111)

Appendix 5: Aliases Used

Episode numbers follow each alias.

ALLEN, Pete 99
ANDERSON, Jack 97
ANDERSON, Tom 105

BAKER, Carl 94
BARLOW, Frank 39
BARRETT, Dr. Thomas 115
BARRETT, Thomas 113
BEAUMONT, Paul 13
BECKETT, Douglas 49
BENSON, Chris 71
BENTON, David 28
BLAKE, George 19
BRODERICK, Pete 34
BROWNING, George 14
BURNS, Tom 57

CARSON, Harry 12
CARTER, Eddie 101
CARTER, Frank 85
CARTER, Tony 90
CARTER, William "Bill" 10
CARVER, Steve 69–70
CLARK, Richard 48
COOPER, Jeff 4–5
CORBIN, Jim 96
CROWLEY, Dan 21
CURTIS, Ed 68

DAVIES, Bob 25
DAVIS, Frank 119
DAVIS, Jack 87
DEXTER, Al 24
DEXTER, Steve 108
DOUGLAS, Bill "Hotshot" 54
DYSON, Stan 117

EDSON, Paul 24
EDSON, Steven 24
EGAN, George 61
EVANS, John 72

FARRELL, Charlie 116
FICKETT, Jack 83
FLEMING, Al 8

FOWLER, Jim "Brains" 2
FRYE, Eddie 50

GARRISON, Bill 112
GLENN, Pete 45
GORDON, Dan 86
GRANT, Bob 87

HAYES, Bill 50
HORTON, Ben 46
HULL, Leonard 56
HUNTER, Paul 51

JOHNSON, Mike 84
JORDAN, Frank 36
JORDAN, Russell 104

KELLER, Paul 81

LEWIS, Ben 118
LINCOLN, James "Jim" 1
LINDSAY, Dick 20
LIVINGSTON, Dave 95

McGUIRE, Jim 75
MANNING, Stuart 42
MARCH, Bill 107
MARLOWE, Tom 109
MARTIN, Bill 52
MAXWELL, Tony 114
MEAD, Phil 57
MILLER, Paul 93
MILLER, Ray 6
MITCHELL, Alan 88
MORRIS, Ed 58
MORROW, David 91
MOSSMAN, Bob 74

NASH, Tom 66
NORTON, George 14

OWEN, Jim 62

PARKER, Jeff 40
PARKER, Jim 106

PAXTON, George 12
PETERS, Nick 60
PHELPS, Larry 29
PHILLIPS, Nick 78
PORTER, George 11
PRIAMOS, Gus 26

REYNOLDS, Harry 55
ROBINSON, Dr. Harry 100
ROGERS, Ben 17
RUSSELL, Ben 103
RUSSELL, Jim 38

SANDERS, Ed 92
SHELTON, Jerry "Shelly" 18
SHERMAN, Johnny 26
SINCLAIR, Jerry 111
SMITH, William 87
SPALDING, Dr. Richard 76
STODDARD, Bob 89

TAFT, Joe 67
TALLMAN, Larry 9

TATE, Fred 65
TAYLOR, Richard 79
THOMAS, Pat 41
TYLER, Gene 110

WALKER, Joe 33
WALKER, Joseph 7
WALKER, Nicholas "Nick" 22–23
WALLACE, Jim 59
WARREN, Joe 63
WATKINS, Bill 73
WHISTLER, Frank 80

YOUNGER, Steve 47

Single-Name Aliases
JACK 87
KELLY 37
MAY 32
PARKER 43
SANFORD 16
TAYLOR 98
WILKERSON 18

Notes: According to an ABC press release, Kimble's alias in episode #31 was Frank Borden, though that name was never mentioned during the episode. In episode #39, Kimble bore I.D. under the name of David Merrill, though he never actually used that alias. Kimble was sometimes referred to only by a nickname, such as "Doc" (episode #27) or "Mister" (3).

Appendix 6: Occupations Held

Jobs or positions held by Dr. Richard Kimble followed by episode numbers of shows.

Truckdriver — Tri-State Trucking, Tucson, AZ (119)
Handyman — Andrea, Pinedale, WA; Salary: $10/day plus board & meals (118)
Truckdriver — Buck Leonard, Leonard Freight, Portland, OR (117)
Doctor — Dr. Howell, Clinica Central, Puerto Vinales, Mexico (115)
Deck hand — The *Prowler*, TX (115)
Deliveryman — Jose Anza, J. Anza Cigars (114)
Chauffeur/handyman — Alan & Norma Bartlett; Salary: $600/month (112)
Parking attendant (112)
Field office assistant — Alex & Pearl Patton, Alex Patton Construction Company, NE (108)
Charter boat deck hand — Gus Hargas, CA (107)
Liquor store clerk — Al Cooney, Ocean Grove, CA (106)
Farm worker — Arthur Brame, Brame Farms/Arthur Brame Industries, PA (104)
Furniture upholsterer — Elco Corporation; Salary: $2/hour (103)
Crewman — Tony Donovan, the *Tillicum*, TX (101)
Bartender — HMS Bounty, Burlington (100)
Carnival roustabout — Matt, Longdale (99)
Film processor — Apex Film Service, PA (97)
Veterinary assistant — Doc Martin, UT (96)
Farmhand — Jacob Lawrence, Monroe County (95)
Apartment superintendent (94)
Bartender — Oliver Enright, Clark City, KY (93)
Teacher's aide — Annie Johnson, Puma County, AZ (91)
Intercom operator, Derrick Barge — Joe Steelman, CA (90)
Bartender — Mr. Hoffman, Little Vienna Restaurant, NY (89)

Appendices: The Character

Cranberry picker — Royal Crest Foods, New England (87)
Flood control worker — Multnomah County Flood Control, Portland, OR (87)
Walnut picker — Mr. Richardson, Richardson's Walnut Groves, CA (87)
Chauffeur — Dr. Mark Ryder, Denver, CO (87)
Deliveryman — Hogue's Tri-City Delivery Service, Phoenix, AZ (86)
Chauffeur — Max Pfeiffer (85)
Farm worker — Jock Sims, Crawford Farms (84)
Motel attendant — Chinese Sunset Motel, Los Angeles, CA (83)
Kennelman — Dr. Motter; Salary: $50/week (81)
Handyman — Rev. Barlow, Santa Elena, NM (80)
Restaurant worker — The Sugar Bowl (79)
Deliveryman — Charlie Paris, Priority Laundromat, NY (78)
Handyman — Lois Carter, Smallgroves, WY; Salary: $20/week plus board & meals (75)
Dishwasher — Edward Hee, Hee's Rice Bowl, Fort Scott, FL; Salary: $1.25/hour (74)
Stockyard worker — Drover City, MT (73)
Custodian — Tony & Carole Burrell, Saturday Morning Club, Sona Falls, WA (72)
Truckdriver/warehouse worker — George Savano, George Savano Auto Parts, Tractor, NJ (71)
Kitchen helper — K's Diner, Temple County, KS (69)
Driver — Peggy Franklin, IA (67)
Chauffeur — George Forster, Ardmore (66)
Lodge attendant — High Desert Inn, AZ (65)
Gas station attendant — Arch Garage, St. Anne (63)
Highway construction worker — Lake City, NY (62)
Zoo attendant — Maj. Alan Fielding, Major Fielding's Jungleland, Morgantown, NE; Salary: $50/week (60)
Citrus grove foreman — Flo Hagerman, Encinas County, CA (59)
Maintenance man — Rutledge, OH (57)
Hospital orderly — Selby, MI (55)
Dispatcher — Gus Hendrick, Bullet Trucking Company, CO (54)
Truckdriver — Inter-South Trucking Company, Bleeker, LA (51)
Handyman — Justin Briggs, Black River, SD (50)
Chauffeur/gateman — Charles & Madge Glenn, CA (49)
Truckdriver — John Harlan, Harlan Fuel Oil Company, Hurley, PA (47)
Private nurse — Norma Sessions, Santa Monica, CA; Salary: $75/week (46)
Spotlight operator — Johnny Haywood, Haywoods Log Cabin, OH (45)
Construction crewman — Jack Glennon, NV (43)
Lodge clerk — Jess Platt, Indian Lake Lodge, Indian Lake, WY (42)
Handyman — Joe Vardez, Joe Vardez Commercial Fishing, Puerto Viejo, CA (40)
Handyman — Sam Braydon, Braydon Farms, Sioux Falls, SD; Salary: $30/week plus board (38)
Farmhand — Max Henderson, Cornell, ID (37)
Gardener — Mike & Laura Pryor, Eugene, OR (36)
Hatchery attendant — Evergreen Fish Hatchery, Northby, WI (35)
Dishwasher — The Iron Horse, PA (31)
Shipper — Willoughby Carloading (30)
Charter boat hand — Charlie Hannah, Weber's Landing, FL (29)
Research technician — Allan Lee Pruitt, Pruitt Plantation Research Laboratory, GA (28)
Farmhand — Belasco Farms, Bellinda, NM (27)
Warehouse worker — Gus Priamos, Konstantine Brothers Distributors (26)
Roller rink attendant — Rollerdrome (25)
Masseur — Greenhurst Health Club, MI (24)
Handyman — Janet Loring; Salary: 83¢/hour plus board & gas (23)
Handyman — Chuck Mathers; Salary: $2/hour (22)
Janitor — Brady's Casino, Lincoln City, NV (22)
Liquor store clerk — Sharp's Liquor (21)
Kennelman — Max Bodin, Bodin Russet Kennels, VA (20)
Lifeguard — Daniel Polichek, The Rainbow, Reno, NV (18)
Mechanic — Tad Crumers, Tad Crumers Farm Equipment, Black Moccasin, NE (17)
Ranch hand — Harlan Guthrie, Westborne, CT (16)
Construction crew timekeeper — Buck Harmon, Highpoint, UT (13)
Stockroom worker — Martin C. Rowland, Denshaw's Department Store, Sioux City, IA (12)
Lumberjack — Larkspur Lumber Company, Seattle, WA (9)
Garage attendant — Ray Lumis, Ray's Garage, Sierra Point, NM (8)
Farm worker — Sindler & Son Produce, Hidalgo Grove, CA (7)
Boxing cut-man — Lou Bragan, Los Angeles, CA; Salary: $75/week (6)
Towel attendant — Los Angeles Memorial

Sports Arena, Los Angeles, CA; Salary: $60/week (6)
Sailmaker — Lars Christian, Lars Christian Sails of Quality, Santa Barbara, CA (4–5)
Deliveryman — Ty Tyson, Tyson's Fuel, Feed & Supply, Hainesville, MO; Salary: $1.10/hour (2)
Bartender — Cleve Brown, The Branding Iron, Hotel Santa Rita, Tucson, AZ; Salary: $75/week (1)

Appendix 7: Romances Engaged In

Following is an alphabetical listing of Dr. Richard Kimble's most serious romances during his life on the run. Episode numbers are in parentheses.

BURNETT, ELEANOR "ELLIE" (32), Stafford, Indiana. Ellie is the daughter of Kimble's late defense attorney, John Burnett. She and Kimble ended their meeting with a kiss of love after aborted plans to run off to Brazil together.

CARLISLE, JEAN (119–120), Los Angeles, California. The fugitive's flight ended in the company of this court stenographer, daughter of Kimble's former golf partner, the late Ben Carlisle.

CARTWRIGHT, SUSAN (89), New York. A waitress, Susan had temporary custody of her 12-year-old nephew, Gary. She told Kimble — whom she knew as Bob Stoddard — she had fallen in love with him, and he confided in her with his true identity.

CHRISTIAN, KAREN (4–5), Santa Barbara, California. She and Kimble — alias Jeff Cooper — planned to fake their deaths and start a new life with each other, but Karen wound up waving good-bye to the man she loved.

FRANKLIN, PEGGY (67), Iowa. Peggy is a divorcée with a young daughter, Nancy. Peggy and Kimble — A.K.A. Joe Taft — drove from Iowa to New Mexico together, sharing a couple of kisses along the way.

HARPER, LAUREL (62), Lake City, New York. Laurel became irate after Kimble — alias Jim Owen — inexplicably broke off their relationship at a roadside inn.

JOHNSON, ANNIE (91), Puma County, Arizona. Annie, a headstrong teacher at an Indian school, helped Kimble — known to her as David Morrow — escape and spent a night in a cave with him.

KING, MARCIA "MARCIE" (29), Key Blanca, Florida. The two began with a mutual dislike, but Marcie eventually fell in love with Kimble, proposing that they flee to Brazil together. They shared a few kisses in her island house.

MARTEN, GAYLE (112). Gayle is a professional musician. She and Kimble engaged in a short-lived romance featuring passionate (by 1967 television standards) kissing scenes. Alas, she was only using him in a scheme to capture her true lover.

MORALES, DR. REINA (115), Puerto Vinales, Mexico. While working together at the Clinica Central, Kimble — alias Thomas Barrett — and Reina fell in love.

REYNOLDS, CORALEE (90), California. Kimble — A.K.A. Tony Carter — ignored stories of a jinx surrounding Coralee and had a brief romance with the waitress.

SESSIONS, NORMA (46), Santa Monica, California. Kimble — known here as Ben Horton — and Norma, a 26-year-old gift shop proprietor, were instantly attracted to one another. She started out using him in a murder scheme but eventually fell in love with him.

WELLES, MONICA (1), Tucson, Arizona. For his first romance, Kimble — alias Jim Lincoln — chose this estranged wife with a son, Mark. Kimble got close enough to Monica to tell the truth about himself.

WELLS, BARBARA (117), Portland, Oregon. Kimble, A.K.A. Stan Dyson, spent a romantic weekend in Washington with Barbara. He did not know she was AWOL from the Women's Correctional Center.

Richard Kimble also encountered numerous other women who either kissed, had crushes on, or shared special relationships with him. Among them:

Tina Andresen (81)
Ruth Bianchi (100)
Cassie Bolin (3)
Louanne Crowell (42)

Andrea Crutch (118)
Janice Cummings (50)
Nedda Donovan (101)
Carol Hollister (34) — she thought Kimble was her late husband
Kate Kelly (84)
Janet Loring (23)
Hallie Martin (45) — a famous balladeer who resembled Helen Kimble
Lucia Mayfield (54)
Chris Polichek (18) — she proposed marriage to Kimble
Alison Priestley (116)
Aimee Renick (47)
Liz Rolande (94)
Lucey Russell (33)
Stella Savano (71)
Joanne Spencer (8)
Marcia Stone (92)
Carla Vardez (40) — a 15-year-old bombshell
Terry Waverley (53) — Helen Kimble's sister

Appendix 8: Injuries Sustained

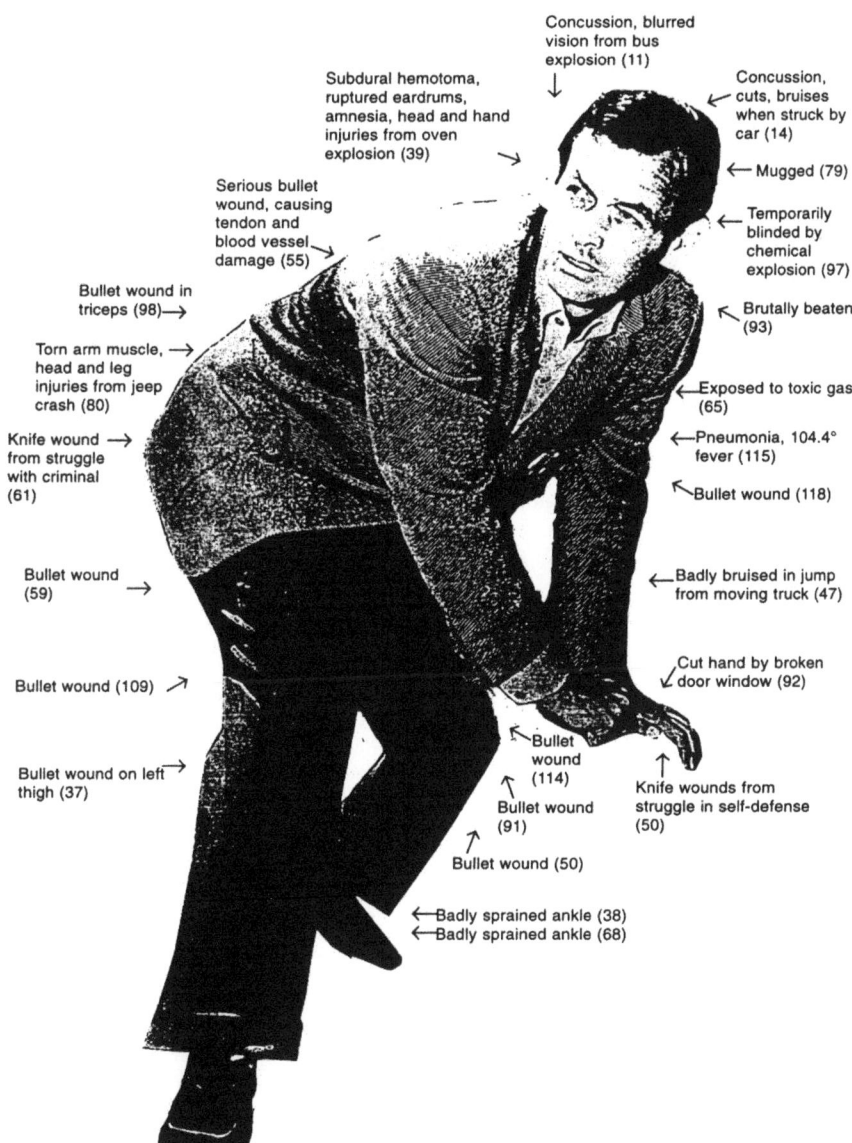

The above details some of the more serious injuries and ailments suffered by Dr. Richard Kimble during his flight from the law in *The Fugitive*. Numbers in parentheses are episode numbers of respective incidents.

Appendix 9: Interesting Facts

No Jones About It. There were 761 different actors and actresses to appear in credited roles on *The Fugitive* (see Appendix 3), but not one was surnamed "Jones." There were six Johnsons: (Arch, Bobby, Georgann, James, Jason, and Kyle), and six Scotts.

By Any Other Name. Dr. Richard Kimble used some 113 different aliases during his flight (see Appendix 5). His most common first names were William (Bill) and James (Jim), used eight times each. George, John (Jack), and Thomas (Tom) were next with six uses each, followed by Ed (Eddie), Frank, Paul, and Steven (Steve) with five apiece. The most common surname was Carter, used four times (thrice within 17 episodes). Two aliases were used twice: Joseph Walker, in episodes #7 and (shortened to Joe Walker) #33; and Thomas Barrett in numbers 113 and (with the title of "Dr." added) 115. The latter was inexplicable: Kimble, who never seemed to have trouble thinking up and using new aliases, recycled one under which he had been identified just two episodes earlier.

All's Welles That Ends Wells. Of Kimble's numerous romances (see Appendix 7), his first was with Monica Welles in episode #1, and his next-to-last was with Barbara Wells in #117.

Moving Target. Kimble suffered through numerous physical problems (see Appendix 8), including nine bullet wounds, during his flight. His left leg took the worst punishment: he suffered four bullet wounds there (in episodes #37, 50, 91, and 114), two badly-sprained ankles (#38, 68), and was struck by a car (14).

The Right Direction. Forty-three different people (see Appendix 2) directed at least one episode of *The Fugitive* each. Jerry Hopper directed 14 episodes, Walter Grauman 11.

Easy to Remember. Richard Kimble, portrayed by David Janssen, used the first name Richard (or Dick) for his alias four times, and the name David three times (see Appendix 5).

Go West, Young Man. Kimble preferred the southwestern U.S. during his travels (see Appendix 4), coinciding nicely with the ABC studio location. He was in California in no fewer than 19 episodes. Arizona was a distant second with seven visits, while New Mexico had five.

Unseen Presence. To the casual *Fugitive* viewer, it may have seemed that the dogged Lt. Gerard was in the vast majority of episodes. Actually, other than in the opening sequence, Gerard appeared in just 38 of the 120 episodes.

When Was She Killed? In episode #4, it is said that Helen Kimble was murdered in 1960. In #32, the date of death is given as September 17. In #39, it is again given as September 17, "two years ago"—presumably 1962, since the episode was aired in November, 1964. Finally, in the concluding episodes, the date of death is reported as September 19, 1961.

How Was She Killed? In the first and last episodes, it is said that Helen Kimble was beaten to death. Almost every other time during the series run that the cause of death is mentioned, it is said she was strangled: in episodes #29, 39, 44, 52, 53, 55, and 58. Episode #94 is the only episode other than the first and last in which Helen is said to have been beaten to death.

Saving on Props. In episode #29, Marcie King has a letter from her father in her purse. In episode #112, the same envelope is used as a prop, appearing in the desk drawer of Gayle Marten.

Who Is Doug? In episode #15, we are introduced to Richard Kimble's family: father, Dr. John Kimble; sister, Donna Taft; and brother, Ray Kimble. In episode #47, Richard composes a letter to his father, closing with "love to Doug and Sis."

Namedropping. In episode #14, we learn that Richard Kimble's middle name is David. Yet, in #65, it is said that Kimble has "NMI"—no middle initial.

Rolling Stone. Kimble tried never to stay in one place too long, but he lasted as long as three months in at least one place. Following are places (episode numbers in parentheses) in which Kimble stayed a month or more:

- Three months—working as acting foreman in the Encinas County, CA, citrus grove owned by Lee & Flo Hagerman (59).
- Two months—working for Gus Priamos in the warehouse of Konstantine Brothers Distributors (26).
- Two months—working as a gardener for the Michael Pryor family in Eugene, OR (36).
- Two months—working as a spotlight oper-

ator and handyman at Haywoods Log Cabin, south of Salisbury, OH (45).

Couple of months — working as a bartender in the Little Vienna Restaurant in New York state (89).

Six weeks — driving a truck for Harlan Fuel Oil Company in Hurley, PA (47).

Six weeks — serving as a chauffeur for George Forster (66).

Five weeks — working at Charlie Paris's Priority Laundromat in New York, NY (78).

Over a month — working as a sailmaker for Lars Christian Sails of Quality in Santa Barbara, CA (4).

One month — working as a handyman for Joe Vardez Commercial Fishing in Puerto Viejo, CA (40).

Polygamy. Kimble's sister, Donna, is married to Leonard Taft. Leonard is played by James Sikking in episode #15, Lin McCarthy in #82, and Richard Anderson in #119–120. Likewise, Lt. Gerard's wife is named Ann (played by Rachel Ames) in episode #4, and Marie (Barbara Rush) in #69–70. They have one child, Phil (Flip), Jr., in episodes #4 and 35, but "children" by #69.

Inter-State Fugitive. The original plans for *The Fugitive* had Richard Kimble hailing from Wisconsin, until the producers discovered that that state did not have the death penalty. Everything was then moved to Indiana, but some of the props from the first season were not changed in time. In episode #12, Kimble's "wanted" poster lists his birthplace as "Beloit, Wisconsin" (future posters list it as Stafford, Indiana). And in #15 Kimble takes a bus to and from his hometown of Stafford; the sign on the bus says "Madison," a Wisconsin city a little north of Beloit.

In Cold Blood. In episode #84, Kimble searches desperately for a blood donor who matches the blood type of Lt. Gerard, who needs a transfusion. Yet, in episode #96, Kimble is said to have blood type O-negative — thus making him a "universal donor."

Picking Up the Scent. In episode #3, two bloodhounds are given an article from Kimble's suitcase, supposedly to pick up his scent. One of the dogs can be seen extracting a biscuit from the cloth.

Three Strikes. Three *Fugitive* episodes use fictional baseball situations as back-drops. In #33, Vin Scully can be heard giving a play-by-play description of a Dodgers-Braves game, but the details described never happened. In #67, a Texas sheriff refers to the Houston Astros losing a game despite out-hitting their opponents, twelve to seven; this never happened before this show's airdate. And in #110 Kimble attends a game in a large stadium; the names announced over the P.A. system do not belong to any major or minor league players from that era.

Don't It Make My Brown Eyes Blue. In episode #11 Kimble becomes a mysterious hero who rescues a group of kids from a burning school bus. The unknown hero is described as having blue eyes, which, according to Gerard, fits Kimble's description. However, Kimble's eyes are brown, as listed on his "wanted" poster, and proven when the show went to color three seasons later.

The Two Wives of Jim Prestwick. In episode #14 Paul Clements talks to Lt. Jim Prestwick about his upcoming party, asking whether "you and Lois" are coming. When Doris Clements spots Lt. Prestwick at the party, she asks, "Where's Sally?"

Flying Backwards. In episode #47 Gerard flies to Pennsylvania on a TWA plane (as we see stock footage from his flight in episode #3). However, the filmclip has been inverted, as we can see the letters "AWT" on the head-rest of Gerard's seat.

Instead of Hempstead. A character in episode #76 is named Willis Hempstead, unmarried daughter of George Hempstead, founder of the show's site of Hempstead Mills. Yet, Willis's surname is listed as "Hampton" in the credits. Likewise, in episode #37, character Patty Sorensen is identified as "Patty Mallet" in the credits.

Not Who He Simms to Be. In episode #48 the main character is identified as Marshal Joe Bob Simms in signs at the park and at the marshal's office. The credits, however, list him as "Sheriff Sims."

The Vast Midwest. The prologue to episode #72 identifies the locale as a "midwestern city." Yet, the rural area's police cars are labeled "Sona Falls, Washington."

Titles. Two *Fugitive* titles were misspelled. Episodes #22–23 were labeled "Angels Travel on Lonley Roads," and #112 was shown as "Goobye My Love."

We'll Beat Whoever It Is. In episode #6 middleweight boxer Joe Smith is preparing for a fight against a contender. Trainer Lou Bragan names the opponent as "Kramer," but the fight poster identifies the boxer as "Kenny Walton."

Too Many Lawyers. In episode #14 we learn that the name of the prosecuting attorney in Richard Kimble's trial was Lester Rand. But in #82 Mike Ballinger is named as the prosecutor in question.

Where Credits Are Due. In episode #87 two different actors are identified as "Second Deputy" in the credits. Also, newsman Doug Bassett is listed as "Donald Bassett."

Right Name for the Part. In episode #88 Paul Sheriff portrays a police officer. And in #97 William Sargent plays a police sergeant.

Book of Numbers. The Bible tells us that there were twelve disciples and that the number "666" represents the devil. Episode #102 was entitled "The Devil's Disciples," and it originally aired on December 6, 1966 — or, 12/6/66.

More Credits. In the credits for episode #109, Sister Veronica is listed as "Sister Vernonica." And in those for #118 the proprietor of Kugler's Pharmacy is listed as "Kuglar."

Car 64, Where Are You? In episode #64 Capt. James Eckhardt recalls being in a car right behind Kimble's as the one-armed man crossed the road. Yet, in the opening scenes for each episode, no car is visible behind Kimble's.

No Comprende. In episode #64 lawyer Burton Green uses a Latin term which puzzles Kimble. As a doctor, Kimble must have learned Latin during his schooling.

What the Doctor Ordered. In episode #70 Dr. Kimble serves wine to Marie Gerard, who had just suffered a serious head injury causing temporary blindness. In #86 Kimble drags Glenn Madison and Pat Haynes from a plane that has just crashed, showing no concern for possible spinal injuries suffered by the two. And, as a *MAD Magazine* spoof of *The Fugitive* pointed out, in recreating the train-wreck scene at the beginning of each episode, "Did it ever occur to you what a Fink Doctor (Kimble) must be to run away from the scene of an accident where hundreds of people need medical attention?"

Two Internships Passing in the Night. In episode #7 we learn that — between medical school and advanced studies — Dr. Kimble interned in New York. Yet in #53 we are told that he completed his internship at County Hospital in Fairgreen, Indiana, where he met his future wife, nurse Helen Waverley.

A Voice Like a Cannon. In almost every episode, the narrator (William Conrad, later the star of *Cannon* and *Jake and the Fatman*) is heard only at the beginning (prolog) and end (epilog) of each episode. However, in episode #9, he opens Acts II, III and IV as well. And in #14 his voice is not heard until the epilog.

A Matter of Timing. The prolog in episode #34 says it has been "26 months since the escape." But the prolog of #39 says the murder was "two years ago" (after which followed his trial and eighteen months in prison, according to episode #1). Kimble thus escaped from jail before the murder was even committed, it would seem.

Don't Tell Mom the Baby-sitter's Dead. Through the entire run of *The Fugitive*, we are led to believe that Richard Kimble's mother, Elizabeth, is deceased. She is never mentioned in the present tense, not even during a visit to his father, brother, and sister, Donna (episode #15), nor in a letter to his father (#47), nor in the episode describing his father's death (#82). However, in the final episode (#120), Donna's husband mentions leaving their kids with "your mother."

Family Reunion. The Fugitive's *real* mother and sister both appeared on the show. David Janssen's mother, Berniece Janssen, had an uncredited cameo as a woman in the motel in episode #47 (Berniece also appeared in the 1993 movie version of *The Fugitive*). David's sister, Jill Janssen, appears in a credited role in #111 and in an uncredited one at the end of #120.

Index

Abbott, Philip 78
Abelar, Mike 197
Academy Award 5
Acosta, Rodolfo 168
Adams, Lillian 148
Addy, Wesley 112
Adler, Jay 24
Aidman, Charles 110
Akins, Claude 49
Alaniz, Rico 101, 184
Albert, Susan 148
Alcaide, Chris 110
Alcaide, Mario 195
Aletter, Frank 110
Alexander, Tommy 140
"All the Scared Rabbits" 115
Allen, Carol 134
Allen, Elizabeth 26, 75, 179
Allen, Lewis 182, 192
Allen, Mark 170, 204
Allman, Sheldon 141
Alzamora, Armand 101
Ames, Rachel 13, 227
Anderson, John 33, 87
Anderson, Richard 76, 98, 114, 161, 204, 227
Andre, E.J. 170
Andrews, Tige 200
The Andy Griffith Show 56
Angarola, Richard 72
"Angels Travel on Lonely Roads" 41
Ansara, Michael 195
Antonio, Lou 18, 100, 175
"A.P.B." 100
"An Apple a Day" 117
"Approach with Care" 170
Arias, Vincent 156
Armer, Alan A. 3, 7

Armstrong, Dave 68, 105
Armstrong, R.G. 11, 88, 115
Armstrong, R.L. 87
Arnold, Monroe 138
Asner, Edward 5, 96, 114, 180
Aten, Laurence 143, 172
Atterbury, Malcolm 60, 137, 170
Atwater, G.B. 93
Avery, Val 90, 105, 141, 180

Baer, Parley 38, 182
Baker, Diane 204
Bal, Jeanne 65
Baldwin, Barbara 121
Baldwin, Walter 117
"Ballad for a Ghost" 79
Balsam, Martin 5, 189
Barclay, Jane 49, 185
Barmak, Ira 140
Barnes, Rayford 96
Barrie, Barbara 82
Barrows, Robert Guy 98
Barry, Donald 70
Bartell, Harry 13
Bartlett, Martine 54
Barton, Dan 38
Barzell, Wolfe 151, 158
Bast, William 115
Batanides, Arthur 36
Baxley, Barbara 172
Baxter, Alan 48
Beckman, Henry 13, 21, 58
Beecher, Bonnie 143, 163
Begley, Ed 5, 56, 98
Beir, Fred 100
Bell, Steven (Steve) 75, 115
Bell & Howell Closeup 7

The Bell Telephone Hour 7, 56
Bender, Russ 87
Benedek, Laslo 33
Benedict, Greg 174
Benedict, Richard 194
Bensinger, Ted 54
Bernardi, Herschel 119
Best, James 26
Bewitched 56
Biberman, Abner 66, 81, 85, 96
Biheller, Robert 119
Binns, Edward 24, 73, 121
Birch, Paul 7, 11, 13, 17, 21, 22, 29, 48, 58, 63, 69, 82, 88, 211
Bissell, Whit 87
Black, John D.F. 17
Blake, Larry 185
Bleecker, Perry 33
"The Blessings of Liberty" 177
"Bloodline" 38
Blyden, Larry 108
Bonanza 56
Bonar, Ivan 192
Boone, Randy 33
Bourbon, Diana 13
Bower, Antoinette 153, 187, 202
Bowman, Lee 75
Bradbury, Lane 105
Bradford, Lane 41
Bradley, Stewart (Stuart) 17, 40
Bramley, William (Bill) 148, 159
Brandt, Thordis 184
Brandt, Victor 190
"Brass Ring" 81
"The Breaking of the Habit" 187
Brenlin, George 128, 159
Brewster, Diane 27, 204
Bridges, Beau 5, 137, 182
Briggs, Don 61
Brinckerhoff, Burt 21
Brinkley, Don 94, 105, 123, 125, 140
Brocco, Peter 58, 159
Broderick, James 180
Brodie, Kevin 84
Bronson, Charles 184
Brooke, Peter R. 76
Brooke, Walter 56, 75, 109
Brooks, Geraldine 19, 93, 190
Brooks, Martin 200
Brophie, Sallie 58
Brough, Walter 179

Brown, Calvin 177
Brown, Lew 38, 143, 156
Browne, Howard 159
Brubaker, Robert 141
Brunetti, Argentina 137
Bryar, Claudia 9, 100, 182
Bryar, Paul 123
Buck Rogers in the 25th Century 4
Bull, Richard 65
The Bullwinkle Show 4
Burchett, Kevin 148
Burke, Walter 165
Burt, Nellie 98, 108
Burton, Jeff 123
Burton, Jhean 141, 179
Butler, Robert 56, 58, 88, 102, 115, 137

"The Cage" 71
Cahill, Barry 75
Caillou, Alan 11
Call, Anthony 85
Callahan, James 146, 174
Callahan, Pepe 184
Campanella, Joseph 54, 121, 182, 204
Cannon 4, 228
Cannon, J.D. 107, 204
Canon, Peter 148
Carabatsos, Steven W. 175
Cardi, Pat 151
Carlson, Richard 51
Carr, Paul 22, 68
Cassell, Seymour 204
CBS Reports/News Hour 105, 156
Challe, William 168
Chambers, Phil 170
Chambers, Richard 54
Chandler, John Davis 11, 180
Chapman, Lonny 143
Charles, Lewis 36, 121
Cheyenne 3
Chiles, Linden 187
"The Chinese Sunset" 141
Christie, Audrey 130
Christine, Virginia 33, 90
Cianelli, Eduardo 159
Cinder, Robert 65
Clark, Dort 24, 56
Clarke, John 101, 119
"A Clean and Quiet Town" 159
Clute, Sidney 166, 189

Coe, Peter 48
Cohen, Larry 69, 87
Coit, Stephen 119
Colasanto, Nick 170
Coleman, Dabney 5, 58, 84, 153, 170
Collins, Russell 33, 60
Colman, Booth 110
Colon, Miriam 195
"Come Watch Me Die" 33
Comi, Paul 49, 107, 204
"Concrete Evidence" 185
Connelly, Christopher 54
Conrad, Michael 170
Conrad, William 4, 7, 228
Considine, John 38
Considine, Tim 166
"Conspiracy of Silence" 112
Constantine, Michael 93, 150, 204
Contreras, Roberto (Robert) 17, 197
Conway, Curt 84
Conway, Russ 194
Cook, Elisha 9
Cook, Perry 190, 204
"Coralee" 153
Corby, Ellen 137, 161
"Corner of Hell" 88
Cornthwaite, Robert 112
Coughlin, Kevin 195
Courtney, Chuck 177
"Crack in a Crystal Ball" 108
Crane, Norma 96
Crawford, John 109
Crawford, Katherine 85
Crawford, Oliver 19, 158, 189
Cross, Dennis 36, 76
Crowell, Jim 185
Crowley, Patricia 9
"Cry Uncle" 73

Dales, Arthur 168
Dallas 5, 204
Daly, James 140, 179
Dana, Barbara 126
Dano, Royal 61
Dapo, Ronnie 119
Darby, Kim 117, 165
Darfler, Gene 117
"Dark Corner" 68
DaSilva, Howard 158
Davidson, James 86

Davis, Michael 101
Davis, Ossie 158
Davis, Susan 115, 159
Day, Johnny 11
Day, Lynda 189
Dayton, June 19, 27, 148
Deane, Edith 1
Deane, Pam 1
Deane, Sarah 1
"Death Is the Door Prize" 158
"Death of a Very Small Killer" 197
"Decision in the Ring" 15
Dee, Ruby 15
Deemer, Ed 76, 110, 159
Delevanti, Cyril 60
Dell, Gabriel 189
DeMave, Jack 202
Dennis, John 96
Dennis, Robert C. 24, 48
Dennis, Sandy 5, 11
Denton, Crahan 9, 68, 126, 167, 175
Dern, Bruce 5, 11, 33, 88, 125, 175
DeSantis, Joe 71
"Detour on a Road Going Nowhere" 75
Deuel, Peter E. 86
deVargas, Valentin 197
"Devil's Carnival" 78
"The Devil's Disciples" 175
Devine, James 93, 119
Devon, Laura 141
Devon, Richard 91
Dexter, Joy 153
Diamond, Bobby 195
Dickinson, Angie 5, 81
Dillard, Mimi 107
Dillon, Robert 175
Dittmar, Joe 2
Dixon, Ivan 69, 199
Dobkin, Lawrence 172
The Doctors and the Nurses 56
Dodd, Barbara 189
Dodson, Jack 130
Dolan, Rudy 28, 68
Dominguez, Joe 72
Donath, Ludwig 177
Donner, Richard 132, 151
Doohan, James 96, 107
DoQui, Robert 146
Dornan, Robert 138
"Dossier on a Diplomat" 198
Doucette, John 63

Douglas, Burt 41, 90
Douglas, Melvyn 5, 148
Douglas, Robert 166
Douglass, Amy 114
Doyle, Robert 33, 119, 180
Drake, Charles 184
Drivas, Robert 56, 161
Dubbins, Don 45
Duggan, Andrew 82, 138
Duggan, Bob 148, 161
Duke, John 45
Duncan, Craig 52
Dunn, James 5, 15
Durren, John 41, 110
Duryea, Peter 56
Duvall, Robert 5, 13, 81
Dymally, Mark 151

Eastman, John 102
"Echo of a Nightmare" 135
Eckstein, George 18, 52, 56, 61, 79, 91, 102, 134, 204
Edwards, James 15
Eitner, Don 95, 137, 182
Eliot, T.S. 131
Ellerbe, Harry 153, 175
Elliott, Russ 96
Ellis, Herb 91, 172
Ellis, Sidney 79
Emerson, Alan 159
Emmett, Jeri 175, 185, 195, 198
Emmy Award 5, 105, 156
"The End Game" 54
"The End Is But the Beginning" 82
"End of the Line" 126
Engle, Roy 180
Ericson, John 81
Erman, John 38
Erwin, Bill 87, 158, 187
"Escape Into Black" 69
Evans, Richard 71
"Everybody Gets Hit in the Mouth Sometime" 93
"The Evil Men Do" 179

Face, Tony 123
Farentino, James 194
Farley, James 190
Farrell, Glenda 21
Farrell, Sharon 88
Farrell, Tommy 40
Fass, George 82
"Fatso" 21
Faulkner, Edward (Ed) 17, 88, 115
"Fear in a Desert City" 7
Fell, Norman 94, 123
Fiedler, John 54
Firestone, Eddie 127
Fix, Paul 79
"Flight from the Final Demon" 44
Ford, Harrison 204
Forrest, Steve 102
Fortier, Marcelle 170, 200
Fortier, Robert 52
Foster, Dianne 87
Foulger, Byron 114
Francher, Hampton 148
Francis, Anne 184
Frank, Joanna 34
Franz, Arthur 119
Franz, Edward 161
Fraser, Elizabeth 135
Frawley, James 153
Freiberger, Fred 180
Fresco, David 184
Frye, Gil 54
The Fugitive (motion picture) 204, 228
The Fugitive Recaptured 2
"Fun and Games and Party Favors" 85

Gallagher, Mel 143
Garcia, Stella 197
"Garden House" 31
Gardenia, Vincent 189
Garland, Beverly 17
Garralaga, Martin 54, 168
Garrett, Betty 69
Garrett, Ed 185
The Garry Moore Show 7
Gehring, Ted 87, 105, 127, 159
Gerard, Merwin 46
Germano, Peter 26, 51
Gerry, Alex 61
Gibbons, Robert 58
Gilchrist, Connie 34
Gilden, Richard 134
Gillespie, Gina 9
Gillis, Jackson 151
Gilman, Sam 197
"The Girl from Little Egypt" 27

Gist, Robert 146
Glass, Ned 105, 141, 167
"Glass Tightrope" 24
Goddard, Mark 85
Golden, Murray 185
Golden Globe Award 56
Goldenson, Leonard 3
Goldman, Lawrence Louis 200
Goldstone, James 65, 73, 78
Gollard, J.T. 198
Gomer Pyle, U.S.M.C. 56
"The Good Guys and the Bad Guys" 125
"Goodbye My Love" 192
Goodman, Ralph 202
Goodwin, Jim 90
Gordon, Don 66
Gordon, Gerald 40
Gordon, William D. 9, 75, 78, 87, 100, 112
Gough, Lloyd 91, 199
Gould, Harold 56, 105, 185
Graham, William A. 13, 46, 49, 52, 105, 126
Grahame, Gloria 5, 51
Grant, Lee 5, 46
Grauman, Walter 7, 41, 71, 76, 79, 82, 108, 114, 118, 226
Greene, Angela 167
Greer, Dabbs 7, 84, 88, 150, 168, 202
Gregg, Sandra 81
Gregg, Virginia 100
Gregg, Walter 161
Gregory, James 168
Gregory, Mary 141
Griffith, James 51, 61, 88
Guardino, Eddie 61
Gunn, Bill 112
Gunsmoke 4
Guzman, Claudio 17
Gwaltney, Francis Irby 88

Hagen, Ross 195
Hahn, Paul 148, 187, 204
Hale, Jean 101
Hale, William 170
Halop, Billy 26
Hamer, Gerald 86
Hamilton, Murray 90, 153
Hamner, Robert 107
Hanmer, Don 128

Haran, Ronnie 78
Harding, June 90, 163
Harmon, John 33, 66, 158
Harris, Michael 189, 204
Harris, Steve 78
Harron, Donald 112
Harry-O 4
Haskell, Peter 98
Hasson, Thomas 41, 86
Hawke, Jonathan 199
Hawkins, Jimmy 18
Hawkins, John 38
Hayes, Adrienne 187
Haynes, Lloyd 132, 159, 204
Hearn, Chick 54
Hebert, Marcelle 130
Heckart, Eileen 5, 41, 187, 211
Heffley, Wayne 96
Heims, Jo 88
Held, Karl 141
Helm, Anne 79
Helm, Peter 17
Helton, Jo 61
Helton, Percy 41
Henderson, Douglas 174
Herbert, Charles 22
Herbert, Pitt 109, 182
Hern, Pepe 17
Hernandez, Robert 197
Hibbs, Jesse 179
Hickox, Harry 22
Hill, Arthur 197
Hill, Steven 146
Hills, Beverly 34
Hingle, Pat 36, 84
Hogan, Robert 61
Holland, Erik 125
Holliman, Earl 125
Holm, Celeste 5, 101, 185
Holmes, Ed 13
"Home Is the Hunted" 29
"The Homecoming" 51
Hong, James 127
Hopper, Jerry 19, 26, 29, 36, 40, 44, 48, 51, 54, 63, 68, 69, 112, 153, 226
Horn, Leonard 144, 148, 150
Howard, Clint 29, 121
Howard, Ronny 5, 73
Howard, Vince 184, 199
Hoyos, Rodolfo 41, 72, 101, 119, 197
Hudson, William 199

Huggins, Roy 3, 7
Hugo, Victor 7
Hume, Edward C. 190
Hyland, Diana 61, 121, 122, 175, 199

Iglesias, Eugene (Gene) 137, 156
Ihnat, Steve 73, 200
"Ill Wind" 143
"In a Plain Paper Wrapper" 151
"The Iron Maiden" 76
Ivers, Robert 150
"The Ivy Maze" 190

Jackson, Mary 51, 95, 150
Jagger, Dean 5, 174
Jake and the Fatman 4, 228
Janssen, Berniece 228
Janssen, David 4, 7, 56, 105, 156, 226, 228
Janssen, Jill 190, 228
Jensen, Johnny 128, 204
Jensen, Marlowe 93, 102, 117, 170, 199
Jenson, Roy 168
Jeris, Nancy 167
Jerome, Stuart 22, 36, 58
Johnson, Arch 9, 135, 156, 226
Johnson, Bobby 161, 226
Johnson, Georgann 128, 180, 226
Johnson, James 107, 174, 226
Johnson, Jason 49, 145, 168, 226
Johnson, Kyle 123, 226
Jolley, L. Stanford 36
Joseph, Allen 134
"Joshua's Kingdom" 165
"The Judgement" 204
Jungleland 102

Kane, Carole 138
Kantor, Leonard 81, 141
Karnes, Robert 102, 159
Kates, Bernard 27, 69
Katz, Michael 2
Kean, E. Arthur 163, 172
Keefer, Don 34
Keen, Noah 95
Keene, William 65
Keith, Brian 5, 7
Keith, Byron 167

Keith, Robert 29
Kelley, Barry 17
Kelley, DeForest 114
Kellogg, John 71
Kellogg, Ray 49, 185
Kemmer, Edward 15
Kemmerling, Warren 168
Kennedy, Don 199
Kent, David 78
Kent, Paul 161
Kenyon, Sandy 41, 88
King, Otto 105
King, Walter Woolf 51
King, Wright 49, 140
Kirkpatrick, Jess 58, 158
Kirkwood, Gene 194
Kleeb, Helen 90
Kline, Robert 174
Klugman, Jack 26, 93
Kneubuhl, John 135, 137, 144, 150, 151
Knight, Shirley 51, 100, 135
Knight, Ted 5, 146, 166
Kobe, Gail 19
Kowal, Jon 148, 189
Krieger, Lee 54
Kronman, Harry 11, 26, 34, 38, 46, 60, 63, 68, 76, 114, 184
Krumholz, Chester 114
Kuluva, Will 13
Kunard, Penny 101

Ladd, Diane 33
Lambert, Paul 76
Lamond, Don 98, 204
Lancaster, Stuart 166
"Landscape with Running Figures" 118
Lane, Rusty 153
Lane, Scott 22
Lang, Doreen 22
Langdon, Betty 128
Lange, Hope 156
Langton, Paul 21
Lanphier, James 192
Larch, John 60, 182
Larkin, John 19
Larson, Glen A. 151
Lasell, John 65, 107, 135, 158
"The Last Oasis" 156
"Last Second of a Big Dream" 102
Latham, Louise 204

Lawrence, Anthony 138
Lawrence, Carol 197
Leary, Nolan 177
Lee, Ruta 41
Leslie, Bethel 52
Lessing, Norman 115, 130
Levinson, Richard 65, 108
Lewin, Robert 135
Lewis, Art 170
Link, William 65, 108
Linville, Joanne 140
Lippe, Jonathan 189
Loeb, Lee 165, 170, 192
Long, Ed 102
Loos, Anne 105
Lopez, Rafael 101
Lord, Jack 5, 192
Lormer, Jon 66, 127
Losby, Donald 7, 73
Love, Phyllis 194
Lucas, John Meredyth 187, 190, 197, 200
Luce, John 132
Lucey, Paul 76
Lukather, Paul 135, 170
Lupino, Ida 21, 24, 31
Lymburn, George 197
Lynch, Hal 115, 175
Lynch, Ken 41, 138
Lyons, Gene 19, 56

McAfee, Kay 1
McCallion, James 127, 179, 202
McCarthy, Kevin 132
McCarthy, Lin 61, 105, 140, 163, 227
McCay, Peggy 31
McCue, Matt 78
McCullough, Andrew 9, 18
McDaniel, Charles 132
McEveety, Vincent 27
McGiveney, Maura 48
McGiver, John 54
Machadah, Zahrini 88
McIntire, Carl 49
McIntire, John 143
McIntire, Tim 143
Macklin, David 87, 195
MacLachlan, Janet 167
McLean, David 33
McLean, Doreen 26, 87

McLiam, John 33, 68, 76, 156
McNally, Stephen 76
MacRae, Elizabeth 68
McVey, Patrick 49
MAD Magazine 228
Madden, Edward 56
Madison, Ellen 45
Madsen, Peter 153, 161
Maguire, Kathleen 56
Malet, Arthur 151
Malone, Nancy 38, 174
Mamakos, Peter 48
"Man in a Chariot" 56
"Man on a String" 60
Manning, Bruce 177
Mantee, Paul 163, 202
March, Alex 134
Marden, Adrienne 63
Margolin, Stuart 54
Marino, Silvia 143, 156
Mark, Flip 46
Marko, Peter 146, 187
Marlowe, Nora 172
Maross, Joe 153, 163
Marshall, Sarah 107
Marshall, Shary 41
Martel, Arlene 177
Marth, Frank 75, 175
Martin, Nan 36, 76
Martin, Quinn 3, 7
Martin, Strother 78
Mason, Marlyn 192
"Masquerade" 96
Master of the Game 4
Matheson, Murray 19
Mathews, Carmen 58
Maverick 3
Max, Edwin 177
Maxwell, Frank 82, 108, 140
"May God Have Mercy" 94
Mayer, Gerald 156, 161, 189, 195, 198
Mayo, John 40, 93, 174
Medford, Don 91, 94, 121, 158, 204
Melville, Sam 180
Menard, Tina 13
Menzies, James 126
Meriwether, Lee 5, 130
Merlin, Barbara 60
Merlin, Jan 177
Merlin, Milton 60
Metcalfe, Burt 91

"Middle of the Heatwave" 107
Mikler, Michael 194
Miles, Vera 5, 7
Milford, John 17, 96, 165
Millan, Victor 167, 168
Millar, Robert 48
Millard, Harry 135
Miller, Denny 170
Miller, Robert Ellis 15
Mills, Mort 17, 90, 112
Les Misérables 7
Mitchell, Dallas 187
Mitchell, Don 148, 190
Mitchell, George 9, 78
Modlin, Elmer 128
Montaigne, Lawrence 101, 112
Montgomery, Ralph 161, 195
"Moon Child" 90
Moore, Joanna 49, 108, 172
Morgan, Read 84
Morris, Greg 105
Morrison, Shelley 121
Morrow, Byron 101, 112
Morse, Barry 4, 7, 56, 105, 156, 202
Morton, Judith (Judee) 119, 161
Morwood, William 40
Moss, Stewart 56
Mullavy, Gregory 128
Mumy, Billy 29
Munk, Robert 172
Murphy, Mary 84
Murphy, Rosemary 161
Musante, Tony 5, 177
Mustin, Burt 84
Mystery Writers of America 105

Naismith, Laurence 102, 130, 202
Nardini, Tom 195
NBC Tuesday Night Movie 105, 156
Nelson, Ed 27, 45
"Nemesis" 63
Nero Wolfe 4
Nettleton, Lois 60, 151, 158
"Never Stop Running" 49
"Never Wave Goodbye" 13
Newell, William 28
Newton, John 91
"Nicest Fella You'd Ever Want to Meet" 84
Nicholson, E.A. 128, 185

Nicholson, Nick 46, 88
Nielsen, Leslie 5, 24, 65
Nielsen Ratings 5, 56
Nielson, James 163
"Nightmare at Northoak" 22
Nisbet, Stuart 119, 148, 180
Noah, James 65, 167
"Nobody Loses All the Time" 172
Nolan, Dani 134, 190
Nolan, James 29, 204
Nolan, Jeanette 143
North, Heather 187
North, Sheree 117, 200
"Not with a Whimper" 130
Nusser, Jim 100
Nyby, Christian (Chris) 22, 173

Oates, Warren 40, 78
O'Brien, Richard 167, 168
O'Connell, Arthur 66, 117
O'Connor, Carroll 5, 45
O'Connor, Tim 19, 46, 71
O'Hara, Pat 172
O'Hara, Shirley 138
O'Hara, U.S. Treasury 4
"The Old Man Picked a Lemon" 101
Oliver, James 141
Oliver, Susan 13
Olivieri, Dennis Joel 135
O'Malley, J. Pat 18, 108, 194
O'Malley, Kathleen 45, 93
"On the Run Newsletter" 1
O'Neal, Kevin 135, 158
"The One That Got Away" 184
Oringer, Barry 156, 180, 194, 197, 202
Oswald, Gerd 165, 168
"The Other Side of the Coin" 182
"The Other Side of the Mountain" 11
Overton, Frank 22

Packard, Ruth 40
Paige, Janis 79
Palmer, Tom 24, 86, 204
Parfrey, Woodrow 58, 78, 114
Paris, Jerry 27
Parke, Lawrence 13
Parker, Warren 24, 101
"Passage to Helena" 194
Patrick, Dennis 52

Patterson, Pat 187
Pellicer, Pina 17
Penn, Leo 184
Pepper, Barbara 22
Pepper, Paul 145
Perez, Raoul 197
Perry, Barbara 40
Perry, Joseph (Joe) 86, 105, 130
Petit, Michel 49
Pettet, Joanna 138
Pevney, Joseph 177
Philips, Lee 13
Phillips, Barney 7, 195
Photoplay Magazine 156
Piazza, Ben 101
Picerni, Paul 36
Pickens, Slim 63
Pierce, Maggie 94
Pine, Phillip E. 81, 134, 172
Pirosh, Robert 21
Pitlik, Noam 46, 79, 119, 177
Pleasence, Donald 145
Pleshette, Suzanne 5, 58, 115
Plowman, Melina 18, 182
Pollack, Sydney 60
Pollard, Rusty 1
Pollock, Dee 78
Pratt, Judson 33
Prescott, Sy 119, 161
Priest, Martin 137
Prine, Andrew 29, 126
Puglia, Frank 195

Quarry, Robert 24
Quine, Don 75, 87, 138
Quinn, Bill 117, 145, 190

Raine, Jack 192
Rainey, Ford 135, 163
Raisch, Bill 4, 28, 36, 70, 132, 159, 167, 172, 190, 204, 211
Ramey, Dianne 73
Randall, Sue 22, 61, 105
"Rat in a Corner" 40
Ratner, Iris 190
Raven Award 105
Raymond, Jim 145, 182
Redmond, Marge 61
Reese, Tom 87

Reindel, Carl 190
Remsen, Bert 13
Remsen, Guy 172
Renard, David 184
Rennick, Nancy 115
Rettig, Tommy 110
Rey, Alejandro 17
Rhodes, Grandon 168
Rhodes, Hari 15
Rhue, Madlyn 48, 161
Richard Diamond, Private Detective 4
Richards, Addison 36
Richards, Paul 100, 141
Richman, Mark 79, 156
Riddle, Hal 100, 192
Riehl, Kay 151, 161
"Right in the Middle of the Season" 173
Riley, Patrick (Pat) 148, 172
Rivero, Julian 72
Roat, Richard 126
Roberts, Stephen 132
Robertson, Ed 2
Robinson, Chris 18
Rodriguez, Percy 194
Rogers, Wayne 5, 141
Roland, Gilbert 48, 195
Roley, Sutton 84
Romero, Carlos 168, 197
Rooney, Mickey 5, 134
Ross, Don 98, 119, 134, 156, 170
Ross, Marion 110
Ross, Sam 161, 173, 182
Rossen, Carol 65, 94, 107, 145, 159
Rosson, Eddie 51
Rubin, Mann 150
Rugolo, Peter 3, 7
Ruick, Melville 141
Rule, Janice 132, 200
"Run the Man Down" 180
"Runner in the Dark" 98
"Running Scared" 140
Rush, Barbara 119, 227
Russell, Bing 27, 63, 98, 105, 151
Russell, Kurt 5, 63, 151
Russell, Mark 148, 165, 190
Russo, Barry 179
Rydell, Mark 159

Salmi, Albert 41
Saltzman, Philip 44, 73, 75, 96, 110, 184

Sanchez, Jamie 156
Sanders, Hugh 11, 79, 100, 135
Sands, Diana 199
Sargent, Joseph 123, 143
Sargent, William 166, 228
Saroyan, Don 128
"The Savage Street" 195
Savalas, George 137
Savalas, Telly 5, 34, 94, 137
Sawyer, Connie 141
"Scapegoat" 87
Schiller, Wilton 3, 156, 163, 204
Schuyler, Richard 76
Scott, Brenda 71, 150
Scott, Henry 134, 161
Scott, Jacqueline 29, 110, 140, 204, 211
Scott, Lorri 190
Scott, Pippa 31
Scott, Simon 163
Scully, Vin 227
Seaforth, Susan 189
"Search in a Windy City" 36
Searls, Hank 13
Seay, James 17, 68, 174
"Second Sight" 166
"See Hollywood and Die" 18
Selzer, Milton 102, 114
Senensky, Ralph 61, 75, 117, 128
"Set Fire to a Straw Man" 121
Seurat, Pilar 168
77 Sunset Strip 3
"Shadow of the Swan" 138
Shannon, Wally 121
"The Sharp Edge of Chivalry" 161
Shatner, William 5, 123
"The Shattered Silence" 202
Shea, Michael 151
Sheiner, David 65, 90, 138, 179
Sheldon, James 11, 34, 135, 138, 140, 141, 180
Shelton, Abigail 7, 95
Sheppard, Sam 7
Sheriff, Paul 150, 228
Sherman, Orville 159, 194
Sherwood, Madeleine 9, 78
Shutan, Jan 101
Signorelli, Tom 179
Sikking, James 29, 102, 163, 227
Silver Bowl 7
Simon, Robert F. 15
Sims, George 182

Singer, Alexander 90, 93, 98, 101, 107, 110, 125, 130
Singleton, Doris 114
Sipes, Glenn 182
Skerritt, Tom 5, 84, 165
Smith, K.L. 93, 199
Smith, Patricia 60, 153, 192
"Smoke Screen" 17
Snyder, Billy 185
Solari, Rudy 45
"Somebody to Remember" 48
Somers, Brett 73
Sommars, Julie 123, 177
Sorel, Louise 91
Sorensen, Paul 65, 150
Sorrells, Robert 78, 115, 175
Soule, Olan 137
Space: 1999 4
Spain, Fay 114
Spruance, Don 102
Stafford, Tim 65
Stanton, Dean 90
Stark, Sheldon 31, 40, 49, 71
Statford, Tracy 93
Stevens, Bard 197
Stevens, Naomi 134
Stevens, Rory 170
Stewart, Peggy 49
Stiles, Jimmy 93, 130, 170
Stokes, Ron 174
Storm, Debi 115
"Storm Center" 52
"Stranger in the Mirror" 123
Stratton, Chet 168
Strickland, Amzie 117
"Stroke of Genius" 137
Strong, Michael 151, 159
Stuart, Maxine 34, 70
Sullivan, Liam 115
"The Survivors" 91
Sutton, Frank 11
Sweet, Katie 66
Swenson, Karl 66, 81
Swoger, Harry 15

Talbot, Nita 134
Tales of the Unexpected 4
Tanner, Clay 52, 148, 187
"Taps for a Dead War" 46
Tartan, James 81

"A Taste of Tomorrow" 150
Taylor, Buck 26
Taylor, Jud 24, 61, 94, 119, 175
Taylor, Vaughn 21, 98, 114, 165
Teal, Ray 9
Tears from a Glass Eye 3
Tedrow, Irene 98
"Ten Thousand Pieces of Silver" 163
"Terror at Highpoint" 26
That's Life 204
Thaxter, Phyllis 75
"There Goes the Ball Game" 189
Thinnes, Roy 168
"This'll Kill You" 134
Thompson, Charles 90
Thompson, Rex 145
Thordsen, Kelly 121, 187
"Three Cheers for Little Boy Blue" 114
Throne, Malachi 40, 112
"Ticket to Alaska" 19
Tiffin, Pamela 27
"Tiger Left, Tiger Right" 65
Tompkins, Joan 85, 189
Townes, Harry 7, 66, 87, 128, 165
"Trial by Fire" 110
Trikonis, Gus 48
Trivers, Barry 24
Troupe, Tom 69
True, Garrison 130
"Tug of War" 66
Turley, Jack 84, 93, 101, 121, 185
TV Guide 1, 7, 204
TV Radio Mirror 7
"The 2130" 148
Tyne, George 134, 177

Ullman, Dan 66, 90, 100, 117, 132, 146, 148, 166, 177
The Untouchables 3, 7

Vaccaro, Brenda 18
Vacio, Natividad 197
Vanders, Warren 51, 75
Van der Vlis, Diana 24, 98
Van Horn, Maya 49
Vanni, Renata 143
Vernon, Glen 40
Vigran, Herb 70
Viharo, Robert 175

Vincent, June 61, 158
Vincent, Russ 26
Vincent, Virginia 40
Voskovec, George 38

Wagenheim, Charles 174
Walberg, Garry 21, 63, 115, 194
"The Walls of Night" 200
Walter, Jessica 146
Ward, Al C. 41, 143
Ward, John 105, 158, 189, 204
Ward, Larry 128
Ward, Skip 204
Warde, Harlan 148, 158, 184
Warden, Jack 5, 185
Warner, Sandra 141
Watson, Bobs 22
Wayland, Len 126, 158
Weaver, Fritz 150
Webb, Richard 26
Webber, Robert 31
Weiss, Arthur 15, 29, 82, 85
Weld, Tuesday 5, 68
Wessell, Richard 26
Weston, Jack 21
"When the Bough Breaks" 61
"When the Wind Blows" 128
"Where the Action Is" 34
White, Christine 76
White, David 19
White, Ruth 11, 91
"The White Knight" 146
Whiting, Arch 140, 168, 204
Whitmore, Stanford 7, 27, 33, 54
Wickwire, Nancy 22, 146
"Wife Killer" 132
Wilcox, Collin 125, 170
Wild, Wild World of Animals 4
Wilke, Robert 168
Wilkerson, Guy 45
Williams, Adam 119
Wilson, Anthony 118
Wilson, Dick 112
Windom, William 190
"Wine Is a Traitor" 168
Wingreen, Jason 18, 41, 76, 114, 148, 185
"Wings of an Angel" 105
Winters, Marc 135, 170, 194
Wintersole, William 134, 175
"The Witch" 9

"With Strings Attached" 144
Witney, Michael 125
Wolfe, Ian 22
Wolfson, Steve 132
Wood, Jeane 200
Wood, Lana 75
Wood, William 40
Woodson, William 138
"World's End" 58
Wright, Ben 172
Wyllie, Meg 115
Wynant, H.M. 96

Yodice, John M. 2
Young, Buck 17, 49, 81, 182
Yuro, Robert 82, 141

Zagor, Michael 204
Zaremba, John 46
Zuckert, William S. (Bill) 41, 87, 119, 179

www.ingramcontent.com/pod-product-compliance
Ingram Content Group UK Ltd.
Pitfield, Milton Keynes, MK11 3LW, UK
UKHW041940140426
5217IPUK00014B/589